DL1113675

An inveterate traveller, **ALEXANDER STEWART** has walked, trekked and tramped in more than 30 countries around the world. In the course of these trips he has researched and written guidebooks for several publishers, including for Trailblazer: *New Zealand – The Great Walks*, *The Walker's Haute Route* and *Peddars Way and Norfolk Coast Path*. As a freelance travel writer and photographer he has also contributed articles and photographs to various newspapers and magazines.

When he isn't escaping the city, he lives in London where he works for WEXAS, the World Expeditionary Association, wondering where to go next.

The Inca Trail, Cusco & Machu Picchu
First edition 1999; this fourth edition 2011

Publisher
Trailblazer Publications
The Old Manse, Tower Rd, Hindhead, Surrey, GU26 6SU, UK
Fax (+44) 01428-607571, info@trailblazer-guides.com
www.trailblazer-guides.com

British Library Cataloguing in Publication Data
A catalogue record for this book is available from the British Library

ISBN 978-1-905864-15-7

© **Trailblazer 2011**
Text and maps (unless otherwise credited)
© **Hugh Thomson 2011**: Text on pp104-16 and pp192-3

Editors: Anna Jacob-Hood & Nicky Slade
Series editor: Bryn Thomas
Typesetting: Nicky Slade
Layout: Anna Jacob-Hood, Nicky Slade & Bryn Thomas
Proof-reading: Nicky Slade & Jane Thomas
Photographs (flora): C1: top left and bottom right © Bryn Thomas
C2 top: middle and right © Bryn Thomas; all others © Alexander Stewart
Photographs (other): © as credited
Cartography: Nick Hill
Index: Jane Thomas

Warning: mountain walking can be dangerous
Please read the notes on when to go (pp23-5) and on mountain safety (pp42-4 and
pp89-91). Every effort has been made by the authors and publisher to ensure that
the information contained herein is as accurate and up to date as possible. However,
they are unable to accept responsibility for any inconvenience, loss or injury sustained
by anyone as a result of the advice and information given in this guide.

Printed on chlorine-free paper by
D'Print (☎ +65-6581 3832), Singapore

THE
Inca Trail
CUSCO & MACHU PICCHU

ALEXANDER STEWART

With additional material by
HUGH THOMSON
ALISON ROBERTS, HENRY STEDMAN,
SOPHIE CAMPBELL & BRYN THOMAS

TRAILBLAZER PUBLICATIONS

Acknowledgements

Lots of people have contributed to my time in Peru being a pleasure and have made working on this book such a joy. Thanks go to members of the INC and SAE who took time to answer my questions, supply information and offer advice. Also to the archaeologists working at Choquequirao and other sites, who generously talked me through developments and recent discoveries. Elsewhere in Peru, special thanks go to Mike Weston, Timoteo Auccapuma, Christian Jara, Julio Vidalon, Elisabeth Hakim, Leo Cusi Loaiza, Carlos Aranibar, Jesus Cardenas, Wilbert Yucara, and Alison Roberts for her work on the Lima chapter of this book.

In Britain thanks to Hugh Thomson for sharing his wide knowledge on the subject and writing the Inca history chapter. Thanks also to Sophie Campbell for her work on the Machu Picchu chapter and thanks as ever to Bryn Thomas for his tireless patience and perseverance with this project; these books simply wouldn't see the light of day without you. Elsewhere at Trailblazer, thank you to the ever-diligent Anna Jacomb-Hood and Nicky Slade for tackling the text, Nick Hill for drawing the maps and sketching the sites and Jane Thomas for the index.

And a particular, personal thank you to Katie, for this, for travelling with me and for more than you can possibly imagine. Finally, Rory, I began this before you were born and as a result you are too little for trekking but some day you will be old enough to start travelling. You can take it down from some upper shelf, dust it down and tell me what you think of it, before we all set off to look for – in the words of Rudyard Kipling quoted by Hiram Bingham in *The Explorer* – 'something lost behind the Ranges. Lost and waiting for you. Go!'

A request

The authors and publisher have tried to ensure that this guide is as accurate and up to date as possible. Nevertheless, things change. If you notice any changes or omissions that should be included in the next edition of this book, please write to Alex Stewart at Trailblazer (address on p2) or email him at alex.stewart@trailblazer-guides.com. A free copy of the next edition will be sent to persons making a significant contribution.

The symbol used at the start of each section of this book is the *Chakana* or Inca Cross, the Inca equivalent of the Tree of Life. The three steps on each side symbolize *Hana Pacha* (the abode of the gods), *Kay Pacha* (the world of men) and *Ucu Pacha* (the underworld or spirit world). The hole through the centre represents the centre of the Inca empire: Cusco; it also stands for the Southern Cross constellation.

Updated information will shortly be available on the Internet at
www.trailblazer-guides.com

Front cover: Machu Picchu (photo © Bryn Thomas)

CONTENTS

PART 7: CUSCO AND AROUND (cont'd)

Around Cusco

PART 8: TRAIL GUIDE AND MAPS

Using this guide   [see inside back cover for key map]

Getting to the trailheads

The classic Inca Trail

Variations on the classic trail

The shorter trails

The Salkantay/Mollepata trek

The Santa Teresa trek

The Vilcabamba Trail

The Choquequirao trek

INTRODUCTION

The mystery of the deep valleys which lie in the quadrant north to north-east of Mount Salcantay have long demanded attention. Separated from Ollantaytambo and Amaybamba by the Grand Canyon of the Urubamba, protected from Cuzco by the gigantic barrier of Salcantay, isolated from Vitcos by deep valleys and inhospitable, high windswept bleak regions called punas, they seem to have been unknown to the Spanish Conquerors and unsuspected by the historians... it appears to have been a terra incognita.

Hiram Bingham, *Lost City of the Incas*

In July 1911 the American explorer Hiram Bingham stumbled across the Inca ruins at Machu Picchu, the archetypal Lost City. None of the world's other great ruins can compare with Machu Picchu's location on a knife-like ridge, amid thick forest, high above a tumultuous river and frequently cloaked in swirling cloud, with the horn of Huayna Picchu punching through the mist, and snow-capped mountains glittering on the horizon. The discovery was the embodiment of many people's fantasies and proved to be the inspiration for innumerable adventure tales.

Bingham was directed to the region and along with his Peruvian guides explored the hillside reputed to conceal the ruins. All at once they 'were confronted with an unexpected sight, a great flight of beautifully constructed stone-faced terraces, perhaps a hundred of them, each hundreds of feet long and ten feet high'. Pushing on, 'without any warning', Bingham happened upon a cave carved into a stunningly sculpted structure whose 'flowing lines...symmetrical arrangement of ashlars, and gradual gradation of the courses combined to produce a wonderful effect...It seemed like an unbelievable dream. Dimly, I began to realize that this wall and its adjoining semi-circular Temple over the cave were as fine as the finest stone work in the world. It fairly took my breath away...'

Prior to the revelation of Machu Picchu, Bingham had explored and uncovered the ruins at Choquequirao. Following up these amazing discoveries, he went on to discover two other Inca sites of great importance, Vitcos and Vilcabamba. Countless other expeditions have explored and searched the region and numerous discoveries have been made, though none as significant as those unearthed by Bingham at the start of the twentieth century.

Discoveries of Inca roads linking these sites have led to the creation of trekking routes for modern-day pilgrims and adventurers to follow. The **Inca Trail** is just one such route, which penetrates the forest and crosses high passes to reach its goal, the ruins at Machu

Picchu. Heavily promoted and justifiably popular, the celebrated trek is almost a victim of its own success. In the wake of stringent regulations imposed to preserve the route, alternative options to reach Machu Picchu have been developed and treks to the other Inca sites have grown up as genuine alternatives to the crowded classic trek: the **Santa Teresa route** avoids the regulations associated with the Inca Trail but still gets you to Machu Picchu following a superb trek through varied landscapes; the **Choquequirao trek** takes you to these remote ruins perched above the Apurímac valley in a location arguably even more dramatic than that of the better-known site at Machu Picchu; the **Vilcabamba trek** explores puna, pampa, pasture, cloud forest and rainforest to lead you to the last refuge of the Incas, the untroubled, unrestored ruins of which are camouflaged and concealed by the forest. Epic **trails joining the various sites** have also been uncovered and now offer the ultimate experience for those with a passion for wilderness and a fascination with the world of the Incas.

So, despite the pressures of mass tourism and the popularity of the better known sites, it is still possible to explore the Cusco region free from crowds. Just take up the challenge and follow in the footsteps of the pioneers!

PLANNING YOUR TRIP

This section is designed to help you plan your trip: to make travel arrangements, calculate how much the trip will cost, and decide both when to go and which trek to take. It also sets out some simple rules to maximize your safety and outlines what to do in an emergency. There is a well-established trekking culture and infrastructure around Cusco. With the use of this book, an internet connection and just a little Spanish it's entirely feasible to organize your entire trip yourself.

Ultimately, though, how you approach your trip is a matter of personal choice and there's no substitute for practical experience when it comes to trekking. That said, the more you plan and prepare, the better equipped you are to deal with events on the ground, allowing you to make the most of the trip.

With a tour group or on your own?

In 2001 the Peruvian authorities outlawed independent trekking in the Machu Picchu Historical Sanctuary and brought in a series of strict regulations as to who could trek the trails to Machu Picchu and how they could tackle them. For a full breakdown of the regulations see p206 but, essentially, you can now only tackle the classic Inca Trail or any trek that joins it by signing up with a tour company or taking an accredited, licensed guide. When the laws were first introduced, it was still possible to sneak onto the trail without paying. Since then the authorities have tightened up security and clamped down on people not abiding by the rules. Don't attempt the classic Inca Trail without a guide or without paying the proper fees. It's highly unlikely that you'll get away with it and all you're really doing is freeloading. Yes, it is expensive to trek the Inca Trail but the costs of maintaining the route are high and the regulations prevent overcrowding, excessive damage and erosion and help to reduce littering. In actual fact the costs are pretty reasonable for a four-day, supported trek. Besides, almost whatever price you pay, it's still worth it.

For those who don't want to be constrained by the regulations, however, there are plenty of options. If you still want to trek to Machu Picchu take the Santa Teresa trek (see p241) which is as yet largely free from regulations. Alternatively, head to the far less-visited ruins at Vilcabamba (see p256) or Choquequirao (see p283). For the really adventurous there are also some longer routes that link the various sites, all of which can be done independently.

How to book

With the advent of tight restrictions on the number of people able to start the Inca Trail each day, your first priority on deciding to tackle the trek is to book as far in advance as possible. Long gone are the days of being able to turn up in Cusco with nothing arranged and put together a trek there and then. Around 200 tourists a day are able to begin the walk to Machu Picchu, and each of these must have a permit that has been secured and paid for well in advance. Competition for these limited places is fierce and the agencies battling for your business often find they can't offer places for the dates you want if you don't plan ahead. Ultimately you should try and make a reservation as far in advance as possible once you know your travel dates; during the peak season from July to August you ought to have things in place up to five months ahead of your proposed departure date. Bear in mind that the departure dates aren't flexible though and you are not allowed to change the name or passport details on the permit.

Your second priority ought to be choosing an agency. Take time over this as it is an important decision: they are, after all, the ones who will arrange everything, supply the equipment and assign you a guide. Only licensed Peruvian agencies are entitled to sell **permits**, so you will have to make a reservation either directly with one of them, or through a foreign tour company. By booking direct over the internet or by phone you will potentially save yourself money by cutting out the middleman. You will also be dealing directly with the people who will be running and arranging your trip, not a Western agent. You can take some satisfaction from the knowledge that whilst the money probably isn't going to the most destitute Peruvians, the money you spend on your trek will at least be going to support the local economy rather than into the pockets of a Western company. For a list of the more-established, respected agencies in Cusco with secure online facilities see pp156-9. Alternatively, for the sake of convenience you may wish to sign up with a foreign tour operator who will make all the arrangements on your behalf, for a fee. However, they will rarely offer you just a trek and nothing else. Nearly all include in the package some sort of airport transfers and accommodation in Cusco. For a bit extra they'll probably even organize your international flights meaning that you can save yourself a considerable amount of time and hassle. For a selection of those who offer the Inca Trail amongst their activities see pp14-16.

If you fall foul of the regulations and are unable to organize a permit for the dates that you targeted, don't worry, simply check out the alternative route options that are outlined on p28 and covered in detail later in this book. Whatever you do, do not be tempted to purchase tours or treks from sales people working in the airports or bus stations. Reputable companies do not operate like this. Always make a final reservation and conduct all payments in an agency office, making sure to ask for a written receipt and contract.

Group service or private service

There are two main types of trek: 'group-service' and 'private-service'. The standard **group-service** is the more popular and involves joining a group of other trekkers from all over the world, so it can be a very social way of walking. However, you can end up with people of very mixed abilities and interests, meaning you may have to walk slower than you'd usually like. The maximum group size is 16 people, although typically there will be 12-14 on the trail. If the group is larger than eight people, the regulations state that there must be two guides. That said, the trend is for smaller groups as it becomes harder for agencies to secure permits, although the cheaper companies bond together to form large groups. This is the cheapest way of doing the trek. Typically treks cost US$420-500 depending on the agency and level of service provided. If you find a trek for less than US$350 the basic maths ought to prove it's not feasible to run a quality trek for this little. At the other end of the scale, prices can double if you book with a foreign tour operator.

The other option is to take a **private-service** trek, which is laid on for just you and your friends. Inevitably, if there are only a few of you this is a much more expensive option as the cost of the guide, cook and porters has to be split between just a handful of trekkers. For larger groups, cost is less of an issue as you can split the price more evenly. Two people on a private-service trek might expect to pay US$800 each, whilst four trekkers would pay US$600 and six people expect to cough up US$500 each. Groups of eight to fourteen people should anticipate spending US$400-450. The maximum group size is still 16, for which each person would pay around US$400. Prices can again vary wildly from company to company depending on the sort of service offered. In addition to smaller groups, you will also receive more attention, probably be treated better and enjoy greater comforts than the group-service can offer. By booking a private-service you are also more likely to get the departure dates you want as the agency can close the booking as soon as you sign up; with a group-service they can't confirm the permits until they are ready to book the entire group, so

---

❏ **On the trail with a trekking group**

Typically a day on any of the trails in the company of an agency-guided trek starts with an early wake-up call and cup of tea in your tent. The porters will then bring a bowl of warm water for you to wash in, whilst breakfast is prepared. The first meal of the day usually consists of a hearty combination of fruit, porridge, bread and sometimes eggs. Following this, the day's walk will begin. During the trek you are only required to carry a day pack containing wet- and warm-weather clothing, adequate water and supplies such as a camera or important documents as the porters or *arrieros* (muleteers/donkey men) will shoulder the bulk of the luggage. In the course of the morning the porters will catch up and overtake you and then will race ahead to prepare lunch at a designated stop. After a brief break in which to eat, the trek continues at a leisurely pace until you arrive at the next evening's campsite, usually well before sunset. This gives you enough time to relax, reflect and unwind before supper and a well-deserved early night.

whilst waiting for the last spaces to be filled may occasionally find they've missed the boat and all the permits have been taken. If that's the case, the trek will be cancelled or they will attempt to offer you alternative dates. Ultimately, you get what you pay for.

Visiting the ruins without doing a trek
It is, of course, entirely possible to visit the ruins at Machu Picchu without undertaking any of the treks described here. Most of the companies listed in Cusco and abroad offer basic tours of the ruins and will arrange to shuttle you from Cusco to Aguas Calientes and from there up to the site itself.

It is equally easy, and potentially cheaper, to get to the ruins simply by using public transport. There is a train service from Cusco to Aguas Calientes and a bus service from there to Machu Picchu. For those on a really low budget there is also now a more arduous, more time-consuming but very cheap way of accessing Aguas Calientes by bus followed by a short section of easy walking (see p177).

TOUR OPERATORS AND TREKKING AGENCIES

Booking direct with an agent in Peru is the cheapest way of organizing your trek. Booking with a company from home though can buy you additional peace of mind and get you a broader package that is likely to include flights and transfers, albeit at a price.

Agencies in the UK and Ireland
● **Amazonas Explorer** (🖳 www.amazonas-explorer.com) are based in Peru (see p157) but offer the Inca Trail and Choquequirao Trek through their agents in the UK, USA and Switzerland.
● **Andes** (☎ 01556 503929, 🖳 www.andes.org.uk) specialize in climbing expeditions but also tailor-make an Inca Mountain trek.
● **Andean Trails** (☎ 0131 467 7086, 🖳 www.andeantrails.co.uk) organize treks for small groups including the Inca Trail, Salkantay and Choquequirao treks, and also offer tailor-made itineraries.
● **Audley Travel** (☎ 01993 838000, 🖳 www.audleytravel.com) offer tailor-made tours.
● **Charity Challenge** (☎ 020 8557 0000, 🖳 www.charitychallenge.com) offer treks to Machu Picchu for a number of charities.
● **Classic Journeys** (☎ 01773 873497, 🖳 www.classicjourneys.co.uk) arrange treks on the classic Inca Trail.
● **Discover Adventure** (☎ 01722 718444, 🖳 www.discoveradventure.com) organize ordinary treks on the Inca Trail as well as treks for charity.
● **Exodus** (☎ 0845 863 9600, 🖳 www.exodus.co.uk) arrange Inca Trail and Choquequirao treks.
● **Explore** (☎ 0845 013 1537, 🖳 www.explore.co.uk) is a large company doing Inca Trail, Salkantay, Choquequirao and Choquequirao to Machu Picchu treks as well as ruins-only trips.

- **Footprint Adventures** (☎ 01522 804929, 🖳 www.footprint-adventures.co.uk) arrange Inca Trail and Salkantay treks.
- **GAP Adventures** (☎ 0844 272 0000, 🖳 www.gapadventures.com) A well-run international organization offering many tours on the Inca Trail.
- **HF Holidays** (☎ 0845 470 7558, 🖳 www.hfholidays.co.uk) offer some treks which include the Inca Trail.
- **High Places** (☎ 0114 275 7500 or ☎ 0845 257 7500, 🖳 www.highplaces.co.uk) operate two trips including the Inca Trail.
- **Imaginative Traveller** (☎ 0845 077 8802, 🖳 www.imaginative-traveller.com) offer several trips including the Inca Trail.
- **Intrepid Travel** (☎ 020 3147 7777, 🖳 www.intrepidtravel.com) offer a variety of treks including Machu Picchu.
- **Journey Latin America** (☎ 020 8747 8315, 🖳 www.journeylatinamerica.co.uk) A well established company for tours to South America, they arrange Inca Trail, Salkantay and Choquequirao treks.
- **KE Adventure Travel** (☎ 017687 73966, 🖳 www.keadventure.com) arrange Inca Trail and Choquequirao to Machu Picchu treks.
- **Last Frontiers** (☎ 01296 653000, 🖳 www.lastfrontiers.com) arrange Santa Teresa treks on behalf of Mountain Lodges of Peru (see p159).
- **Llama Travel** (☎ 020 7263 3000, 🖳 www.llamatravel.com) specialize in good-value trekking trips to Peru, including the Inca Trail.
- **Mountain Kingdoms** (☎ 01453 844400, 🖳 www.mountainkingdoms.com) offer a variety of treks including tailor-made ones.
- **Naturetrek** (☎ 01962 733051, 🖳 www.naturetrek.co.uk) organize a Macaws and Machu Picchu trek.
- **Peregrine** (☎ 0844 736 0170, 🖳 www.peregrineadventures.com) are an Australian outfit offering a variety of treks and cycling trips in the region.
- **Pura Aventura** (☎ 0845 225 5058 or ☎ 01273 676712, 🖳 www.pura-aventura.com) arrange Inca Trail treks.
- **Red Spokes** (☎ 020 7502 7252, 🖳 www.redspokes.co.uk) organize cycling trips in Peru as well as the Inca Trail trek.
- **Spirit of Adventure** (☎ 01822 880277, 🖳 www.spirit-of-adventure.com) arrange the Inca Trail and Choquequirao to Vilcabamba trek with other activities including white-water rafting and mountain-biking.
- **Tucan Travel** (☎ 020 8896 1600, 🖳 www.tucantravel.com) is one of the largest tour operators in the area and organize everything from 7- to 65-day trips. They also have offices in Sydney and Cusco (Av de Sol 616, Office 202).
- **W&O Travel** (☎ 0845 277 3366, 🖳 www.wandotravel.com) arrange tailor-made treks on the Inca Trail, Salkantay and Choquequirao routes as well as on the Santa Teresa trek on behalf of Mountain Lodges of Peru (see p159).
- **Walks Worldwide** (☎ 0845 301 4737, 🖳 www.walksworldwide.com) offer the Inca Trail and a Salkantay Luxury Lodge Trek.
- **World Expeditions** (☎ 0800 074 4135, 🖳 www.worldexpeditions.co.uk) arrange Inca Trail and Choquequirao to Machu Picchu treks as well as a rather

unusual Salkantay to Km77 trek that, following a brief train ride, continues from Km104 to Machu Picchu.

Agencies in Continental Europe
● **Austria** El Mundo Reiseburo (☎ 0316 810698, 🖳 www.elmundo.at).
● **Belgium** Allibert Trekking (☎ 02 526 92 90, 🖳 www.allibert-trekking .com); Joker (🖳 www.joker.be) has ten offices in Belgium; Divantoura (☎ 09 223 00 69, 🖳 www.divantoura.be) Agents for Explore, see p14.
● **Denmark** Inter-Travel (☎ 33 15 00 77, 🖳 www.inter-travel.dk) Agents for Explore, see p14.
● **France** Allibert Trekking (☎ 08 25 09 01 90, 🖳 www.allibert-trekking.com) has branches in Chamonix, Chapareillan, Paris and Toulouse as well as Belgium and Switzerland; Club Aventure (☎ 08 26 88 20 80, 🖳 www.clubaventure.fr).
● **Germany** Neue Reise Theke (☎ 03 51 479 3710, 🖳 www.reisetheke.de).
● **Netherlands** Trotamundos (☎ 043 350 0308, 🖳 www.trotamundos.nl) Agents for GAP Adventures – see Canada below. Adventure World (☎ 023 5382 954, 🖳 atc@euronet.nl) Agents for Explore, see p14.
● **Switzerland** Allibert Trekking (☎ 022 849 85 51, 🖳 www.allibert-trekking .com).

Agencies in the USA
● **Adventure Center** (toll free ☎ 800-227-8747, 🖳 www.adventurecenter.com).
● **Adventure Life** (toll free ☎ 800-344-6118, 🖳 www.adventure-life.com) arrange budget tours and treks.
● **Andean Treks** (☎ 800-683-8148, 🖳 www.andeantreks.com) have an office in Cusco and many years of arranging tours and treks throughout Peru.
● **GAP Adventures** (toll free ☎ 1-800-708-7761 or ☎ 1-888-800-4100, 🖳 www .gapadventures.com) A well-run international organization offering many tours on the Inca Trail.
● **Holbrook Travel** (☎ 352-377-7111, toll free ☎ 800-541-7111, 🖳 www.hol brooktravel.com) No treks but they do stay in the upscale Machu Picchu Pueblo Hotel (see p202).
● **Wilderness Travel** (☎ 510-558-2488, toll-free ☎ 1-800-368 2794, 🖳 www .wildernesstravel.com) A company with a fine reputation; specializes in cultural, wildlife and trekking tours including the Inca Trail and Salkantay Trek.
● **Wildland Adventures** (☎ 800-345-4453, 🖳 www.wildland.com) are a leading eco-tourism operator offering itineraries including the Inca Trail and the Amazon.
● **World Expeditions** (contact World Expeditions Canada; see also p15).

Agencies in Canada
● **GAP Adventures** (toll-free ☎ 1-888 800 4100, 🖳 www.gapadventures.com) A well-run international organization offering many tours on the Inca Trail.
● **Trek Escapes** (☎ 1-866-338-8735, 🖳 www.trekescapes.com) An agent for a number of trekking companies with offices in: Calgary (☎ 403-283-6115, 🖳 cal gary@trekescapes.com); Vancouver (☎ 604-734-1066, 🖳 vancouver@trekes

capes.com); Edmonton (☎ 780-439-0024, 🖳 edmonton@trekescapes.com) and Toronto (☎ 416-922-7584, 🖳 toronto@trekescapes.com).
● **World Expeditions** (toll free ☎ 1-800-567-2216, ☎ 613-241-2700, 🖳 www .worldexpeditions.ca) also has a branch (Expéditions Monde) in Montreal (☎ 514-844-6364, toll-free ☎ 1-866-606-1721, 🖳 www.worldexpeditionmonde.com). See p15.

Agencies in Peru
See Cusco, pp157-9

Agencies in South Africa
● **Shiralee Travel** (☎ 028-313 0526, 🖳 liesel.maree@harveyworld.co.za) Agents for Explore, see p14.

Agencies in Australia
● **Adventure Associates** (☎ 02-8916 3000, 🖳 www.adventureassociates.com)
● **Adventure World** (☎ 1300 295 049, ☎ 02-8913 0755, 🖳 www.adventure world.com.au).
● **GAP Adventures** (toll free ☎ 1300 796618, 🖳 www.gapadventures.com) A well-run international organization offering many tours on the Inca Trail.
● **Inca Tours** (☎ 02-4351 2133 or toll-free ☎ 1-800 024 955, 🖳 www.inca tours.net).
● **Peregrine** (☎ 03-8601 4444, 🖳 www.peregrineadventures.com) Offer a number of treks and cycling tours in the region.
● **Tucan Travel** (☎ 02-9326 6633, ☎ 1-300-769249, 🖳 www.tucantravel.com) is a major operator in the region; see p15.
● **World Expeditions** (☎ 02-8270 8400, 🖳 www.worldexpeditions.com.au) **Sydney**. Also in Melbourne (☎ 03-8631 3300, 🖳 travel@worldexpeditions .com.au); Brisbane (☎ 07-3216 0823, 🖳 adventure@worldexpeditions.com .au); and Perth (☎ 08-9486 9899, 🖳 holiday@worldexpeditions.com.au); see p15.

Agencies in New Zealand
● **Adventure World** (☎ 09-524 5118, toll-free ☎ 0800 238368, 🖳 www.adven tureworld.co.nz).
● **GAP Adventures** (toll free ☎ 0800 333307, 🖳 www.gapadventures.com) A well-run international organization offering many tours on the Inca Trail.
● **World Expeditions** (☎ 09-368 4161, toll-free ☎ 0800-350354, 🖳 www.world expeditions.co.nz). See p15.

PORTERS, ARRIEROS AND GUIDES

In most instances you are likely to tackle the treks described here with an agency or tour company from Cusco, indeed in some cases this is the only way of undertaking the treks. The agency will supply you with guides, porters or mules. However, at the time of writing, there were still a number of treks that you could set out on independently, or with *arrieros* (muleteers) and mules that

(continued on p20)

❏ PORTER WELFARE

Roughly 7000 porters now service the needs of the tens of thousands of tourists who walk the Inca Trail each year. These people have often been exploited in the past and frequently worked with inadequate, inappropriate clothing and gear for derisory wages. While this situation has changed there are still improvements to be made and unscrupulous agencies to be weeded out. There are now several organizations dedicated to the issue of porter welfare who are campaigning for better working conditions and reasonable rates of pay.

As an individual trekking to Machu Picchu or any of the other sites in the area, there are several things you can do to improve the plight of those making your trek possible. **Let the agency in charge of your trek know that the welfare of porters is important to you**. Make sure they understand that you consider it an important factor when it comes to selecting an agency to run your trek. Porters need fair wages, decent meals and warm, dry overnight accommodation. There is still room for improvement with all of the agencies, but some are markedly better than others. Those offering the classic Inca Trail trek for less than US$350 won't have the porters' best interests at heart or be paying them adequately. Ask how much the porters are paid – the Porters' Law passed in 2002 states a wage of s/42 per day for the four-day classic Inca Trail. Unfortunately, the law has been described as 'unimplementable' and sadly most agencies are ignoring this rule and typically issuing salaries of around s/25-30 per day. This should include food rations and transport to the trailhead although some agencies expect porters to pay for anything more than basic rations and for their own transport to the trailhead or the journey home, a cost that can reduce their income considerably. The law also states that porters should not carry in excess of 25kg, a figure that includes a 5kg personal allowance for items such as blankets and clothes. Although strictly enforced, some companies make great efforts to get round this particular regulation. Don't stand for such sharp practice and say something if you see an abuse being perpetrated. Also enquire about the standard of equipment used by the porters; do they have waterproof clothing? Do they all sleep in tents with integral floors and have access to sleeping bags and mats? Showing you care about such things will encourage all operators and agencies to treat their porters fairly.

On the trek, try to interact with your porters. Take time to talk to them and learn something about their lives. Many have low self esteem so be bold and initiate the process, share some coca leaves and pick up a few words of Quechua (*Allillanchu?* means 'How are you?' whilst *Añáy* means 'Thank you'). The porters often have colourful stories to tell and can offer you a real insight into Andean traditions and culture. At the end of the trek make sure you tip your porters and that they get the money that is intended for them. Tipping directly to each individual member of the team ensures they receive a fair share. Show them you appreciate the work they have done on your behalf by thanking them verbally and individually.

Report unscrupulous trekking agencies

If you witness porter abuse, neglect or encounter unscrupulous agencies taking advantage of their porters bring it to the attention of the guide. Upon your return to Cusco, make an official complaint at the agency office, ideally in front of other potential clients, and if sufficiently bad, submit a report to the South American Explorers Club (see p130), the International Porter Protection Group or Andean Travel Web (see opposite). Equally, do let us know if you've had either a particularly good or poor experience on your trek. Your observations will mean that agencies are forced to face the fact that the issue is important and that in order to continue to do business they must respect those porters working for them and look after them properly.

Of course, if you are trekking independently and hiring guides, arrieros or porters directly, you personally need to take responsibility for the welfare of the team you hire, and again abide by the basic guidelines set out above.

International Porter Protection Group (IPPG)

Although not based in Peru the IPPG (🖵 http://ippg.net) is a volunteer organization that is dedicated to improving the conditions of mountain porters in the tourism industry worldwide. The comprehensive website outlines a number of measures that you can take to ensure you have a positive effect on your porters and their welfare. In addition, on their website, the IPPG recommend you ask the following when booking the Inca Trail:

● Does the company follow the IPPG's five guidelines on porter safety? These are:

1. Adequate clothing for protection from bad weather and high altitude should be provided to porters. This may mean windproof jackets and trousers, suitable footwear, socks, hats and gloves.

2. Porters should have access to shelter, either in a room, lodge or tent (the trekkers' dining tent is not acceptable as it rarely has an integral floor and is not usually available until late evening, meaning that the porters potentially have to wait in inclement weather without shelter), sleeping bags and mats and cooking equipment.

3. Porters should have the same access to medical care as tourists and also be covered by some form of insurance.

4. Adequate procedures should be in place for medical evacuation of porters.

5. Porters should carry no more than 25kg according to Peruvian law. Weight limits might need to be adjusted taking into consideration altitude, weather conditions and the state of the path. Child porters should never be employed.

● What is the company's policy on equipment and health care for porters?

● What does the company do to ensure its staff are properly trained to look after porters' welfare?

● Does the company ask about the treatment of porters in its post-trek questionnaire?

● If booking the trek from outside of Peru or through a middleman or agent who hires another agency to run the trek itself, you should also ask about the company's policy on training and monitoring porter care by its ground operator in Peru.

Unfortunately the excellent **Inka Porter Project** (Porteadores Inka Ñan) which was dedicated to improving conditions for porters and arrieros in the Andes is no longer operational, although the website still contains a lot of useful guidelines. Visit 🖵 www.porters.nu to watch a documentary following the working day of a porter; it also explores the history and political struggle of the porters and aims to increase awareness and give porters a voice.

Andean Travel Web

🖵 www.andeantravelweb.com/peru is a great source of information about Cusco and the attractions in the area including all of the trekking opportunities. The non profit-making organization also runs community projects and is dedicated to raising awareness of the issue of porter welfare.

In Cusco you can donate clothing or school equipment at their office (La Casa Cultural, Avenida Pardo 540). The office overheads are covered by a tour agency, Peru Treks and Adventure (see p159), which means that all of the proceeds from your donations reach the communities.

you have hired yourself. These include the Santa Teresa, Vilcabamba and Choquequirao treks as well as those routes linking Vilcabamba with Choquequirao and Choquequirao with Machu Picchu.

Hiring arrieros and porters

Arrieros can be hired in Cusco. However, the best deal and the best way of supporting the local economy is to hire your team of muleteers from the start of the trek or town closest to the trailhead. For the Salkantay and Santa Teresa treks look for arrieros in Mollepata (see p231); for the Vilcabamba trek or Huancacalle to Cachora via Choquequirao trek try Huancacalle (see p261); for the Choquequirao trek or Choquequirao to Machu Picchu trek recruit your arrieros in Cachora (see p287).

At the time of hiring, negotiate a fair price for a fair service. Don't exploit the local populace and don't haggle ridiculously hard for the sake of a few *soles* (see p87). The arriero may insist on taking a second mule. This is not a con trick to get you to part with more money, it is an insurance factor should one mule go lame or get injured, or should you need to ride at any point due to exhaustion. At the time make sure you agree exactly what is expected of the arriero. Also agree where he will sleep and who will feed him; you may be required to provide shelter and meals for the duration of the trek. Bear in mind that you will need to factor in a sum for the time it takes the arrieros to return home after the trek, and you should allow for a tip too if they provide particularly good service.

For an arriero or porter the rate is around s/30 per day, equivalent to US$11/£7. A tip in the order of 5-10% of the total fee is reasonable, but consider how hard the guy worked on your behalf and remember that he is usually very poorly paid, so give generously.

Getting to Peru

BY AIR

Getting to Peru by air is relatively straightforward and by far the most common means of accessing the country. Airlines with routes to and from Peru include Aerolineas Argentinas, AeroMéxico, Air Canada, Air France, Alitalia, American Airlines, Avianca, British Airways, Continental Airlines, Copa Airlines, Delta Airlines, Iberia, KLM, LAN Airlines, Lufthansa, TACA and Varig. Fares vary according to the airline, the time of year and the route you take but are generally quite costly. The two high seasons and thus the most expensive fares are from mid-December to mid-January and July to mid-August. The majority of the agencies listed on pp14-16 will be able to organize tickets on your behalf; otherwise check out their various websites to see if you can secure a discount by booking online. For a full online guide to flights in and out of Peru visit ⌨ www.traficoperu.com. International plane tickets are expensive in Peru as a result of high taxes so you are better off buying an open return if you don't know when you'll be coming back rather than trying to purchase a one-way ticket home once in Peru.

From Europe

Currently, there are no direct flights from the UK or Ireland to Peru. Flights generally connect with others operating out of gateway cities such as Madrid and Amsterdam. Alternatively they fly via cities in the USA or possibly via other Latin American countries. Flight times are between 16-22 hours depending on the route. Prices begin at a little more than £500 but rise very quickly.

For the best deals look at websites such as: ⌨ www.opodo.co.uk, ⌨ www.ebookers.com, ⌨ www.expedia.co.uk or ⌨ www.cheapflights.com. Otherwise, good places to start looking include: Flight Centre (☎ 0844 800 8660, ⌨ www.flightcentre.co.uk); North South Travel (☎ 01245 608291, ⌨ www.northsouthtravel.co.uk); STA Travel (☎ 0871 230 0040, ⌨ www.statravel.co.uk); Trailfinders (☎ 0845 058 5858, ⌨ www.trailfinders.com); Travel Bag (☎ 0871 703 4698, ⌨ www.travelbag.co.uk).

From the USA and Canada

Direct flights to Lima operate out of Atlanta, Dallas, Houston and Los Angeles although the major gateways are Miami and New York. Return tickets cost US$1200-1600. Air Canada can book you all the way through from Toronto, and operate connecting flights from Montreal, Vancouver and Calgary to Toronto. Fares start from CAN$1400-2000. For good deals try: Air Brokers International (☎ 1 800 883 3273, ⌨ www.airbrokers.com); Exito Travel (☎ 1 800 655 4053, ⌨ www.exitotravel.com); STA Travel (☎ 1 800 781 4040, ⌨ www.statravel.com); Travel cuts (☎ 1 866 246 9762, ⌨ www.travelcuts.com).

From Australia and New Zealand

There are no direct flights from Australia or New Zealand to Peru. Flights are generally via the USA or an alternative South American gateway. Tickets from Australia cost A$1900-2600 whilst fares from New Zealand begin at NZ$2400. Both Flight Centre (⌨ www.flightcentre.com.au or ⌨ www.flightcentre.co.nz) and STA Travel (⌨ www.statravel.com.au or ⌨ www.statravel.co.nz) have offices throughout Australia and New Zealand.

OVERLAND

The Darien Gap separating Panama and Colombia is uncrossed by either roads or railways. This missing chunk of the Pan American Highway effectively prevents all but the most adventurous from travelling overland to Peru. There are routes to Peru from neighbouring South American countries though. Although this isn't quite as straightforward as it might appear, it is possible to access Peru from Bolivia, Brazil, Chile, Colombia and Ecuador.

From **Bolivia** buses from La Paz cross overland into Southern Peru. It is also possible to cross the border on Lake Titicaca and then access Cusco from

Puno. Overland travel from **Brazil** to Peru is possible via Iñapari or through the jungle to Puerto Maldonado which is a short flight or a long bus ride from Cusco. Alternatively catch a ferry from Manaus to Iquitos, a thrilling journey that takes around 10 days, and from where you can fly to Cusco.

The Pan American Highway crosses from **Chile** to Peru between Arica and Tacna on Peru's south coast. Buses from Tacna then go to Arequipa or Puno from where you can connect with others going on to Cusco.

The route into Peru from **Colombia** is hardly ever used but is feasible, crossing from one country to the other at Leticia and then pushing upriver to Iquitos. The Pan American Highway pushes south from **Ecuador** into Peru via Tumbes, from where there are flights and onward bus services to Lima.

Budgeting

The major expense on a trekking trip to Peru, unless you opt for a couple of nights in Cusco's Hotel Monasterio (top suites US$1590 per night; see p168) at the end of your trek, is the trek itself. Although for a budget, independent trek on one of the less popular routes you can get away with saving a little and cutting costs, for an outing on the classic four-day Inca Trail set aside at least US$420 for a basic trek, more if you use a better agency with a well-established reputation or want to trek without any other walkers. Once on the Inca Trail though you won't have to pay for anything other than the occasional soft drink or snack from one of the locals' stands along the way.

Away from the trails and the mountains, Cusco can cost virtually as little or as much as you want it to. In the main, transport, food and accommodation, the biggest three expenses in most people's travels, are reasonable and good value. You can of course treat yourself to a first-class train ride, a Michelin-starred meal and de luxe accommodation, all of which are readily available in both Lima and Cusco. As a guide, budget travellers can probably get by on less than US$30 per day, whilst up to US$60 buys you a better meal and the odd taxi ride as well as a private hot shower in a more salubrious place to stay. More than US$90 should mean that you enjoy a comfortable stay and eat very well. A fully guided tour run by an international agency will almost certainly cost you far more though.

ACCOMMODATION

As with most things, you get what you pay for, and cheap, non-tourist accommodation is often available in rather grubby, sleazy parts of town. Basic tourist accommodation starts at around US$5 per night, though, and a comfortable double room should cost you US$15-35. At the other end of the spectrum, rooms in five-star international chain hotels can easily set you back US$300 whilst for luxury accommodation the sky's the limit. The seasons impact heavily on prices, and in Cusco during the height of the season (June to August), you may find prices increase by up to 25%. The same thing happens around a major celebration or fiesta (see p81).

FOOD

By roughing it in the countryside, eating locally sourced produce bought at market or from villagers, you can get by on very little. Even in major towns food can be dirt cheap if you stick to the street vendors who ply their wares at all hours of day and night or take advantage of the good set menu deals available in local restaurants, although hygiene standards are not always of the highest. You ought to be able to find a good meal in a decent, clean restaurant for less than US$10. Top end venues with superb reputations and food to match, of which there are plenty in Peru, will naturally set you back rather more.

TRANSPORT

Public transport costs are usually very reasonable in Peru, even for long-distance journeys. You are of course at the mercy of cramped, dilapidated buses and dozy drivers, but this is the reality of public transport here. Then again, rates are so reasonable it seems churlish to complain. Additional comfort and safety comes at only a slightly higher price if you opt to travel by private, luxury bus.

The exception to the good-value rule is the train from Cusco to Aguas Calientes (see p357), which has far higher rates than you might expect as it is a monopoly and caters to a captive audience of eager tourists.

When to go

The trekking season in Peru typically runs during the dry season from April to October when there is likely to be the most sunshine and least rain on the trails. During this period the trails get particularly busy between June and July and it can be hard to secure permits for some of the most popular treks such as the classic Inca Trail without a lot of advance planning. To maximize your enjoyment and escape the worst of the crowds target April-May or September-October for your trip.

At other times of year it is still possible to tackle most of the trails but be aware that in the wet they can become very much trickier propositions than in the dry, and the changeable and occasionally awful weather means that some of the treks are a wash out. The Vilcabamba Trail is particularly affected by bad rain and during continued wet periods you may struggle to find an agency willing to make the trip. If considering trekking independently, you should be an experienced trekker before setting off on some of the more arduous, out-of-the-way routes at this time of year.

Remember that although Machu Picchu itself is open year-round and can be an enchanting, mysterious place when shrouded in cloud and clear of crowds, the classic Inca Trail is closed completely in February.

LIMA – CLIMATE CHARTS

Max/min rainfall (mm)

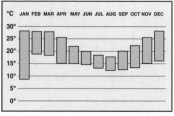

Max/min temperature (°C)

CUSCO – CLIMATE CHARTS

Max/min rainfall (mm)

Max/min temperature (°C)

FOR HOW LONG?

The popularity of the Cusco region amongst trekkers is entirely understandable. Amongst some exceptionally dramatic scenery are hidden ruins and lost cities to rival anywhere else in the world. The treks described and detailed in this book take between two and nine days to complete, with the majority taking four to six days. When calculating how long your trip needs to be, remember to allow a day to travel to and from Cusco from Lima (more if you decide to travel overland rather than fly) and a couple of days in Cusco to aid acclimatization. This last factor is very important and will improve your chances of enjoying and succeeding on your trek and reduce the likelihood of you suffering from altitude sickness and inadvertently endangering your life. Since this is South America you may also want to build in a contingency day in case there are problems with the flights in either direction.

If you haven't pre-booked your treks and are arriving in Cusco hoping to put something together on spec, allow at least four to six weeks to secure a place on the classic Inca Trail because of the complicated regulations and restricted numbers permitted to start the trek each day. Bear in mind that during the peak season it will take you far longer than this to actually secure a slot. You should be able to put together a trek on one of the other routes within two to five days, though.

Route options

[**See Route Options map overleaf**]. The treks described in this book offer you a selection of routes to Machu Picchu, many people's focus when visiting Peru, which take various lengths of time and cater for people of varying ability and interest levels. The legendary trek has become a 'must do' for many travellers. However, the popularity of the trek has meant that the trail and the ruins along it have had to deal with an increasing number of visitors. To counter the detrimental effects of this influx, the Peruvian government has imposed a strict limit on the number of people able to start the trek at any one time. The result has been that lots of people have fallen foul of the regulations and been unable to tackle the trek.

The good news, though, is that there are a number of alternative treks in the Cusco region, many of them on original Inca trails to other, less well-known but similarly stunning sites such as Choquequirao and Vilcabamba, routes and ruins that may be more appealing in some respects as you don't have to share them with 500 other people every day. There are also two much longer, more difficult expeditions that actually link several of the key Inca sites and provide you with a wonderful, broad experience of the region, its history and its archaeological remains.

THE CLASSIC INCA TRAIL   [3-4 days, see pp209-223]

This is the trek that most people think of when picturing Peru: it has become synonymous with the country. Beginning at Km88 on the railway line to Aguas Calientes, the trek follows an original Inca path uncovered in 1911 by Hiram Bingham and developed in 1944 by Dr Paul Fejos, past the restored ruins at Patallacta, Runcu Racay, Sayacmarca, Phuyu Pata Marca, Intipata and Huinay Huayna to arrive eventually at Machu Picchu. The 43km (26½ mile) trek takes **3-4 days** and is reasonably gruelling; although some of the trek is through exquisite cloud forest and rich subtropical jungle, other stages are through exposed mountain scenery and the path also crosses two steep-sided passes at 4200m/13,750ft.

This trail is subject to the Inca Trail regulations and permits must be secured well in advance of departure. It is closed completely during February.

Chaunquiri

Espíritu Pampa
(Vilcabamba)

Vilcabamba Trail
A challenging 3-4 day trek (allow 6-9 days in all) between Huancacalle and Chaunquiri via the ruins of Vilcabamba – the real Lost City of the Incas.

Río Vilcabamba

Pucyura

Pampaconas

Huancacalle

Vilcabamba
La Nueva

Panta
△

*Abra de
Choquetecarpo*

Arma

Santa Teresa Trek
Currently permit free, this 3- to 4-day trek follows the forested Santa Teresa valley to the foot of Machu Picchu mountain.

Huancacalle to Choquequirao Trek
An epic 8- to 9-day link route, enabling you to visit two great sites. Spectacular and crowd free.

*Quebrada
Totora*

Yanama

Maizal

Corihuarachina
△

Totora

Pincha
Unuyoc

Choquequirao

**Choquequirao to
Machu Picchu Trek**
Links the top two sites in a superb but challenging 8- to 9-day trek.

Choquequirao Trek
From Cachora to Choquequirao and back takes 4-5 days, descending into then climbing out of the breathtakingly sheer Apurímac Valley.

*Río
Cachora*

Cachora

Curahuasi

To Abancay

Sayhuite

PLANNING YOUR TRIP

Route Options

To Quillabamba

Chaullay

Rio Santa Teresa

Santa Teresa

La Hidroeléctrica

Machu Picchu

Aguas Calientes

km104

Riverside Trail
Km88 to Machu Picchu in 2-2½ days. Quiet and easy.

Veronica △

Lucmabamba

5

1
2
3
4
6
7
8
9
10
11
12

3rd pass

2nd pass

km88 km82 Chilca (km77)

La Playa

Hatun Poccos

Patallacta

Ollantaytambo

Inca Trail
The Classic Route takes 3-4 days and begins at Km88. Other tours start at Km82 or Km77.

1st Pass: Dead Woman's Pass

Huayllabamba

To Cusco

△ Palqay

Paucarcancha

Inca Canal

Rio Humantay

△ Humantay

Rio Cusichaca

Rayampata

Chaullay Ccolpapampa

△ Salkantay

Pass

Tucarhuay △

Inca Chiriaska Pass

Salkantay Pampa

Cerro Soray △

Soray Pampa

Salkantay Trek
Excellent 6-day trek from Mollepata to Machu Picchu. Quite strenuous when crossing the Inca Chiriaska Pass. Superb views of Salkantay.

Zurite

To Cusco

Rio Blanco

Limatambo

Marcocasa/ Cruz Pata

Keyed Inca Trail Sites
1 Wayna Picchu
2 Intipunku
3 Choquesuysuy
4 Intipata
5 Paltallacta/Llactapata
6 Winay Wayna
7 Phuyu Pata Marca
8 Chachabamba
9 Concha Marca
10 Sayac Marca
11 Runcu Raccay
12 Machu Quente

Mollepata

Rio Apurimac

0   10   20km

0   5   10   15 miles

VARIATIONS ON THE CLASSIC TRAIL

There are two straightforward variations to the classic Inca Trail. The first (see p223) begins at the village of Chilca, which stands at Km77 on the railway line before tracking alongside the Urubamba River to join the original trail from Km88. Dry and dusty, it isn't all that interesting and not really worth the additional day's hike unless your tour happens to begin from here. The other option (see p225) is to begin at Km82, which offers half a day's more riverside stroll than the Km88 option, but is less monotonous than the Km77 stretch. You also get to visit the ruins at Huillca Raccay, which overlook Patallacta. Trekkers on both these routes are at the mercy of the Inca Trail regulations and must secure a permit well in advance.

SHORTER TRAILS

For those pushed for time or not inclined to mount a four-day trek to Machu Picchu, there are several options that allow you to get a sense of the approach route to the ruins and then explore the site itself without having to resort to the shuttle bus from Aguas Calientes.

Km104 and the Purification Trail   [2 days, see pp227-8]

There are two route options from Km104 on the railway, both of which take two days to complete, although only one of these is actually spent trekking. From the Inca ruins at Chachabamba you can either scale a steep hillside on a narrow, exposed path to reach Huinay Huayna and then join the classic Inca Trail for the final approach to Machu Picchu, or you can head down the river to Choquesuysuy before tackling an arduous three-hour climb to Huinay Huayna along a route nicknamed the 'Purification Trail'.

People using either of these routes used to be able to stay at the Trekker's hostel at Huinay Huayna, but this is now no longer the case. Consequently you must descend through Machu Picchu to stay in Aguas Calientes before returning to explore the site the following morning. Both options are subject to the Inca Trail regulations and trek permits must be reserved well in advance. The route is open during February though, when the main, classic approach to Machu Picchu is shut.

Km88 Riverside Trail   [2-3 days, see pp229-30]

From Km88 on the railway line it is possible to follow the Río Urubamba all the way to Km104, from where you are able to ascend to Huinay Huayna via one of two routes. The scenic stroll avoids the tough climbs associated with the classic Inca Trail but it also avoids all of the ruins that you would otherwise encounter along the route, making it a far less attractive option. This trek is also subject to the Inca Trail regulations and should be arranged well in advance.

OTHER TREKS TO MACHU PICCHU

There are two other methods of trekking to Machu Picchu. One is an extended hike that begins with a genuine wilderness experience and a chance to explore the slopes of Mt Salkantay, the sacred mountain of the Incas, before joining the classic Inca Trail for its final three days; the other is an excellent, charming alternative to the classic trail that is currently unregulated and therefore is very popular with those who have fallen foul of the strict Inca Trail regulations.

The Salkantay Trek   [6-7 days, see pp230-41]

The name Salkantay derives from the Quecha word 'Salka', meaning wild, savage or invincible. It is an apt name for the mountain under which this trek, a dramatic extension of the classic Inca Trail, begins. Typically it takes 6-7 days and combines wonderfully a stretch of wilderness walking largely free from crowds and the rather more popular and crowded classic pilgrimage. Also known as the Mollepata Trek by some agencies, trek providers and writers, this trail ascends from the village of Mollepata into the mountains where it climbs over a 4950m/16,235ft knife-like pass on the eastern shoulder of Mt Salkantay. From here it descends into the valley of the Urubamba and joins the classic Inca Trail at Huayllabamba before continuing along the traditional route to reach Machu Picchu. Because it joins the Inca Trail, the Salkantay trek is also subject to the Inca Trail regulations and requires you to have a permit, secured well in advance.

The Santa Teresa Trek   [3-4 days, see pp241-56]

This route to Machu Picchu, via the 'backdoor', has become increasingly popular with those who have fallen foul of the Inca Trail regulations and failed to book far enough in advance to secure a trek permit for the classic Inca Trail. It is also usually quieter and less heavily used than the traditional route although as more and more people discover it so the amount of traffic on the trail increases. It's also the only route where there is the option to stay in lodges rather than simply camp, assuming that you choose to trek with the agent that owns the properties (see p159).

The 3- to 4-day trek begins from Mollepata and climbs over a pass (4700m/15,420ft) on the western shoulder of Mt Salkantay before descending into the very attractive, forested Santa Teresa Valley. From here it clambers over a ridge into the Aobamba Valley and then joins the Urubamba Valley, finishing at the foot of Machu Picchu mountain. Although there are hardly any Inca ruins along the trek, it is a very scenic walk through some of the region's most picturesque landscapes. The sprawling, partially uncovered yet highly significant site at Llactapata and the fact that the trek finishes on the doorstep of one of the finest archaeological sites in the Americas are some compensation though. At present, and despite rumblings to the contrary, this route remains free from the Inca Trail regulations and you are able to trek it independently and arrange your own guide and porters. You do need to pay s/129 (approximately US$46) for an INC permit at Soraypampa if your agency has not incorporated the cost into the total fee; this is in addition to the entrance fee for Machu Picchu. Some agencies might try to avoid the checkpoint so as not to pay the fee but this is not to be condoned.

THE VILCABAMBA TRAIL
[6- to 9-day trip with 4 days of walking, see pp256-82]

This remote, rarely tackled trek follows the low-level route the Incas took as they fled from the conquistadors deep into the jungle, where they built the last capital of Vilcabamba. The trek itself takes roughly four days but because the path is rarely used it's sometimes overgrown, often muddy in places and prone to damage by landslips so it's worth factoring in additional time. You will also need to take into account the time it takes to get to the out-of-the-way trailheads at Huancacalle and Chaunquiri too, and might want to include additional days in Quillabamba or Huancacalle. To be safe, set aside six to nine days for the entire expedition.

The ruins at Espíritu Pampa, thought to be the site of Vilcabamba, are less immediately spectacular than those at Machu Picchu or Choquequirao, because they lie buried in the thick jungle and haven't been particularly cleared or restored. Instead they have a different type of appeal, and much of the magic and reward for walking this route comes from the jungle that you pass through and the varied flora you are able to see. Since the route isn't currently subject to any regulations you may trek it independently or arrange your own guides and arrieros to help shoulder the burden.

THE CHOQUEQUIRAO TREK   [4-5 days, see pp283-98]

This trek travels from Cachora to the ruins at Choquequirao, the first major Inca site uncovered outside Cusco and yet one that is still to be fully explored. Having reached the ruins at the end of the second day you then retrace your steps and walk out along the same trail. With a day at the ruins to explore this extensive site you should reasonably expect the trek to take 4-5 days.

The trek is physically quite demanding as it requires you to descend 1500m/4920ft into the sheer Apurimac Valley in order to cross the Apurimac River, only to then have to climb 1800m/5900ft up the similarly steep opposite cliff to access the ruins perched on a ridge far above. It's hot and dry, and there are few points at which to collect water along the route so you must be prepared to carry additional supplies for much of the trek. However, the vertiginous valley is spectacular and the ruins themselves, which resemble Machu Picchu in many respects, are fascinating, meaning that the trek is set to replace the classic trail as the serious hikers' alternative. It isn't currently covered by any regulations, although this may well change as its popularity grows.

COMBINING ROUTES

Many of these routes can be combined, tackled in stages or done in the opposite direction. The exception is the classic Inca Trail which must be tackled in the direction described in this guide. There are also numerous alternatives in the mountains and valleys around Cusco. Two of the finest combination routes are the longer, more adventurous paths that connect Huancacalle to Choquequirao, and Choquequirao to Machu Picchu. Neither of these routes is regulated at present and both can be trekked independently with a team you have sourced and hired yourself.

Choquequirao to Machu Picchu Trek   [8-9 days, see pp298-311]

This is potentially the finest outing described here. The 8- to 9-day trek links two of the most spectacular Inca ruins by way of a stretch of stunning countryside. From Cachora the path follows the Choquequirao route to the ruins perched precariously high above the Apurímac valley. Descending past the ruins at Pinchu Unuyoc the trail tumbles down one hillside only to have to clamber steeply up another, before crossing the Abra San Juan and going down to Yanama. From here it cuts away east and climbs through a section of pretty puna to cross another pass in the lee of a number of giant glaciated peaks before dropping into the jungle to join the Santa Teresa Trek at Ccolpapampa and approaching Machu Picchu via the 'back door'.

Not for the faint hearted, the route represents quite an undertaking but it does provide you with two exceptional archaeological sites and leads you though a wide range of Peru's vegetation zones so that you'll experience a huge amount of native flora.

Huancacalle to Cachora Trek   [8-9 days, see pp311-324]

This epic trek, which takes 8-9 days and can be done in either direction, sets off from Huancacalle, via the archeological sites at Vitcos and Ñusta España to cross the high pass at Choquetecarpo and descend into the valley beyond, where it passes through the remote, traditional hamlet of Yanama. Beyond here it climbs and descends steeply to cross the Abra San Juan and breach the valley of the Río Blanco before arriving at the partially reconstructed ruins at Pinchu Unuyoc. A further steep ascent leads to Choquequirao, perched high above the plunging Apurímac valley. After a day exploring the site join the Choquequirao Trek trail as it plunges into and then rears out of the deep canyon to arrive eventually at Cachora. Tough and occasionally tricky to follow, this route is a real challenge. The rewards, though, are spectacular and you will spend much of the walk free from crowds.

If tackled in reverse, finishing at Huancacalle, there is the opportunity to then push on to Espíritu Pampa following the route outlined in the Vilcabamba Trail description to complete a spectacular traverse that would probably take more than two weeks to complete.

❏ **Other activities**
The Cusco region offers far more than simply trekking. Unless your schedule is tight, you should consider trying to take in some of the other world-class activities available on the city's doorstep. For a list of activities that includes mountain-biking, white-water rafting, ballooning, sky-diving and trips to the rainforest as well as a list of the agencies that specialize in organizing them see pp160-1.

What to take

Walking in the Andes should not be taken lightly regardless of which trek you choose. An ill-fitting boot or a rucksack that won't fit properly can cause discomfort and potentially spoil your trip.

Try to travel light but strike a compromise between weight and what is really essential, making sure that you have sufficient appropriate clothing to be safe and comfortable. A lot of people make the mistake of overpacking. Given the quality and advances in modern gear, there's no reason to take enormous amounts of equipment or clothing with you. Don't forget that you can always pick up additional things in Peru.

Weight is a vital consideration on treks where you are responsible for carrying your own bags. On those trips where either porters or mules will be carrying most of your luggage, don't use this as an excuse to take unnecessary things just because someone else will be shouldering the load.

FOOTWEAR

Your top priority whilst trekking ought to be the condition of your feet. This will have the single biggest impact on your enjoyment of the trek and your ability to tackle some of the longer, more arduous stages.

Some people manage in a pair of stout trainers but these will not protect your ankles, are not waterproof and could result in you having bruised and sore feet after some of the more gruelling days spent crossing rocky or uneven terrain. Sections of the treks are rough and bumpy and you will definitely have to negotiate stretches of scree, scramble over loose boulders, cross wet, smooth rocks, wade through small streams and possibly trudge through patches of snow. Therefore you will need footwear that is supportive without being too restrictive or rigid, is waterproof, has sewn in tongues, and soles that can grip even in wet conditions. Ideally you should have a pair of sturdy **boots**. Get a pair that have a little room at the toe end to assist circulation and prevent your toes getting crushed or bruised in the course of prolonged periods of descent. Whatever you buy, make sure that your shoes are properly broken in well ahead of the start of your trek; otherwise you may end up with blisters.

Sandals or **flip flops** are also a good idea to give your feet a bit of a respite at the end of the day. They might also come in useful when crossing small streams.

Some people choose to wear **gaiters** on some of the tougher sections of track to help keep water, mud and other debris out of their boots. They will also stop your shins from getting scratched by the undergrowth. Telescopic **trekking poles** that have shock-absorbing springs in are also a good idea, particularly for steep downhill sections of track as they can give much-needed support to your knees. Whether you use one or two poles is down to personal preference.

❏ **Old clothes required**
If you have a little spare room in your luggage and can squeeze in some old or unwanted clothes, there are various agencies in Cusco that will accept donations and distribute the clothes to porters or local villages. A good place to start is the office of Andean Travel Web (see box p19), which makes collections and regularly hands out clothes, school equipment and Christmas presents to small communities in the region.

CLOTHES

Since the treks described in this book take you across a range of landscapes and altitudes you will need to carry clothes that are appropriate for a range of temperatures and conditions. Adopt the simple but effective technique of layering. The base layer should keep the skin comfortable and dry. The second, insulation layer should trap and retain body heat in order to provide extra warmth, whilst the outer layer must protect you against the wind, rain, snow and even sun.

It is vital that the **base layer** dries easily and helps to conduct sweat away from the body. T-shirts made of synthetic materials do the best job of 'wicking' moisture away from the skin. Wool, silk or cotton are less useful for this layer.

Fleece is the most desirable material for the **insulation layer** since it is light, wind-resistant and quick drying. Wool is also a good insulator but dries very slowly and can become very heavy when wet. Try to ensure that, since you'll be bending and stretching as you work your way across uneven terrain, your lower back is adequately covered.

Your legs need to have as much freedom of movement as possible. Shorts offer the most flexibility. Lightweight, tough trousers are also essential and ideally should be made of rip-stop fabric. In general avoid thick, heavy trousers, especially denim jeans as they restrict movement and can be very difficult to get dry.

The Andes get a lot of rainfall so good **waterproofs** are essential, even in summer. The weather can be highly unpredictable in the mountains and rain can occur pretty much all year-round. Modern raincoats made from lightweight, waterproof, highly breathable fabric allow water vapour to pass through the jacket from the inside to the outside but stop water from leaking in. In this way condensation is prevented from forming on the inside of the coat, which would quickly drain away body heat. The arms of the jacket should be long enough to fit over warm under-layers and the coat should have a long enough tail that your lower back isn't exposed when bending or stretching forward. The coat also ought to have a roomy hood that can be drawn tight but that still provides you with peripheral vision. A variety of pockets in which to store maps, snacks, etc is also useful.

A **hat** provides vital protection against the elements. A wide-brimmed version is a good idea to shield your eyes from the harsh mountain sun. A woolly hat can be useful for keeping your head warm in the evenings or when the temperature drops. Take a pair of **gloves** to keep your hands warm and your fingers flexible at higher altitudes or in less than perfect conditions.

EQUIPMENT

Rucksack

Comfort is the key when choosing a rucksack for a multi-day trek. Modern packs are available in a variety of sizes. Get an experienced shop-assistant to fit you with the right-sized pack before buying one.

The hip belt ought to support about a third of the weight of the pack, with the rest being carried on your shoulders. Make sure that the straps are adjustable so that you can alter them to suit the terrain: when climbing it is better to take the weight on your shoulders, whilst when descending it is often more comfortable to release the shoulder straps slightly and tighten the hip belt.

Try not to buy a pack that is too large, otherwise the temptation is to try and fill it. The pack should have easily accessible compartments for the items you want most often, such as water bottles, guidebook, maps and snacks. Straps and buckles on the outside of the pack can also be useful for securing trekking poles or other bits of temporarily unnecessary kit. All materials should be robust and long lasting. Stitching on the pack must be high quality and any zips should be resilient and smooth running.

In very heavy rain even the most waterproof packs can leak. As a precaution you should use a heavy-duty waterproof inner liner to protect your gear and a pack cover to sluice off the majority of the rain. For further protection put your things into plastic shopping bags or waterproof 'stuff sacks', which ought to guarantee that everything stays dry.

Sleeping bags and mats

A **sleeping bag** is an essential piece of kit since you will be camping along the treks. Some agencies will hire out or provide sleeping bags as part of the package that they offer. However, if you want to use your own bag rather than sleep under someone else's bedding, a lightweight, compact sleeping bag offering three-season comfort in temperatures of -5°C ought to be sufficient unless you are particularly prone to the cold in which case a four-season bag may be more appropriate.

Equally useful and certainly worth taking is a **sheet sleeping-bag** – essentially a sheet folded and sewn along two sides – to use as an inner liner for your main bag, since they offer an extra layer of warmth, are easy to wash and keep the inside of the main sleeping bag cleaner.

Sleeping mats are also a good idea and can immeasurably improve the quality of a good night's sleep by cushioning you and by insulating you from the cold ground. Old fashioned foam mats are OK but you are better off with a modern, self-inflating Therm-a-rest. These can puncture so consider taking a repair kit with you too.

Tent

All agencies are obliged to provide tents for the treks you undertake with them. These ought to be of serviceable quality and completely sufficient for your trip. If you are considering trekking independently, make sure you have a lightweight, robust tent that packs up compactly. You need to seal the seams to stop rain getting in. If you decide to travel independently once in Peru, it is possible to hire tents from a number of agencies and equipment stores in Cusco.

Stoves, pans and crockery

On an organized trek the agency is also obliged to provide all of the cooking equipment and enough crockery and cutlery for the entire group. However, should you want to trek independently, you will need to take your own. Butane gas stoves such as the camping-gaz ones with the small blue cylinders are perfectly adequate although you may want to buy cylinders containing a butane-propane mix that will work more effectively at altitude. These are readily available in Cusco. Take light aluminium pans that can be stored one inside the other. Plates aren't necessary as long as you don't mind eating from the pan. Do take cups and cutlery though, as well as some sort of wire scrubber to clean the dirty dishes. All of this can be bought or hired in Cusco.

FOOD

Dehydrated or vacuum-packed food is a useful quick energy source or a treat along the trail. There's no need to bring much from home, though, as there are lots of opportunities to buy food in Cusco. Agencies will provide all the main meals for organized treks and probably produce fruit and sweets at opportune moments as well. If you are setting out alone, take food that doesn't weigh too much but which delivers large amounts of carbohydrate. Potato, *quinoa* (an Andean grain) and polenta are all good sources, as are pasta and dried noodles. Dried sausage or tinned meat is also a good idea. Herbs and spices as well as salt and pepper can help add flavour to otherwise uninspiring suppers. Soups or porridge are a good way of getting additional hot food and liquid into your body whilst nuts, chocolate and boiled sweets are a good way of raising your spirits, getting a quick boost or winning friends.

TOILETRIES

Take only those toiletries that you think you'll actually need. You should aim to be well equipped but don't bring bulky items: take the smallest bottles possible. That said, before you set out on the actual trek make sure you take everything you might need. Whilst Cusco has several chemists, you are unlikely to find one in the smaller towns at the trailheads for each trek and certainly won't come across any once the trek has actually begun.

A checklist of toiletries should include: **a bar of soap** (keep it in a bag or container; liquid soap is a good idea for washing clothes); **towel** (most outdoor shops now sell special low-bulk, highly absorbent towels); **toothbrush** and **toothpaste** (take only as much toothpaste as you'll need – buy a small tube or take a part-used one to save space and weight); **toilet paper**; **pre-moistened tissues** (for example 'Wet-Wipes'; useful in a number of situations); **nail scissors**; **earplugs** (may help if sharing a campsite with a crowd of snorers); **lip balm** (essential on higher sections of the trek where the track is exposed to full sun); **tampons**; **contraceptives**.

MEDICAL KIT

Your medical kit should cover most eventualities though hopefully you won't have to use any of it. However, most people find they need to dip into their supplies sooner or later to sort out everyday ailments, such as blisters, caused by trekking. Perhaps most importantly, do not forget to take an adequate supply of any **prescription drugs** that you might need.

A basic medical kit should comprise **hydrocolloid blister pads** and **zinc oxide tape** with a strong adhesive for securing dressings or bandages. **Plasters** are good for covering and protecting minor cuts and injuries. **Sterilized gauze** is useful should you need to soak up blood or pus from a cut or graze. It is also useful in keeping a cut clean and free from infection. **Antiseptic cream** or spray will prevent minor infections from developing. **Anti-inflammatory painkillers** such as Ibuprofen are helpful in easing the discomfort of bruises or sprains. **Hydrocortisone cream** is a good aid if you suffer from heat rash. **Deep heat spray** will ease minor sprains and help to loosen or warm-up sore muscles. **Hypodermic needles** are essential tools for piercing blisters; use a sterilized needle to dig out a splinter that doesn't have a head/end proud of the skin for a tweezer to grip; **tweezers**, though, can be helpful for less delicate work. A pair of small, sharp **scissors** is also a good idea. **Bandages** may be needed to cover more substantial wounds or to support damaged joints. An **elasticated knee support** is helpful for weak knees and useful on the long pounding descents.

High factor **sun-cream** is vital, as the sun at altitude can be very harmful. **Aloe vera** is also useful in the wake of sunburn and to ease the discomfort of windburn, rashes or grazes. Although not strictly necessary, you may wish to take **multivitamin tablets** to supplement your diet in the course of the trek.

MISCELLANEOUS ITEMS

As well as the essential items you may also want to bring a few other bits and pieces. A **watch** is very useful for gauging how far and fast you have travelled as well as keeping track of time. **Sunglasses** help to cut out the sun's glare and will protect you from reflected light. A **penknife** with all of its various blades and tools is invaluable as is a **water bottle**, preferably with two-litre capacity. The modern Platypus or Camelbak system, whereby a pouch is connected to a tube so you can drink while you walk, is a good idea as it encourages you to drink more. **Water purifying tablets** or iodine drops are a good idea if you haven't time to boil the water before drinking it. A reliable, compact waterproof **torch** is a good idea, as are extra **batteries** for it. A **head torch** is an even better idea as it means that your hands are still free. **Matches** and a **lighter** are necessary to ignite cooking gear or start a fire. A **whistle** may prove to be a vital survival aid should you get lost or injured and need to attract attention. A stretch of **string** has several uses – to fasten things to the outside of your pack, for example, or to act as an impromptu washing line.

A **compass** or **GPS unit** may be useful if you're trekking independently and could become essential in bad weather as the tracks are poorly defined in places.

Finally, you must remember to take degradable **rubbish bags** with you since it is important that you pack any rubbish out of the mountains and get rid of it responsibly in a town.

PHOTOGRAPHIC EQUIPMENT

Mountains and landscapes are notoriously difficult to photograph well. The results often don't capture the scale or grandeur of the Andes and the powerful sweep and subtle colours of the hillsides quite often don't translate well to prints.

Good quality, **compact cameras** are light, tough and take adequate photographs. **SLR** or **digital SLR** cameras and a couple of lenses offer more scope for creativity and increase your chance of capturing the delicate light and effects found in the mountains. Don't forget your **battery charger**; as there's nowhere to use it on the trail you may need **spare batteries**. A **zoom lens** will afford you a greater degree of compositional flexibility without adding too much weight to your bag. A **lens hood** will reduce the glare from the sun, whilst a **UV filter** will cut through the high-altitude haze. A **polarizer** will also cut through the haze and deepen the blue of the sky as well as add colour and depth to lakes and coasts. For self-timer or longer exposure shots a small, lightweight, sturdy **tripod** is a good idea and a remote **shutter-release cable** is a good investment too.

A **carrying case** that can be attached to your belt or waist strap is useful since it means that your equipment will be readily accessible yet still be well protected. If you have to stop, drop your pack and rummage about for your camera you may be less inclined to use it. Make sure your camera bag is waterproof since there is quite a high likelihood that you'll get rained on.

Take extra **memory cards** if you need them but note that most internet cafés will usually also offer a service whereby they download the photos off your camera card and burn them onto a CD.

MAPS

Good quality, trekking-scale maps of Peru are not all that easy to come by. The IGN (Instituto Geográfico Nacional) in Lima produces a series of 1:100,000 scale topographic maps of the country that have contours at 50m intervals as well as spot heights. The legend includes all standard information such as settlements and roads plus a great deal of terrain and vegetation detail. These are also available from the South American Explorer's Club (see box p130), which also produces a 1:25,000 scale map of the Inca Trail showing contours, spot heights and places of particular interest along the route. Some specialized map shops outside of Peru also sell both IGN and South American Explorer Club maps. Stanfords in the UK sells both through its shops (12-14 Long Acre, London WC2E, and 29 Corn St, Bristol BS1) and online at 🖥 www.stanfords.co.uk.

The IGN maps that you need for the classic Inca Trail are 2444 (27-r) and 2344 (27-q). For the Vilcabamba Trail you will also need the north-western section of 2344 (27-q) as well as 2244 (27-p) and 2245 (26-p). For the trek to and from Choquequirao search out maps 2343 (28-q) and 2344 (27-q). Be aware that old editions of (27-q) do not show Mollepata, the start point for both the Salkantay and Santa Teresa treks, although the hamlet is featured on the new version of the map.

For the longer treks linking several sites, you will need to track down additional maps. For the route from Cachora to Machu Picchu via Choquequirao you'll need maps 2343 (28-q) and 2344 (27-q), whilst to get from Cachora to Espíritu Pampa via Choquequirao or in reverse from Vilcabamba to Choquequirao and then on to Cachora, you will need Nos 2343 (28-q), 2344 (27-q), 2244 (27-p) and 2245 (26-p). There is also a more general 1:200,000 scale map available of the region to the north of Cusco. Although this scale is inadequate for trekking, it does help to put the area into context.

ITMB Publishing (🖳 www.itmb.com) also produces a detailed road map of *Cusco and South Peru*, updated in 2009. As well as the main map featuring neighbouring towns such as Pisac, Calca and Urubamba, there is a detailed town plan of Cusco at 1:11,000 scale and an inset of the Inca Trail at 1:50,000 scale, in addition to an annotated plan of the ruins at Machu Picchu. Cusco town plans are also available from Editorial Lima 2000, whilst ITMB produces a decent street map of Lima.

RECOMMENDED READING

For a good introduction to Peru's history and culture, see *The Peru Reader: History, Culture, Politics* (Duke University Press). It's a fascinating anthology covering a wide range of subjects.

Guidebooks
Each of the major publishers has a guidebook to Peru. Best of these are the *Footprint Guide to Peru* and the *Rough Guide to Peru*. Lonely Planet also produce a very comprehensive *Peru* guide and their *Trekking in the Central Andes* highlights selected treks in Peru, Bolivia and Ecuador; Lonely Planet's *Quechua Phrasebook* is recommended. Charles Brod's *Apus and Incas* (Inca Expeditions) guide to trekking in the Cusco region is available in Cusco, where you can also find Peter Frost's *Exploring Cusco*.

Expedition reports and travelogues
Lost City of the Incas by Hiram Bingham (Phoenix) is a reprint of the classic account of the rediscovery of Machu Picchu. A rip-roaring adventure story, although bear in mind that many of his theories about the site have not stood the test of time (see p329). For more on Hiram Bingham, his rediscovery of the site and the controversy surrounding the artefacts shipped home, see Chris Heaney's *Cradle of Gold: The Story of Hiram Bingham, A Real Life Indiana Jones, and his Search for Machu Picchu* (Palgrave MacMillan).

Earlier trip reports and accounts of expeditions include *Peregrinations of a Pariah* by Flora Tristan and *Peru, Travel and Exploration in the Land of the Incas* by E George Squier (Macmillan).

Hugh Thomson's *The White Rock: An Exploration of the Inca Heartland* is a fascinating account of a modern explorer and archaeologist at work as the author and colleague Gary Ziegler search for and rediscover the Inca site at Coca Cota in the Vilcabamba region. There's good information on the Incas in general and on past explorers, whilst his *Cochineal Red* (both Phoenix) is a thorough investigation of earlier civilizations. In *A Sacred Landscape: The Search for Ancient Peru* (Overlook) Thomson explores Moches, Chavin, Nasca and other ancient civilizations of Peru with an interesting description of the recent archaeological work at the Inca site of Llactapata, near Machu Picchu.

Classic travelogues include those by Ronald Wright, *Cut Stones and Crossroads* (currently out of print) and Matthew Parris, *Inca Kola* (Weidenfeld and Nicholson). *Three Letters from the Andes* by Patrick Leigh Fermor (John Murray) is an enthralling, typically lyrical account of the author's trip to Machu Picchu that perfectly captures the landscape and people he encounters. *Eight Feet in the Andes: Travels with a Mule in Unknown Peru* (John Murray), describing a journey made in 1983, is Dervla Murphy at her best.

The Incas

There are countless books on the Incas, with titles aimed at everyone from children to academics.

The definitive text is John Hemming's *The Conquest of the Incas* (Macmillan), which ranks as one of the great pieces of historical writing. Hemming's book *Monuments of the Incas*, featuring stunning black and white photography by Edward Ranney, was updated in 2010 and reissued by Thames and Hudson.

The Last Days of the Incas (Simon & Schuster), by filmmaker and journalist Kim MacQuarrie, reads like a riveting novel and covers not only the Conquest but also the exploits of more modern adventurers rediscovering Machu Picchu and Vilcabamba.

Although the Incas had no form of writing there are some fascinating near-contemporary Spanish accounts. The most thorough is by Pedro de Cieza de Léon, a soldier who arrived in Peru in 1548 and recorded the conquest in *The Discovery and Conquest of Peru* (Duke University Press). Garcilaso Inca de la Vega, the son of an Inca princess and a Spanish conquistador, wrote *The Royal Commentaries of the Inca* (Andean World), originally published in 1609. It's most interesting for its description of Inca customs and culture, and of Peruvian flora and fauna. The version readily available in Peru is illustrated with some of the naïve drawings by Felipe Huamán Poma de Ayala originally published in his *Nueve Crónica y Buen Gobierno*.

'Do you eat gold?' asks the Inca. 'I eat gold', replies the Conquistador.

FELIPE HUAMÁN POMA DE AYALA, FROM HIS *NUEVE CRÓNICA Y BUEN GOBIERNO* (c1600)

Michael Moseley's illustrated archaeological survey, *The Incas and their Ancestors* (Thames and Hudson) is excellent. Maria Rostworowski de Diez Canseco's *History of the Inca Realm* provides a Peruvian perspective on the Incas that is scholarly yet accessible. *Art in the Andes, from Chavin to Inca* (Thames and Hudson) by Rebecca Stone-Miller is authoritative and well illustrated.

Machu Picchu and other Inca sites

Machu Picchu by John Hemming (Readers' Digest Wonders of Man Series) is a fine book on **Machu Picchu** and its position in Peru's history. *The Machu Picchu Guidebook* by Ruth Wright and Alfredo Zegarra (Johnson Books) is a good contemporary guide to the site and its features.

Machu Picchu, Unveiling the Mystery of the Incas (Yale), edited by Yale archaeologists Richard Burger and Lucy Salazar, was published to coincide with the Machu Picchu exhibition at the Peabody. Apart from the excellent photographs and the catalogue of 120 objects from the site, the book is also interesting in that it includes Hiram Bingham's original 1913 report of the rediscovery and a scholarly modern overview of Machu Picchu and its significance.

Johan Reinhard refines the theory of Machu Picchu as a cosmological, hydrological and sacred geographical centre in the fourth edition of *Machu Picchu, Exploring an Ancient Sacred Center* (Nuevas Imágenas).

The Machu Picchu Historical Sanctuary by Jim Bartle and Peter Frost (Nuevas Imágenas) is an attractive illustrated look at the region. *Realm of the Incas* by Max Milligan (Idlewild) includes a more sumptuous selection of photographs covering far more than just Machu Picchu.

Recently published, *Stone Offerings, Machu Picchu's Terraces of Enlightenment* (Lightpoint Press) is an award-winning photographic book by architectural photographer Mike Torrey. The beautiful photos were taken over a few days at summer and winter solstice. Though quite expensive it would make a perfect souvenir.

In comparison with Machu Picchu, however, there is precious little written about **Vilcabamba**. Vincent Lee's *Forgotten Vilcabamba – Final Stronghold of the Incas* (Sixpac Manco Publications) is by far the most comprehensive book on the site and its history and also contains a number of detailed diagrams of the ruins. Lee also produced an earlier guide, *Sixpac Manco – Travels amongst the Incas*, which contains some of the same information. Gene Savoy described his explorations of the region in *Antisuyu* (Simon and Schuster). John Hemming dedicated a number of chapters in *The Conquest of the Incas* to Vilcabamba and Hugh Thomson also provides good historical information and descriptions of the ruins in *The White Rock*.

Field guides

There aren't many readily available, good quality, compact field guides for Peru's flora or fauna. If you don't mind carrying fairly bulky books, John Dunning's *South American Birds*, the comprehensive *Birds of the High Andes*

❑ SOURCES OF FURTHER INFORMATION

Peru

A great place to start is perusing the comprehensive visitor information listed on Andean Travel Web (🖳 www.andeantravelweb.com/peru) which focuses on Cusco but also provides good-quality information on Lima, Arequipa, Hauraz, Trujillo, Lake Titicaca, Paracas and the Amazon.

Otherwise, for general information, try: 🖳 www.peru.info, the website of the official government tourism agency; or 🖳 www.perulinks.com which has thousands of links on a multitude of topics; 🖳 www.travel-library.com/south_america/peru has exhaustive listings and links for Peru; 🖳 www.yourperuguide.com is also worth looking at. Do bear in mind that many 'official' sites are nothing of the sort, just agencies looking to advertise treks and tours.

● 🖳 www.traficoperu.com Detailed information on topics as diverse as flights, accommodation, places to eat and car hire

● 🖳 www.paginasamarillas.com.pe Online version of Peru's yellow pages

● 🖳 www.saexplorers.org South American Explorers Club website (see box p130)

● 🖳 www.livinginperu.com Expat guide to local news and events

● 🖳 www.amerispan.com Decent general site for information on studying in Latin America

Cusco

🖳 www.cuscoperu.com is a listings site for Cusco with recommendations and links in English. 🖳 www.cuscoonline.com is also worth a look. The local university runs 🖳 www.unsaac.edu.pe, which is only available in Spanish.

Machu Picchu and the Inca Trail

For information on Machu Picchu and the Inca Trail try the Andean Travel Web site (see p19); the South American Explorers Club website 🖳 www.saexplorers.org; 🖳 www.ex.ac.uk/~RDavies/inca also has details and many links. Otherwise the personal sites of Hugh Thomson (🖳 www.thewhiterock.co.uk) and Gene Savoy (🖳 www.genesavoy.org) are worth a look. 🖳 http://incas.perucultural.org.pe offers a Peruvian perspective on the Incas.

---

by Jon Fjeldsa and Niels Krabbe, or the *Field Guide to the Birds of Peru* by James Clements and Noam Shany are worth tracking down. Most useful, though, is the *Field Guide to the Birds of Machu Picchu* by the ornithologist and Cusco resident Barry Walker. Although it's tricky to come by, you should be able to find a copy at the airports in Lima or Cusco or in bookshops in Cusco.

If you're after more than just birds, *The Travellers' Wildlife Guide to Peru* by David Pearson and Les Beletsky contains superb illustrations of more than 500 of Peru's most common insects, amphibians, reptiles, birds and mammals. The *Bradt Guide to Peruvian Wildlife*, by Gerard Cheshire, Barry Walker and Huw Lloyd, covers fauna found in the High Andes and focuses on Cusco and the Sacred Valley. There's also a good section on orchids and birds in Peter Frost's and Jim Bartle's *Machu Picchu Historical Sanctuary*, to which Barry Walker has also contributed.

Other books

The Heights of Machu Picchu is Chilean poet Pablo Neruda's epic, inspired by the ruins. It's been called the single most important piece of South American poetry, with comparisons to TS Eliot's *The Waste Land*.

The Royal Hunt of the Sun is Peter Shaffer's gripping play about the fall of the last Inca, Atahualpa. *To the Last City* (Chatto and Windus) by Colin Thubron is a fictional account of a journey to Vilcabamba that perfectly captures the atmosphere of the place and the trek.

For children, try *The Angry Aztecs and the Incredible Incas* by Terry Deary, in the Horrible Histories series, which has history mixed in with thrilling tales.

Health precautions, inoculations and insurance

Any form of outdoor physical activity carries with it the possibility of accidents and trekking in the Andes is no exception. However, there are certain golden rules to follow on the trail that will help to minimize the risk of accidents or getting lost. To avoid unpleasant or unwanted surprises, always plan each day's walk carefully, study a map and familiarize yourself with the route, the type of terrain to be covered and the length of time you expect to be trekking. There are also a few pre-trek preparations that you can take to further ensure that your walk is trouble-free, as described below.

FITNESS

Whilst a reasonable level of fitness is a good idea, there's no need to go overboard on training for trekking the Inca Trail. You will, however, enjoy the treks a lot more if you are fitter.

Pre-departure fitness preparation

If you lead a largely sedentary existence it is wise to do some pre-departure exercise before trekking. Any type of exercise is better than none at all just to confirm that you can walk for more than a couple of hours at a time, and for more than one day.

The most efficient way to get fit for the trek is to walk up and down hills, preferably carrying at least a partially loaded pack. Climbing a staircase repeatedly will have a similar effect. Jogging helps to build up stamina and endurance. By at least walking regularly your body is becoming attuned to the rhythms and rigours of life on the trail.

The longer treks, from Vilcabamba to Choquequirao or Choquequirao to Machu Picchu, also require a certain mental resilience as well as physical fitness. Embarking on a trek lasting eight or nine days is a very different proposition to one lasting four or five days. If you have significant doubts about your ability to complete the trek think carefully before committing to it, since there are no opportunities to bail out along the route once you have begun.

HEALTH

Hopefully the worst complaint you'll have to endure is **sunburn**. The high Andean slopes are exposed and, as a result of the thin atmosphere and the reflection of sun off snow, ice or water, you will find that you burn very easily, even on an apparently overcast day. Wear a hat and use high-factor sun-cream to avoid getting burnt. Sun can do just as much damage to your eyes so protect them by wearing sunglasses.

The cold can be just as hazardous when trekking. The weather in the mountains is highly changeable and you should be prepared for sudden drops in temperature. Cold, wet and windy conditions can sometimes be the cause of **hypothermia**. General awareness, being properly equipped and the ability to react to the symptoms promptly should prevent a serious incident.

Blisters are the bane of trekkers and their most common complaint. Friction between the boot and the foot causes a protective layer of liquid to develop beneath the skin. This can take four or five days to heal properly. As with so many things, prevention is far better than cure. By taking the necessary precautions in advance you ought to be able to avoid them altogether. Firstly, make sure that you break in all footwear well in advance of the trek. Wear proper walking socks. Never trek with wet feet as this is a sure-fire way of getting blisters. If your boots get soaked wear plastic bags over dry socks in order to prevent them from becoming wet too. Change into dry socks when you take a break on the trail. Most importantly, never ignore the feeling that your boots may be rubbing; cover the sore area with zinc-oxide tape, a plaster or a specialized blister pad. This will act as an additional layer of skin and should stop the chafing. Vaseline, or at a push lip salve, when rubbed onto a sore toe or heel, can also stop abrasion and delay the onset of a blister.

There are minor adjustments that you can make to your boots depending on the terrain that will help to stave off blisters. Whilst going uphill tighten the upper section of your boot and loosen the laces slightly across the foot. Conversely, when descending, loosen the upper part a little and tighten the laces across the foot.

Should you develop blisters use a clean hypodermic needle to burst them. Allow the blister to dry out, then apply antiseptic cream and a dressing to keep it covered and free from infection.

Inoculations

Before travelling to Peru make sure you have had the following inoculations: **tetanus**, **polio**, **diphtheria**, **tuberculosis**, **hepatitis A** and **typhoid**. If it was a while since your original shot check whether you require a booster. If you are going to the jungle (below 2000m) or intend to tackle either the Vilcabamba, Choquequirao or one of the routes linking either Choquequirao to Vilcabamba or Machu Picchu you should also take a course of anti-**malaria** tablets and consider having a **yellow fever** jab. Some doctors will also suggest you have a **rabies** inoculation if you are intending to tackle one of the longer treks as you may be several days' walk from the nearest transport or the closest hospital.

However, the inoculation won't actually stop you getting the disease, it'll simply buy you more time to get to a hospital.

For a full list of the current requirements or recommended jabs look at the US Center for Disease Control website (🖥 www.cdc.gov), ask a doctor or visit a travel clinic. In the UK you can get the latest advice and vaccinations from the Nomad Travellers Store & Medical Centre (three clinics in London and branches in Bristol, Manchester and Southampton, see 🖥 www.nomadtravel.co.uk for address details) or from clinics run by Trailfinders (☎ 020 7938 3999, 🖥 www .trailfinders.com/services, 194 Kensington High St, London) and Masta (🖥 www.masta-travel-health.com). Travel clinics will, of course, charge for any inoculations they give.

HIGH-ALTITUDE TRAVEL

One of the most common complaints on the various treks described here is **Altitude Sickness** (AMS). Cusco stands at 3360m/11,000ft above sea level and the highest pass described on one of the routes is 5000m/16,400ft. At these altitudes the air pressure is substantially lower than at sea level, having dropped by about one tenth for every 1000m/3300ft of altitude gained. Altitude sickness is caused by the body's inability to get enough oxygen at higher elevations. Since all of your vital organs need oxygen to function, this can be a serious condition and, if ignored or left untreated, it can be fatal. However, it is also very common (some of the top hotels in Cusco even have supplementary oxygen in the rooms) and entirely preventable. For a full rundown on the causes, symptoms and treatments of altitude sickness read the section on p90 carefully.

Before you go, if you suffer from heart or lung problems, high blood pressure or are pregnant, you must visit your doctor to get advice on the wisdom of trekking through the Andes.

Acclimatization

The safest way to avoid any problems with altitude is to acclimatize properly (see p90). The worst thing that you can do is fly in from Lima, which is at sea level, try to start a trek the following day and expect your body to be able to cope with the change in altitude. At the very least take a couple of days out to relax in Cusco and allow your body to adjust to the higher elevation. Within a couple of days you'll find moving about much easier and after two weeks you'll barely notice the altitude at this level at all.

INSURANCE

Before setting off make sure you have travel insurance or are covered by your domestic policies. When choosing travel insurance make sure that the type of policy you plump for covers you for trekking the trails described in this book. Most will automatically but some might not, so read the small print carefully. For complete peace of mind, take out insurance especially tailored for trekkers or mountaineers. The British Mountaineering Council (☎ 0161 445 6111, 🖥 www.thebmc.co.uk) offers this type of insurance for its members.

PERU

Facts about the country

Peru! There it was: vast, mysterious, grey-green, dirt poor, infinite, wealthy, ancient, reticent.   **Mario Vargas Llosa**

There are few countries on earth that can rival Peru for diversity. The stories and legends associated with it have fired people's imaginations for centuries, luring visitors to its shores since the Spanish came looking for treasure in the 16th century. Frequently portrayed as the land of unimaginable riches, the bloodiest conquest, the most heart-wrenching ballads and the most merciless revolutionaries, this country of superlatives also boasts the second-highest mountain range in the world, some of the driest deserts, part of the world's largest jungle and endless empty beaches within its borders. Despite these rugged, inhospitable extremes, Peru also ranks as one of the great centres of ancient civilization; the Incas are just one of a long line of highly developed cultures to have evolved and thrived here.

The country has had a chequered recent past coloured by a brutal ruling regime and terrorism. However, it has emerged from these troubled times and is now battling to entrench democracy and to achieve economic progress and growth. The signs are currently positive and although the country is still finding its feet as a modern nation (unemployment remains rife and the lack of real opportunities is a major concern), as confidence in the country grows, so the likelihood of stability becomes more real.

Despite apparent advances and a willingness to embrace the influences of a wider world, though, the country remains firmly rooted in its indigenous traditions and celebrates its ethnic origins and sense of self. Peruvians are rightly proud of their heritage and the cultural riches their country has to offer.

GEOGRAPHICAL BACKGROUND

Peru is the third-largest country in South America. Covering an area of 1,285,000 square kilometres, it is approximately eight times smaller than the USA and five times the size of the UK.

Geographical regions
Uniquely in South America, there are three distinct geographical regions: *costa* (coast), *sierra* (highlands) and *selva* (jungle).

South America started life conjoined with other continents before splitting away. Mountains were forced up by the collision of two tectonic plates, with the fault line where the two plates pushed together lying offshore and running parallel with the coast. This fault line is the cause of Peru's frequent earthquakes. The formation of the Andes, the longest continuous mountain chain in the world, produced a temperate climate at higher altitudes, whilst the lowlands became dominated by tropical and semi-tropical conditions. The mountains are studded with volcanoes, many of which are extinct but a few occasionally still grumble to themselves.

In cross section, from east to west, the southern Andes have a distinctive profile. In effect, following the coastal desert there are two parallel mountain ranges separated by a high-altitude plain or steppe, which give way to the jungle.

Coast Peru's coast, all 1500 miles of it, is dry and barren, and at the mercy of the Humboldt (or Peru) Current and the unique conditions that it creates. The Humboldt Current is an ocean stream that flows in the direction of the Equator and can extend up to 1000 kilometres offshore. The nutrient-rich water supports an extraordinary abundance of marine life, even though it is very cold. In fact, the water is sufficiently cold to generate a mass of chill air above it. This cold coastal air blocks the warm moist winds blowing in from the Pacific, ensuring that hardly any rain falls on the coast, although clouds and fog are produced. This gloomy mist, which lies heavily over Lima for some of the year, is known as *garúa*. The current is largely responsible for the aridity that prevails along Peru's coast and for creating a long thin strip of desert, the Atacama, behind the barrier, which now stretches from Peru into Chile and extends 20-100km inland.

Highlands The *sierra*, Peru's central highland regions, which are synonymous with the country, are dominated by the *Cordillera de los Andes*. The Andes, which are the backbone of Peru, form a region called La Sierra. The word comes from the Latin *serra* and literally means 'saw'. There are several branches of the Andes in Peru, including the *Cordillera Blanca* (White Range) that fronts the Amazon, the *Cordillera Negra* (Black Range) that fronts the coast and the smaller but no less dramatic *Cordillera Huayhuash*. Some of the world's highest peaks, including Huascarán (6768m) and Yerupája (6634m) can be found amongst these ranges. The mountain slopes to the east have been heavily eroded by water which has left them jagged and precipitous with sharp ridges rising between steep valleys. The slopes to the west have suffered comparatively little due to the scarcity of water so are more even and rolling. Further south the ranges extend into the ridges of Vilcabamba and Vilcanota, which include Mt Salkantay (6271m).

Characteristics of this rugged region include steep, deep valleys and high plateaus known as the *altiplano steppe*, or alpine zone. These enormous enclosed plains, trapped by the ranges to either side of them, are in turn distinguished by barren grasslands, *puna*, where coarse grasses clump together for survival in the cold air and poor soil. Almost half of Peru's population lives scattered across the sierra despite the brutally inhospitable terrain and thin, freezing air.

❏ **El Niño**

Peru is at the mercy of a weather condition known as El Niño. This is an important temperature fluctuation in the surface temperature of the Eastern Pacific Ocean, which can have profound effects on the west coast of South America. The name *El Niño*, from the Spanish for 'little boy', refers to Jesus because the phenomenon is usually noticed around Christmas. There is an opposite effect called *La Niña*, meaning 'little girl'. The condition is very difficult to predict but historically has occurred at irregular intervals of two to seven years and has usually lasted one or two years.

Essentially, El Niño is a change in the weather which is caused by an alteration in the currents of the Pacific Ocean. A rise in air pressure over the Indian Ocean coupled with a fall in air pressure over the Eastern Pacific means that trade winds in the south Pacific head east. Warm air rises near Peru and warm water spreads from the west Pacific to the East Pacific taking rain with it. The cold Humboldt Current is replaced by El Niño's warm tropical waters, meaning that the damp sea winds are able to roll over the desert, causing torrential rain. An El Niño is most often associated with very wet summers (December to February) when heavy downpours cause serious flooding and can cause enormous devastation. Usually many people die or are made homeless as a result. Other parts of the world are also affected, with drier than usual conditions experienced in southeast Asia and northern Australia increasing bush fires, worsening haze and dramatically reducing air quality.

In addition to the climatic effects, El Niño reduces the upwelling of cold nutrient-rich ocean waters and diverts the Humboldt Current that supports so much of Peru's marine life. At this point, all the fish swim south to colder waters. The local fishing industry can therefore suffer terribly during a prolonged El Niño event.

Although the mechanics of the phenomenon are understood, no-one knows what triggers it, and so it is very difficult to predict. Without any means of preparing for it, there is no way to counter the effects. During the last major event, 900 people died and an estimated US$90 billion damage was caused across the world. Worse has happened though and it has been suggested that a strong El Niño led to the demise of the great Moche and Tiahuanaco civilizations, and that the destruction of the fertile farm lands of the Chimú in a similar event led to them having to expand and conquer their neighbours.

Jungle *La selva* is the isolated rainforest region in the eastern part of Peru between the foothills of the Andes and the Amazon basin. Largely unexplored, it contains some of the finest, untouched rainforest in the world, including the Manu National Park, considered to be the world's most bio-diverse rainforest. The region where the forest begins on the foothills of the mountains is poetically described by locals as *Las cejas de la selva* or 'eyebrows of the jungle'. This subtropical region is where much of Peru's coffee is grown.

Climate

Temperatures on the **coast** fluctuate but it is almost always dry. During the summer months, from December to April, temperatures reach 25°C to 30°C. Winter is from May to November when typically the cooler temperatures reach 10°C. Winter is characterized by cloud, fog and what little rain that does ever fall, does so at this time. Temperatures in the **central highlands** are more consistent, rising to 20°C during the day and falling to below freezing during the night. However, the quantity of rainfall varies, with most falling during the wet season from November to March. During these months the evenings tend to be warmer as a result of the cloud cover. June to September tends to be relatively dry. The **jungle** has similar wet and dry seasons to the sierra, being driest from April to October and wettest from November to March. It's hot and humid almost all year round though. (For information on when to go see pp23-5).

HISTORICAL OUTLINE

With the Incas taking centre stage it's easy to forget that their time in Peru's long and complex history was relatively short. Their empire, the pinnacle of a series of other notable Pre-Colombian civilizations in South America, was little more than a century old before it was spectacularly brought down in the incredible clash of cultures with the Spanish *conquistadors* in 1532.

Peru – beginnings and the first cities in the Americas
Man first crossed the Bering Strait from Asia over 15,000 years ago and gradually moved south through the Americas. The first traces of human existence in Peru can be dated back to at least 9000BC and the first cultures emerged along the coast where food was abundant in the form of fish. Notable amongst these coastal peoples are the **Chinchorro** who appear to have been the first people in the world to practice mummification. Unlike for the Incas, Chinchorro mummification was for the masses; many have been found, with the earliest mummy radiocarbon dated back to 5500BC.

These coastal groups gradually developed a farming culture, growing corn and cotton in the pastures of the valleys near the coast and domesticating the llama, alpaca and guinea pig. The settlements grew, in particular along the Supe river north of Lima, and by 3000BC a civilization known as the **Norte Chico** had emerged that was contemporary with the civilizations developing in Egypt and Mesopotamia. The earliest cities in the Americas were here in Peru, including **Caral** which was the capital of a group of 18 city states. The ruins of Caral near Barranca can be visited and include six stepped pyramids, raised ceremonial platforms and amphitheatres, dated to around 2500BC. Evidence of cassava (yuca) and sweet potatoes show that there were links with the Amazon and that some kind of trade must have been going on from around this time.

One of the striking things about these early South American civilizations is how sophisticated they became without discovering things like pottery making. Currently the oldest ceramic sample was found in the valley of Viru, near Trujillo, and dated to 1800BC.

The Chavín – Early Horizon period (1000-200BC)
Until the dating of the city of Caral (above) to around 2500BC, archaeologists believed the site at **Chavín de Huantar**, in the Cordillera Blanca highlands north-east of Caral, to be the earliest example of an urban culture. Chavín culture arose here around 900BC and thrived for about 700 years. This was during what is known as the Early Horizon period, 'horizon' because it's the time when

a number of artistic, architectural and religious styles from several different cultures appear to come together. Shared artistic styles also suggest common belief systems. Metallurgy developed during this period: gold, silver and copper ornaments found near Chiclayo show Chavín-style motifs.

It's been suggested that there may have been some cultural contact between the Olmecs of Central America and the Chavín as both worshipped a fearsome fanged jaguar-man god – a stylized symbol that is a feature of Chavín art. The Chavín religious cult was widespread in Peru, eventually stretching two-thirds of the way along the coast and inland to the central highlands. The religion appears to have involved the use of psychotropic drugs, probably made from the San Pedro cactus which is often shown in carvings. A shaman would take the drug to aid his transformation from human to animal.

The Chavín dominated Peruvian culture in this Early Horizon period yet since there do not appear to have been wars involving them it seems that this was achieved without force on their part. However, it's been suggested that the powerful **Sechín**, a contemporaneous culture centred on Casma, 380km north of Lima, may have ensured the spread of the cult having adopted it themselves.

Nazca and Moche – Early Intermediate period (100-600AD)

As the influence of the Chavín waned, in what is known as the Early Intermediate period (100-600 AD) regional cultures began to dominate: in the north, the Moche, and in the south, the Nazca.

Paracas-Necropolis, named after the cemetery 260km south of Lima, was the first phase of Nazca culture and lasted from 300BC to 200AD. It's characterized by exquisite textiles of wool and cotton embroidered with hundreds of detailed figures, wrappings for some of the mummies found in this cemetery. The **Nazcas** are famous today for the Nazca Lines, giant patterns and pictures etched into the desert plain that can best be appreciated from the air. This has led to some far fetched theories about their creation. Eric von Daniken in *Chariots of the Gods* suggested that they were laid out by alien visitors as runways for their spacecraft. Maria Reiche, who made a life's work of their study, believed that this was an enormous observatory. More recent studies suggest that they may have been processional routes linking shrines and water sources. Nazca pottery, colourful and striking in design, is also significant.

In the north of Peru, the warlike **Moche** rose to power, creating an empire that extended along the coast from Piura to Casma and lasted from 100AD to 800AD. It's unlikely, however, that this 'empire' was anything more than a large group of autonomous states linked by a shared culture but you can clearly see how it paved the way for the Incas. Organizational skills involved in building monumental structures were honed in the creation of the massive Temple of the Sun at their capital near Trujillo.

Again, as with the late development of pottery in South America, it seems incredible that a culture could develop to this level without the invention of writing. For record keeping, though, it's likely that the Moche used *quipus*: strings of coloured threads each with a number of knots as counters, as did the Incas. Moche culture was sophisticated and their fine colourful pottery features scenes from daily life: religious ceremonies, battles, hunting and fishing. There are pots with amazingly lifelike human faces as well as the wide range of the pornographic ceramics for which they've become famous.

The demise of the Moche may have been the result of a prolonged drought and then flooding caused by El Niño in the 6th century AD.

Huari-Tiahuanaco (600-1000AD)

As in the Early Horizon period with the association between the Chavín and their religious cult and the militaristic Sechín who helped spread it, there appears to have been a similar interaction between the cult practised at Tiahuanaco and the Huari (Wari) from around 600AD. The people of Tiahuanaco, though, also sought to actively expand their empire so that by the end of the first millennium a large part of Peru was under the control of two cultures – the Huari and the Tiahuanaco.

The site at **Tiahuanaco**, by Lake Titicaca and now in Bolivia, was the capital of that civilization and amongst the impressive ruins you can still see the Gateway of the Sun, the monumental doorway carved with the Gateway God, Viracocha. Although this area had been inhabited since 1500BC it was not until after it had developed as a cultural and religious centre (300BC to 300AD) that it began to expand, creating an empire which eventually encompassed the northern third of Chile, part of western Bolivia and an area of Peru which included Arequipa.

The **Huari** were originally based in the central highlands, with their capital near Ayacucho. They were powerful empire builders, dominating the coast and central highlands of Peru from south of Nazca and Cusco almost to the border with modern Ecuador. Their legacy for the Incas was in their urban and agricultural infrastructure: terraces for efficient cultivation of mountain slopes, drains and canals to control water, and roads to link all parts of their empire.

Chimú and other regional cultures (1000-1400AD)

The repressive Huari were not popular and the unity imposed on much of the country by them began to disintegrate at the start of the second millennium. Regional states, including that of the **Chachapoyas** at Kuélap in the northern highlands), the **Chanca** north of Lima and the **Chimú** near Trujillo, began to replace them. The Chimú built Chan Chan; covering more than 20 sq km this is the world's largest adobe city and was the largest pre-Hispanic city in the Americas. The Chimú were conquered in 1450 by Inca Túpac Yupanqui, Pachacutec's son.

Incas (1200-1542AD)   [see Inca History, pp104-116]

The **first eight Incas** (strictly speaking the term refers to the ruler though it has come to mean the people) cover the period from about 1200 to the early 15th century, a time when their power and influence was limited to the Cusco area. It was not until 1438 under **Pachacutec** (see p108) that the drive began to create an empire that was soon to become the largest in pre-Columbian America, stretching north as far as Colombia, south into Chile and Argentina and east into Bolivia.

The Spanish and the conquest of the Incas [also see pp113-16]

It's likely that the Spanish unknowingly unleashed an advance attack on the peoples of South America in the form of smallpox which swept south across the continent from Colombia. Some, however, believe it may have been a local sand-fly disease. Whichever it was, it claimed the Inca emperor **Huayna Capac** in 1527 and it's estimated that by 1550 it had decimated between 50% and 75% of the population. On his deathbed Huayna Capac further weakened his empire by dividing it between his sons, **Atahualpa** and **Huascar**, pitting them against each other in a civil war.

The Spanish advance on the Americas was rapid after the voyages of Columbus between 1492 and 1503 to the Bahamas, the Caribbean islands, Central America and Colombia. In 1502, **Francisco Pizarro** sailed from Spain with 2500 other colonists in 30 ships. By 1519 he had risen to become mayor and magistrate of Panama City. No doubt inspired by the rumours of gold and silver in the lands to the south he organized his own expedition with Diego de Almagro. He made some preliminary voyages between 1524 and 1528 before returning to Spain to organize funds for a full-scale expedition and to crave the indulgence of the Spanish crown.

Granted the title of Governor of Peru, Pizarro landed near Tumbes in northern Peru in 1532 and marched south with a force of 106 foot-soldiers and 62 horsemen. Having defeated his brother Huascar, Atahualpa was also in the north, at Cajamarca with his army of 80,000 men. That meeting which sealed the fate of the continent is described on p104. In the resulting **Battle of Cajamarca**, on 16 November 1532, Pizarro famously trapped Atahualpa and greedily held him ransom for enough gold and silver to fill three rooms. Even though the ransom was fulfilled Pizarro realized that he could not keep the Inca

Pizarro and Almagro set sail.
FELIPE HUAMÁN POMA DE AYALA, FROM HIS *NUEVE CRÓNICA Y BUEN GOBIERNO* (c1600)

emperor alive and, after a mock trial convicted him of treason and of killing his brother. He had him executed in July 1533. Peter Shaffer's play, *The Royal Hunt of the Sun*, is a moving recreation of these final events.

Pizarro nominated a puppet ruler, **Túpac Huallpa**, and marched south to take Cusco. Túpac died on the march and so Pizarro replaced him with his brother, **Manco Inca Yupanqui**, who had come from the capital to meet them. Cusco fell in 1534 and the following year Pizarro founded Lima. Manco Inca attempted to retake Cusco, laying siege to the city in 1536 before retreating into the jungle around Vilcabamba. It was not until 1573 that the Incas were finally subdued.

Viceroyalty of Peru (1542-1826)

With Peru conquered and a handful of seditious conquistadors crushed in 1542, Spain sought to consolidate its hold on the country. In due course the

Viceroyalty of Peru, as the colony was known, became the most prized asset in Spain's South American empire. Lima, founded in 1535, became increasingly important, with traders all along the coast using its port to send goods out of the country. Over the next 200 years the capital developed into the main political, social and commercial centre for all of the surrounding countries. By contrast, Cusco became a relative backwater.

The *encomienda* system of rule The rulers of the new colony were the Spanish-born viceroys appointed by the Spanish crown. Immigrants from Spain were given most of the prestigious positions and power was contained by these individuals, who installed a feudal system of rule.

A theoretically fair system of rule, the *encomienda* system, was authorized by the Spanish crown. The premise was that the crown governed and owned everything. This meant that the conquistadors could extract tribute for the crown and personal services for themselves in exchange for converting indigenous people to Christianity. In return for the salvation of their souls, the Indians were forced to give up their bodies and work for the Spanish. In theory, the Spaniards could benefit from the labours of the Indians who lived on the land that they oversaw for the Spanish crown, but neither they nor the Indians could own the land, and the Indians were not to be treated as slaves. Nor could the Spaniards live on this land or pass it on to family or next of kin. Crown agents, *corregidors*, were appointed to supervise and enforce these rules.

Of course, in practice the system failed. The royal administrators found themselves in constant conflict with the *encomenderos*, who had no intention of fully emancipating the Indians or of treating them as equals. Fundamentally the colony was too far from the crown to be properly supervised. Greed inevitably surfaced and those Spaniards holding land were set on making as much money as they could, regardless of the conditions their labour force endured. As governor of Peru, Pizarro gave large groups of Indians to his allies and friends, effectively creating the basic colonial land tenure structure that the crown had set out to avoid. Much of Imperial Spain's wealth was subsequently built from the maltreatment of the descendants of the Incas.

Some of the stories which became known as *La Leyenda Negra* (the **Black Legend**) telling of the violence and brutality, meted out by the Conquistadors on their new colony and its inhabitants, were no doubt true but they do not tell the whole story. The Incas are often portrayed as a harmonious people who endured countless atrocities and abuse at the hands of the Spanish, but they were a warlike, vicious society themselves: if the shoe had been on the other foot, Atahualpa acknowledged that he would have had no qualms about brutally incarcerating the Spanish if he had captured them. Nonetheless, the atrocities endured after the conquest need to be recounted and recorded as this period was full of terrible violence. The most horrific incidents related to the giant silver mines at Potosí (now a bleak town in Bolivia), which were discovered in 1545. Forced off their land and conscripted into working in the mines, convoys of pressed Indian labour were driven from their homes to work themselves to

PERU

death. Hundreds of thousands of Indians died as a result whilst Spanish coffers were filled with the necessary cash to finance wars across Europe.

Spain loses control The Spanish empire struggled to fully assert itself over its colonies and the crown's laws were frequently flouted. Coupled with this, locally born Spaniards (*Creoles*) became resentful at the fact that they were not entitled to any of the perks or positions of power that the immigrant Spanish enjoyed in Peru. It wasn't until the transition from the Hapsburgs to the Bourbon kings at the start of the 18th century that the empire was able to re-establish control.

Dramatic changes were made to the way that Peru was governed. Control was centralized, laws preventing Creoles from taking up positions of power were tightened and the Jesuits were driven out entirely. Spain's South American territories were also divided up. The creation of Viceroyalties to the north, east and south of Peru meant that the area to be governed by the Viceroy of Peru was decreased and so became more manageable. Trade regulations were also revamped, and Lima lost its protected status as the country's main docks. Existing taxes were increased and additional levies implemented.

Uprisings in the 18th century These changes and the tightening of control inevitably resulted in resentment. Over the next hundred years a series of protests and rebellions on various scales broke out. In 1740 **Juan Santos Atahualpa** roused a group of forest Indians to revolt and successfully repelled attacks on his stronghold in the high jungle. He never succeeded in extending his power or gaining additional control though, and died in 1756. A more important insurgence, drawing on the existing unrest, broke out in 1780. The *mestizo* José Gabriel Condorcanquí symbolically adopted the nickname **Túpac Amaru II**, and whipped up anti-Spanish feeling. Initially just a demonstration against the high charges and duties demanded as well as the harsh employment laws, his rebellion took on a more significant note when he imprisoned a corregidor, massacred a group of 600 Royalist soldiers and attempted to instigate Inca rule. The empire's response was rapid and brutal, with troops from Lima despatched to quell the uprising. Within a year, following a decisive battle at Checacupe, Túpac Amaru was taken into prison, tortured and put to death, although the uprising he inspired staggered on until 1783.

Although ultimately unsuccessful, Túpac Amaru II had demonstrated that there were deficiencies in Spanish rule and that a high level of popular unrest existed. Historians now consider his rebellion an important precursor to Peruvian independence.

Towards independence The late 18th century saw profound changes all across the world. The North American colonies gained their independence from Britain and France suffered a revolution. Liberal ideas spread across the globe, and South America took notice, recognizing that there now existed the potential to throw off the shackles of colonialism. Inflammatory articles and newspapers began to appear in Lima, and discontent became rife. Peruvian nationalism gained momentum and began to take shape as the philosophy of the Enlightenment pervaded the whole of the country.

The Peninsula War for control of Europe's Iberian Peninsula saw Napoleon cross Spain to attack Portugal before turning on his erstwhile Spanish allies in 1808. The beleaguered Spanish crown called for assistance from its colonies. In return for aid, the colonies demanded a relaxation in the regulations preventing Creoles from holding responsible positions of power and an increased recognition of their general rights, a step that meant that Peru tasted early stages of independence. By the time that Ferdinand returned to the Spanish throne in 1814, much of South America was in upheaval and Royalist troops were struggling to maintain control. **San Martín** first liberated Argentina then in 1817 liberated Chile. At the same time **Simon Bolívar** had ejected the Spanish from Venezuela and Colombia. By this stage it was just a matter of time before one of these great liberators reached Peru.

Independent Peru

San Martín, anxious to protect his territories and deprive the Spanish of the prized silver mines at Potosí, arrived first from the south, in 1818. Having persuaded an English naval officer, Lord Cochrane, to attack Lima, San Martín landed in Pisco and marched on the capital. Battling north he reached Lima in time to witness the Viceroy escape with the few Royalist troops he still had. Entering the city without a struggle, he proclaimed independence on 28 July 1821.

San Martín assumed political control as 'Protector of Peru' and initiated some immediate changes, declaring freedom for slaves' children, abolishing Indian service and actually outlawing the term Indian. However, with the Royalists still controlling chunks of the north of the country his changes were largely superficial.

Travelling north, San Martín tried to enlist the aid of Bolívar in routing the remnants of the occupiers. Bolívar, a man predisposed to megalomania, turned down the advance, intent on securing his own fame by achieving victory alone. Relenting, San Martín handed the initiative to his opposite number, who mopped up the last patches of resistance to independence in 1824.

Bolívar absorbed Peru into his vast Andean Confederation, which included Colombia, Venezuela, Ecuador and Bolivia. However, a year after his withdrawal from the country to return to Colombia, the Peruvians abandoned his constitution and in 1826 installed **General La Mar** as president. There quickly followed a series of *caudillos* (military leaders) who assumed power in the absence of any civilians. Plots, counterplots and coups ensued, with **General Gamarra** seizing power in 1829, a move that set the tone for the rest of the country's history. Voted out of office four years later, Gamarra staged another coup in a bid to regain power, but was overwhelmed and exiled. Nonetheless, the military seized control.

In 1835-36 **Santa Cruz** invaded Peru from Bolivia and installed himself as Protector with the ambition of uniting the two countries. Chile and Argentina, in alliance with Gamarra, intervened and at the battle of Yungay in 1839 reinstated Peru's independence. Gamarra was installed as president once again, and promptly attacked Bolivia. In 1841 he was slain at the Battle of Yngavi. Peru went on to have six presidents in the course of the next four years.

Finally, in 1845, **Ramón Castilla** came to office. Riding a wave of enthusiasm and prosperity heralded by the export of *guano* (bird excrement) fertilizer, Castilla oversaw a period of prosperity and real growth. By the early 1860s more than three-quarters of the Peruvian government's revenues were derived from the export of guano. Money was invested in the rail network and a programme of schooling and teaching the indigenous people went a long way to emancipating the slaves. A second term in office saw him develop sugar and cotton as export commodities as the rich guano reserves ran out and cheaper alternatives were discovered. Sadly his successor, **Balta**, couldn't sustain the growth and enormous, ill-conceived expenditure on railways and other engineering works left Peru on the brink of economic collapse. On the back of the 1872 elections the military staged another coup, which was overthrown by a civilian mob and led to the country's first civilian president, **Manuel Pardo**, coming to power.

Despite the proclamation of independence, Spain refused to officially relinquish control of Peru. In 1864 a company of soldiers captured the Chincha Islands, which were responsible for much of the guano that fuelled Peru's early wealth. In alliance with Chile, Ecuador and Bolivia, Pardo went to **war with Spain**. Although the Spanish shelled Lima they never made land and eventually retreated. Finally, in 1871 a ceasefire was agreed, but it wasn't until 1879 that the country formally recognized its former colony's status as an independent country.

The War of the Pacific

Peace and stability didn't last long. As Peru's economy collapsed under the weight of foreign debt, the country's problems were exacerbated by deteriorating relations with Chile and a squabble over nitrate-rich deposits located in Bolivia. When hostilities between Bolivia and Chile boiled over into war in 1879, Peru offered to act as a go-between, having made a secret pact with Bolivia to support each other. In retaliation, Chile declared war on Peru. Early Peruvian victories at Iquique and the sinking of the Chilean corvette *Esmeralda* were offset by the loss of the ironclad frigate *Independencia*, followed by the loss of Tacna and Arica. Further victories on land and at sea saw Chilean forces occupy Lima at the start of 1881. The treaty of Ancón in 1883 ended the dispute but saw Peru cede control of its southern provinces to Chile for 10 years. However, it wasn't until 1929 that an agreement was reached under the terms of which Tacna was returned to Peru, while Chile kept control of Arica and the rich nitrate deposits found there.

British bailout

Following the War of the Pacific, Peru was virtually bankrupt. With the loss of the nitrate rich territories the country's coffers soon ran dry and by 1890 Peru was unable to pay its foreign debts. An international plan to bail out Peru saw the creation of the Peruvian Corporation in London, which assumed the enormous debt in return for control of the economy. Foreign companies assumed control of the rail network and valuable guano production, and were given free access to the country's main ports. Despite the embarrassment and indignity of being bailed out, Peru did stabilize and a semblance of peace returned. The development of copper production buoyed the economy and reforms including direct suffrage, public education and municipal elections helped to ease the plight of the ordinary peasant.

In 1908 one of the big businessmen, **Augusto Leguía**, was elected president. During his tenure foreign investment increased and the capital was modernized, yet he made few concessions to support the poor and resentment swelled. Minor rebellions followed and in 1931, a year into his fourth term, he was ousted by a military coup.

APRA and the army

During the years Leguía had been in power, the labour movement had steadily been growing in strength. The worldwide Depression in the early 1930s hit Peru hard as demand for its main exports declined drastically. At this time an originally Marxist movement, the **APRA** (Alianza Popular Revolucionaria Americana), stepped up its activity and resistance to what it saw as the financial hegemony of the United States. The group's founder, **Víctor Raúl Haya de la Torre**, stood for election in 1931 calling for state control of the economy and nationalization of key industries, but was defeated. APRA, convinced that the group had been robbed, instigated disturbances in Trujillo targeting the sugar barons there. Fifty military prisoners, including ten officers, were killed in the violent uprising and the brutal retaliation by the army saw almost five thousand people massacred in the desert. In revenge, APRA assassinated the president in 1933.

The organization was promptly banned, but went underground, operating secretly and becoming one of the largest and best-organized political parties in Peru. Legalized again in time for the 1945 election, APRA nominated a more neutral candidate than the contentious Haya de la Torre, who went on to win a majority in both the Senate and the Chamber of Deputies. No sooner was he in office than **President Bustamente** announced his independence from APRA. Unable to control inflation though, he increasingly relied on the army to consolidate his position until inevitably a military coup removed him from office. APRA was banned once more and its members clamped down on so they couldn't continue to work, even clandestinely.

Agrarian reform and military rule

By the time of the 1956 elections a new political threat had emerged. The **National Youth Front** demanded radical reform. Only with the support of an unholy marriage of convenience between a weakened APRA and their traditional enemy, the army, was the then president **Manuel Prado** able to defeat the group's leader **Fernando Belaúnde Terry**. Strikes and disturbances persisted, particularly in the remoter parts of the country, and a bloody revolt led by **Hugo**

Blanco broke out in the Cusco region. Peasants seized control of land and began to work their own plots. Landowners were forced to bribe the peasants to come back to work or risk going bankrupt. Although arrested in 1963, Blanco had laid the foundations for agrarian reform.

Following the deadlocked 1962 elections where Haya de la Torre, Belaúnde and General Odría all polled approximately a third of the votes, the army predictably took control. Fresh elections were called in 1963, by which time neither APRA nor the National Youth Front posed a serious threat to society, and Belaúnde swept to power. In order to appease the increasingly agitated campesinos he set about a series of radical agrarian reforms and distributed 500,000 acres of land to the people who were finally entitled to work it for themselves rather than for an absent landlord.

In 1968 the military once again intervened and seized control. Belaúnde was deported and a military regime installed. Relationships with the then Soviet Union and Eastern European countries were developed and various land reform initiatives were launched. The regime took over control of industry and handed more land out to the campesinos. Large estates were taken over and reorganized as cooperatives. In 1973 the educational system was overhauled, rural schools were built and the equality of women was recognized. However, the fishing crisis of the 1970s, when stocks dwindled, coupled with the decline in the world price of copper and sugar resulted in increased national debt. Ultimately the army handed back control voluntarily by calling a democratic election in 1978.

Rise of terrorist groups

A new constitution was sketched out and Haya de la Torre eventually became president. His tenure was short lived though and he was replaced in 1980 by Belaúnde, who set about reorganizing the economy along free-market lines. However, his policy to further develop the Amazon and exploit the wealth there failed to stem the rise in inflation, which reached 100% in 1983-84. At the same time, two terrorist groups, the Maoist inspired **Sendero Luminoso** (Shining Path) and the Marxist **MRTA** (*Movimiento Revolucionario Túpac Amaru*), began to make their presence felt (see box p58). Inflation ran riot as the value of the sol collapsed.

In 1985 APRA swept to power and **Alan García** was elected president. An ambitious economic programme to cut taxes, reduce interest rates, freeze prices and devalue the currency was intended to solve many of Peru's deep-rooted economic and social problems. The short-term boom this produced led to far worse problems in the long-term and García's resolution to only pay off a tenth of Peru's foreign debt simply led to international banks suspending future loans. The situation rapidly deteriorated, with terrorists and the military, including a right wing death squad comprising disaffected army personnel and police officers and known as the *Rodrigo Franco Commando*, engaged in a bloody, violent battle that inevitably harmed the campesinos caught in the crossfire more than it did either group actually involved in the struggle. García's abortive attempt to nationalize the banks simply plunged Peru further into disarray and ensured that by the time he eventually went into exile, hounded by allegations of corruption, the country was bankrupt.

❏ Terrorism – the Shining Path and the MRTA

Peru has been menaced by two main terrorist movements: the **Sendero Luminoso** (Shining Path, also known as the Partido Comunista de Perú, Communist Party of Peru) and the MRTA (Movimiento Revolucionario Túpac Amaru, Túpac Amaru Revolutionary Movement). Founded in 1970 along the lines of the Chinese Gang of Four by Abimael Guzmán (aka Comrade or Presidente Gonzalo), Sendero Luminoso are Maoists opposed to global capitalism who have abandoned the possibility of democratic change. In 1976 the group adopted armed struggle as the only means of achieving its ends and bringing about revolution in Peru. Support for the group comes from the large number of disaffected campesinos in the country, especially farmers and families scratching a living in the group's traditional heartland, the highlands around Ayacucho.

Ruthless and savage, the Sendero actively persecuted anyone not allied with them or who didn't actively agree with their philosophy. The revolution was proclaimed through 'teachings' and by terrorizing rural communities into acquiescing, whilst funding came from the cocaine trade and protection rackets. At their height during the 1980s and 90s, members numbered in their thousands and carried out attacks on business interests, local officials, police stations and anything deemed to be interfering with or oppressing the peasantry. Members met secretly and would simply melt back into the obscurity of their villages when put under pressure. Guzmán himself lived mainly underground, rarely seen even by members of his own organization. Nowadays their numbers are vastly reduced, although there is still some limited support for the group abroad and an old website 🖳 www.blythe.org/peru-pcp that is maintained online as an archive for historical and political research. The Committee to Support the Revolution in Peru (CSRP) also have a site 🖳 www.csrp .org, which distributes the writings of the Communist Party of Peru.

Guzmán was captured in 1992 and still languishes in jail. The events leading up to his capture in his Lima hideout were made into a book, *The Dancer Upstairs* by Nicholas Shakespeare, which subsequently became a film staring Javier Bardem. In 2003 a ruling that the anonymous trial by military personnel that convicted Guzmán was unconstitutional led to him being retried and again convicted to life in prison. Other rulings delivered by military panels during the Fujimori years have been overturned or annulled though.

The urban-based, Marxist **MRTA** first found support in the shanty towns around Lima. Although more moderate than the Sendero, they have never been as well supported and indeed their capacity and confidence was rocked by an army ambush in 1988 that saw 62 militants killed. They first came to the world's attention on 17 December 1996 when they successfully infiltrated the Japanese ambassador's residence disguised as waiters. They held the building under siege for 126 days, with over 300 hostages including Fujimori's brother and a number of Peru's highest ranked officials, whilst calling for the release of hundreds of jailed comrades. Four months into the siege, Fujimori authorized Peruvian forces to storm the building. All but one of the hostages were rescued alive, whilst all of the terrorists were killed. Later, in 2003, the soldiers involved in the resolution of the stand-off were tried for massacring the terrorists in cold blood, but were acquitted on the basis that they had been involved in a military confrontation. Regardless, the MRTA remains a broken entity today.

1990s – the reign of Fujimori

The 1990 election became one of Peru's most pivotal. In the run-up there were four main candidates: the popular and internationally renowned author **Mario Vargas Llosa** with his right-wing coalition; **Luís Alvacastro**, general secretary of APRA; **Alfonso Barrantes** in charge of a left-wing group; and **Henry Peace** of the United Left. The left were severely split and after five disastrous years in power APRA stood little chance of regaining the presidency, leaving Vargas Llosa the clear favourite. In the event, a brand new, unknown political party, Cambio 90 (Change 90), led by a young college professor of Japanese descent, **Alberto Fujimori**, proved the stiffest challenge. In a notable upset, the unfancied Fujimori defeated the favourite Vargas Llosa.

Once in power, Fujimori reneged on his promises, assumed complete control and rewrote the Peruvian constitution, declaring that he needed a freer hand to introduce market reforms and combat terrorism. He also adopted most of Vargas Llosa's policies. Ever since it has been known as the **President's Coup**, since that is essentially what it amounted to: a bloodless coup d'état.

Fujimori's successes Fujimori embarked on a series of economic reforms designed to turn the country around. Although the prices of many staples such as flour and fuel trebled, he did manage to get hold of the economy and restore international faith in Peru. His greatest success and the turning point that enabled him to stand for a second term was the capture of Sendero Luminoso leader Abimael Guzmán in September 1992. Even though Fujimori was unaware of the operation by the secret anti-terrorist police to grab Guzmán at his Lima hideout, he milked the success, publicly displaying the captured terrorist in a giant cage, dressed in a cartoonish prison outfit, and successfully convincing the international media that Peru was no longer a country where terrorists were set to take over.

The Peruvian people responded to his successes and Fujimori secured almost two-thirds of the votes in the 1995 election, when he defeated the former head of the United Nations **Javier Pérez de Cuellar**. Continued economic success, inflation dipped from a record rate of 2777% in 1989 to 10% in 1996, and a peace treaty with Ecuador after skirmishes in 1995, 1997 and 1998 over ownership of oilfields on what the Peruvians claim is their side of the border followed, but at considerable cost to human rights. Despite international aid agencies confirming widespread poverty and unemployment in Peru and the devastating effects of El Niño in 1998, the economy remained buoyant in the run-up to the 2000 elections.

Fujimori loses control Here Fujimori pushed his luck by once more rewriting the constitution in order to permit himself an unprecedented third term in office. Despite a stranglehold on the media Fujimori encountered strong opposition from **Alejandro Toledo**, who represented the interests of Andean communities and cities. Following a hotly contested election full of untruths and deceit, in which a smear campaign accusing Toledo of abandoning an illegitimate daughter and being financially unreliable surfaced amidst allegations of vote rigging and fraud, Fujimori claimed 49.87% of the vote, missing outright victory by 14,000 votes. Toledo withdrew from the contest in protest and Fujimori embarked on an historic third term.

No sooner had he settled back into office though then he was forced to resign. Video tapes were leaked to the press of Fujimori's sinister chief assistant, **Vladimiro Montesinos** head of the state intelligence agency SIN (*Servicio de Inteligencia Nacional*), bribing congressmen. In total around 2700 so-called 'vladivideos' came to light, revealing the extent to which Montesinos had exerted control over the army, the intelligence service and the cocaine mafia through bribes, extortion, intimidation and threats of violence. Montesinos fled to Panama just as it was revealed that he had squirreled away more than US$50 million of what is thought to be drug money in foreign bank accounts. He suc-

---

❏ Truth and reconciliation

In 2003 Peru formally petitioned Japan for Fujimori's extradition to face multiple counts of bribery, corruption and being an illegal president. The same year, the Truth and Reconciliation Committee reported into the civil war of the 1980s-90s stating that almost 70,000 Peruvians had been killed. There were also accusations Fujimori made a US$15 million pay-off to Montesinos when he lost his job; established a programme of forced sterilization of campesino women; and was linked to the Grupo Colina death-squad, who were responsible for a number of assassinations and kidnappings in the early 1990s. Since Peru has no formal extradition treaty with Japan there was no way of removing Fujimori, a Japanese national, and bringing him to trial to face charges. That is until he voluntarily left the country to mount a campaign to be elected president of Peru in 2006, claiming that he would be fully exonerated.

Upon entering Chile he was arrested on an extradition warrant and returned to Peru, the first time a court anywhere in the world had ordered the extradition of a former leader to be tried in his home country for human rights violations. Following trial in 2007 Fujimori was sentenced to six years in jail for abuse of authority stemming from an illegal search of an apartment belonging to Montesinos' wife, which he ordered without a warrant. He was also fined the equivalent of US$135,000. In a separate trial for human rights abuses, the charge being that he ordered the murder of 25 people at the hands of military death-squads, he was found guilty and sentenced to 25 years. In 2009 Fujimori was convicted of embezzling and sentenced to a further 7½ years in prison, having admitted to paying Montesinos $15 million (£9 million) in government funds illegally. It is thought that he admitted the charge to avoid a protracted trial that might harm his daughter's candidacy for the 2011 presidential elections. Keiko Fujimori is currently a front runner (ahead of Luis Casteñda of the National Solidarity Party, ex President Toledo and Hunaca). If she wins she has stated that she will pardon her father.

Montesinos fared little better. Having been traced to Venezuela, captured there and returned to Peru in 2001, he was convicted in 2003 of embezzlement (on relatively minor counts) and sentenced to nine years' imprisonment; he has since received a further tariff of five and eight years on additional counts of bribery and abuse of power, as well as a further 15 years for corruption and conspiracy. He is on trial again for alleged involvement in the death-squad killings as well as running guns to the Colombian rebel group the FARC, apparently with CIA support. Montesinos also refutes the allegations.

cessfully evaded capture until 2001 when he was held in Venezuela and returned to Peru to stand trial (see box opposite).

Fujimori clung to power for a further two months. On a routine tour he stopped in Japan and in November 2000 sent his resignation as President of Peru to Congress. He then revealed that he had been a Japanese national throughout his time as president, a disclosure that meant he had illegally spent 10 years at the top since by law the Peruvian president must be a Peruvian national.

Peru in the 21st century

Fresh elections were called in 2001, with the centrist **Toledo** narrowly defeating Alan García, the man who had so badly damaged Peru's economy in the late 1980s. Toledo stood on a manifesto promising the creation of a million new jobs and a strong, stable economy. Carefully exploiting his Andean ancestry he adopted the nickname Pachacutec after the great Inca emperor. Sadly he was unable live up to his namesake. Having inherited a sceptical, pessimistic populace, a damaged domestic set-up with slow growth and worsening social conditions, Toledo found his popularity rapidly falling. His pledge to create a million jobs remained unfulfilled, unemployment remained a serious problem, taxes increased, pledges to increase salaries fell through and the benefits of what little economic changes he did make failed to filter down to the populace at large.

Crippling strikes, violent street demonstrations and a series of major confrontations in 2002 and 2003 prompted him to call a state of emergency, whilst a series of scandals forced him to reshuffle his cabinet and relaunch his administration. Toledo's approval rating slumped to less than 10%, the lowest of any South American leader and lower even than the disgraced Fujimori (31%), who continued to broadcast a radio show on Radio Miraflores from his home in Japan, despite an international arrest warrant for his involvement with the death squad Grupo Colina.

Return of García in 2006 elections Sensing an opportunity, **Fujimori** returned from Japan in 2005 to stand for President in the 2006 elections. He was arrested in Chile on an extradition warrant to face long-standing accusations of corruption and human rights abuses. (He is now serving a 25-year jail sentence in Lima). With Fujimori constitutionally banned from appearing on the ballot, the 2006 election became a stand off between the populist **Ollanta Humala**, an indigenous Andean ex-army officer who had served under Fujimori and was backed by Venezuelan President Hugo Chávez, and the ex-president **Alan García** who pledged to rein in public spending and not fritter away the benefits of a positively expanding economy.

Voters, suspicious of Chavez's influence, clearly forgave García for putting Peru on the road to ruin in the 1980s and elected him back into office, much to the chagrin of Chávez who had championed Humala as part of his vision for South American socialist solidarity. Relations between Peru and Venezuela further soured after the election result, when Chávez refused ties with the García administration and accused him of being an American lapdog. In contrast, foreign investors and external observers reacted positively to the result. García's cabinet included APRA members and independents as well as six women. García, styling himself as a mature pragmatist, delivered a degree of stability and prosperity and on the back of economic growth, low inflation and a sensible spending policy, business leaders predicted an Andean renaissance.

However, he made little impact on the crippling poverty affecting so many Peruvians. Inevitably the huge numbers of people living on less than a dollar a day began to lose patience with empty promises and the president's approval rating fell. Demonstrations, strikes and street protests in the run up to the first anniversary of García's return to power soured what had appeared to be one of South America's great political comebacks.

The forced resignation of his entire cabinet in 2008 on the back of allegations of bribery and corruption further tarnished his reputation. An ill-advised law to allow foreign companies to exploit natural resources in the Amazon, passed in 2008, was revoked in 2009 following protests, roadblocks and confrontations between police and Amazon tribes, one of which left more than 30 people dead and 150 hurt near the town of Bagua. García accused the tribes of impeding progress; the tribes claimed they see little benefit from the push to develop Peru's rich natural reserves. Subsequently García also rejected a law that would give indigenous people more power to stop oil and mining projects on their lands. The law was passed by Congress but sent back by García, saying it went too far and that he couldn't let indigenous communities stop development that would benefit all Peruvians. The controversy and outcry continues, causing social friction and endangering the country's stability and prosperity.

In the run-up to the 2011 elections a stay in office for García seems very unlikely. Candidates include Humala, Toledo, Kuczynski and Keiko Fujimori, daughter of the disgraced former president.

THE PEOPLE

The vast majority (almost three-quarters) of Peru's 29 million inhabitants live in cosmopolitan modern cities. Nonetheless, the society is deeply rooted in the past and just under half the population is **Quechua**. The Quechua living in rural areas prefer to be known as *campesinos* (rural labourers) rather than *indios* (Indians), a term which is considered derogatory. Around a third of the population are *mestizo*, with mixed Spanish and Amerindian heritage and parentage.

Other groups include the **Aymara** living around Lake Titicaca and the **indigenous** tribes living in the Amazon, who number around 250,000.

There is also a small black **Afro-Peruvian** population, mostly living on the coast south of Lima and descended from those unfortunate enough to be brought to Peru as slaves, and a small **Asian** community made up of Chinese and Japanese immigrants. Descendants of the first Spanish families and other European immigrants constitute a small **Caucasian** population.

Life expectancy is 68 years for men and 72 for women.

Education and literacy

About 20% of adult Peruvians living in the countryside are illiterate compared with 4% of urban dwellers. Education is now free and compulsory for both sexes up to the age of 16 – a boon for the 30% or so of Peru's population under the age of 14. This is understandably difficult to enforce in remote rural areas. Nonetheless, the government estimates that most of the country's children have access to primary education, two-thirds go to secondary school and around 25% go on to tertiary education. Publicly funded schools don't have a great reputation and resources are very scarce, so those who can afford it tend to send their children to private schools.

Language

Spanish is the official language of Peru and spoken in all but the most remote areas (for a list of useful words and phrases see pp349-52). However, for a large percentage of the population this is a second language, and **Quechua** (or *Runasimi*, 'the people's mouth'), the official language of the Incas, whom it actually predates, is the indigenous first language. Most of the people who still speak Quechua are concentrated around Cusco and elsewhere in southern Peru. In and around Lima or the other major tourist destinations such as Arequipa and Cusco, English is also understood by some people. In the countryside surrounding Lake Titicaca a handful of people still speak Aymara, an ancient language dating to before the Incas.

There was no written version of Quechua until the 16th century and so no standard way of transcribing it exists. Even now it is only fitfully being introduced into schools. As a result you will see the same words written differently. For instance, Inca can be spelt Inka, Cusco is sometimes written as Cuzco or Q'osqo and Sacsayhuaman sometimes shown as Saq'saywaman. The spellings in this book are consistent, if not the only versions of these names.

Religion

From the 16th century onwards the Inca religion was displaced by Roman Catholicism as the conquistadors steadily converted the local population. Nowadays, around 90% of Peru considers itself **Roman Catholic**. The Peruvian church is also the cradle of 'Liberation Theory', a Socialist interpretation of Christianity designed to support the poor.

Although the vast majority of the population ostensibly claim to be Catholic, the reality is that few attend regular church services and a large proportion of this figure practise a form of **Pagan Catholicism**, whereby Catholicism is fused with a series of indigenous, animist beliefs such as the worship of deities from the natural world, including mountains, animals and plants. Viracocha (the creator) is often thought of as the Christian God whilst Pachamama (the earth mother) is represented by the Virgin Mary and seemingly Catholic services generally have many layers of meaning.

Some 6% of the population now state that they are **Protestant** and the greatest threat to Catholicism in Peru comes from the predatory evangelical Protestant groups throughout the country. Some of these churches are American imports whilst others are homegrown organizations such as the IEP (Evangelical Church of Peru), which have been active for more than a hundred years.

POLITICS AND ECONOMICS

Politics

Every five years presidential elections are held and at the same time the 120 Congressmen are selected. The president is then responsible for choosing his ministers. Peru is split into 25 departments, each governed by prefects that are also chosen by the president. Departments are further subdivided into provinces, which are further broken up into districts that are in turn run by mayors elected every five years.

Current politics

Alan García, leader of the left-wing social democratic party **APRA**, was elected to power in 2006, winning approximately 53% of the vote, and began his second term in office having previously governed Peru in the late 1980s. Voting for him was dubbed 'voting for the lesser of two evils': although people had a very negative impression of García, they were scared of the implications of Venezuelan President Hugo Chávez's support for his opponent Humala. The result represents a spectacular turn-around for García whose first tenure saw Peru slide towards bankruptcy and ended with him in exile for nine years in Colombia waiting for corruption charges dating to his first term to expire.

The next elections will be in 2011 and candidates include Humala (see p61) for the nationalist **Alianza Gana Perú** (including the Nationalist, Socialist and Communist parties), Toledo (see p61) for the **Alianza Perú Posible**, former mayor of Lima Luis Castañeda Lossio for the right-wing **Solidaridad Nacional** (including Fujimori's old Cambio 90 party), Keiko Fujimori (the ex-president's daughter) for the right-wing **Fuerza 2011** and Pedro Pablo Kuczynski for the **Alianza por el Gran Cambio**.

In general there is widespread cynicism connected with traditional political parties in Peru.

Human rights

During the hostilities between Sendero Luminoso and the army, countless numbers of campesinos were caught up in the ensuing violence. On the one hand the terrorists used force to cajole and bully the inhabitants of villages to comply with their message and on the other the military massacred anyone suspected of collaborating with the enemy. At the height of the conflict, there are thought to have been 10-15,000 secret Sendero members, against whom were ranged more than 6000 troops and anti-terrorist police. During the struggle, thousands of innocent people 'vanished' or were murdered. In 2002 the Truth and Reconciliations Commission, which was set up by Toledo to examine atrocities committed in the 1980s and 1990s by the Sendero Luminoso, MRTA and the Peruvian army, began reporting on the horrific incidents. At the inauguration of the Commission a spokesman summed up the task ahead saying, 'What is absolute, what is definitive is that people were unjustly killed and human rights were violated. We are not trying to open Pandora's Box, we are trying to air things that have been forgotten and stink.'

In 2003 the commission reported back, its chairman remarking that, 'The report we hand in contains a double outrage: that of massive murder, disappearance and torture; and that of indolence, incompetence and indifference of those who could have stopped this human catastrophe but didn't.' In all, 69,280 Peruvians had been killed or had disappeared during the conflict, more than doubling the number used in the past to catalogue the violence and making it one of Latin America's most brutal wars. Ayacucho, the Sendero heartland, bore the brunt of the losses, with campesinos accounting for three quarters of the victims. Both the terrorists and the army were blamed for the loss of life. For more on this watch *State of Fear*, a powerful documentary based on the findings of the Commission that tells the story of Peru's war on terror.

An ongoing lawsuit against the government concerns the issue of forced sterilization. As part of a family planning policy during the civil war up to 300,000 sterilizations were performed without the consent of the women. The case was shelved but in 2010 some of the victims from the province of Anta refiled their case.

The economy

Peru's economy reflects its varied geography. The country has bountiful mineral deposits and a range of climates that allows the production of a wide range of produce. Poor economic guidance, political instability and crippling inflation have in the past brought the country virtually to its knees, though. Currently things are much healthier and the economy is thriving. Nonetheless, the gulf between those who have and those have not is still vast, and there are still a lot of desperately poor Peruvians with little or no prospects.

Fujimori privatized large chunks of state-owned industry and overhauled the tax system. Toledo also followed a pro-market policy. Following the early reforms and a shift to a free market economy the growth rate for real GDP soared to 13% before stabilizing around 7% by 1997. The worst El Niño of the 20th century and the Asian economic crisis in 1998 halved this figure but since 2001 Peru's economy has been one of the fastest growing in South America. Aided by market-orientated economic reforms and a series of privatizations GDP has grown steadily from 4.8% in 2004, 6.7% in 2005 and 8.0% in 2006. Higher world prices for minerals sustained the 7.5% growth in 2007 and 9.8% in 2008 before a dramatic fall in 2009 to 0.9%.

Recent economic expansion has been driven by construction, mining, export growth, investment and a swell in domestic demand. The country's chief exports are minerals and metals; Peru is the world's second largest producer of silver and also mines a significant amount of gold, copper, zinc and lead. Mineral exports have consistently accounted for 50% of the country's export revenue, peaking at 62% of total earnings in 2006. The overdependence on min-

❏ Coca and cocaine

Coca leaf (*Erythroxylon coca*) has been part of Andean life for thousands of years and is deeply intertwined into the practical and spiritual fabric of Peruvian society. Illustrations of people using coca can be found on the portrait pots of the Nazca and tools associated with its use date from the Moche culture. In Inca times it was so prized that only the nobility were allowed to use it, but since the arrival of the Spanish, who first tried to ban the practice then realized the value of allowing the indigenous population to chew coca, it has filtered down into common usage.

When a quid of leaves is chewed with a mixture of lime or quinoa and potash called *llipta*, it acts as a stimulant to help suppress hunger, thirst and fatigue. It also eases the effects of altitude, helps to calm nausea and fortify the body. What's more, it provides the recommended daily dose of iron, calcium, vitamin A and phosphorus so it's hardly surprising that local people still believe that it's a universal panacea.

Coca farming Until 1996 Peru was the world's largest coca leaf producer. Overtaken and now a distant second to Colombia, the country still cultivates 34,000 hectares of coca per year. Easily purchased in Andean markets, it is used by people in all walks of life for many different purposes. The leaves contain 14 alkaloids, one of which is the narcotic cocaine. It has been said though that coca leaf has as much to do with cocaine as an elephant does to ivory – it is the base ingredient from which the final product comes, nothing more. The leaf in its original, unprocessed form is perfectly legal in Peru and widely used by farmers and labourers involved in back-breaking work, as treatment for everything from toothache to childbirth, in religious ceremonies and as offerings to the *Apus* and as innocuously as in a cup of tea (Mate de coca, see p79). This is not true of the cocaine that can be derived from it.

Discovery of cocaine First isolated in the 19th century by a scientist called Gaedake, the cocaine alkaloid was initially received as a great scientific discovery and heralded as a pain-killing drug of great potency. Coca wine and other coca-containing preparations were widely sold as medicines and tonics, with claims of a wide range of health benefits. The original version of Coca-Cola was among these.

Cocaine trafficking After the addictive nature of the drug was realized these products became illegal. Unfortunately its abuse and restriction has created a monster. The main problem in Peru is the enormous wealth that production of the drug can bring. Production is generally run by organized, largely Colombian, gangs of narco-terrorists, whose lawless, brutal practices hold sway over some of the remoter sections of Peru. Much of the cocaine base is shipped to neighbouring Colombia for processing into cocaine, while finished cocaine is shipped out from Pacific ports to the international drug market. Increasing amounts are also making their way across the border into Brazil and Bolivia for distribution in Europe. Since the 1980s the USA's Drug Enforcement Agency (DEA) has put political and economic pressure on Andean countries in a bid to eradicate the problem of cocaine trafficking and abuse by wiping out coca production in the Andes. This broad strategy overlooks the traditional value of the coca leaf to the Andean communities and ignores the poverty that drives campesinos without a viable alternative source of income to try growing it: coca is five or six times more valuable per kilo than coffee. The internal perception in Peru is that cocaine is a problem of the urban Western world, where the demand is generated. The suspicion is that the war on drugs is cynically fought in the highlands of the Andes, largely out of sight and unreported, rather than in the West itself, because there are no voters or people to upset.

erals and metals inevitably exposes Peru to global price fluctuations. Other important exports include fishmeal, petroleum, textiles and coffee.

Peru's major trading partners are the US, with whom they signed a free trade agreement in 2006, China, the EU, Chile and Japan.

On the home front, services make up the largest percentage of GDP (54%), followed by manufacturing (14%), agriculture (7.8%), mining (5.7%) and construction (6%). Annual inflation is around 2%.

Continuing economic problems Despite the apparently rosy outlook, there are still deep-rooted problems in Peru. The country's wealth is concentrated in the hands of a few and the vast majority of people still have very little. Underemployment remains a serious issue and has remained stubbornly high: in 2009 the rate was almost 50%. Almost half the population lives below the poverty line and 20% earn less than US$2 per day. In contrast, the richest 10% of the population hold more than a third of the country's wealth.

The environment
Just like anywhere else, Peru is struggling to reconcile the need to embrace a developing economy and the need to conserve ecologically sensitive parts of the country. The major issue confronting the country is the ongoing oil programme that is devastating chunks of the Peruvian rainforest. Sections of the rainforest have been cut down since the time of the Incas, but never at this rate or over such a large area, and never at such cost. Conservationists and eco-tourism operators are battling to prevent the programmes and the associated problems of deforestation and environmental degradation, but they are up against substantial adversaries.

In 2003 the government granted oil companies greater access to indigenous lands throughout much of the Andes. Since then, the rainforest and jungle has come under intense pressure, particularly the area to the north of Quillabamba. There are 11 trillion cubic feet of oil and gas buried beneath the jungle, but it is an area rich in bio-diversity and inhabited by native tribes, many of which have had little or no contact with the rest of the world. International pressure and outcry scared off a number of investors, including Shell, but a gas-production consortium took over what became known as the Camisea Project. Two 800km gas pipes opened up the forest to migrants, loggers and developers; pipelines from the Camisea fields known as Block 88 in the lower Urubamba region cut through the Vilcabamba range and carry oil and gas to an export terminal on the coast, at Paracas. Planned for many years, the project finally got the green light from ex-president Alejandro Toledo in the belief that it would bring great economic benefits to Peru. Since then the government has quietly issued a decree entitling the project to commence oil and gas development in previously protected reserves. Allegedly tribes in these areas have been forcibly removed from ancestral lands, and the common problems associated with deforestation have become apparent, with landslips and increased erosion threatening the hillsides. Communities and farmers in the area have also been hit by infectious diseases and outbreaks. Nonetheless, there is extensive pressure from the gas companies to open up adjacent areas such as the neighbouring Block 56, located on the tribal lands of the Machiguenga indigenous communities, for a project labelled Camisea 2. Local groups and indigenous tribes are up in arms at the prospect, and cite liquid gas and diesel spills as reasons to stop the project. According to a report in 2006 the pipeline was poorly constructed by unskilled labourers, using old, corroded pipes, which meant that in the first 18 months after it became operational, the pipeline ruptured four times. Campaigners also report a decline in the number of fish and animal populations in the region since the start of the project. In 2008 García opened the Amazon to foreign prospectors, a move that caused more than two months' of protests and road blocades that culminated in casualties on both indigenous and police sides of the stand off, before the ill-advised law was revoked.

Other problems include the melting of Peru's numerous tropical glaciers. Global warming is likely responsible for the fact that the glaciers are shrinking since they are melting faster in the dry season than they are being replenished in the wet. The glaciers feed many of Peru's major waterways. If the glaciers disappear there is a very real danger that the rivers will dry up and the land and people dependent on them will suffer. Desertification is a serious threat and the consequences are dire.

CULTURE

Writing

Although Peru has a powerful literary tradition, very few Peruvian writers ever make it into English. To track down some of the harder-to-find titles you may have to look in bookshops in Lima (see p132) or Cusco (see p153).

Many of the classic records of the conquest are written by the conquistadors, but there are also Peruvian accounts offering a different perspective. **Garcilaso Inca de la Vega** and **Felipe Huamán Poma de Ayala** (see p39) are the two best examples.

The best known contemporary Peruvian writer is **Mario Vargas Llosa**, whose novels and commentaries stand comparison with those of other great South American literary figures. Essentially a novelist, Vargas Llosa has also written about Peruvian society and culture. The best examples of his complex, meandering narratives are the rather disturbing *Death in the Andes* (Faber and Faber) which deals with the Sendero Luminoso and Peruvian politics, *Aunt Julia and the Scriptwriter* (Picador), a comic novel about a Bolivian scriptwriter who arrives in Lima to write radio plays, which is full of insights into Miraflores society, and *A Fish in the Water* (Farrar, Straus and Giroux) which describes Vargas Llosa's unsuccessful attempt to run for presidency.

Daniel Alarcón is a Peruvian-American author whose work has been featured in the New Yorker magazine. His collection of short stories, *War by Candle Light* (Harper Perennial), touch on a number of aspects of life in Lima, whilst his novel *Lost City Radio* (Fourth Estate) is a thinly veiled look at the disappearances and turmoil associated with the Sendero Luminoso.

❏ Quipus

The Incas never created a written version of their language. Nonetheless, they were able to communicate complex ideas and record enormous amounts of information by using quipus.

Quipus, which were used by early Andean societies and adopted by the Incas, are essentially a series of different coloured strings with knots tied in them. The colour, position and number of knots in the string could then be read by trained, skilled interpreters. Quipus may have just a few strands, but some have as many as 2000. A group known as Quipucamayocs, the accountants of the Inca society, created and deciphered the knots. They were capable of simple mathematics as well as recording information such as keeping track of *mit'a*, a form of taxation. The system was also used to record the census and to keep track of the calendar.

Record keeper with his quipu.

FELIPE HUAMÁN POMA DE AYALA, FROM HIS *NUEVE CRÓNICA Y BUEN GOBIERNO* (c1600)

Today there aren't all that many quipus left in existence, as the Spanish suppressed the use of them and destroyed a large number. Historians are still attempting to decipher the knots and their messages. Most people maintain that the quipus only recorded numbers, but there is some evidence to support the theory that actually they contain far more information and were effectively written records or books.

José Maria Arguedas is an indigenous author who writes about native Andean people in his novels *Los Ríos Profundos* (*Deep Rivers* – Pergamon Press) and *Yawar Fiesta* (Quartet Books). **Ciro Alegría** also carefully depicts Andean communities in *El Mundo es Ancho y Ajeno* (*Broad and Alien is the World* – Merlin Press). **César Vallejo** is one of South America's great poets and one of the most innovative Spanish-language poets in the world. His romantic imagery and unusual use of language make his poems both beautiful and powerful.

Visual arts

During the late 16th, 17th and 18th centuries a form of painting known as the **Cusco School** flourished in Peru. Formal European subjects and themes such as religion were reinterpreted by indigenous artists who had been taught by Spanish masters such as Juan Iñigo de Loyola, who arrived in 1545. These largely anonymous local artists drew on Spanish Mannerism to create paintings of unique and extraordinary beauty that mixed religious and native Andean imagery. The best examples include sumptuously dressed holy figures and archangels armed as soldiers of heaven. The hallmark of Cusco painting is the lack of perspective in the dramatic images, the predominance of red, yellow and earth colours and the application of gold to imitate the appearance of embroidered designs. The best examples can be seen in Cusco Cathedral. In the San Blas district of Cusco you can buy paintings in this style.

Martín Chambi is the best known Peruvian photographer. His images of Cusco, surrounding villages and communities and the first iconic photographs of Machu Picchu taken in 1920 are internationally renowned. Described by Mario Vargas Llosa as, 'a true inventor, a veritable force of invention, a recreator of life', Chambi was a prolific portrait photographer but also captured landscapes exquisitely. These he sold mainly in the form of postcards, a format he pioneered in Peru. In 1990 the Smithsonian Institution published a collection of his pictures, *Martín Chambi – Photographs 1920-1950*. Phaidon also published a collection of his photographs in 2002.

Peruvian cinema suffered as a result of a decision by the then prime minister Fujimori to overturn a law promoting domestic films. Ever since then the industry has remained under funded.

Music and dance

Music and dance are big parts of Peruvian life. Traditional music is a fusion of intercontinental styles using a mix of instruments to produce a generally soulful sound. Key instruments include the *queña*, bamboo flutes of varying lengths; *zampoñas*, double-rowed pan pipes; *charangos*, ten-stringed mandolins with a box made of armadillo shell, as well as drums, guitars, harps and brass instruments.

In the Andes, *huayno* is the staple musical form. This traditional, infectious rhythm relies on wind instruments and lyrics that fuse joy and sorrow. A Spanish version of huayno known as *musica folklórica* also use string instruments such as mandolins and harps. The traditional huayno tune *El Condor Pasa*, originally written in the 18th century to mark the death of the rebel Túpac Amaru II, achieved international fame when covered by Simon and Garfunkel and still endures today. However, the style has also fused with other sounds such as rock and Colombian *cumbia* to evolve into *chicha*, a form popular in the working class districts of cities or in the shanty towns and Andean villages. Lyrics focus on love in all its forms but also the harshness of Andean life, drawing on themes such as displacement, exploitation and hardship for its power. The best-known chicha bands include Belem and Los Shapias.

From the coast rises up the sound of *criolla*, which has its roots in both Spain and Africa. The most famous criolla style is the *vals peruano* (the Peruvian Waltz), which is faster than its European equivalent and full of complex guitar melodies, making it ideal for dancing. The best exponents of this form are Chabuca Granda, Susana Baca, Eva Ayllón and the band Peru Negro. Both Baca and Ayllón are also excellent exponents of *landó*, a bluesier style of criolla. Ideally both these styles should be heard live in order to capture the full energy and passion within the music. The bars, clubs and *peñas* in Lima are the best places to catch a performance.

The national dance is the *marinera*. Performed to criolla it is a flirtatious courtship between a man and a woman who circle each other. Other routines include the closely related *zamacueca* and the rather simpler *zapateo*, which translates literally as foot-stomping.

Media

The most established daily newspapers are *El Comercio* (🖳 http://elcomercio .pe), *Expreso* and *La República* (🖳 www.larepublica.com.pe). There are also a multitude of tabloid-style papers whose staple material is sex and sport with gruesome accidents or horrific murders thrown in for good measure. Slightly out-of-date US and English newspapers can also be found in Lima. For travel journalism pick up the magazine *Rumbos* (🖳 http://web.rumbosdelperu.com).

There are nine main terrestrial channels in addition to a wide range of cable TV stations such as CNN and BBC World. The bulk of domestic television content is imported Spanish-language soap operas or locally made low-budget talk and news programmes. The main television networks are slowly regaining their news credibility in the wake of a series of scandals whereby the chief executives took money from Fujimori's spymaster Vladimiro Montesinos in exchange for positive coverage. These bribes were all caught on film and when the videos surfaced in 2001 the country was gripped by what became known as the 'Vladivideos' (see p60).

Radio is a very popular form of entertainment and in the mountains is often the only way that people can keep abreast of the news. As well as the state run Radio Nacional there are three main national stations, all based in Lima.

Sport

Fútbol (soccer) is the most fanatically followed sport in the country, watched with an almost unparalleled zeal by hordes of spectators. The main teams, Alianza, Cristal and Universitario are from Lima (the classic local derby is Alianza versus Universitario), but Cusco giant killers Cienciano won the Copa de Sud America against Argentinean favourites Boca Juniors in 2004, sparking wild celebrations in the city. Unfortunately Peru hasn't qualified for the World Cup since 1982 and on two occasions has been squeezed out by local rivals Chile and Ecuador. Although most Peruvian teams will be unknown to you, key international players such as Claudio Pizarro and Nolberto Solano have played in the UK, most recently for Chelsea and West Ham respectively; Nolberto Solano returns having just signed for Hartlepool United.

Other sports struggle to compete for attention, but bullfighting and surfing have dedicated followings.

Practical information for the visitor

DOCUMENTS AND VISAS

Citizens of the EU, USA, Canada, Australia and New Zealand do not currently need a visa to enter Peru and are entitled to remain in the country as tourists for up to 183 days. Check with your local Peruvian embassy before departure to ensure that this is still the case as the situation does periodically change.

Before entering the country you will have to complete a *Tarjeta de Embarque/Tarjeta Andina de Migración* (**TAM/tourist** or **embarkation card**) on the plane or at the border crossing. In theory you must have a return ticket before being given a card but in practice this is rarely checked. Keep the card and your passport with you at all times when moving about the country, particularly in remote areas. It is also law to carry these documents on the Inca Trail. If you lose the card you may be fined.

As you enter the country the immigration officer will stamp your passport to authorize a stay of 30, 60, 90 or 183 days; note **that this cannot be extended** so ensure you request more time within the maximum period if there's the slightest possibility that you might need to stay longer.

If you need to **extend your stay**, you can cross one of Peru's borders and get a new tourist card when coming back in to the country.

Should you need a **tourist visa**, it will cost around US$38 or equivalent (prices vary according to your nationality), and you will need two passport photos, a return ticket and proof that you have enough money to finance your stay in Peru.

MONEY

Currency

The Peruvian currency is the *nuevo sol* (s/), usually called just the *sol*. This is broken down into 100 *céntimos* (cents). Since being tied to the US$ the sol has for many years been relatively stable and traded consistently at s/3.30-s/3.50 to US$1 although with the uncertainty surrounding the forthcoming election it has currently fallen to s/2.76.

During the 1980s and early '90s Peru suffered very high inflation, running at thousands of percent at one stage, and the currency was devalued twice, changing from the sol to the *inti* and then again to the nuevo sol. Some of the old notes may still be in circulation but they are worthless. Fortunately they look very different to the new notes, which have 'nuevo' clearly printed on them.

Notes in circulation are s/200, s/100, s/50, s/20 and s/10. Coins come in s/5, s/2, s/1, s/0.50, s/0.20 and s/0.10 denominations. Always ask for small bills when changing money or receiving local currency as the larger bills can be hard to break in remote communities or small towns. Make sure that all the notes are in good condition as some hotel owners or shopkeepers will refuse worn, torn or otherwise damaged currency.

There are **two currencies in the Peruvian economy**, nuevos soles (s/) and US dollars ($) and you can work with both. Use dollars for the big stuff (flights, international restaurants, big hotels, treks) but keep some soles for the small stuff (local shops/businesses, transport and restaurants especially in places outside Cusco and Aguas Calientes).

❏ Rates of exchange		
	PERU	
	NUEVO SOL	**US$**
Au$1	s/2.94	US$1.07
Ca$1	s/2.83	US$1.02
€1	s/3.90	US$1.42
NZ$1	s/2.03	US$0.80
UK£1	s/4.47	US$1.63
US$1	s/2.76	–
For up-to-the-minute rates of exchange check the Internet: 🖥 www.xe.com/ucc		

You will get a better rate if you withdraw dollars at an ATM and change them into soles rather than withdrawing soles. Most banks have 24-hour ATMs which accept foreign credit and debit cards. Be sure to retrieve your card since there is no warning sound to remind you to do so.

Other forms of money

There are lots of **ATM**s (cash machines) in Lima and Cusco where it is possible to withdraw money on your Visa or MasterCard. Using your **credit** or **debit card** through an ATM that has Cirrus, Maestro or Plus system logos on it ought to give you access to your bank account. Cash withdrawals can usually be made in either US dollars or nuevo sol. Some banks will charge you for using this service so check if your bank makes a handling fee before leaving home.

Credit cards are also widely accepted in moderate to expensive hotels, shops and restaurants in larger towns and cities although you should not rely on this means of payment once outside Lima or Cusco. Visa is the most commonly accepted card.

Travellers' cheques are a safe alternative to cash. Stick to US dollars for ease and convenience, as these are most widely accepted and will give you the best exchange rate when it comes to cashing them. American Express travellers' cheques are the most widely recognized and have offices in Lima and Cusco.

Banks and casas de cambio

Banks and **cambios** are usually open during weekdays (9am-noon and 4-6pm). Generally, try to get to the bank earlier in the day and avoid going on Friday afternoons. Casas de cambio are generally open all day. Changing money here is straightforward as long as you have your passport with you to prove your identity.

Money changers often loiter outside banks or congregate on street corners where there are banks or ATMs. Some wear jackets or badges with logos suggesting that they are official or regulated *cambistas* (money changers) licensed by the local municipality. However, they rarely offer better rates than those you can obtain from a bank and are far more likely to try and short-change you.

❏ **Airport tax**
For most people this should now be included on their ticket but if not you may have to pay cash at the airport to cover an **international departure tax** of US$31. On internal flights, such as the flight from Lima to Cusco, there is a **domestic departure tax** of US$6.80.

GETTING AROUND

Travelling between cities

There are regular **flights** between Lima and Cusco as well as other major towns such as Arequipa, Iquitos, Puerto Maldonado and Trujillo. The domestic airline network is frequently in turmoil though and service providers often spring up and then fail. The most established, reliable operators include: **LAN Peru** (🖳 www.lan.com) which flies to the most touristy destinations; **TACA** (🖳 www.taca.com) which has a limited service between Lima and Cusco; **Star Peru** (🖳 www.starperu.com) which has flights to Cusco and a handful of less obvious cities as well; and **Peruvian Airlines** (🖳www.peruvianairlines.pe)/. (See also box p140).

A popular alternative to flying is to travel overland by **bus**, the norm for most Peruvians. Services are regular and reasonably reliable although the buses can vary immensely in terms of quality from luxury coaches to scruffy ex-US school buses. There are scores of competing companies with the biggest names operating the most frequent long-distance routes. The main companies are **Cruz del Sur** (🖳 www.cruzdelsur.com.pe) and **Ormeño** (🖳 www.grupo-ormeno .com.pe). Slowly Peruvian cities are adjusting to having a single bus terminal and centralizing the arrival and departure of the numerous operators, but these may still be clustered around a square. It is also possible that the departure point is in an entirely different place to the ticket office so make sure you check where the bus is leaving from. Arrival and departure times are loosely timetabled so take the journey times quoted with a pinch of salt.

Since the privatization of the railways in the late 1990s **train** services have ceased to be the cost effective means of travel they once were. **PeruRail** (🖳 www.perurail.com) has daily services between Cusco and Aguas Calientes (below Machu Picchu) and between Cusco and Puno. The extension from Puno to Arequipa has been suspended but still occasionally runs as a charter service (see p358). There is also a weekly seasonal service operated by **Ferrocarril Central Andino** (🖳 www.ferrocarrilcentral.com.pe) from Lima to Huancayo in the central highlands. This only runs from mid-April to the end of October but climbs to 4781m in the course of the trip.

As a last measure it's possible to **hitch** a ride, although this isn't the safest way to travel and shouldn't be attempted alone. However, there aren't many private cars on the roads, buses are cheap and trucks often charge for giving a lift in rural areas, so hitching is a pretty impractical way of travelling.

Local transport
Walking is usually a safe and practical way of exploring a city. Alternatively jump in a **taxi**. Taxis don't usually have meters and will try to charge whatever they think they can get away with. Always ask what the fare is in advance and fix a price for the journey. If it seems outrageous don't be afraid to haggle: offer to pay half to three-quarters of the fare. Tipping is neither the norm nor expected. Official, regulated cabs called by telephone are usually more expensive than the private cars with a taxi sticker in the window flagged down in the street, but are generally more reliable. People travelling alone, especially women, should always use a regulated taxi. Share taxis for longer trips often wait by main junctions or roundabouts to collect multiple fares.

Local **buses** are almost always beaten-up old bangers, but they are astonishingly cheap. *Micros* or *combis*, also known as *colectivos,* are minibuses or minivans that hustle for business on the streets of most towns. Stickers on the outside identify the route and the destination, and although the system appears chaotic, they will cover almost everywhere in a city. A conductor leans out of the door calling for business, and once on board you must squeeze into place or risk standing the entire journey. Fares are collected once you're on the move. Safety and personal health aren't usually top of the driver's priorities and you will often endure a pretty hair-raising ride.

Hiring a car
Driving in Peru is not for the faint hearted. It's a long way from place to place, traffic jams in Lima are horrendous, pollution is a real problem, the roads aren't especially good and other road users are often aggressive and bad-tempered. There are major car hire firm offices in Lima and a handful of larger cities, including Cusco. A driver's licence from your own country is usually sufficient unless you want to hire the vehicle for more than a month, in which case you will require an International Driving Licence. You will also need a credit card and usually have to be aged 25 or older.

Rates vary considerably from company to company and fuel is extra. For sound advice on motoring in Peru contact the Touring y Automóvil Club del Peru (🖳 www.touringperu.com.pe).

ACCOMMODATION
Price
Prices in this book are split into three categories; **budget**, **mid-range** and **expensive**. Hotel prices are particularly changeable and may well vary in comparison to those quoted here. Nonetheless you will be able to make comparisons between the relative price brackets.

Prices are quoted for single/double/triple rooms (**sgl/dbl/tpl**) and the description will include relevant information about whether bathrooms are attached (**att**) or shared/communal (**com**), other facilities and the availability of breakfast. Budget rooms begin at US$5-15 for a room. Mid-range options are from US$15 to US$70. There has been a real explosion in this price bracket reflecting the growth in domestic and international tourism. Expensive hotels are defined as those charging more than US$70 per night. They may also add 10% for service and 18% for tax. If you're travelling in the low season you may be able to negotiate a cheaper rate. Try asking '*tiene algo un poco más económico?*' (Have you got anything a bit cheaper?). Paying cash might also get you a discount.

Standards

Peru boasts the standard range of South American accommodation options, from five-star top-end hotels to basic rooms and shared dorms in hostels. Peruvian hotels are entitled to call themselves *residencials*, *hostals*, *hotels*, *pensións* or *hospedajes* and must identify themselves with a plaque posted outside indicating the type of establishment, even though this makes no difference to the standard of accommodation on offer. There is no universal standard of grading accommodation in Peru. You might find yourself in a filthy, basic bolthole in a dangerous part of town overseen by an intimidating hotelier, or you could end up in a charming, atmospheric colonial mansion so your best bet is to actually look at a room to see whether it suits you before you hand over your money.

Camping is often possible, and is usually free, except in formal campsites.

FOOD

Peru has the most extensive menu on the continent and some of the world's top chefs. Yet mention Peruvian food to most people and the few that have heard of it might think of guinea pig, but the country's cuisine is about so much more than that. Lima is now one of the top gastronomic capitals of the continent with some world-class restaurants serving the *Novo Andina* cuisine pioneered by the chef and restaurateur Gastón Acurio.

Even in smaller regional restaurants Peruvian cooking can be very appealing; there's nothing finer than sitting in a darkened *picantería* (a traditional local restaurant often serving spicy food) with a steaming plate of *chicharrones* (fried pork and pork skin), and a mug of *chicha de jora*, the country's famous fermented maize beer.

And *cuy* (guinea pig), be it fried, baked or barbecued, is actually very tasty.

Meat

Meat dishes are numerous and varied. Most common are *lomo cordon bleu* (beef loin steak stuffed with cheese and ham), *lomo milanesa* (beaten into a thin steak and fried in breadcrumbs), and *lomo a lo pobre* (fried with an egg on top). Chicken is often served like this or simply roasted. *Parilladas* (a mixed grill and a restaurant that sells grilled meat) are generally very good.

More interesting dishes include *lomo saltado* (strips of beef stir-fried with onions, spicy orange peppers, tomatoes and soy sauce, served with rice and fried potatoes), *anticucho* (beef-heart kebabs cooked on a skewer over hot coals and served with a range of spicy sauces), *causa rellena* (a lightly spiced potato cake mixed with tuna or chicken), *aji de gallina* (shredded chicken stewed in a rich, gently spiced cream sauce) and the coronary-inducing *chicharrones* (deep-fried chunks of pork or pork skin; the original hot pork scratchings).

❑ **Ceviche**
Ceviche (cebiche; fresh, raw white fish marinated in a mixture of lime juice, hot peppers and red onion known as *leche de tigre* or tiger's milk, and often served with two types of maize and sweet potato) is usually a lunch dish, deliciously light and tasty. Many countries in South America lay claim to ceviche, but to suggest that it is anything but a Peruvian creation whilst in Lima or elsewhere along the coast is likely to get you into serious trouble.

How to make ceviche
1kg soft white fish (lemon sole or halibut, alternatively mix half fish and half shellfish)
2 large onions, sliced
1 or 2 chillies, chopped
juice of 6 limes
1 tbsp olive oil
4 tbsp fresh coriander
Seasoning to taste
Method: Wash and cut the fish into bite-sized pieces. Place in a dish with the onions, chilli and coriander. Mix up a marinade using the lime juice and olive oil and season to taste. Pour over the fish and store in a cool spot or refrigerator. How long you leave it for is a matter of taste. Some restaurants serve it after less than ten minutes, sashimi style; to 'cook' it through thoroughly will take about an hour. Serve with boiled sweet potatoes and corn on the cob.

Most unusual for many foreigners is the tradition of eating *cuy*, that popular childhood pet, the guinea pig. Considered a delicacy, it's usually fried or baked, prepared with *huarcartay* (an aromatic Andean herb), cumin and garlic and tastes a little like duck but with a unique gamey flavour. It is generally served whole, head, paws and all, as if it has just been run over in the traffic and peeled off a car wheel, and can be quite fiddly to eat.

Once scorned by the middle classes as being fit only for the poor peasant farmers, alpaca steak is now a staple on many *Novo Andina* menus.

Fish
Peru has excellent fish that includes *congrio* (conger eel), *corvina* (sea bass), *lenguado* (sole) and shellfish. Try the Peruvian version of fish and chips, *jalea* (fried whitebait) which is served with fried *yuca* (cassava or manioc), fried yellow peppers and a dollop of spicy *aji* sauce, *chupe de camarones* (traditional creamy prawn chowder), and that famous traditional Peruvian dish, *ceviche* (see above).

Other dishes
It was Viracocha's sons who discovered the **potato**, having been sent to Lake Titicaca by their Creator father to bring back the plants that grew there, so goes the Inca myth. It's not far from the truth, though, in that research shows that this is where the earliest potatoes evolved. Hunter gatherers learnt to farm the tubers that grew there about 7000 years ago. Some 200 species of wild potato are found in South America and there are now an astounding 5000 varieties cultivated in the Andes. Popular dishes include: *causa*, made with yellow potatoes,

lemons, hard-boiled eggs, olives, sweet corn, sweet potato and cheese and served with an onion sauce; *papas a la Huancaina*, a cold appetiser of potatoes in a thick, spicy cheese sauce; and *papa rellena*, where a potato is baked then fried before being stuffed with meat, olives, onions, boiled egg and raisins.

You should also try *chuño*, freeze-dried potato. It was the Incas who developed freeze-drying as a way of preserving potatoes which were then stored as a reserve if other crops failed. They freeze-dried them by leaving them out on winter's nights in sub-zero temperatures.

Quinoa used to be highly important within Andean civilizations, second only to the potato. In contemporary times its value is again being recognized because of its high nutritional and protein content, making it an unusually complete foodstuff.

In markets you'll see some of the amazing range of **maize** in a variety of colours and sizes that's available here. Unlike the puny corn found elsewhere, Peruvian corn comprises giant white kernels bursting with flavour and juice. Corn has been planted in Peru for over 3000 years. The ancient farmers achieved a degree of sophistication in the selection and creation of new varieties that adapted to varying terrains and climates. Corn is cooked in a number of ways; on the cob, *choclo* or *choclo con queso* (with a piece of cheese), boiled, ground with a pestle and mortar, toasted or fermented into *chicha* (see p80). You'll find cornmash pastries (*tamales* and *humitas*), savoury or sweet and in a wide range of colours.

Soups are often hearty and filling. Try *yacu-chupe*, a green soup made from potatoes, cheese, garlic, coriander, peppers, eggs and onions or the pleasantly spiced *sopa a la criolla*, made with thin noodles, beef hearts and bits of egg and vegetables.

As well as the wide range of Peruvian dishes you'll find excellent approximations of other cuisines: pasta is often freshly made and Chinese food (*Chifa*) is usually good.

Dessert

There's a wide range of options available for the sweet tooth, and the Peruvian tooth can be very sweet indeed. Most common puddings are *picarones* (light

---

❏ Health warning

You should always be conscious of where your food has come from and how it has been prepared otherwise you run the risk of contracting diarrhoea. Beware of tap water unless you are absolutely confident of the source, and if necessary boil or purify it before drinking. To be on the safe side, buy bottled water. Don't then get caught out by using ice that could have been made from contaminated water.

All food that can't be peeled or shelled should be washed in purified water. Stay clear of salads as they may have been washed in tap water. Ice cream from a reputable brand ought to be okay, unless the vendor has allowed it to melt and refreeze. Freshly, fully cooked food is generally safest, and try to stay clear of reheated dishes. That said *ceviche*, which isn't technically 'cooked' but marinated in lime, is perfectly safe if served fresh in a reputable restaurant.

fried doughnuts with honey) and the jelly-like *mazamorra morada* (a sweet-tasting dish made from purple maize). When in Lima make sure to try Suspiro de Limeña (see p136), a classic dessert from the city.

In addition to all the standard citrus fruits and recognizable fruits such as bananas, guavas, pineapples, papayas, mangoes and passionfruits there are also four unusual varieties; the custard-ish *cherimoya* (custard apple), *guanabana* (soursop), the gloopy *granadilla* (similar to passionfruit) and the native powdery, peachy *lucuma* (eggfruit).

Taxes and tipping

Expensive restaurants will add 19% tax to the bill. They may also add a 10% service charge which is meant to go to the waiter meaning that tipping is unnecessary. However, the money often doesn't reach the people who've earned or deserve it so you might want to consider leaving a cash tip as well. In budget or moderate restaurants tipping is normal although not obligatory.

> ❑ **Mate de coca**
> This herbal tea is made by submerging the leaves of the coca plant in hot water or by using a pre-prepared tea bag. The tea is greenish yellow and has a slightly bitter flavour. Although legal in Peru, most countries do not distinguish between the coca leaf and any other substance containing cocaine, so the possession of coca leaf, even as a tea bag, is prohibited. If you try to take some home you run the risk of arrest and a possible prison sentence.

DRINK

Non-alcoholic

Tea is widely drunk. It is usually served without milk but with sugar and lemon. Herb teas are also popular. *Mate de coca* made from coca leaves, is readily available in the cafés and restaurants in Cusco and helps to alleviate the symptoms of altitude sickness. **Coffee**, surprisingly for a coffee-producing country, is pretty poor and is either served as coffee essence, to which you add hot water, or instant coffee. Milk is again served separately. However, there are also plenty of places in Cusco that will now serve you a cappuccino or espresso. **Bottled water** is sold widely and should be drunk when you aren't confident of the water source or haven't had a chance to purify or boil the water yourself (see p91). The usual range of **soft drinks** is available, with the addition of *chicha morada*, made from purple maize, and the ubiquitous, home-grown, iridescent Inca Kola, which outsells the imported American equivalent in Peru. Try it just once to discover the sickly sweet, bubblegum flavour.

Alcoholic

Peruvian **lager** is pretty drinkable. There are numerous bottled brands including Arequipeña, Cristal, Cusqueña and Pilsener that are all brewed to about 5% alcohol content and all taste quite similar. For a change try the sweetish dark ale Cusqueña Malta.

Peruvian **wine** is yet to reach the same heights as its South American neighbours, and lack of infrastructure and poor marketing probably mean interna-

---

❏ **Pisco Sour**
2fl oz Pisco
Half a lemon or one lime
1 egg white, whisked
1 tablespoon of sugar

Beat the egg white and sugar together. Add the Pisco and lemon juice and blend. Serve the cocktail over crushed ice and garnish with a dash of angostura bitters.

tional sales are a way off; you're better off sticking to Chilean or Argentinean wine instead. If you are feeling adventurous try the Tacama, Ocucaje or Vista Allegre red or white wines from Ica.

Chicha is a maize wine that dates back to the time of the Incas but is still drunk today in the rural Andes. Nicknamed 'the champagne of the Incas', and made from a specific type of yellow maize called *jora*, it actually tastes like a type of cloudy pale cider. The name derives from the Spanish *chichal*, meaning 'saliva' or 'to spit', which refers to the Andean people's early methods of production: for centuries they found saliva an effective means of converting starches in the maize grains into fermentable sugars. Nowadays sugar is used to kick-start the process. Houses that brew and sell chicha can be identified by the red plastic bags hung outside on the end of long poles, not unlike pub signs.

Pisco is a potent clear spirit distilled from grapes. Usually drunk as part of a Pisco Sour cocktail, it can be deceptively strong. Chileans consider it their national drink as well and there is plenty of friction between the two countries over the origin of the drink.

ELECTRICITY

220 volts, 60Hz AC. Power cuts and surges are not unusual so it's worth bringing a surge protector for any valuable equipment such as laptops. Peruvian wiring often leaves a lot to be desired, particularly in bathrooms.

TIME

Peru is five hours behind GMT (UK winter time), in line with Eastern Standard Time in the USA.

POST AND COMMUNICATION

Telephone

To make international calls from Peru first dial the international dialling code and then add your country code, STD and the number required. If you want to make calls from your mobile phone abroad, check with your phone provider what the charges and coverage are. You can make international phone calls from public phones in the street operated by Telefónica-Peru, but only with a phone card. These are readily available from shops advertising *tarjeta telefónica* (telephone cards) or from touts hanging around phones selling them. There are standard phone cards or ones where you have to dial a number, usually ☎ 147, and then enter a PIN printed on the card – simply follow the instructions that follow from the operator or recorded message to make the call. Often internet cafés also have private phone booths where it is possible to make cheap local and international calls.

For the operator dial ☎ 100; for directory enquiries dial ☎ 103; for the emergency services dial ☎ 105; for the international operator dial ☎ 108.

To call Peru from abroad dial your international access code and then ☎ 51. Add ☎ 1 for Lima or ☎ 84 for Cusco.

Email

Email and internet access is readily available in large towns and even smaller places have a smattering of cyber cafés. Although internet cafés open and close with alarming rapidity, there are usually lots to choose from and some hotels and hostels now also offer internet access. There is free wi-fi for members of the South American Explorers Club (see p130) at their clubhouse in Lima.

Post

Post in Peru, branded Serpost, is slow but generally reliable. Letters to Peru take between one and two weeks to arrive whilst letters to Europe or the USA from Peru take between ten days and three weeks to be delivered. Stamps are

PERU

❑ **Holidays and festivals**

1 Jan	New Year's Day (all Peru but major fiesta in Huancayo)
6 Jan	Fiesta de Ollantaytambo (Cusco)
14 Jan	Feria de Pampamarca (Cusco): agricultural fair
April	Maundy Thursday, Good Friday and Easter (all Peru)
1 May	Labour Day (all Peru)
7-9 June	Qoyllur Riti (Cusco): pilgrimage to the glaciers of the high Andes
June	Corpus Christi (all Peru, but Cusco in particular): on the ninth Thursday after Easter 15 statues of saints and virgins are paraded around Cusco's streets
24 June	Inti Raymi (Cusco): old Inca festival of the winter solstice which is now a major tourist attraction in Cusco.
29 June	San Pedro y San Pablo (St Peter and St Paul; all Peru)
15-18 July	Fiesta de la Virgen del Carmen (Pisac, Pucara and in particular at Paucartambo, 110km northeast of Cusco)
28-29 July	Independence Day (all Peru)
30 Aug	Fiesta de Santa Rosa de Lima (Lima)
4 Oct	Fiesta de la Virgen del Rosario (Lima and Cusco)
18 Oct	El Señor de los Milagros (Lima): day of religious processions
1 Nov	Todos Santos, All Saints' Day (all Peru)
2 Nov	Dia de los Muertos; day when Peruvians remember their dead
5 Nov	Birth of the first Inca, Manco Capac (Puno); week-long festival centred on this date
8 Dec	Immaculate Conception (all Peru); religious processions in honour of the Virgin Mary
24 Dec	Santurantikuy (Cusco): literally 'saints for sale', was originally a market where figurines for nativity scenes were sold; now a general market; elsewhere the day is a pre-Christmas holiday
25 Dec	Christmas (all Peru)

frequently available in the same places that sell postcards. Main *correos* (post offices) have **poste restante** and American Express offices will hold mail addressed to their customers. To pick up mail you will need your passport. When it comes to looking for mail check to see if it has been filed under any of the names on the envelope as post is not necessarily sorted by surname. To minimize confusion make sure that all correspondents clearly print and underline your surname on the envelope.

SHOPPING

Fabrics

The Andean people have always placed great store by intricately woven textiles and fabrics have a long history amongst indigenous culture. Rugs, ponchos, clothes and wall-hangings are all readily available from markets such as those at Chinchero, Pisac and Ollantaytambo.

Alpaca wool is widely used and most shopkeepers will proudly tell you that the fabric you're holding comes from 'baby alpaca'. The quality varies enormously. Modern dyes are less subtle than traditionally applied ones. If you singe a couple of fibres and it smells like burning plastic the material is acrylic. If it smells very bad when wet it's probably llama as alpaca is odourless whether wet or dry.

The finest wool is from **vicuña**. The national animal of Peru was once hunted almost to extinction; in 1974 only 6000 remained but conservation has led to them being taken off the endangered list: there are now more than 350,000. Their wool is expensive because they can be shorn only every three years.

Arts and crafts

Andean crafts and folk art, ceramics, wood carvings, hand-tooled leather, gold and silver jewellery and *arpilleras* (appliqué pictures of Peruvian life) are all good buys and can be picked up at many of the markets or shops in larger towns. Never buy the framed insects seen for sale in Cusco, though. They are often endangered species and the trade in them depletes the resources of the Amazon. If you are tempted, then remember that if they are restricted or protected species customs will confiscate them from you. Genuine 'Inca' artefacts are often nothing more than cheap knock-offs, and any actual relics you find must not be taken out of the country – it's illegal to export them.

Bargaining

Haggling and bargaining are often part of the ritual when shopping for goods at markets and fairs. Foreigners, including those with backpacks, are seen as rich, and in comparison to the many Peruvians who live below the poverty line, they really are. Prices can therefore sometimes be inflated. However, the vast majority of Peruvians are not out to take advantage of you. When buying hand-crafted goods remember that the seller has probably toiled to produce the exquisite textile or carving that you are interested in, and recognize the craftsmanship, skill and time that have gone into producing your souvenir. The tiny saving you might make by aggressive haggling could actually represent rather

---

❏ **Tourist Protection Service**
If you think that you've been ripped off contact **Indecopi**, the government-run Tourist
Protection Service (☎ free 0800 4 2579) at Portal Carrizos 250 on Plaza de Armas in
Cusco to report the incident and make a complaint. See p133 for details of the police
service in Lima.

---

more to the person you are bargaining with. The seller may even be forced to
sell their goods at any price in order to survive. Do not take advantage of this
and only bargain when you feel that the price really is too high. Remember; pay
the fairest price, not necessarily the lowest price.

SAFETY

Pickpockets and opportunist thefts are the biggest problem for travellers.
Usually thieves work in teams and target anyone who looks to have money. One
of them will distract you using any number of ingenious techniques to get your
attention. Most frequently, someone will trip or fall into you, an old lady might
collapse in front of you or someone may spit or stick chewing gum to your
clothes. Whilst you are distracted an accomplice relieves you of your wallet,
opens your bag with a razor or simply grabs it and runs. Muggings and assaults
do happen too but are less common.

By not flaunting your valuables and staying alert in crowded or busy areas,
such as markets, bus depots or train stations, you can reduce the risk to yourself. Be careful when travelling at night and if necessary take a taxi rather than
walk. A moneybelt is a good way of concealing your cash. Alternatively, make
sure that you carry your cash in several different places in order to minimize the
risk of losing it all. Some people go to the lengths of lining their packs with
chicken wire or mesh to prevent bag slashers from opening up their packs.

Be on your guard when seemingly confronted by a policeman. Always ask
to see identification and at no point simply hand over your passport or documents. If you can help it, avoid getting into a police car and instead insist on
walking to the police station.

Should the worst happen, try to stay calm, remember that they are just after
your money, and hand it over. It's not worth getting killed for. If you are a victim of crime or do get ripped off, report it to the tourist police, who generally
speak English and are usually helpful. Make sure that you get a police report for
your insurance claim.

Bearing all of this in mind, most people still have no problems when visiting Peru. Take care and you will probably be fine.

On the Inca Trail

A lot of agencies and guidebooks imply that the Trail is rife with opportunistic
criminals and tent slashers waiting to steal your possessions. These tend to be
exaggerated claims and theft itself is now uncommon on the Inca Trail, as long

as you take a series of basic precautions. Don't take unnecessary valuables with you. Make sure not to take jewellery or large quantities of cash along (do remember to take your passport though as it must be shown at checkpoints). Carry any valuables that you do take in a safe pouch and make sure that you keep your camera in sight at all times, especially at meal times. When camping, remove temptation by ensuring that all your belongings are stored inside the tent, not outside or around it.

DRUGS

The possession of drugs in Peru, essentially marijuana or cocaine, is considered a very serious offence and usually leads to draconian penalties. There is no bail for serious charges and you may be imprisoned for some time before coming to trial. If you are suspected or convicted of trafficking in drugs the sentence can be up to 15 years in prison. Avoid having any casual conversations with someone who offers you drugs, as the person you are speaking to may be a police informant or plainclothes officer.

MINIMUM IMPACT

3

Minimum impact trekking

Tourism is a vital source of income for Peru and, directly or indirectly, a great many Peruvians benefit from the increasing numbers of trekkers and tourists flocking to the country. However, there are undoubtedly problems along the Inca Trail and the other trekking routes in the region that are caused by the arrival of hordes of visitors. Litter, erosion, pollution and the destruction of the landscape and the Inca archaeological sites are all sadly the realities of large numbers of people visiting these areas. The INC does nominally try to keep the place clean, but unfortunately their actions aren't all that effective. Whilst it's easy to blame the authorities for the decline of the pristine wilderness, trekkers are equally at fault. People on the trails also have to take responsibility for their own litter and actions, and each individual should remember that their thoughtlessness and selfishness potentially has consequences for everyone else.

ENVIRONMENTAL IMPACT

Damaged vegetation, litter, polluted waterways, deteriorating facilities and an increase in erosion are all indications that trekkers have had a negative impact on the landscape. Fortunately, people are now much more conscious of the potential impact that they have on the environment and are more likely to adopt a considerate, responsible attitude whilst trekking or otherwise enjoying the landscape. It's important that we all maintain this new-found responsibility.

Pack it in, pack it out
All waste must be carried off the mountain. Human detritus is one of the most significant threats to the natural environment. Unsightly and unhealthy, accumulated rubbish is a hazard for people and wildlife alike. If you are with an official group, in theory all you have to do is hand the litter to the team members who will then ensure that it is removed from the trail. Unfortunately this isn't always the case and more unscrupulous guides or porters may dump or drop rubbish along the route. Keep an eye on your team and make sure they understand that it is important to you that they adhere to this rule. In addition, don't give them batteries to dispose of; keep hold of them and take them back home where there are proper facilities for getting rid of them. If you are trekking independently, take rubbish bags with

you to carry all your waste and be conscious of the amount of litter you are like-ly to generate when preparing to trek. If you come across litter along the trail you should pick it up and remove it, if at all possible, in order to set a good example.

Bury your excrement

Where possible, always use the purpose-built toilet blocks along the trails or at the campsites. If you are trekking on one of the routes that doesn't have facili-ties, or are caught short on the trail, stick to the following rules: make sure you're at least 20m away from both the path and any water source or stream; take a trowel with you so that you can dig a small hole to squat over and cover the hole with plenty of soil once you're done; dispose of your toilet paper prop-erly either by burning it or burying it deeply in the same hole. Better still pack it out along with everything else, having taken the precaution of double-bagging (preferably in a zip-lock bag) the offending article.

Don't pollute water

The Andean waterways and lakes are fragile ecosystems. Contamination can easily lead to deterioration in water quality. Equally, no-one wants to bathe in other people's bathwater. Or cook with it, do their laundry in it or indeed drink it. Yet this is the consequence for the local people if you wash your hair or body or clothes in the mountain streams, no matter how romantic an image this might conjure up. Your guide will almost certainly provide you with a bowl of warm water at the start and end of the day for you to wash with. Dispose of this care-fully, at least 20m away from any other water source or stream, and wait until you finish the trek to have a proper wash.

Erosion

In general, the Inca trails are clearly marked and easy to follow. Try to stay on these paths wherever possible. The continued use of shortcuts, particularly on some of the steeper sections of trail, erodes the slopes. From the various passes it is very tempting to descend quickly and directly, and you may see people, especially guides, doing just that. Faster and possibly more fun, the shortcuts nonetheless destroy the fabric of the hillside and cause irreparable damage. Tedious as it may sound, stick to the marked paths.

Camping

When camping try to have as little impact as possible on the countryside. Ask permission if near to a farm or small holding. Confine yourself to as small a space as is realistic and do not spread yourself out unduly. Don't litter the area and when you strike camp make sure you tidy everything up and leave the site as you found it, undisturbed.

Campfires

Whilst a campfire sounds very appealing and the stuff of true camping expedi-tions, the reality of an out-of-control fire means that it just isn't worth the risk. There's absolutely no need to light a fire on any of the treks described here: for cooking you or your guides ought to use a portable stove, whilst for heat you should simply put on another jumper or layer of clothes.

Don't camp in the ruins
The ancient stones are being badly damaged by trekkers who like the idea of spending a night amongst the Inca sites. Litter and human waste are not the only problems of this selfish action. Campfires damage the walls and clumsy campers dislodge and remove the stones themselves. You do not belong amidst the ruins and you cannot stake a claim to them by sleeping amongst them.

Don't pick flowers or disturb fauna
Leave the flora and fauna alone. The Cusco region, a dedicated UNESCO natural World Heritage Site, is full of stunning flowers and some extraordinary bird and animal life. It is illegal to remove anything from the trails or the sanctuary, so leave it all where it belongs for others to enjoy as well.

ECONOMIC IMPACT

The economic importance of tourism for Peru is undeniable. However, not everyone benefits equally. If you book an organized trek through a foreign operator, the bulk of your money stays outside the country. Book a trek through an agency in Cusco, and a far greater proportion of the money remains in the city. The porters and trek team may not be from the city, although they will benefit from the opportunity to work. If you trek independently where possible, you will contribute far more to the local economy. Employ a local porter or arriero. Some independent trekkers feel that being burdened by their pack is part of the experience, but it is far more useful to the region if you hire help, and if arranged whilst there, can be a surprisingly simple, cheap way of putting something back and making your trip more enjoyable.

Pay a fair price for a fair service
Recognize the worth of a service to you and pay a reasonable rate for it. Do not attempt to bargain porters or arrieros right down and do not haggle overly aggressively. They are paid poorly for back-breaking work, yet are worth every sol to the success of a trek (see porter welfare, pp18-19). However, do not believe the market traders and touts who tell you that goods have a fixed price!

CULTURAL IMPACT

The places that you are visiting are of great spiritual, historical and cultural importance. Show these places the respect that they deserve. To fully appreciate and understand the cultural history and value of the place that you are visiting you ought to spend some time learning about its people and history (see pp48-71).

Whilst you are trekking try to be considerate to other visitors and users of the countryside. Try to keep noise to a minimum. As a general rule, be selfless and remember that you are only visiting.

Encourage local pride

Encourage local pride by giving Peruvians a balanced view of life in your home country. In answer to queries about how much you earn, reply honestly but put the figures into context by comparing how much it costs to rent a flat or buy certain types of goods. Tell them what you think is good about their lifestyle – the extraordinary surroundings, the lack of real crime, the clean air – and comment on what appeals to you about their lifestyle. If you particularly enjoyed your stay or trek be sure to let them know.

To give or not to give?

Giving to beggars can perpetrate an attitude of dependency. Be careful not to load up with sweets or other gifts to answer the children's begging requests. Although handing things out might make you feel good in the short term, it can lead to a detrimental effect on the recipient, resulting in low self-esteem and an associated idea that the west and tourists hold the answer rather than their own culture. Additionally, there are no dentists in the rural communities and giving sweets to children here is not helpful.

If someone has done something helpful, consider rewarding them, but be careful as to how you do it. Requests for pens and other school equipment are harder to refuse, but donations should really be made to a school rather than an individual to ensure equal distribution.

You should also be wary of handing out medicines along the trails. Strong or prescription medicines may be taken incorrectly and do more harm than good. If you have additional or left over medicines donate them to an agency or organization that can distribute them to a hospital instead.

Ask permission before taking a person's photograph

Respect their privacy and if they aren't comfortable or happy with the situation then leave them alone. Ideally you should not pay people for posing. If you offer to send someone a copy of the photo you've taken, make sure you get the address and follow through your promise.

Don't flaunt your wealth

Your wealth, however poor you may be by the standards of your home country, is far in excess of that of most Peruvians, so don't make a big issue of it and certainly don't flaunt it. Take care of valuables and put them away so as to remove temptation. When camping make sure that all your equipment is out of sight inside the tent, especially at night.

Don't lose your temper

Peruvians rarely lose their rag, and you should work hard to control your temper as well, even when things aren't working out as you might have hoped they would. Be polite and the chances are the courtesy will be returned.

Safe trekking

SAFETY

Although there are hazards in the mountains, a properly prepared expedition with the right equipment and a bit of common sense should not be troubled by them.

Weather

The weather in the Andes is very changeable. You should expect rain whatever the season and ought to carry warm clothing at all times, even if it seems to be a sunny day, since temperatures can plummet and conditions change very quickly. As a general guide, check the weather forecast with your agency or online before setting out and keep an eye on the weather as you walk. For more information about the climate, see p24.

Keeping on course

Although the majority of trails in the Cusco region are well trodden, there are also plenty of areas where you will come across very few people and where the track has disappeared, particularly on the Vilcabamba trek or longer routes linking Vilcabamba to Choquequirao or Choquequirao to Machu Picchu. Bad weather can also mean that a path previously simple to follow becomes obscured and much harder to trace. In thick cloud or fog do not leave the path.

An accurate topographic map and a compass are good ideas, as long as you know how to use them. Similarly, a handheld GPS (Global Positioning System) can help you to find your way.

Tell someone where you're going

If you are planning on trekking independently, before you set off on your trek, tell someone responsible, at your hotel or hostel for example, where you are going and when you expect to return. They should be aware of what to do if you don't come back, and how long they should wait before raising the alarm.

Beware of the dog

Rural dogs can be dangerous, some may even carry rabies, but are more often just a nuisance. If confronted by an angry, barking dog often just bending down as if to pick up a stone is enough to cause them to turn tail – this is what the locals do and the dogs are used to being pelted.

HEALTH IN THE MOUNTAINS

Trekkers often revel in the horror stories about the diseases encountered on treks and trips to the developing world. Whilst Peru does have a handful of serious health problems, you are very unlikely to be affected by them and if you follow simple guidelines you'll minimize the risk to yourself.

MINIMUM IMPACT & SAFE TREKKING

Acute mountain sickness (AMS)

Altitude sickness (or Acute Mountain Sickness, AMS) is a potentially fatal condition and must not be underestimated. The higher you go above sea-level, the
lower the barometric pressure, resulting in less oxygen reaching your lungs with
each breath. This in turn means that less oxygen is passed into your blood. It
generally occurs above 3000m/10,000ft, but can affect people at lower elevations: it is the **speed of ascent** and not the actual altitude that causes AMS. The
human body takes several days to acclimatize to an increase in altitude. There
are no hard and fast rules as to how long this takes, as individuals are affected
differently.

AMS and High Altitude Pulmonary Oedema (HAPE) and High Altitude
Cerebral Oedema (HACE), the serious, life-threatening conditions that can occur
as a result of it, are entirely preventable though, if certain precautions are taken:
- Don't exceed the recommended rate of ascent.
- Drink plenty of liquid, at least four litres per day in some form.
- Eat well, even if at altitude you find you lose your appetite.
- Avoid overexertion by climbing slowly and steadily.
- Look out for early symptoms of AMS and react to them.

Mild symptoms are uncomfortable, but not dangerous, and will pass in a
couple of days. As well as breathlessness and an irritating dry cough, you will
have a headache and feel nauseous. In more serious conditions you may start to
vomit. Increasing tiredness, confusion and a reduction in coordination are more
advanced symptoms. Initially ascend slowly, stopping frequently. Remember, it
is the speed of ascent, not altitude itself that causes AMS. Drink plenty of liq-
uids to prevent dehydration. Eat light meals and avoid alcohol. Use a light
painkiller but do not take sedatives or strong painkillers, which may mask the
onset of more serious symptoms.

If the conditions persist or if you have any reason to suspect that you are suffering from AMS, you should consider descending at once. Even dropping down
500m/1600ft can have a beneficial effect. If you find yourself still struggling,
descend further immediately, even during the night. See p44 for more on AMS.

Hypothermia

Also known as exposure, hypothermia develops as a result of someone being
extremely cold. If they are hypothermic, they'll stumble, be confused, slur their
speech, act oddly and be very cold to the touch. They may be oblivious to the
fact that they are in danger. To try to prevent the onset of the condition or the
deterioration of the casualty, try to warm them up, most usually by getting them
out of wet clothing or by sharing bodily warmth.

Sunburn and sun-stroke

The strong Andean sun burns quickly. Protect against sunburn by wearing a hat,
sunglasses and a shirt with a collar. You'll also need sunscreen as the sun is
strong, and even an apparently cloudy day is no guarantee that you won't get
burnt. Occasionally, if a person's temperature is driven dangerously high, they
can develop sun-stroke. A victim of this will be delirious and confused, whilst

their pulse will be racing and their breathing fast and erratic. Try to reduce their temperature gradually by fanning, sponging them with a damp cloth and shading them. If they lose consciousness you must try to get them to a doctor as quickly as possible.

Care of feet, ankles and knees

Whilst trekking, your feet are your most valuable tools. A twisted ankle, sore knee or septic blister can severely spoil your trek so take precautions to prevent them. Wear comfortable boots with good ankle support. Don't carry too much or over-stress your joints. Avoid walking in the dark. Wash and dry your feet thoroughly and change your socks regularly. If you do feel a blister developing, act immediately to prevent it from getting worse.

● **Blisters** Prevention is far better than cure when it comes to blisters. If you feel a tingling sensation or 'hot spot' developing stop at once and cover the irritated area with a piece of moleskin or Second Skin. If a blister does form either burst it with a sterilized needle and apply a dressing or build a moleskin dressing around the unburst blister to protect it.

● **Sprains** Reduce the risk of a sprain by wearing boots with good support. Mind your step as you walk over rough or uneven terrain too. If you do sprain an ankle, soak it in cold water and keep it bandaged. Aspirin is good for reducing swelling and easing the pain.

● **Knee problems** Sustained sections of steep downhill trail can result in sore, strained knees. When descending this type of trail take small steps and tread carefully to lessen the impact and jarring on the joints. Knee supports can give some assistance, and trekking poles can also help for long descents, particularly if you have a previous history of knee problems.

Chapped skin and lips

Carry moisturizer or Vaseline to apply to chapped skin. Use lip balm to soothe cracked or dry lips.

Food

To improve your chances of not getting sick when eating, maintain a high standard of hygiene. Essentially, if you can't cook it, peel it or wash it in clean, purified water then you should be wary of it.

Water purification

Always boil, filter or purify your drinking water. This will help to reduce the risk of picking up a water-borne illness such as giardia, but will also reduce the number of non-returnable, non-reusable, non-biodegradable and very environmentally unfriendly plastic mineral water bottles found all over the routes. Iodine tablets or iodine drops are ideal for treating water; simply follow the instructions on the packet or bottle. A portable water filter chemically or mechanically cleans the water, but isn't necessarily thorough enough to remove all bugs or impurities. If you treat your water yourself you reduce the risk of it simply being warmed up in a kettle and can be absolutely sure that it has been purified.

FLORA & FAUNA

4

The Machu Picchu Historical Sanctuary is a UNESCO World Heritage Site and, unusually, it's a World Heritage Site for both architecture and wildlife. The Sanctuary covers some 325 sq km in an area of wilderness banded to the north by the watershed of the Mt Veronica massif, in the east and west by the Cusichaca and Aobamba Valleys, and in the south by the ridgeline of the Salkantay massif.

The area represents one of the world's most biologically diverse regions: 10% of Peru's entire biodiversity is represented within the confines of the Sanctuary alone. This includes around 200 species of orchid, more than 700 species of butterfly and over 400 species of bird. Of the 9000 or so registered bird species in the world, those found in Europe and North America account for around 1400. Peru accounts for almost 1800 on its own, of which 120 are endemic to Peru. The Sanctuary plays host to almost 5% of the world's known bird species.

The reason for this is the great variety of ecosystems generated by the wide range of altitudes found within the Sanctuary. The mouth of the Aobamba River lies at 1725m, whilst a mere 20km away the peak of Mt Salkantay grazes 6271m. The high mountain ridges generate microclimates that are particularly favourable to the evolution of certain species. The 4546m altitude span results in a broad scope of temperatures being available for different species to dwell in whilst regular rainfall and frequent cloud and mist mean that the region is also humid for much of the year.

The Sanctuary is classified into ten distinct 'Life Zones', which range from the permanent snows of the high peaks through two types of high altitude grassland to seven zones of forest. The best known and most recognized zones are the treeless, mountain grassland environment known as puna and the cloud forest, which harbours four Life Zones and is most commonly characterized by a dense and varied mass of trees, smothered in lichens, bromeliads and orchids and surrounded by tree ferns and bamboo. The Sanctuary is also home to some of the few remaining native Andean *Polylepis* forests, which are found on steep slopes and cliffs at higher altitudes; the classic Inca Trail passes through one such section during the ascent to Dead Woman's Pass.

See pp40-1 for details of field guides to the region.

FLORA

In the Andes flowers and plants from the valleys and highland plains grow alongside each other as a result of the variations in altitude and climate found there. Consequently the region boasts a wide range of habitats and microhabitats, and features a huge diversity of wild species.

Trees

There are a number of beautiful trees found throughout the cloud forest. **Aliso** (*Alnus jorullensis*) grows up to 20m tall and is frequently found on the banks of rivers and streams between 2500-3800m. The Incas and the Spanish used its large trunks as beams and lintels in buildings. Today, doors, windows and fruit crates are made from its pale yellow wood. The smaller **chacpa** (*Oreocallis grandiflora*) ranges in height from 2-6m. It has a host of pink flowered heads that can readily be seen in the Cusichaca Valley on the early stages of the Inca Trail. Baskets are made from the small, flexible branches and locals chew the leaves in order to prevent tooth decay. The thorny **tara tree** (*Caesalpina spinosa*) is very common in the Cusichaca Valley. It is unusual in that it bears fruit all year round. These fruits contain tannin, used for tanning leather. They are also used to ease throat pain. The tara is most easily recognized by the characteristic orange/red seedpods it produces that resemble tough-skinned broad beans. The **chamana** (*Dodonaea viscosa*) is also found in the Cusichaca Valley. It is a smaller shrub that grows to 2m and is covered in abundant foliage. It is the perfect plant for binding the soil along the steep mountainsides. The wood burns well even when fresh as it contains an oily substance that is flammable. The similar sized **llaulli** (*Barnadesia horrida*) is a thorny bush that can be found in the ravines adjacent to the Urubamba Valley between 2900-3800m. The local farmers cultivate it as a hedge and use it to make a lattice on the roofs of their adobe huts upon which tiles are laid. The pink, daisy-like flowers are good for alleviating respiratory problems and bronchitis.

The town of Chilca, in the Urubamba Valley, gets its name from the **chilca bush** (*Bacharis latifolia*), which is abundant throughout the valley between 2500-3400m. Balls of white flowers form at the end of the branches in clusters. The leaves and flowers are used to make a yellow/green dye for wool. A ball of ash and calcium, called Llipta, which locals chew with coca leaves, is made from its ashes. The town Mollepata, the start point for the treks over Mt Salkantay, is so called because the Incas cultivated molle trees in the region. The name literally translates as 'The place of the Molles'. The **molle** (*Schinus molle*) is a 6-7.5m tall tree that is attractive enough to be used as an ornamental plant. The Incas used resin collected from it to embalm their mummies. Today, the tree's wood is used in carpentry and its ashes used as tanning product and in the production of soap. Oil extracted from its leaves is used in perfumes and by the toothpaste industry. Honey, vinegar, tincture and condiments are all made from the small red fruits that the tree produces. Other attractive ornamental trees include the **rata rata** (*Abutilon sylvaticum*), the pink and white conical flowers

FLORA & FAUNA

of which are used to decorate city plazas and gardens but is found wild in the Cusichaca Valley around Huayllabamba, and the **unca** (*Myrcanthes oreophyl*), which grows up to 15m tall and has very pretty, large white flowers with many filaments. The Incas used to make *keros*, ceremonial vases, from its heavy, white wood, whilst today it's used in furniture making. The bright red splashes of colour visible around the towns of Pisac, Calca and Urubamba in the Sacred Valley are likely to be flowering **pisonay** (*Erythrima edulis*). This giant, leafy, 15m tall tree is native to the high jungle but the Incas acclimatized it to the highlands and considered it to be sacred. However, the real giant of the forest is likely to be the **eucalyptus** (*Eucaliptus globulus*). This imported tree grows up to 30m tall and is the most industrialized, commercialized and useful tree to the Andean people as it grows very quickly in comparison to Andean trees. Its wood is used in the building and mining industries and to make furniture, posts and railway sleepers. Its leaves are used to cure colds and to produce menthol on behalf of the drug and food industries.

Finally, keep your eyes peeled for the **kantu** (*Cantua buxifolia*), known locally as *Flor del Inca*, Peru's national flower. This red and yellow tubular flower, which opens out like a trumpet, grows on a shrub that stands up to 4m tall and grows between 2300-3800m. The Incas dedicated this plant to the Sun God and used the pattern of its flower on their pottery, textiles and ceremonial vases. Kantu are often grown as ornamental plants in town plazas, such as in Cusco and are a common sight throughout the Sacred Valley.

Orchids

The Machu Picchu Historical Sanctuary is famous for the quantities of orchids that flourish there. Over 70 genera and around 250 species thrive in the moist, humid confines of the Sanctuary. However, much of the region remains unexplored and there are undoubtedly more to be discovered, possibly for the very first time.

Although orchids abound, numbers around the Inca trail and in particular at Machu Picchu itself, have dwindled significantly over recent years as a direct consequence of illegal collection by visitors. The biggest threats though are from deforestation and forest fires, such as the huge blaze in August 1997, which destroy valuable orchid gene banks and prime habitat as well as altering and annihilating entire ecosystems. A particular case in point is the unsympathetic and extensive clearing that occurred around Intipata on the Inca Trail (see p221), which resulted in the loss of unique habitat for the rare orchid *Telipogon papilio*, which now faces extinction in the Sanctuary. Conserving these orchids is everyone's responsibility. There is currently no single organization responsible for their preservation in Peru although INRENA (the Ministry of Agriculture), INDECOPI and PromPeru share the obligation. Until this commitment is taken seriously though it remains extremely difficult to manage the conservation of Peruvian orchids.

The observant or interested trekker should spot orchids at any time of year. The most likely places to come across these exquisite flowers are off the beaten track though, especially in the cloud forest between 1800-3000m. Most flower during the rainy season, from October to March. The diversity of species on show is stunning.

The most widespread and populous genus is *Epidendrum*, of which there are around 30 species in the Sanctuary. The most common is *Epidendrum secundum*, known locally as **huinay huayna**, meaning 'forever young', a reference to the fact that this diminutive, striking orchid flowers almost all year round. The small splashes of vibrant colour are most readily spotted around the ruins of Huinay Huayna on the Inca Trail, which is named after the plant. Its abundant flowers are red, pink, yellow or violet. Other species include the delicate and fragrant *Epidendrum ciliare*, which grows on trees and rocks at the lower elevations of the Sanctuary, and *Epidendrum coronatum*, which grows in open areas amidst other plants at altitudes between 2800-3200m.

Also commonly seen on the forest border and on open slopes are the *Odontoglossum sp*, whose bright yellow flowers are distinctively shaped and protected by brown or purple sepals.

Once widespread, *Masdevallia veitchiana*, known locally as **huakanki**, which means 'you'll cry', has been collected almost to extinction. One of the most striking orchids, its purple and orange flowers with three slight pointed petals are very distinctive and still sought after. The orchid requires open sunny areas and can still be seen at Huinay Huayna on the Inca Trail, where it clings to rocky outcrops carpeted in moss. It flowers from May to July. The bamboo orchid, *Sobralia dichotoma*, also known as the **Inca orchid** or *Flor del Paraíso*, is visible around Machu Picchu by virtue of the fact that it grows so tall (up to 5m) and has large, showy, 8cm diameter purple flowers that bloom from July to September and can easily be seen above the surrounding foliage. At the other end of the scale is one of the world's smallest orchids, a *Stelis* whose flower is barely 2mm wide.

Shrubs and flowers

Familiar plants frequently seen whilst out walking in the UK, Europe and the US can be spotted in the Sanctuary, too. **Broom** (*Spartinum junceum*), a member of the sweet pea family, was introduced from Spain in 1580. This yellow flowering shrub grows well in grasslands up to 3500m. The plant is cultivated in order to produce dye, firewood and for use as decoration. Its bright flowers are used medicinally to treat rheumatism, oedema, liver diseases and abscesses. They also serve as makeshift confetti in parades. **Lupins** (*Lupinus sp*) are another common shrub found throughout the grasslands in the area. Its blueish, lavender flowers are shaped like pea flowers and have bright yellow centres. The leaves, flowers and stems are used for a cream or green coloured dye. **Ladies' slipper** (*Calceolaria engleriana*) is a member of the snapdragon family. The flowers of this 2m tall shrub resemble tiny 2cm slippers – the Latin name is derived from *calceolus*, meaning 'slipper'. In Quechua the plant is called *pucllu*, which means 'bag' or 'sack' and again refers to the shape of the flowers. Its Spanish nickname is *globitus*, meaning 'little balloons', because you can pop the flowers between your fingers. Various species are used by local people in tea as a cure for uterine problems or as a diuretic. Also readily identifiable are the flowers of the **wild potato** (*Solanaceae sp*). This erect, clambering herb has violet flowers with five points and protruding yellow anthers. There are some 135 species of this genus in Peru alone, growing in rocky or wooded areas.

A type of **lily**, *Bomarea dulcis*, grows around boulders in grassy areas. The plant produces between two and five dangling two-inch flowers that resemble tubular bells. The sepals of these are reddish pink but have darker edges. The Quechua name for this plant is *milli milli*, meaning 'twins' and describes the two flowers often seen hanging together. The equally distinctive, purple-violet dangling flowers of *Brachyotum grisebachi* can be readily seen on the edges of the cloud forest near to water. This 2.5m shrub has many branches and produces masses of the distinctive flowers, which are occasionally worn by local people as ear decorations. **Begonias** (*Begonia bracteosa*) flourish within the Sanctuary and the red, white or pink flowers of various species can be seen on numerous dry, sunny, stepped slopes. **Bomareas** can be seen in two colours. The showy orange bracts of *Bomarea aurantiaca* and the deep red bracts of *Bomarea coccinea* are particularly visible in the humid cloud forest around Phuyu Pata Marca on the Inca Trail and in the jungle surrounding the Santa Teresa Valley.

Daisies, **fuchsias**, **elders** and **buttercups** are also prevalent. More unusual is the **datura** (**moonflower**), *Brugmansia arborea*. There are two types, which have white and red/green flowers. Both are hallucinogenic and toxic if consumed.

Other plants

Bromeliads, relatives of the pineapple, can be seen throughout the Sanctuary. Several types of cacti are also common. The **agave cactus** (*Agave americana*) is a broad plant with bluish spiked succulent leaves that grows on the dry mountainsides. The Incas made ropes and knitted suspension bridges from the leaf fibres. They also made sandals from it. Local people now use it to form an impenetrable hedge and in the production of products such as soap. The **prickly pear cactus** is cultivated in order to obtain carmine, a natural red colourant used in food, and pharmaceutical and cosmetic industries. Carmine is obtained from the cochineal, a parasitic insect found in the cactus. The fruits of the cactus are delicious and are sold in many of the towns in the Sacred Valley.

There are two types of common **grasses**. *Stipa ichu*, the golden or brown stems of which grow in tussocks on the puna from 3000-4500m, is a tough, ubiquitous grass used to make roofs on huts, insulate beds and tents and as animal feed. The other is *Certaderia nitida*, which stands much taller and looks like a fox tail. A type of succulent grass, *Plantago rigida*, grows in round, rigid cushions. Inflexible leaves grow in star shapes in high swampy areas between 4500-4800m. Trekkers often use these cushions as stepping-stones across boggy areas. The Quechua name, *qachqa oku*, refers to the plants texture (*qachqa* means 'rough') and habitat (*oku* means 'wet'). This plant is the favoured foodstuff of alpacas.

Moonflower
Brugmansia arborea

Tailed Phragmipedium orchid
Phragmipedium caudatum

Ulluypiña
Eustephia coccinea

Begonia
Begonia bracteosa

*Odontoglossum
mystacinum* (Orchid)

Kantu/Cantuta
Cantua buxifolia

Bromeliad
Bromeliaceae

Huinay Huayna orchid
('Forever young')
Epidendrum secundum

Huakanki orchid
('You'll cry')
Masdevallia veitchiana

Llama llama
('Flames')
Oreocallis grandiflora

Flor del Paraíso
(Inca orchid)
Sobralia dichotoma

Lupin
(Tarwi, Chocho)
Lupinus sp.

Ladies' slipper
(Zaptitos: 'Little shoes')
Calceolaria engleriana

Wild potato
Solanum aloysifolium

Red datura/moonflower
Datura sanguinea

Broom (Retama)
Spartium junceum

❑ **The Festival of the Snow Star**
The Andean bear, known as *ukuku* in Quechua, is important in Andean folklore and plays a vital role in the Festival of the Snow Star at Qoyllur Riti, a village on Nevado Ausangate near Cusco. Once a year, typically in early June on the full moon before Corpus Christi, thousands of pilgrims gather high in the mountains. Each group is accompanied by an ukuku, a dancer in a wool mask and shaggy tunic who represents the bear. The ukuku is thought to live on the edge of two worlds. He is portrayed as a mischievous clown and a trickster, but is also a savage, supremely strong guardian sent to guide the pilgrims across the glaciers and protect them from the souls of the damned that wander the ice. According to legend the bear earns his manhood by confronting and defeating one of these souls, and the role of the ukuku is now seen as a traditional rite of passage for young men.

The festival dates back to the days when Peruvians made pilgrimages to placate the spirits or *apus* of the mountains with sacrifices. Legend has it that there's always a death during the pilgrimage and the apu is satisfied. It is the responsibility of the ukuku to bring down the healing properties of the apu in the form of glacial ice.

FAUNA

Mammals

Although you may have heard of the **Andean (or spectacled) bear** (*Tremarctus ornatus*), the only member of its family found in South America, it is very shy and consequently difficult to see. Measuring 1.5-2m from head to tail, this black bear which gets its nickname from its creamy face markings and dark eye rings, is classified as 'vulnerable' because its territory has been reduced by deforestation, farming and other human activity. The bear survives in this hostile situation by being willing to eat anything, a policy that occasionally gets it into trouble when it raids maize crops at the edge of cloud forests. Typically though, these harmless animals feed on cacti, orchid bulbs, fallen fruit and assorted leaves, although they also prey on small animals such as rabbits, mice and nesting birds. However, the bear's favourite food is bromeliads; it will construct rudimentary platforms in order to clamber up trees, like Paddington reaching for marmalade, to be able to get at these plants. Having feasted, and without any natural predator (except man), the bear often just falls asleep.

Even more enigmatic and tricky to spot are **puma** (*Felis concolor*). These powerful, tawny cats are usually solitary animals that prefer habitats with dense underbrush and rocky areas perfect for stalking and ambushing prey. Once revered by the Incas as a symbol of power and elegance, their numbers have declined due to hunting and the loss of habitat and they are now rare in this region. The **culpeo fox**, known locally as *zorro*, is more common. This bold, versatile scavenger preys on rodents including Andean **skunks** and **weasels**, rabbits and birds, although it will also make do with carrion. There are two types of high-altitude grassland deer, the endangered **Andean huemal**, or *taruka* as it is called in Quechua, and the rather more common **white-tailed deer**. The Sanctuary is also home to **pudu** (*sachacabra* in Quechua), secretive pygmy deer that are nocturnal and consequently rarely seen during the day.

Mountain **viscachas** (*Lagidium peruanum*) look a lot like rabbits but are in fact close relatives of the chinchilla. These bushy tailed rodents with long furry ears are widespread, but blend easily into the background, their grey and brown fur perfect camouflage against the rocks that they like to sun themselves on. There are also large colonies living amongst the ruins at Machu Picchu.

Llamas (*Lama glama*) and **alpacas** (*Lama pacos*), are the most regularly seen animals in the Sanctuary. Relatives of the Old World camel, both species were domesticated many thousands of years ago by pre-Columbian Andean tribes who recognized these hardy creatures could carry substantial loads as pack animals and also represented a useful source of food and warm wool. Llamas are the most common and strongest of the Andean camelids. They stand 1.9m tall and can carry up to 60kg. The alpaca, known as *pacocha* in Quechua, has a smaller and more rounded silhouette than a llama. In general alpacas have more and better-quality wool than llamas, the most desirable being from baby alpaca, which is soft and fine. Alpaca meat is also being promoted and many of the restaurants in Cusco will serve it. These two camelids have two wild relatives, **guanacos** (*Lama guanicoe*), which stands just over a metre tall at the shoulder and has a grey face, short ears and a white belly, and **vicuña** (*Vicugna vicugna*) which are smaller, graceful-looking creatures with inquisitive eyes, tawny brown fur on their upper parts and longer white fur on the throat and underside, reputed to be the finest animal wool in the world. Both of these are rarely seen in the Machu Picchu Sanctuary having been shot and trapped extensively by hunters and poachers, but are fortunately more common in the south. They are now protected species in Peru and although still vulnerable, their numbers have started to increase again.

❏ The Peruvian paso

The Spanish conquistadors were responsible for introducing the horse to South America. Initially used to intimidate the Inca troops who hadn't encountered horses in battle before, they were then used for transportation and breeding. Breeds included the jennet, an ideal light riding horse, the barb, which had great stamina and the Andalusian, an elegant, strongly-built breed favoured as a warhorse. Horses with good endurance and a smooth gait were particularly prized, a pair of characteristics that led to the selective breeding of the Peruvian paso, noted for its good temperament and comfortable ride.

Instead of a trot, the Peruvian paso performs an amble somewhere between a walk and a canter. The four beat lateral gait – right hind, right front, left hind, left front – accounts for the smooth ride since it causes none of the vertical bounce associated with trotting. The gait, which is natural and doesn't require training, also makes the horse very stable as there are always two and sometimes three hooves on the ground. The horses have great stamina and spirit, known locally as 'brio', and are able to cover great distances without tiring, travelling at a comfortable canter over uneven terrain. They are also willing to work and very biddable, making them an incredibly useful steed.

The past thirty years have seen a resurgence in the Peruvian paso's fortunes and the annual National Show just outside Lima to find the most elegant and beautiful horse in the country has developed into a major event in Peruvian cultural life.

Insects

Peru is justifiably famous for its **butterflies**: a fifth of the world's butterfly species is found here. Some 1300 species have been recorded in the community of Pakitza, in the Manu National Park and over 1200 species have been noted at a community 235km away on the Tambopata River. Incredibly, only 60% of these species overlapped. Scientists estimate that there must be more than 4000 species in the country, only about 3600 of which have currently been registered. Considering that North America boasts 679 species and Europe a mere 441 species, this is an astounding number.

The Andean highlands at more than 5000m are home to relatively few species. Those that do survive here are specially adapted to the rigorous environment. Tropical forests are the preferred habitat of most butterfly species. Trekkers on the Vilcabamba Trek are likely to see the most diverse array of butterflies, often encountering huge swarms congregating together.

Unfortunately, you are also likely to become very well acquainted with the **midges** that can be encountered throughout the Sanctuary, but most especially in the Santa Teresa Valley. They also plague the approach to Choquequirao.

Reptiles

Few reptiles are known about, as the forest tends to be so dense and inaccessible. Keep a look out for **snakes**; coral snakes, bushmasters and the rare velvet fer-de-lance are endemic to the Sanctuary. They are all poisonous and should not be approached if encountered. Fortunately most snakes found in the Andes are non-venomous. Most frequently encountered are harmless whipsnakes: slender green snakes with yellow underbellies. **Frogs** of the genus *Atelopus* also live in the forest above 2000m.

Birds

The Incas believed that birds were the messengers of the *apus*, the gods who lived on the summits of mountains. The condor, being the most impressive bird, was associated with the highest peaks whilst less stirring birds were considered to carry the thoughts and words of spirits residing on lower mountains.

The Sanctuary has an impressive array of avifauna for such a compact area. Many birds have relatively small altitudinal ranges, meaning that each of the Sanctuary's ten habitats is home to species that are found in no other zone. More than 400 species are known to exist in the Sanctuary and more than 200 of these can be readily observed along the Inca Trail or on the treks to Vilcabamba and Choquequirao. The *Polylepis* woodland contains some of the rarest birds, including tit-spinetails and high altitude hummingbirds, but the cloud forest is home to the greatest diversity and here you can expect to see tinamous, guans, parakeets, hummingbirds, wrens, jays, swallows, quetzals, woodpeckers, flycatchers and tanagers. The best way to spot these birds is to look for them at the correct time of day. Although you can see birds at any time, your best chance is first thing in the morning or at dusk, when they are singing and most active. Be quiet as you walk through the forest and stop periodically to look around carefully. To improve your chances further, bring binoculars on your trip.

● **Andean condor** The emblematic **Andean condor** (*Vultur gryphus*) is actually an enormous vulture, boasting the largest wing span of any land bird. Some individuals have spans in excess of 3m and measure well over a metre from their bill to the tip of their tail. They can weigh up to 11kg. The adult plumage is uniformly black, with the exception of a white ruff surrounding the base of the neck. The head and neck are blackish red and bald, an adaptation for hygiene given that the bird primarily feeds on carrion and rotting meat. When in flight, it can be identified by its sheer size and characteristic silhouette: the finger feathers at the tips of its wings point forward. Condors prefer relatively open areas that allow it to spot carrion from the air and favour rocky cliffs and outcrops on which to nest. Although considered a mountain bird, it is more common on the coast.

ANDEAN CONDOR

The Andean Condor is a national symbol of Peru and plays an important role in indigenous folklore and mythology. More recently it has endured a swathe of negative press, and stories abound of birds harrying travellers, killing livestock and even snatching small children whilst shepherds tended to their llama flocks. Writers including Bruce Chatwin (*In Patagonia*) and George Squier (*Peru – Travel and Exploration in the Land of the Incas*, 1877) documented instances where they came under attack from condors. Hiram Bingham recounted in *Lost City of the Incas* that local shepherds had to wage a constant battle with condors that had no difficulty in carrying off a sheep. Even today some of the less discerning newspapers occasionally run stories about condors snatching away unguarded infants. If you come across a condor in captivity or happen to see a stuffed specimen, a quick look at their ineffective, talon-free feet, akin to those of an enormous domestic chicken, which have been adapted for walking rather than holding or carrying objects, will debunk the notion that they could carry off anything substantial, let alone a small child or sheep wriggling to be free.

● **Birds of prey** The bigger birds in the high Andes are usually raptors or birds of prey. Look out for the **American kestrel** (*Falco sparverius*), a pair of **Aplomado falcons** (*Falco femoralis*) or a **mountain caracara** (*Phalcoboenus megalopterus*). The kestrel, colloquially known as a sparrow hawk, is a small falcon, averaging around 20cm from beak to tail, with blue-grey wings, a white head with blue-grey cap, white cheeks and a pair of vertical black face markings. Its breast and tail are a brownish, rust-colour. The medium-sized falcon is 10-20cm longer but very slim. It has a dark blue-grey head, long, light brown pointed wings, a tapering tail with narrow white or grey bars and a paler breast. The caracara is larger still, measuring up to 50cm from beak to tail. It has

MOUNTAIN CARACARA

characteristic black, white and grey wings, a black and white tail and the bare skin of its face is an orangey colour. A highly opportunistic scavenger, it can often be seen walking on the ground in search of carrion and can often be found near human habitation. Other species to spot include a number of types of **hawk**, most common of which is the **red-backed hawk** (*Buteo polyosoma*), and the **black-chested buzzard eagle** (*Geranoaetus melanoleucus*). It is a big, bulky, powerful looking bird measuring up to 80cm from beak to tail. Its plumage is predominantly a blue-hued grey colour, with black edges to its wings and a black neck and head. It is identifiable in flight by the short, wedge-shaped tail that scarcely protrudes from its broad wings.

● **Guans** These large pheasant-like birds can be seen or more frequently heard, crashing about in the trees of the humid montane forests. The most common is the **Andean guan** (*Penelope montagnii*). This turkey-sized bird, with orange-brown plumage and a red wattle, lives in the trees and feeds on fruit, seeds and other vegetable matter, rarely descending to the ground.

BLACK-CHESTED
BUZZARD EAGLE

● **Motmots** These beautifully coloured birds are related to kingfishers. They occur in all types of forest as well as on open areas of grassland. Colourful, long and slender, they are medium sized birds with long, broad bills that are somewhat curved down at the end. The most distinctive feature though is their tail. In most motmots, two central feather shafts grow much longer than the others. The **Highland motmot** (*Momotus aequatorialis*) grows up to 48cm and has a turquoise-blue forecrown and green underparts. It can be seen all along the Urubamba Valley, often perched on riverside boulders, and around Aguas Calientes. Similar, but slightly smaller and with brown underparts, is the **blue crowned motmot** (*Momotus momata*).

● **Tanagers** Amongst the forests' most common and visible birds, tanagers often congregate in small flocks near human habitation to feed in fruit trees. They are noted for their colourful plumage and few other species can compete with the broad spectrum of colours found on their feathers. There are 135 species recorded in Peru, 60 of which can be seen around Machu Picchu. Those most commonly spotted along the Inca Trail are the **blue-and-yellow tanager**, the **blue-gray tanager**, the **saffron-crowned tanager**, the **fawn-breasted tanager** and the **silver-beaked tanager**.

● **Trogons** Although less well known than other gaudy birds, trogons are often considered to be the most visually impressive birds. The largest of the species, the quetzals, are the most dazzling. Males are consistently more colourful than the females and have metallic or glittering green, blue or violet heads, backs and chests. Their breasts and undersides are contrasting bright red, yellow or orange. The females usually have darker brown or grey backs and heads, but they share the brightly coloured chests of the males. The long characteristic tail is squared off and striped black and white on the underside. Look out for the green-headed **collared trogon** (*Trogon collaris*) and the similar **masked trogon** (*Trogon personatus*), which can be distinguished by the thicker bars on its tail feathers.

● **Wrens**   These are small, brownish birds that tend to skulk in thick undergrowth. The Latin name of the genus, *Troglodytes*, refers to a cave dweller, a reference to the wren's predilection for nesting in holes and crevices. They are very vocal and have attractive singing voices. The typical sound heard at Machu Picchu is the song of the **Inca wren** (*Thryothorus eisenmanni*), which is native to Peru and whose distinctive spotted breast marks it out from other types of wren.

● **Hummingbirds**   Almost everyone can identify hummingbirds, which evolved in the Andes. They are mostly tiny birds, usually clad in iridescent metallic greens, reds, violets and blues. These tiny, nectar-drinking birds rely entirely on their wings for locomotion since their feet and legs are too weak for anything but perching. There are more than 130 species of hummingbird in Peru, the majority of which are found in the Andes. The most commonly spotted hummingbird along the Inca Trail or in Cusco gardens is the **sparkling violetear** (*Colibri coruscans*), which has a violet-blue chest and violet ear that extends to its chin. It is a tireless singer. The slightly larger **green-and-white hummingbird** (*Leucippus viridicauda*) is regularly recorded around Machu Picchu, where it can be determined by its white chest. The world's largest hummingbird is the surprisingly muted (at least in comparison to its relatives) **giant hummingbird** (*Patagonia gigas*), which can measure more than 20cm from the tip of its long bill to the end of its tail. You will also come across **sunangels**, **sapphirewings**, **coquettes**, **goldenthroats**, **sunbeams** and **coronets**, each of which is as beautiful as its name promises.

● **Waterfowl**   In mountain streams as well as along the Urubamba River, you can find **torrent ducks** (*Merganetta armata*). Uniquely adapted to swimming, diving and feeding in the fast rushing waters that cascade off the mountains, the ducks rarely stray far from the streams and even nest in crevices between boulders on the water's edge. Male torrent ducks have striking black and white striped heads and red beaks, and females have orange underparts, grey backs and a yellow bill. **Andean gulls** (*Larus serranus*), the only gulls to be found in the high Andes, also live along the Urubamba or can be found on the higher elevation tarns. You can also see the **Andean (or ruddy) duck**, which is rust-red with a spiky black tail, and has a white face with a black cap and wide blue bill, and the **crested duck**, a sleek grey with a touch of red on the wings. Heavily built **Andean Geese**, with white plumage and small pink bills, prefer being on land to swimming so that they can graze, whilst black and white **giant coots** are common on the water. Elegant **puna ibis** (*Plegadis ridgwayi*), which have dark purplish-brown feathers and a chestnut face, can often be seen around Cusco and along the first stages of the railway trip to Machu Picchu foraging slowly and probing the shallow waters and mud with their distinctive long, curved bills.

● **Other birds** The magnificent **cock of the rock** (*Rupicola peruviana*), with its prominent fan-shaped headdress of bright orange or scarlet feathers, is Peru's national bird. The female of the species is significantly darker and browner though. Frequently seen along the railway tracks around Machu Picchu, it is also common in the forests surrounding Espíritu Pampa, where gatherings of males compete for breeding females by displaying their gaudy plumage, bobbing and making a series of calls.

Other stunning, noisy birds often spotted are **parakeets**, which can often be seen and heard around Aguas Calientes or in the forests along the Vilcabamba trek. On the ground you can see furtive **tinamous**, a type of partridge. Prior to the introduction of the chicken by the Spanish, the Incas domesticated tinamous for their meat and eggs. At one stage these birds were so common that they gave their name to the town in the Sacred Valley: Pisac means 'partridge'.

Swifts and **swallows**, with their distinctive swept-back wings and pointed tails, have easily identifiable silhouettes as they flash overhead. Woodpeckers, such as the **bar-bellied woodpecker** (*Venilioris nigriceps*) and **crimson-mantled woodpecker** (*Piculus rivolii*), are recognizable due to their shape and habit of drilling in tree trunks. The attractive **Andean flicker** (*Colaptes rupicola*), a fairly common, largish woodpecker (33cm from beak to tail) with a light brown head and black cap, grey and dark brown feathers and a yellow breast, lives in puna and scrubland where, rather unusually, it nests in earth banks and old adobe buildings.

5

THE INCAS

Hugh Thomson

The Imperial Landscape
A Reading of Inca History in the Sacred Valley

When the Inca emperor Atahualpa first met the Spanish conquistadors, he offered them a drink from a *qeros*, a drinking flask, in the
traditional ceremony of reciprocal toasting that had always been
practised in the Andes. The Spaniards refused, showing him a Bible
instead – which Atahualpa, insulted by
their refusal to drink with him, spurned.
What was this 'writing' anyway, these
scribbles on a piece of paper? Nor had
the Spaniards arrived with the traditional gifts, so the Inca emperor sent them
an insulting present of ducks gutted and
filled with straw. This, went the infer-
ence, was what he could do to the conquistadors whenever he wanted. The
Spaniards, in their turn, were outraged
at Atahualpa's insult to the Bible.

A more telling instance of the clash
and mutual misunderstanding of civilizations could not be imagined.

But before we become too self-con-
gratulatory and assume that we understand such things in ways the brutal
Spaniards did not, it is as well to
remember that an encounter with Inca
civilization is still almost the nearest we
can find to experiencing an entirely
alien mind-set – and as result we can
misunderstand them just as easily.

Ancient Peru is one of the oldest

*Conqvista en los banos
estava Atagvalga Inga.*
Conquistadors (Sebastián de
Benalcázar and Hernando
Pizarro) confront Atahualpa
Inca at the royal baths,
(Cajamarca).

FELIPE HUAMÁN POMA DE AYALA,
FROM HIS *NUEVE CRÓNICA Y BUEN
GOBIERNO* (c1600)

civilizations on earth; yet it is also one of the most isolated. Until
the relatively late arrival of the Spaniards in 1532, the Incas and the
many cultures that preceded them had a unique way of looking at
the world – one that excluded writing, the wheel and many other
necessities of the so-called 'Old World', but managed to build mag-

nificent monuments and a stable society in a terrifyingly unstable landscape.

And their relationship to that landscape is consequently very different. When you travel down the Sacred Valley and on towards Machu Picchu, you are passing through a region of extraordinarily stratified history. The eminent Andeanist Susan Niles has said that, given they were unable to record their history in writing, 'in many ways, the Incas sought to make history visible'; that is, the buildings they left behind were to remind their successors of their achievements. This is true of course of many monuments around the world, from the Pyramids to Les Invalides, but for the Inca Emperors it had the added urgency of being the only way they would be remembered: they carry no inscriptions.

Thus the so-called 'Sacred Valley' – the term was not used by the Incas themselves, as is often assumed, but was a marketing invention of 1950, designed to promote a driving rally held in the valley that year – could just as much be described as the Imperial Valley. From Huchuy Cusco, with its first essay at the architecture of the Inca 'royal estate', the *moya*, to the greatest example of all, Machu Picchu, the Urubamba valley is studded with calculated reminders of the imperial presence, and not just in the buildings but in the way the terraces and actual river have been landscaped and controlled; 'terraformed', as the archaeologists like to say.

Take Machu Picchu for instance: while almost certainly built by the emperor Pachacutec, probably as a winter retreat for the court from the rigours of more upland Cusco, it was also a reminder to new subjects he had conquered in the surrounding valleys that the Incas were here to stay; not only that, but as an additional humiliation those same new subjects were doubtless forced to build this new symbol of occupation by the Inca – and on a site that must have posed extreme engineering problems, as we know from the depths of the foundations and the bulwark terracing needed to support the spectacular city on a mountaintop.

Their labourers built with extraordinary facility and speed. When the Spaniards appointed a 'puppet Inca Emperor', having murdered his predecessor Atahualpa, they were astonished when a palace was constructed for him in what seemed to them little less than a day. But then the Incas were always a tribe in a hurry, and to understand them fully one needs to appreciate their historical imperative.

*Amojonadores deste reino,
vna Cavcho Inga,
Cona Raqvi Inga.*
Surveyors of this kingdom:
Una Caucho Inca and Cona
Raqvi Inca.

FELIPE HUAMÁN POMA DE AYALA,
(c1600)

The Incas were prodigious builders, accomplished engineers and skilled architects. Without the art of writing, they left their history in stone. They were able, however, to keep records of accounts and taxes using quipus, coloured knotted strings (see p69).

Coreon major i menor.
Hatvn Chasqvi, Chvrv Mvllo
Chasqvi, Cvraca.
Couriers of greater and lesser rank: Hatun Chasqui (chief courier), Churu Mullu Chasqui (the courier who carries the conch shell), Curaca (local chasqui).

FELIPE HUAMÁN POMA DE AYALA, (c1600)

The vast size of the Inca empire meant that it required efficient communications to maintain control. The Incas built a network of paved roads covering more than 14,000 miles (22,500km) and stretching from north of Quito in modern Ecuador to south of Santiago in Chile. Since there was no knowledge of the wheel or any horses, transportation was by porter or by using llamas as pack animals. Communications were provided by teams of **chasquis** (couriers). They would run in relays between tambos (way stations) and it is said that they moved so quickly that they could bring fresh fish from the sea up to Cusco without it spoiling.

Birth of the Inca empire

It was only after 1400AD that the Incas began to expand out of their heartland around Cusco, and so their empire lasted for little more than a century before being brutally cut short by the Spaniards. The Incas were the last in a whole series of cultures pre-dating the Spanish Conquest that stretched back to around 3000BC. The world has taken a while to appreciate the achievements of these more shadowy, earlier Peruvian civilizations, not least because the Incas downplayed the achievements of preceding civilizations and in some cases ignored them completely.

The Spanish chronicler Pedro de Cieza de León quoted his Inca sources as telling him that 'before them, there were only naked savages and that these natives were stupid and brutish beyond belief. They say they were like animals, and that many ate human flesh, and others took their daughters and mothers to wife and committed other even graver sins.'

This manipulative distortion of history was so successful – the same myth was repeated by other chroniclers like Garcilaso de la Vega in the early seventeenth century – that the truth has emerged comparatively recently. Far from imposing order on an unruly bunch of savages, the Incas were the latest dominant tribe (and a short-lived one at that) in a series of Andean civilizations that had flourished over the preceding 4000 years: the Moche in the north of Peru, with their magnificent pottery, the Huari of the central states and the Tiahuanaco culture near Lake Titicaca were just a few of the cultures who had attained a high level and on whose achievements the Incas had often built.

The Incas were just one of a number of competing tribes in the area around Cusco, before beginning to build up their substantial empire under a series of dynamic and capable emperors. At its height Tahuantinsuyo, 'the land of four quarters' as their empire was called, spanned the Andean spine of the continent from Colombia to Chile.

To call it 'an empire' is strictly speaking misleading, if familiar – it was in some ways more like an extensive trading association controlled by the Incas. Nor were all Inca conquests military: Tahuantinsuyo can be compared to an aggressive modern corporation offering overwhelmingly compelling reasons to each client tribe why they should join – consumer benefits. The Incas also made it clear to any opponent that they would win whatever happened, because they always did. Cieza reported one Inca Emperor as saying to a prospective new tribe, 'these lands will soon be ours, like those we already possess.' Given the Indians' often fatalistic turn of mind, this proved effective diplomacy and many tribes capitulated without a fight. The Inca use of history to legitimize their leadership and facilitate such conquests was adroit.

Nowhere is this more evident than in their 'creation myths': one of these claims that the original Adam and Eve of the Inca line, Manco Capac and his sister Mama Ocllo, had emerged from the Island of the Sun (now in Bolivia) on distant Lake Titicaca. This island, revered as the birthplace of the sun, had been a place of pilgrimage for the earlier Tiahuanaco civilization whose buildings were still so admired on the *altiplano*. By claiming that they too had come from the Island of the Sun, the Incas were harnessing the cultural power of an earlier mighty civilization, from the stones of whose great ruins, they implied, they somehow drew some of their own strength.

A Sacred Landscape

Stone was far more than just a building material for the Incas: they worshipped some of the great naturally occurring boulders in the region – like Chuquipalta, the 'White Rock' near Vitcos, or Qenko – making them into *huacas* (shrines) with elaborate carvings. Such stone monuments were a reminder to themselves and others of their mountain origins and dynastic power.

In another Inca creation myth, Lord Viracocha formed the first man out of stone. Later, when the greatest of all Inca emperors, Pachacutec, successfully defeated the rival Chanca at the birth of his imperial Inca dynasty,

De Ingas
Mango Capac Inga.
The first Inca, Manco Capac.
FELIPE HUAMÁN POMA DE AYALA,
(c1600)

Astrólogo Pveta Q save del
sol y de la luna...
Astrologer and Shaman who studies the sun and the moon and the stars in order to know when to plant the fields. (Note that he carries a quipu, marking his astrological calculations with knots on the strings).
FELIPE HUAMÁN POMA DE AYALA,
(c1600)

THE INCAS

he was said to have summoned 'the very boulders around Cusco' to rise up and fight with him in a desperate defence of the capital against the invaders.

There is an idea in the West that stone must imply some notion of permanence, but this is not necessarily true in the Andes, which is not a static landscape. In an area of incipient volcanic activity and landslides, with recurring and violent El Niño activity over the millennia, the landscape has always been changing. For the Incas, stone was a much more volatile, organic medium. This sense of stone as a life-force is crucial to understanding the Inca architectural and sculptural aesthetic. That old, tired phrase about 'the living stones' of some great site suddenly becomes a powerful, resurrected cliché when we look at Inca sites.

The sheer primacy given to monumental stonework by the Incas is remarkable. In doing so, they again claimed descent – and legitimacy – from the great Tiahuanaco civilization whose ruined city with its monoliths was still so admired across the Andes. Pachacutec even brought Colla stone masons all the way from Lake Titicaca to try to replicate the look of Tiahuanaco at some of the ambitious sites he built, like Ollantaytambo; we know because the masons rebelled against the harsh working conditions.

Growth of the Inca Empire

The phenomenal growth of the Inca Empire is attributed by many chroniclers to the achievements of this one man: Pachacutec, who according to these accounts, deserves to be as well known as Alexander the Great or Napoleon.

El noveno Inga, Pachacvti Inga Ivpanqvi.
The ninth Inca, Pachacutec.
FELIPE HUAMÁN POMA DE AYALA, (c1600)

Originally known as Inca Yupanqui, Pachacutec was a younger son of the emperor Viracocha. During Viracocha's reign in around 1438, the Chanca, a rival tribe to the north of Cusco, attacked the Incas with such ferocity that Viracocha and his designated heir, Inca Urcon, fled the capital – some believe to the site of Huchuy Cusco, the fascinating early estate built on the hills above Calca, one of the least visited and most evocative of the sites along the Sacred Valley. Only a small band of captains led by Inca Yupanqui remained to give a last-ditch defence.

It was now, according to the myth he later assiduously propagated, that Pachacutec called 'on the very stones of Cusco' to fight alongside them. Not only were the Chanca sent packing, but Inca Yupanqui (who then adopted the soubriquet Pachacutec, 'Transformer of the Earth', and took the throne from his disgraced father and brother) embarked on an ambitious programme of conquest that initiated the imperial phase of Inca culture. Within a generation the Incas had grown from an anonymous small tribe of the Cusco valley to become the dominant force of the Andes.

During his long reign from c1438 to 1471, Pachacutec's achievements seem almost to beggar geographical comprehension: he led the first wave of conquests over to Bolivia and Lake Titicaca; his son Topa Inca, working under his direction, followed with further expansion north up to Ecuador, until the empire stretched to an area the size of Continental Europe.

Fiesta de los Ingas. Varicza, Aravi del Inga. Canta con sv pvca llama.
Fiesta of the Incas. Dance, song of the Inca. He sings with his red llama.

FELIPE HUAMÁN POMA DE AYALA, (c1600)

Pachacutec was also acutely conscious of the need to create his own myth and legitimize his new dynasty. In the words of the chronicler Juan de Betanzos, 'he decreed the remembrance of history'. After his victory over the Chanca, he gathered the stones that were supposed to have helped him in his fight and set them up as carved rocks, or *huacas*, in places where they could be worshipped. He enthused the Incas with the idea that they were a people of power, of destiny, and created an elaborate hierarchy devolving down from his own position as the 'Sapa Inca', the emperor. The nobility became a separate tier in this hierarchy and were allowed to wear ear-plugs as a distinguishing feature. Tribes living close to Cusco were accommodated within this concept by being made *Incas de Privelegio*, 'Honorary Incas'.

He also ensured that impressive monuments were erected – from stone of course – to this idea of an imperial destiny. Inca leaders had always been expected to build (one of the slurs perpetuated about the disgraced Inca Urcon, the brother that Pachacutec had usurped, was that he was too weak to leave a building to his name). But Pachacutec took this principle to new, grandiose extremes. He ordered the construction of Sacsayhuaman, of the temple-fortress at Ollantaytambo and, it seems probable, of Machu Picchu and Pisac. Any one of these sites would be a substantial monument; cumulatively they represent a quite exceptional achievement.

Pachacutec was said, according to later Inca accounts, to have laid down all the basic framework for the institutions of state over his long reign of approximately thirty years – institutions which his successors were ritualistically to preserve in his name. For the first time, the peoples of the coast and the mountains were given a unified administration that allowed peaceful trading and co-operation, with Quechua as the *lingua franca*. Where there had previously been darkness, so this story went, the Inca Empire brought order.

This account of Pachacutec, however, needs to be treated with some care. It is a seductive idea – an empire carved out by the sheer will-power of one individual, single-handedly turning the tide of a nation's destiny – and as such appealing to Spanish chroniclers reared on just such chivalric exploits them-

Travaxa: Zara, Papa Hallmai Mita.

Work in January. Maize, time of rain and digging. Month of the biggest feast.

FELIPE HUAMÁN POMA DE AYALA, (c1600)

Travaxa: Zara, Papa Apaicvi Aimoray.

Work in July. Maize and potatoes. Month of the harvest and distribution of the lands.

FELIPE HUAMÁN POMA DE AYALA, (c1600)

selves. Pachacutec was undoubtedly a dynamic and capable leader. But what has come down to us is very much the 'official version' of the history, carefully propagated by his own descendants; a usurping family, they had an interest in denigrating the achievements of their predecessors, who consequently may have received short shrift (just as the Incas were prone to ignore the influence of preceding civilizations).

As the old English saying goes: 'Treason shall never prosper, for if it prosper it is no longer treason.'

While Pachacutec initially concentrated on the southern Andes and Bolivia, his son Topa Inca began the expansion into the northern ranges and Ecuador that was to have such a profound consequence for 'the land of the four quarters'.

The Incas had a prolonged love-affair with the warm climate of Ecuador: fertile land, the trade in exotic desirables like seashells and the attractions of the local girls combined to make it irresistible to the aesthetes from the highlands. Successive emperors spent more and more time campaigning there. The rhythm of such campaigns allowed plenty of time to enjoy the place: the normal, very civilized practice of pre-Columbian peoples was for fighting to pause during harvest-time to allow both sides to gather in crops (when the Spaniards arrived, they disconcerted the natives by ignoring this convention). Cieza de León also reports that the Incas often found it too hot to fight in the summer.

Topa Inca, like his father, was a formidable builder: it is likely that he was responsible for Choquequirao, the spectacular site high above the Apurímac which emulates, or competes with, Machu Picchu; he also built an estate at Chincheros, the great walls of which support the later church plaza built by the Spaniards.

In Ecuador he founded the city of Tumipampa (modern day Cuenca), where his son Huayna Capac, the future emperor was born. When Huayna succeeded to the throne, Ecuador clearly appealed to him more than the harsher climate of the Inca heartland. He chose to stay for many years in his birthplace of Tumipampa, and was said to have preferred it to Cusco as a capital. This did not stop him from ensuring that a substantial country palace, Quispiquanca, was built for him in what is now the town of Urubamba, beside the modern road ascending to the Chicón glacier; the site has recently been restored and is impressive if little visited, despite the nearby location of the best restaurant in the valley, the Huacatay (see p194).

By Inca standards Huayna seems to have been a bit of a *bon viveur*, perhaps because of his Ecuadorian upbringing: he was said to be able to drink three times as much as any of his subjects. When asked how it was that he never became intoxicated, he replied that 'he drank for the poor, of whom he supported many.'

Andas del Inga. Pillco Randa.

The Inca's red litter, used in war. Here Huayna Capac is shown going to war with the Cañari in northern Ecuador.

FELIPE HUAMÁN POMA DE AYALA, (c1600)

Yet the push up into Ecuador by the Incas can with hindsight be seen as an expansion too far. In just three generations, under first Pachacutec, then his son Topa Inca and finally his grandson Huayna Capac, the Inca empire had grown from an enclave around Cusco to one that stretched right along the Andes. In the process it had become fatally distended. The endless campaigns that Huayna waged in Ecuador had created a permanent standing army in the north, with powerful generals, a disruption to the normal Inca convention that armies were temporary and centred on Cusco; he had also fathered several sons there, which had serious dynastic implications.

In around 1527 came disaster: a fatal epidemic (opinions vary as to whether it was European smallpox that had swept down the South American coast from the north, or a local sand-fly disease, bartonellosis) killed as much as half the population of twenty-five million, including Huayna Capac himself.

The cracks in the Incas' new empire quickly started to show. Huayna had been away in the north for over ten years. His legitimate successor and son, Huascar, was based back in Cusco. Now a contingent of Incas in Quito led by his son Atahualpa (who may well have had an Ecuadorian mother) decided that they were far enough away both from Cusco and Huascar to declare independence.

The resulting civil war between the Ecuadorian and Peruvian sides of the Empire was devastating. It was the turning point in Inca fortunes, much more so than the Spanish Conquest of 1532, which simply exploited the wreckage it caused. The two sides were evenly matched: as the legitimate contender, Huascar had all the resources of the Cusco state behind him; Atahualpa was the more experienced soldier, with a strong Ecuadorian power-base and a ruthless streak – indeed far from being the passive and noble Indian sometimes portrayed, Atahualpa was one of the most brutal of all Inca emperors. Atahualpa eventually defeated Huascar and had him killed, but not before the country had

Conqvista preso Atagvalpa Inga.
Atahualpa in prison, Cajamarca.
FELIPE HUAMÁN POMA DE AYALA, (c1600)

been laid waste. Despite the civil war, Huascar still ensured that a country palace was built for him at Calca.

The epidemic and then the great Inca civil war so weakened Tahuantinsuyo that by 1532, when the Spaniards arrived, they could simply walk in and take it. The conquistadors, as so often, were incredibly lucky. After landing on the coast, at Tumbes, they travelled south down the Royal Road towards the Inca capital, moving through a civilization which had been fatally weakened by first disease and then internal divisions.

After the famous meeting with Atahualpa, in which the *barbudos*, the bearded ones, and the emperor so signally failed to understand one another, it was not long before Francisco Pizarro and his men kidnapped Atahualpa in the main square at Cajamarca; after extorting a huge ransom of gold and silver from the Inca, they executed him regardless and marched on Cusco to claim the Empire for themselves.

The power of the mummy

The astonishing expansion of the Incas across a few generations before the arrival of the Spaniards can only partly be explained by dynamic leadership. Other factors contributed to their success: a facility for trade, their opportunism and an occasionally overlooked factor – the curious Inca laws of dynastic inheritance.

When each Inca emperor died, his estate (or *panaca*) continued to maintain his household as if he were still alive – he remained 'resident' in his old palace as a mummy, to be brought out on feast days or for the coronation of his successors, and each of those successors would therefore have to build themselves a new palace. When a new emperor was crowned, the mummies of the whole previous dynasty of dead Inca emperors were carried in procession alongside him, along with their fingernail and hair trimmings, which had been scrupulously preserved while they were alive. The sense of a 'living' dynastic succession must have been overwhelming.

(Opposite) Unable to record their history in writing, the Incas sought to make it visible in the form of beautiful and dramatic buildings and stonework full of symbolism. **Top**: Dawn breaks over a typical trapezoidal archway amidst the ruins of Pisac (see p189), in the Sacred Valley. **Middle**: Vast concentric rings and agricultural terraces created by the Incas as an experimental farm at Moray (see p194). They were able to construct terraces for cultivation on even the steepest slopes, demonstrating their supreme engineering skills. **Bottom**: The Incas showed mastery over their medium in their use of stones of enormous size, dressed to fit perfectly together without the use of mortar. This wall is in Cusco on Hatun Rumyoc. (Photos © Alexander Stewart).

At the time of the Spanish Conquest there were twelve such *panacas* in existence. Each mummy would have its own litter, bearers and attendants from that *panaca*, and a pavilion would be erected for them on the main square where the coronation took place. In a ceremony that built on the traditional consumption of vast quantities of alcohol by the Inca's new subjects, the incoming emperor, the 'Sapa Inca', would also exchange toasts with each of his dead ancestors, with the mummy's attendants drinking on behalf of the corpse.

It is clear that the 'mummy lobby' had grown very powerful towards the end of the Inca Empire and precipitated a bitter divide in Cusco. Huascar Inca, who had a reforming agenda during his brief tenure as emperor, tried to limit what he saw as the abuses that had grown up. According to the chronicler Bernabé Cobo, 'So many nobles were involved in serving these dead bodies, and their lives were so licentious, that one day Huascar Inca became angry with them and he said that there should be an order to have all the dead bodies buried and to take all their riches away from them. He went on to say that the dead should not be a part of his court, only the living, because the dead had taken over the best of everything in his kingdom.'

Entiero de Chinchaisvios.
Chinchaysuyu burial.
FELIPE HUAMÁN POMA DE AYALA, (c1600)

Here a Chinchaysuyu mummy is being carried to its burial chamber. The Inca region of Chinchaysuyu was the northernmost part of the empire, in north Equador and southern Colombia. Atahualpa's mother was from this area.

It must have been particularly galling for each new emperor that the mummy of his predecessor got to keep all his land, wealth and particularly palaces, so that the incoming Inca would have to build a new one. The main square of Cusco when the conquistadors arrived was witness to this: each side was lined with the palaces of past Incas, still inhabited by their mummies. Indeed there had been no space left for Huascar on the square itself and he had been forced, to his fury, to build a new palace on the hill above; he caused outrage at one point by threatening to confiscate one of the palaces of his dead forebears instead, according to Pedro Pizarro, one of the liveliest of Spanish chroniclers.

(Opposite) Top: The Coricancha in Cusco (see p146) was the Incas' Temple of the Sun, the grandest building in the entire empire. After the conquest the Dominicans built their monastery, Santo Domingo, right on top of it in a symbolic show of dominance of their religion. The superiority of the fine Inca masonry is obvious and it was also shown to be more technically advanced in the earthquake of 1950 when the monastery collapsed but the Inca stonework remained unharmed. **Bottom:** Somewhat fanciful giant mural in Cusco depicting the rise and fall of the Incas. (Photos © Alexander Stewart).

Much the same applied to the country palaces. One probable reason why Machu Picchu seems to have been abandoned by the time of the Spanish Conquest is that after the death of Pachacutec, it reverted to his *panaca*, not the incoming new Emperor, and therefore went into a gentle decline, without the imperial resources to maintain such a grandiose site.

And therein lies a powerful engine for continual Inca expansion: the fact that the mummy of a departed Inca and his *panaca* continued to own his palaces and land even after his death was a powerful incentive for every new emperor to go out and conquer new lands, since he would not simply be inheriting them.

The guerrilla campaign after the Spanish conquest

The Incas did not just roll over and die after the arrival of the Spaniards in 1532, despite the initial success of the conquistadors. After Atahualpa's death, the Spaniards decided to install a puppet emperor on the throne, a brother of his called Manco; this proved to be a costly error. After a few years of obedience, Manco revolted, calling troops up from all over Tahuantinsuyo for one last blowing up of the fire from the dying embers.

Pedro de Cieza de León described the conquistadors' dismay at suddenly seeing the strength of Manco's forces camped around Cusco: 'So numerous were the [Indian] troops who came here that they covered the fields, and by day

Conqvista. Milagro del Señor Santiago major, após-tol de Jesu Cristo.
St James the Great, Apostle of Jesus Christ.
(St James comes to the aid of the Conquistadors and saves Cusco).

FELIPE HUAMÁN POMA DE AYALA, (c1600)

it looked as if a black cloth had been spread over the ground for half a league.' Many of Pizarro's comrades had gone to Chile on an expedition, while others were in the newly-founded city of Lima. The remaining Spaniards were taken by surprise and trapped in the streets of the town, while the Incas gathered outside the walls and in the great fortress above at Sacsayhuaman.

By setting fire to the roofs of Cusco and keeping up a punishing siege, the Incas came close to defeating the Spaniards. There were fewer than two hundred of the conquistadors, and of these, as Pedro candidly admits, only the cavalrymen really mattered, as the Spaniards on foot were no match for the agile Indians: 'the Indians hold the infantrymen in slight account'.

It was the European horses which were the Spaniards' only hope if they were to hold over 100,000 Inca soldiers at bay. On open ground, an armoured Spanish horseman with steel weapons against a native infantryman was like a tank against an archer. But in the cramped streets of Cusco, the horses were no longer so agile or effective. The Indians built palisades to contain them, and used slings to hurl burning cloth at the buildings where the Spaniards were sheltering. The defenders realized they were in an impossible position.

They mounted a despairing charge and rode up to take Sacsayhuaman, before Manco could assemble even more native troops for the siege. However much one might dislike the motives or morals of the conquistadors, this was a bold and brave move given how few of them there were and the overwhelming superiority of the Incas.

The Incas under Manco were forced to retreat. He led his men into the wild Vilcabamba area to the west of Cusco from where he and his successors remarkably managed to hold out against the Spanish for another forty years, waging intermittent guerrilla attacks. It is in this area that some of the most deliberately inaccessible Inca ruins can still be found, like the settlement at Espíritu Pampa which more intrepid trekkers reach in a descent from Vitcos, a site originally built by Pachacutec but later reoccupied by Manco as a symbol that he was continuing in his ancestor's great tradition, however straitened his circumstances.

Manco used the emotive power of the mummies during his exile, carrying the surviving bodies of previous Inca emperors with him into the Vilcabamba, as well as the Punchao, the sun-shield. Even though the mummies were captured by the Spaniards and brought back to Cusco, they passed back into native hands and continued to be used by the underground resistance movement for the next twenty years.

In some ways, Manco Inca is the forgotten hero of Inca history. His predecessor Atahualpa is remembered as the emperor whom Pizarro and his men first seized and ransomed for rooms full of gold and silver before executing, while the name of Túpac Amaru, the very last Inca, lives on for its symbolic value and has been sporadically revived as the focus for later resistance groups. But Manco was a more admirable character than either of them. When he was placed as a puppet on the throne by the Spaniards, he had already survived both a brutal civil war and the Spanish Conquest, which along with the epidemic had managed to lay waste one of the world's great empires in less than ten years. The world he had known had crumbled around him. Out of the ashes, and with some consummate political manoeuvring, he somehow managed to rally a rebellion which, if not ultimately successful, at least gave heart to his people.

La Preción de Topa Amao Ynga.
Túpac Amaru is led into Cusco.
FELIPE HUAMÁN POMA DE AYALA, (c1600)

Modern Peru and the Inca legacy

The sense of landscape and buildings as important repositories of history still runs deep in the Peruvian psyche. When President Toledo – the first Peruvian president of Indian origin – was inaugurated, he chose to do so at Machu Picchu rather than as previously in Lima, a very deliberate nod to the Inca tradition.

Certain aspects of the Inca world-view – the belief in cooperative labour by communities, their superb agriculture and husbanding of shared resources, a spirituality rooted in stone and maize and the mountains, and in a sacred landscape – are still part of the Quechua inheritance, despite the intervening imposition of three hundred years of Spanish rule.

Now the *indigenismo* movement of the early 20th century and recent political initiatives have sought again to place the Inca empire and its beliefs at the heart of Peru's sense of national identity, with a great national pride in their pre-Columbian achievements.

This has had one desirable outcome, in that the conservation and promotion of archaeological monuments has proceeded apace: from Choquequirao to Vitcos and even the formidably jungle-covered site of Espíritu Pampa, the visitor will see evidence of sustained reconstruction, if sometimes perhaps a little too over-enthusiastic. Only a few historic sites, like Huchuy Cusco, are still neglected, although these have the virtue of an atmospheric, overgrown setting as a result.

The recent work of historians and archaeologists like John Rowe, Susan Niles, Brian Bauer and Richard Burger has given us more of an insight into the historical events that shaped the spectacular Inca architecture of their heartland around the Sacred Valley. But we still know less about the Incas and their predecessors than we do of other ancient civilizations, partly because of their illiteracy but also because we have come to a true study of their culture surprisingly late.

It would therefore be a mistake to underestimate the difference in outlook between the Incas and ourselves, and the difficulties in bridging that divide that still remain. When offered a cup by the Inca world, as the conquistadors were by Atahualpa, we should choose to drink deeply if we want to understand them.

Elements of the above article are drawn from Hugh Thomson's books on Peru: *The White Rock: An Exploration of the Inca Heartland* and *Cochineal Red: Travels through Ancient Peru* (both Weidenfeld & Nicolson).

In addition to writing the above books, Hugh Thomson has led several research expeditions to the area around Cusco and made the first reports of some previously unknown Inca sites. For more information see 🖥 www.thewhiterock.co.uk.

LIMA

6

Alison Roberts

Lima is everything you've heard it described as; a sprawling, polluted South American city ringed by squatter settlements and clogged with tooting traffic. Humidity is high, rain is a rarity and for six months of the year the city seldom pokes its head out from under a grey blanket of fog, known as *garúa*. Already home to eight million people, it is a magnet for migrants who swap rural poverty for the urban kind and eke out an existence performing circus tricks at traffic lights.

As the main gateway to Peru, however, most tourists haul up in Lima at some point and many at the start and end of their trip. Although not a destination in its own right, those who make the most of their time here will be richly rewarded since Lima has a few surprises up its sleeve.

Widely reputed to be the 'gastronomic capital of Latin America', in the last few years there has been a boom in the city's dining scene and in particular in *Novo Andina* cuisine which draws on the country's enormous biodiversity for its traditional and unique ingredients and on the country's cultural mix for its international influences. 'Fusion food' is fabulous and when it comes to fine restaurants you'll be spoilt for choice in Miraflores: indeed you may find yourself wishing you could extend your stay to sample more menus.

Central Lima is the city's historical and cultural heart. Its magnificent colonial churches and mansions are a reminder that Lima was once described as the 'City of Kings' and, until the middle of the 18th century, was the capital and most important city in the continent's Spanish territory. This legacy is recognized today by UNESCO.

A strip of parkland skirts the Pacific cliff tops of Miraflores and Barranco and when the weather is fine there is nowhere better to take a stroll or to walk off that long lunch. A Lima sunset is also something special and can be enjoyed at one of a number of beach bars, perhaps with a Pisco Sour.

Lima's middle class is growing and has affluent aspirations. Larcomar commercial centre is testament to this; with panoramic views of the Pacific coastline it's a relaxing place to while away an afternoon shopping, attracting Lima's fashionable set to its designer stores while its multiplex cinema and open-air food court are popular for a family night out.

This section guides you towards the city's finest restaurants, shops, bars and museums and gives you an idea of how best to spend the 'head and tail' of your trip. What better way to start your holiday

Civdad La Villa de Callav.
City of Callao, Gateway to
Lima.
FELIPE HUAMÁN POMA DE AYALA,
(c1600)

than with an exploration of the country's history, culture and cuisine and what better way to end it than with a celebratory night out and a spot of souvenir shopping?

A BRIEF HISTORY

Lima was founded by the Spanish conquistador Francisco Pizarro on 18th January 1535. It was initially called *La Ciudad de los Reyes* (The City of Kings) because its foundation was decided on 6th January, the feast of Epiphany, but the native name *Lima,* thought to derive from the Quechua name *Rimac* (talker), persisted; the river still retains the Quechua version. Lima soon became the most important city in the Spanish viceroyalty of Peru and flourished through trade. In 1551 the National University of San Marcos and first university in the New World opened. Tragically, much of Lima's colonial architecture was damaged by earthquakes in 1630 and 1684. Indeed the city was almost completely destroyed by another earthquake in 1786. An elaborate rebuild followed (only 20 houses had been left standing), funded by wealth generated from Potosi's silver mines.

After the Peruvian war of independence Lima became the capital of the Republic of Peru. That same year (1821) the liberator, José de San Martín, founded the National Library but during the War of the Pacific (1879-84) it was turned into barracks and saw many of its valuable books and manuscripts destroyed by Chilean troops who occupied Lima for almost three years.

The city expanded in the 19th century following the economic boom in *guano* (seabird droppings) exports but since the 1940s the rapid growth resulting from immigration from Andean regions (in the 1990s thousands fled terrorist activity) has not been matched by formal job opportunities. Around 350,000 now live in Villa El Salvador, a squatter settlement to the south of the city and a world away from being described as La Ciudad de los Reyes.

Lima's historic centre was declared a World Heritage site in 1991 and in 1997 Alberto Andrade, Lima's then mayor, launched a campaign which saw restoration work begin on the historic centre, parks planted, streets cleaned, police vigilance increased and, more controversially, street vendors kicked out. Today Lima is the 19th most populous city in the world and home to a third of Peru's population.

WHAT TO SEE AND DO

Lima has plenty of sights which can easily be visited on foot. The following **walking tours** will lead you to some of the highlights, although there is much to be enjoyed en route, as well as the warm-up they provide for hikers of the Inca Trail.

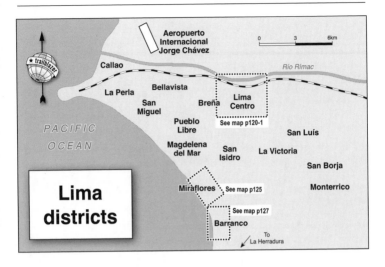

Lima districts

Follow the **Lima Centro tour** (below) to see the best of Lima's colonial architecture, including its historic cathedral and colourful China Town, or opt for a long lazy lunch followed by a clifftop stroll and admire the sunset in **Miraflores** (see p124). Perhaps you'd prefer a spot of retail therapy alongside a dip into some of the museums in **Barranco** (see p126), or skip the shopping and go for the culture in earnest with the museums of the **Pueblo Libre** district (see p128). Whichever walk you choose, you'll get a real flavour of Lima's history and diversity.

Lima Centro – colonial architecture, city views, China Town
[SEE MAP PP120-1, ONE DAY]

With a full day of exploration ahead why not fuel up with a **buffet breakfast** at the **Hotel Sheraton** (Av Paseo de la República 170). Waiters tour the tables with coffee refills and the spectacular spread includes fruit, cereal, pastries and a Creole and Oriental food station.

It's time to get moving. Turn left out of the hotel and head straight up **Jirón Belén** (there's a pistachio-coloured building on the corner). After a block, look left to spot a blue church with a giant snowflake window (**Iglesia Recoleta**), which stands in **Plaza Francia**. Continue straight ahead until you reach **Plaza San Martín** which is ringed with white wedding-cake mansions and one pink one. In the centre of the plaza is a **statue of General San Martín** on a horse. The plaza is particularly delightful in October/November when the jacaranda trees are in bloom. Keep to the left side of the plaza passing **Teatro Colón** (once a luxurious and respected theatre, it became a cinema in the 1950s and closed in 2003) and the **Gran Hotel Bolívar** which dates from 1924 and is famous for its Pisco Sour (try one on the return leg).

Lima Centro

To Cerro San Cristóbal

Jr Marañón

Jr Cajamarca

Jr Trujillo

Jr Francisco Pizarro

Rio Rimac

LIMA

Railway station

Post Office

Santo Domingo

Jr Conde de Superunda

Hostal Roma

WALKING TOUR

Jr Callao

Jr Chancay

Av Taca

Jr Huancavélica

Jr Angaraes

Jr Ayacala

Jr Rufino Torrico

Jr Cañete

Av Emancipación

Jr Ica

El Cordano

Palacio de Gobierno

Tourist Info office

T'anta

Plaza de Armas

Jr Carabaya

Jr de la Unión

Jr Camaná

Jr Guillema

Jr Cusco

Jr Puno

Jr Ocoña

Av Nicolás de Piérola

San Francisco

Hostal España

Jr Ancash

Jr Azángaro

Jr Junín

Jr Lampa

Jr Huallaga

Jr Ucayali

Jr Miró Quesada

Cathedral

Hotel Maury

Palacio Torre Tagle

La Merced

Inka Path

Museo de la Inquisición

Plaza Bolívar

Av Abancay

Jr Ayacucho

Trailblazer

Jr Andahuaylas

Jr Ucayali

Jr Paruro

Barrio Chino

Wa Lok

Salón China

Mercado Central

Jr Cusco

San Pedro

Casa Goyeneche

Jr Miró Quesada

Av Abancay

Av Nicolás de Pierola

Av Grau

Metro supermarket

Jr Cusco

Jr Lampa

Jr Puno

Jr Azángaro

Parque Universitario

Jr Leticia

Jr Montevideo

Jr de la Unión

Plaza San Martín

Estadio Futbol Bar

Jr Pachita

Av Roosevelt

Jr Cotabambas

Av Grau

Gran Hotel Bolívar

FINISH WALKING TOUR

Jr Ocoña

Av Nicolás de Pierola

Jr Belén

Miguel

To Miraflores

Plaza Francia

Iglesia Recoleta

WALKING TOUR

Paseo de la República

Plaza Grau

Parque de la Cultura

Sheraton

START WALKING TOUR

(Paseo Colón)

Museo de Arte de Lima

Av Garcilaso de la Vega

Jr Quilca

Jr Dávalos

Jr Lisson

Av Washington

Av Uruguay

Av Bolivia

Av España

Av 9 de Diciembre

Alfonso Ugarte

Av Portugal

Plaza Bolognesi

Las Brisas de Titicaca

LIMA

0   100   200   300m

Continue straight up pedestrianized **Jirón de la Unión** which is crowded day and night with shoppers and families visiting its cinemas, arcades and fast-food joints and spot the many places serving *pollo a la brasa* (roast chicken and chips). Be sure to look up though, as behind the commercial fronts are sorbet-coloured, icing-frosted colonial mansions.

After three blocks stop to admire the apricot and primrose-coloured façade of **Iglesia de La Merced** (8am-noon & 5-8pm daily, free admission). Built on the site of the first Mass celebrated in Lima in 1534, the church was originally a smaller wooden construction but has been destroyed and rebuilt several times owing to earthquakes. Step inside to escape the heat of the day and marvel at the magnificent altar.

Continuing along Jirón de la Unión you can't help but notice the enclosed wooden balconies that adorn many of the colonial facades. In 1997 Alberto Andrade, Lima's then mayor, launched the *adopte un balcón* campaign in an effort to save the characteristic balconies. Look out for the plaque at **No 461**.

Lima's **Plaza de Armas (Plaza Mayor)** is a UNESCO World Heritage site. In the centre is a **fountain** dating from 1650. The **Palacio de Gobierno**, built in 1937 on the site of Pizarro's palace, is the residence of Peru's president (at noon you can watch the changing of the guard).

The first stone of the original cathedral was laid by Pizarro in 1535 and construction of the primitive building was completed in 1538. Since then the **cathedral** (Mon-Fri 9am-5pm, Sat 10am-1pm, s/10) has been damaged by countless earthquakes and was almost entirely destroyed by one in 1746. The existing building was completed in 1755. Inside, the ornately carved choir stalls are worth a look or search for the coffin which supposedly contains Pizarro's remains. There is also a **museum of religious art** (10am-4.30pm Mon-Sat, s/5).

A white horse-drawn carriage and driver in top hat and tails can be hired if you fancy taking a spin around the plaza (s/3) or perhaps you'd prefer to catch one of the many tourist buses up to **Cerro San Cristóbal** (every half-hour 9am-8pm daily, s/5), a viewpoint from where, on a clear day, you get a good appreciation of how big, busy and bone-dry Lima is. The one-hour round trip crosses the River Rimac, passes **Plaza de Acho** (a bullring with a brief bullfighting season in late October and November) and heads into a slum district of brightly painted houses, before slowly climbing up. There is a giant yellow cross at the top which is illuminated at night.

Back at the plaza stroll along **Pasaje Ribera el Viejo**, stopping at one of the pavement cafés to refuel (*T'anta*, see p138, is a good choice) before reaching the church and convent of **Santo Domingo** (9-11am & 3-6pm, church free, convent s/5), which contains the tombs of two Lima saints; Santa Rosa de Lima and San Martín de Porres, the first black saint.

Directly opposite the church is a salmon-pink and cream arcade, part of **Lima's old post office** and somewhere to pick up a couple of postcards or send an email. Walk through, turn right, and you're back at Plaza de Armas, then pass the palace and turn left up **Jr Carabaya** with its green-painted 'Narnia' lamp posts.

Straight ahead is Lima's main railway station, **Estación de los Desamparados**. Services from here are now limited just to weekly trains in the tourist season to Huancayo in the Central Highlands.

If you feel it's time for a rest pop into *El Cordano*. This bar first opened in 1905 and stepping through the saloon-style doors you'll see the décor hasn't changed much. Pull up a wooden chair at a marble-top table and order a *jamon de norte* (carved ham) roll (s/8).

Follow the road round and ahead is **San Francisco Church and Monastery** (▣ www.museocatacumbas.com; church 7-11am & 4-8pm daily, museum 9.30am-5.30pm daily, s/7). This historical site is definitely worth a visit. You can see it only on a guided tours but they leave frequently from a cool, peaceful waiting room decorated with colourful Sevillian tiles. The catacombs are an obvious highlight for the ghoulish; mind your head and peer into crypts of creatively arranged and precisely sorted bones. There is a dark wood library of ancient texts and in the refectory hangs a painting of the last supper with a slight difference; the disciples are eating *cuy* (guinea pig; an Andean delicacy).

If you fancy a spot of late lunch or early supper why not head to China Town. Continue up **Jr Ancash** to **Av Abancay**, turn right, pass **Plaza Bolívar** and the Peruvian Congress building, then turn left up **Junín** for one block, passing the **Museo de la Inquisición** (▣ www.congreso.gob.pe/museo.htm; 9am-5pm daily, free). In the 16th century this housed the Inquisition which was responsible for eliminating heresy and blasphemy in the New World; you can visit the dungeon cells where those accused awaited judgement and punishment.

Turn right down **Ayacucho** which leads to the **Mercado Central**. Pass the shops of colourful underwear, take a left down **Ucayali** and walk through the **Chinese gate**. Be sure to look down at the tiles celebrating those 'hatched, matched and dispatched' in Lima.

Retrace your steps along Ucayali past the hardware stalls of wooden spoons and saucepans and cross Av Abancay. After one block you will arrive at the Jesuit church of **San Pedro** (7am-noon & 5-8pm daily, free) built in 1624. Its simple exterior masks the magnificence of its golden altars. At No 363 Ucayali **Palacio Torre Tagle** is a strawberry-pink colonial mansion. Look out for Toby jug faces peering down from an exquisite wooden balcony. Opposite at **No 358** you can take a peek through wrought-iron gates at the plant-filled patio of another colonial mansion, **Casa Goyeneche**, restored by Banco de Credito in 1971. Passing the imposing Roman columns of the Banco de Credito and Banco del Reserva del Peru turn left along **Carabaya** to go back to **Plaza San Martín**.

Cross the plaza and head for **Gran Hotel Bolívar** (see p136). Your Pisco Sour is well earned but before you hit the bar check out the stained-glass cupola in the entrance hall and 1920s Ford parked in reception. Flop down on the worn, brown, leather sofas. You'll find the midnight-blue walls and carpets surprisingly soothing.

Miraflores – a long lazy lunch, cliff top stroll and sunset view
[HALF DAY]
Lunch – allow two hours or more!

Cliff-top stroll – allow an hour and be prepared for the weather to change. The coastal cloud quickly rolls in and when it does it's chilly, but when the view is great then so are the chances of getting sunburned.

Limeños love nothing more than eating and drinking with friends and family. Lunch is the main meal of the day and a leisurely affair most often enjoyed at a *cebichería* (seafood restaurant). To get a better appreciation of this side of Lima life take a long lunch yourself; after all you are on holiday. **Av La Mar** is a thirteen-block strip of some of Lima's most popular lunch spots (see p137) including *La Mar* (No 770) and *Pescados Capitales* (No 1337). This corner of Miraflores is a 'must' for those wanting to try *cebiche* (ceviche) or *tiradito* (without onions and the fish is sliced finely and then flattened) for the first time, since the quality of ingredients and service is assured and the recipes are traditional but with a twist, so are more suited to an international palette.

Leaving Pescados Capitales turn right and then immediately right down **Choquenchanca**. Walk three blocks (after one block you will pass a small **produce market** on your left) to **Malecón de la Marina**. Turn left and follow the cliff-top path.

For a slightly shorter walk, from La Mar cross over the road of the same name and walk for three blocks down **Merino** to Malecón de la Marina. Turn left and follow the cliff-top path.

This delightful walk winds its way through a string of grassy flower-filled parks where locals come jogging, cycling and to walk their dogs, and around an urban workout of sports pitches, skateboard parks and tennis courts. For those eager to exercise after an indulgent lunch there are regularly spaced pull-up bars. For those not so inclined there are frequently sited benches.

A short flight of steps leads down to a chessboard path. Follow this to get a closer look at the **Pacific** and the **Nazca line shaped flower beds**. There are also paths that drop down to the beach road: although tempting, it is not regarded as safe and it's advisable to take a taxi instead.

There's a **lighthouse**, a grassy headland off which the **paragliders** leap ($40 for a 15-minute tandem flight between the lighthouse and Larcomar, noon-6pm daily, wind permitting!) and **Parque del Amor** where couples canoodle in the shadow of a statue of lovers in a passionate embrace and behind a wall of colourful mosaic tiles and poetry.

Cross the bridge and you'll see the silver chimneys and patio umbrellas of **Larcomar** rise from the cliff. Take an escalator down into the belly of this shopping centre and fill yours with an ice-cream (*lucama*, eggfruit, is a favourite flavour with locals). There's no better spot for a sunset drink than *Mangos'* terrace (see p136) which perches over the Pacific waves.

Miraflores

0   100   200m

Where to stay
1 Inka Lodge
2 Hotel Antigua
3 Flying Dog Hostel
4 Casa Andina
5 El Patio
6 Kúsillu's
7 José Antonio
8 Friend's House
9 Inka Hostel
10 Tinkus Hostel
11 Hostal Buena Vista
12 La Castellana

Pescados Capitales
Choquenchanca
Produce market
START WALKING TOUR
Malecón de la Marina
Mendiburu
Oscar Valdez
Cordova
Perez Aranibar
START WALKING TOUR
Merino
La Mar
WALKING TOUR
Av La Mar
Lord Nelson
La Red
Santa Cruz
Santa Cruz
Primavera
Bandelli
Lastres
Tupac Amaru
Figueredo
Berlín
Plaza Morales Barros
Marqués de Torre Tagle
Huaca Pucllana
La Tabla
Huaca Pucllana
Aviación
Madrid
José Gálvez
Francia
Ramón Zavala
Roma
Jorge Chávez
Bolognesi
2 de Mayo
Julio Elcorrobarrutia
Elías Aguirre
La Bodega de la Trattoria
Av José Pardo
General Borgoño
Enrique Palacios
Plaza República
Independencia
Lighthouse
1
Piura
Coronel Inclán
Atahualpa
Malecón Cisneros
Huaringas
2
Plaza Bolognesi
Av Grau
Germán
Recavarren
O Bar
Cocodriloverde
SAE Club
Post Office
Venecia
Tripoli
Italia
Federico
Bellavista
Berlín
M Olaya
Av Arequipa
4
Thouars
Mercado del Indios
Rodrigo
Segundo Muelle
Parque del Amor
Malecón Balta
Malecón 28 de Julio
Av Mariscal Oscar Benavides – Diagonal
3
Parque Kennedy
Ovalo
Il Cappuccino
La Trattoria di Mambrino
Bar Habana
Bar Bobo
Manuel Bonilla
Porta
Ocharán
Rafael
Craft stalls at Parque
José Larco
Astrid & Gaston
5
Diez Canseco
Alpaca III
Pasaje el Suche
Av 6
Jazz Zone
10
El Alamo
Metro
Juan Fanning
8 7
José Gonzales
Colón
Manco Capac
28 de Julio
Vivanda Kennedy
Av La Paz
11
del Solar
9
Killaii
12
FINISH WALKING TOUR
Larcomar Shopping Centre
(Gótica, Mangos, TIC & Cinema)
Av Armendariz
Av José Larco
Fores
The Corner
Alcán
Santa Isabel
San Fernando
San Martín
Grimaldo
Benavides
Av República
Olcay
Alfaro
Antigua Bodega Dalmacia
T'anta
Av Vasco Núñez de Balboa
San Antonio
Av Reducto
Paseo de la República
Parque Reducto
Ramón Ribeyro

PACIFIC OCEAN

LIMA

Barranco – seaside suburb, sandwiches and shopping
[HALF DAY]
Barranco was once a seaside resort for Lima's wealthiest families wishing to escape the stifling summer heat downtown. Many of its magnificent mansions are still standing and, despite their neglected and crumbling appearance, provide a snapshot of what was once a very fashionable neighbourhood.

Starting at **Parque Muncipal**, in front of lemon-coloured art café *Iskay,* walk south down **Av San Pedro de Osma** passing **Museo Galeria Arte Popular de Ayacucho** (10am-6pm daily, free but you need to ring the bell) on the right and **Museo de la Electricidad** (🖳 http://museoelectri.perucultur al.org.pe; 9am-5pm daily, free) on the left; in front of which is a tram which used to run between Barranco, Miraflores and Lima Centro.

You can continue walking for a couple of blocks, to No 423, to reach **Museo Pedro de Osma** (🖳 www.museopedrodeosma.org; Tue-Sun 10am-6pm, s/10). Once the fancy beach-house residence of the Osma family and worth a look in its own right, it now houses an impressive private collection of colonial paintings, sculptures, textiles and silverwork. There's not a deckchair in sight.

Alternatively take a left up 28 de Julio (right if you're retracing your steps having visited the museum) and another left to bring you back to Parque Muncipal. Pop your head into *Juanito's* (Av Grau 274, p138) to see a traditional *bodega* (bar that also serves snacks) and try one of their sandwiches. Cross the park, stopping to admire the red biblioteca on your left, the equally red church on your right, the pool with Romanesque statue and fountain and locals promenading in the purple shadow of the jacaranda trees.

Follow pedestrianized **Paseo Chabuca Granda** straight ahead (passing the bodega on your left which has a display of plastic cocktails outside) and then take the steps down (don't cross the bridge). Follow cobbled **Bajada de los Baños** towards the sea. This shady walkway is flanked by what were once grand houses and boughs of bougainvillea. It makes for an enjoyable stroll but turn back before reaching the end as this area has a nasty reputation for crime.

Climb back up the steps and cross the wooden **Puente de los Suspiros**, or Bridge of Sighs. Legend has it that a girl of nobility, living in one of the mansions, fell in love with a road sweeper but her father would not allow her to see the boy so she waited and watched for him at her window. Those who walked across the bridge could hear her sorrowful sighs. Turn left and pass the raspberry coloured, almost roofless, **Ermita Church**. Another legend suggests that fishermen, lost at sea in thick fog, had their prayers answered when a luminous cross appeared on the cliff top and guided them safely home. The church was later built on the very same spot. There are a number of bars here with great ocean views, perfect for admiring the sunset so maybe you'd prefer to end the walk here and wait for the show.

Back at the bridge there is a **Statue of Chabuca Granda**, a Peruvian singer and composer. One of the bars at the *mirador* is named after her best-known song *La Flor de la Canela*. Follow the steps up, cross the road and walk down **Junín** for a couple of blocks until you see the ocean. Follow the palm trees and

Barranco

Where to stay

1 The Point
2 Second Home Peru
3 Kaminu
4 Barranco's Backpackers Inn
5 La Quinta de Allison

0   100m

Av El Sol-Oeste

Diez Canes co.

WALKING TOUR

La 73

Tweddle

Av San Martin

Av Miguel Grau

Av Pierola

Bar Cala

Av Pierola

Miraflores

Av Sáenz Peña

Dédalo

Santa Rosa

San Antonio

Sargento Pimiento

Av Bolognesi

Pazos

Junín

Martinez

Cavero

Colina

Circuito De Playas

Canta Rana

Antica Trattoria

Domeyer

El Libertador

1

Posada del Angel

2

Union

Bajada de los Baños

Statue of Chabuca Granda

Ermita Church

Chala

K'antu

Bank $

Sanchez Carrion

La Noche

Juan Pazos

La Victoria

Bank $

Parque Municipal

Juanito's

Bars and sunset viewpoint

Paseo Chabuca Granda

3

La Estación

Puente de los Suspiros

Museo del Electricidad

Biblioteca & TIC

Panama

28 de Julio

4

Iskay

Posada del Angel

Mochileros

Museo Galeria Arte Popular de Ayacucho

5

Av San Pedro de Osma

Herrera

To Museo Pedro de Osma, 350m

trailblazer

LIMA

strip of parkland along the cliff top. Ahead you can see Miraflores and its skyscrapers. Below are the beaches and surfers. Shortly you will see a blue and red tiled staircase on your right which leads to **Av Sáenz Peña**, a wide boulevard of some of Barranco's finest buildings. Usually the *D'Anafria* ice-cream men are here on their yellow tricycles, blowing their duck whistles in case you hadn't noticed them. It's a nice spot to sit or have a look around the craft gallery **Dedalo** which has a garden *café*.

You can either return to Parque Muncipal along **Av San Martín** (the second right off Av Sáenz Peña) passing a couple of handmade clothing boutiques, or continue along the cliff top, weaving through the park and listening to the crashing waves below until you reach **Av El Sol Oeste**. Walk up the street for two blocks and stop for a snack at *La 73* (see p138) or catch a taxi (s/5) down to *Bar Cala* (see p139) on the **Circuito De Playas** and finish with a sunset drink.

Under no circumstances should you walk down to or back from the beach road.

Pueblo Libre museums – a little light learning and lunch
[HALF DAY]

The Pueblo Libre district is to the south-west of Lima Centro. Start at the **Museo Nacional de Arqueología, Antropología e História del Perú** (🖥 http://museonacional.perucultural.org.pe; Plaza Bolivar, cnr San Martin & Vivanco, Tue-Sun 9.30am-5pm, s/10) which is housed in a colonial mansion. The extensive collection of pre-Columbian artefacts is displayed chronologically in rooms dedicated to a specific era and leading off two peaceful courtyards. Next door, yellow **Quinta de los Liberatores** was once the home of both San Martín and Bolívar (see p54).

Cross **Plaza Bolívar** passing a giant stone bust of the man himself and a central fountain. Turn right and immediately left. The vivid orange church of **Santa María Magdelena** (7.30-9am & 6-9pm and all day Thu) is unmissable in all senses of the word. There are dazzling altars on three walls of the scarlet interior. The steps down to the catacombs can be seen through an iron grate. Fresh bread smells waft from *Pandería Don Alejo* next door, if you're feeling peckish.

Cross back over the road. On the corner of **Av San Martín** is *Antigua Taberna Queirolo* (🖥 http://antiguatabernaqueirolo.com; Mon-Wed 10am-11pm, Thu-Sat 10am-midnight, Sun 10am-4pm). Opened in 1880 by an Italian immigrant the dark wood décor, tiled floor and marble-top bar are reminiscent of that time. Although wine and Pisco are no longer made on the premises (in 1963 the vineyard moved 150km south of Lima to the Cañete valley) there is a shop next door or you may prefer to try before you buy and join the regulars for a spot of lunch (choose your sandwich filling from the glass cabinet at the bar).

Continuing up Av San Martín look down at your feet and you'll see a blue line painted on the pavement. This leads to the next museum. It's a good 20-minute walk but the area is safe. First you must turn left and pass *El Bolivariano*, another option for lunch. The building dates from 1780 when it was a convent. Cross the road and the blue line will take you past Metro supermarket, left through a residential area, right for a block until you reach a park, walk through the park, then right, left, right until you reach **Av Bolívar**.

Museo Larco (💻 www.museolarco.org; 9am-6pm daily, s/30) is immediately on your right (No 1515) behind a high white wall smothered in bougainvillea and honeysuckle.

The museum is worth visiting as much for its tranquil garden setting and relaxing restaurant *Café del Museo* (same hours as museum) as for its collection of pre-Columbian finds. Fabulous milky quartz and lapis lazuli necklaces and painfully big silver nose plates are kept in the 'vault' room. There's also a staggering number of ceramic jars with spouts on display. Choose a favourite and if you're struggling there are more shelves in the storehouse. It is, however, the 'erotic pottery' that the museum is perhaps most famed for. As you enter, the lights automatically turn on. Don't worry if you're not sure what you're looking at as there's an explanation for every position and expression. After all that steamy stuff you'll need a drink to cool down.

More museums

● **Museo de la Nación** (Av Prado Este 2466, San Borja, Tue-Sun 9am-5pm, s/7) will get you in the mood for Machu Picchu as you weave your way around the floors of pre-Columbian exhibits and explanations.

● **Huaca Pucllana** (see map p125; Calle General Borgono cuadra 8, Miraflores 9am-5pm, closed Tue, s/7) is an adobe pyramid built in about the 5th century AD by the Lima culture as a ceremonial centre. Roam around to your heart's content.

The classy *Huaca Pucllana Restaurant* (☎ 445 4042, 💻 www.resthuacapucllana.com) has tables metres from the site. At night it's a magical spot to be.

● **Museo de Oro** (💻 www.museoroperu.com.pe; Alonso de Molina 1100, Monterrico, daily 11.30am-7pm, s/33) is a dazzling display of ancient gold artefacts that will have you humming Spandau Ballet's 'Gold' as you admire all that glitters. Rumours suggest some of the pieces, however, may not be the real deal. There is also a huge collection of weapons.

● **Museo de Arte de Lima** (MALI see map p121; 💻 http://www.mali.pe; Paseo de Colón 125, Lima Centro, 10am-8pm Tue-Fri & Sun, 10am-5pm on Sat, s/12 for foreigners) has art collections from the pre-Columbian period to the present. There's also a *café* where you can discuss your favourite piece.

PRACTICAL INFORMATION

Arrival

By air All flights into Lima arrive at **Aeropuerto Internacional Jorge Chávez**, (💻 www.lap.com.pe) in the district of Callao, about 16km north-west of the centre. If you arrive off an international flight, having reclaimed your luggage, you will be directed by airport staff to press a button. Keep your fingers crossed that you get the green light indicating you are free to go. If you are unlucky enough to get the red light you will have to wait for your bags to be opened and searched; this is Customs Lima style. There are ATMs, *casas de cambios* (foreign-exchange office) and left-luggage facilities at the airport.

A taxi is the easiest and most convenient way to get into the city. Once in the arrivals hall for both international and domestic flights you don't need to worry

❏ **South American Explorers Club (SAE)**
Founded in 1977, this almost-legendary club for travellers in South America provides a wide range of help and backup services for members including emergency assistance, trip planning advice, luggage storage, help finding a trekking or travel partner, poste restante or mail forwarding, free events and lectures, help finding volunteer work, a book exchange and a library of books in English, and maps and detailed trip reports from travellers.

At the clubhouse there's free wi-fi, free tea and coffee and even short local phone calls are free. Members also benefit from a wide range of discounts throughout Peru; pick up a list at the clubhouse. The volunteer staff here are a mine of useful information and advice.

A non-profit organization, SAE (☎ 445 3306, ⌨ www.saexplorers.org) is at Calle Piura 135 in Miraflores. They're open Mon-Tue & Thur-Fri 9.30am-5pm, Wed 9.30am-8pm, Sat 9.30am-1pm; closed on public holidays. Membership costs from US$60 per year (US$90 for couples) and you can sign up on the spot.

There are also clubhouses in Cusco (see p156); Quito, Ecuador; and Buenos Aires, Argentina.

about finding one since you will instantly be approached by touts; these work for official taxi companies and wear their ID around their neck in a plastic pocket.

Taxi Green (⌨ www.taxigreen.com .pe) charges s/40 to Central Lima/ Miraflores and s/45 to Barranco. Payment is up front. It is advisable to use official taxis from the airport.

A cheaper option is to leave the arrivals hall and, just across the road in front of the terminal building, you will spot the crowd of unofficial taxi drivers waiting for a fare. You will need to negotiate a price, especially since they know you are a new gringo in town, and shouldn't pay more than s/20 to Central Lima and s/35 to Miraflores/Barranco.

Avoid a station wagon cab since your luggage can be seen. Lima's traffic is notoriously heavy and your hotel transfer could take up to an hour.

By bus There is no main bus terminal in the city so each company has its own depot. Generally the bigger and better bus companies are located along Javier Prado Este, in La Victoria (a taxi to Miraflores/Central Lima from here should cost around s/7); the cheaper companies are in Central Lima.

Orientation
Lima is a huge city forming a continuous urban area with the seaport of Callao in the north. Although composed of almost 50 districts, those of interest to tourists are within a relatively small area.

Lima Centro is the city's historical and cultural heart and has a political function. One of the city's main arteries, **Avenida Paseo de la República/Via Expressa** leads south from Lima Centro passing through the financial and business district of **San Isidro** and onto **Miraflores**, a modern clifftop suburb of shops, restaurants and hotels which are mostly clustered around **Parque Kennedy** and **Av Larco**.

Further south is the former seaside resort of **Barranco**, now a charmingly arty quarter and notorious night spot.

The more traditional neighbourhood of **Pueblo Libre**, with its collection of museums, lies to the north of Miraflores and Barranco and west of Lima Centro. The most populous parts of the city are to the extreme north and south and the growing gap between rich and poor is clearly evident between neighbourhoods. The wealthy residential areas of La Molina and Monterrico are away from the coast, south-east of the centre.

Getting around

The driving on Lima's roads is like 'Wacky Races' and it's best to just sit back and trust your driver since he negotiates the traffic on a daily basis. Don't be afraid, however, to ask him to slow down. After all you're paying.

Taxis You'd be forgiven for thinking every vehicle in Lima is a taxi since it certainly seems that way. Get hold of a luminous taxi sticker, slap it on your windscreen and, hey presto, you're a taxi too.

Since most taxis are 'unofficial' it is advisable to think before hopping into a cab. Most restaurants have valets and security guards who will gladly flag down a taxi for you, put you in it, and take down vehicle details. Alternatively stop the bright yellow ones as these are registered with the **Metropolitan Lima Taxi Service** (although anyone can paint their cab yellow).

Taxis in Lima are comparatively cheap and certainly convenient. Always negotiate your fare before setting off and pay on arrival. Any journey within Miraflores/Barranco should cost s/4-8, from Miraflores to Central Lima/Pueblo Libre/San Borja s/8-12 and out to Monterrico about s/15.

Combis If you want to travel around Lima like a local jump on board a *combi* (minibus). They're very cheap but also very slow since they will drop off and pick up passengers absolutely anywhere along their route, giving you a chance to get to know the people you're squashed up against, although watch roaming hands in your pockets.

A useful route is **Av Arequipa** which joins Miraflores and Central Lima (runs east off the Parque Kennedy roundabout). If travelling from Miraflores look for a sign in the wind-screen stating 'Todo Arequipa' or 'Wilson' as their destination. If travelling to Miraflores look for 'Todo Arequipa' or 'Miraflores/Larco/Schell'. It costs s/1 to make any journey within a district and s/2 to travel between districts.

Tours **Mirabús** (☎ 242 6699, 🖳 www.mirabusperu.com, main ticket office Av Larco 345, ticket stand at Parque Kennedy) is a red double-decker open-top bus which cruises around Lima's sights. The company offers several tours including daily one-hour tours of Miraflores, a two-hour evening tour (Wed-Sun 6pm, 3 hours, s/55) of Lima Centro and its floodlit colonial buildings, with a refreshment break at Hotel Sheraton and entrance to the magical water circuit (see box p139) and its fountain jets set to music; and a three-hour trip (Tue-Sun 10am, s/55) to Pachacamac, a Pre-Columbian ceremonial temple in the Lurin Valley, about 30km south of the city.

Car rental **Budget** (☎ 442 8703/442 8706, 🖳 www.budgetperu.com, Canaval y Moreya 569) has branches at the airport as well as in Lima Centro, Miraflores, Barranco and San Borja.

Hertz (☎ 445 5716, 🖳 www.hertz.com.pe, Jr Cantuarias 160) has branches at the airport and in Miraflores. **Avis** (☎ 434 1111, 🖳 www.avisperu.com, Av Javier Prado Este 5233) has branches at the airport and in Miraflores. **National** (☎ 578 7878/575 1111, 🖳 www.nationalcar.com.pe, Av Costanera 1380) also has a branch at the airport.

Banks

In Miraflores there are banks all the way along Av Larco such as **BCP** and **Banco Continental** (Mon-Fri 9am-6pm, Sat until 12.30pm). In Lima Centro there is a branch of **Interbanc** (Mon-Fri 9am-6pm, closed Sat) on Jirón de la Unión and at the Parque Muncipal in Barranco. There is also a BCP ATM here.

The banks will change money but you get a better exchange rate in the casas de cambio (Lac Dolar, Av La Paz 211, Miraflores, and Jr Camaná, Mon-Fri 10am-2pm & 3-6pm, Sat 10am-2pm).

On every street corner there are *cambistas* (street changers) clutching wads of money, a calculator and sometimes wearing a blue or green bib with a dollar or Euro sign on the back. They will give you a better rate still but unless you are confident in your

❏ **Embassies and consulates**

Argentina (☎ 433 3381, 🖳 embajada@terra.com.pe), Av Arequipa 121, 28 de Julio 828; **Austria** (☎ 442 0503, 442 1807, 🖳 lima-ob@bmaa.gv.at), Av Central 643, 5th Floor, San Isidro; **Australia** (☎ 222 8281, 🖳 www.australia.org.pe), Av Víctor Andres Belaúnde 147, San Isidro; **Belgium** (☎ 241 7566, 🖳 www.diplomatie.be/lima), Angamos Oeste 380, Miraflores; **Bolivia** (☎ 422 2095, 🖳 postmast@emboli.org.pe), Los Castaños 235, San Isidro; **Brazil** (☎ 512 0830, 🖳 www.embajada brasil.org.pe), Av José Pardo 850, Miraflores; **Canada** (☎ 319 3200, 🖳 www.canadainternational .gc.ca/peru-perou), Bolognesi 228, Miraflores; **Chile** (☎ 710 2211, 🖳 http://chileabroad .gov.cl/peru), Javier Prado Oeste 790, San Isidro; **Colombia** (☎ 441 0954, 🖳 www.em bajadacolombia.org.pe), Av Jorge Basadre 1580, San Isidro; **Ecuador** (☎ 212 4161, 212 4171, 🖳 www.mecuadorperu.org.pe), Las Palmeras 356, San Isidro; **France** (☎ 215 8400, 🖳 www.ambafrance-pe.org), Arequipa 3415, San Isidro; **Germany** (☎ 212 5016, 🖳 www.lima.diplo.de), Av Arequipa 4210, Miraflores; **Ireland** (☎ 446 3878, 🖳 irish consulperu@yahoo.ca), Avenida Paseo de la República 5757B, Miraflores; **Israel** (☎ 418 0500, 🖳 http://lima.mfa.gov.il), Natalio Sánchez 125, 6th Floor, Santa Beatriz; **Italy** (☎ 463 2727, 🖳 www.amblima.esteri.it), Av Gregorio Escobedo 298, Jesús María; **Japan** (☎ 219 9500, 🖳 www.pe.emb-japan.go.jp), Av San Felipe 356, Jesús María; **Netherlands** (☎ 213 9800, 🖳 www.nlgovlim.com), Av Jose Larco 1301, 13th Floor, Miraflores; **New Zealand** (☎ 422 7491, 🖳 alfonsorey@gmail.com), Los Nogales 510, San Isidro; **Spain** (☎ 513 7930, 🖳 www.mae.es/consulados/lima), Calle Los Pinos 490, San Isidro; **Sweden** (☎ 442 8905, 🖳 konslima@speedy.com.pe), La Santa María 130, San Isidro; **United Kingdom** (☎ 617 3000, 🖳 www.ukinperu.fco .gov.uk), Av José Larco 1301, 22nd Floor, Miraflores; **USA** (☎ 618 2000, 🖳 http://lima .usembassy.gov), Av La Encalada 17, Surco.

ability to detect fake notes (the serial number of the genuine notes you are given will end in the same letter so check for one that doesn't) it is advisable not to change money this way.

If you need money wired to you there is a branch of **Western Union** (🖳 www .westernunion.com.pe) on Av Larco.

Books

Ibero Librerías (🖳 www.iberolibros.com) stocks coffee-table books on Peru and a selection of English-language paperbacks and guidebooks. There are branches at Av Larco 199, Miraflores; Av Oscar R Benavides 500, Miraflores; and Av Malecon de la Reserva 610, Tda 127, Larcomar, Miraflores.

Communications

● **Internet** Many hostels and hotels offer free internet use for guests; otherwise Lima is well connected with *cabinas publica*

(internet kiosks) widely found. **Refugio Internet** has two branches on Av Larco and in Lima Centro internet is available in the Post Office Arcade. Generally it's about s/2 for an hour.

● **Telephone** Blue and green **Telefónica** phone booths are numerous in commercial areas of the city and take coins.

Another way to call is to buy a pre-paid phone card from a supermarket or bodega. This is also an economical way to call home but you will need to buy a *tarjeta larga distancia* for this. To use the card, scratch the silver panel to reveal the secret code and then dial the short number at the start of instructions. A voice recording will ask you to type in the secret code. It will then inform you how much money is left on the card and ask you to dial your desired number. Before you are put through the voice tells you how many minutes you have. When calling the UK from a residential line a s/10 card can last as much as an hour but from a public phone box about 20 minutes. At a *locutorio* (communications centre) you can use a phone booth.

● **Post** The main **post office** is in Lima Centro just off Plaza de Armas; in Miraflores there is a post office (Mon-Sat 8am-8pm and Sun 9am-1pm) close to the Indian Market at Petit Thouars 5201.

It costs s/6 to send a card to Europe and takes about a week to arrive. Be careful though if you slip a letter inside, your card will be weighed and cost more.

Emergencies

● **Police** Lima is a big city in a less developed country. Crime happens but it's not something to be paranoid about especially if you take the same sensible precautions you would in any city; don't flash your wealth, don't carry valuables, be on your guard in crowded places and at ATMs and don't walk in unlit, unfamiliar places at night. Also, do watch your bag in restaurants as it could be kicked from under your chair. To avoid this some restaurants' chairs have a strap with which to secure your bag. In touristy areas there is a great police presence, plus security cars and bikes keeping the streets under constant surveillance. Again this is nothing to be anxious about; in fact it should be a comfort.

If you are a victim of crime you can contact the **Tourist Police** (Jirón Colón 246, Miraflores, ☎ 243 2190, 24 hours).

● **Medical** It is goes without saying that you should buy medical insurance before travelling to Peru otherwise medical treatment will be costly. Either way you will be asked to pay before you receive treatment.

Clinica Anglo Americana (☎ 616 8900, 🖳 www.clinangloamericana.com.pe; Calle Alfredo Salazar 350, San Isidro) and **Clinica Ricardo Palma** (☎ 224 2224, 🖳 www.crp.com.pe; Javier Prado Este 1066, San Isidro) are closer for Miraflores and **Clinica San Felipe** (☎ 219 0000, 🖳 www .clinicasanfelipe.com; Av Gregorio Escobedo N 650, Jesus Maria) is closer to Lima Centro. All have some English-speaking staff.

Pharmacies, such as Botica Fasa and Inka Farma, are open 24 hours. They are numerous along Larco (Miraflores), Jirón de la Unión (Lima Centro) and Av Grau (Barranco); you'll be amazed what you can buy without a prescription.

● **Earthquake** During your stay in Lima you may experience an earth tremor which sounds and feels a bit like a truck is headed your way.

In the unlikely event of an earthquake the procedure in Lima is to evacuate buildings but if this isn't possible look for the green signs marked with a giant 'S' for seismic. These identify the (supposedly) safest spots.

Laundry

Ask your hostel or hotel if they provide a laundry service as many do, otherwise there's Lavanderia Lava Queen (Larco 1158, Miraflores) and Press To in the Metro Supermarket in Lima Centro.

Tourist information

There are stalls in Parque Kennedy and Larcomar and there is a tourist office behind the Plaza de Armas, on Pasaje Ribera el Viejo in Lima Centro and in the Biblioteca building in Barranco. They do dish out free maps and odd brochures but speaking to fellow tourists and your hotel/hostel staff is likely to be more rewarding.

WHERE TO STAY

There are three main areas of tourist accommodation in Lima: Miraflores has the greatest selection of hostels and hotels. Base yourself here for restaurants and shopping. There are budget choices in Barranco, for those who prefer to be close to the nightlife, and a range of accommodation options in Lima Centro, for those seeking proximity to the city's historical sights, although care should be taken in both neighbourhoods at night. (See also p83.)

Miraflores   [see map p125]
Budget *Kúsillu's Hostel* (☎ 444 0817, 🖳 www.kusillushostel.com, Av Larco 655) has light rooms with colourful jungle murals. It is friendly and popular and there are plans to build another floor of accommodation. Guests have use of the rooftop terrace, modern kitchen and internet. A dorm bed is $9 and rooms cost $11/22 (att).

LIMA

If you want to hook up with fellow travellers and be a step away from fast-food joints and 'pizza alley', *Flying Dog Hostel* (☎ 447 0673, 🖥 www.flyingdogperu.com, Martir Olaya 280) is a good choice. There are three other branches of the hostel dotted around Parque Kennedy but this one has more private rooms. It's well maintained with helpful staff and all the usual backpacker services. A dorm bed costs s/30, a double room s/90 (att) and a triple s/135 (att).

Friend's House (☎ 446 3521, 🖥 friendshouse_peru@yahoo.com.mx, Jr José Gonzales 427) is painted apple green, faded but friendly and more like a family home than the other hostels. Breakfast and use of the kitchen are included. It is close to Larcomar's shops and cafés. There is another branch around the corner at Jr. Manco Capac 368 which offers dorm beds too (s/20). Rooms cost s/35/48 (com) and s/40/70 (att).

Mid range A peaceful oasis retreat in the heart of the action, *El Patio* (☎ 444 2107, 🖥 www.hostalelpatio.net, c/Ernesto Diez Canseco 341) has charming, sorbet-coloured rooms leading off a flower-filled patio, perfect for a spot of relaxing reading. A continental breakfast is included and a laundry service, currency exchange, and suites with kitchenette are available. Gorgeous; highly recommended. Rooms cost from s/120/150 (att) with a s/15 deduction for cash payment.

Inka Lodge (☎ 242 6989, 🖥 www.inkalodge.com, Elías Aguirre 278) is a couple of blocks from Huaca Pucllana and about a 10-minute walk from the heart of Miraflores. The décor is unmistakably Inca themed, with masks, murals and interesting information panels. Rooms are spotlessly clean and sparklingly new. Breakfast is included and guests can make use of the free internet, lockers, kitchen and laundry service. This small hostel is an excellent choice and has dorm beds at s/36 and rooms for s/69/78 (com).

Friendly *Tinkus Hostel* (☎ 255 7593, 🖥 www.hoteltinkus.com, Av La Paz 608) is centrally located and good value, although not for those with an aversion to orange since this is the colour scheme throughout. A continental breakfast is included and there is a laundry service and wi-fi. Rooms cost s/100/125/150 (att).

Just across the street from Larcomar Shopping Centre and its view of the ocean is *Inka Hostel* (☎ 445 2178, 🖥 www.inkahostel.com, Av José Larco 1178). It is brightly decorated with citrus shades. Some of the rooms have small terraces and cost $35/40/50 (att).

Set behind wrought-iron gates, *Hostal Buena Vista* (☎ 447 3178, 🖥 www.hostalbuenavista.com, Grimaldo del Solar 202) is a bright choice. Catch up with your letter-writing on one of the patios under the shade of a royal blue garden umbrella. Free internet, breakfast and kitchen use is included. Rooms cost s/105/135/165 (att).

Just next door is *La Castellana* (☎ 444 3530, 🖥 www.castellanahotel.com, Grimaldo del Solar 222), which looks like a magnificent colonial mansion from the outside but the décor is dated and dark. The rooms are spacious and clean and cost s/189/225/264 (att).

Expensive *Casa Andina* (☎ 447 0263, 🖥 www.casa-andina.com, Av Petit Thouars 5444) opened in 2007 and is part of a countrywide chain of hotels. In a central location, it's opposite the Indian Market, round the corner from Parque Kennedy. It's a stylish place with wi-fi, air-con, laundry service, currency exchange and a buffet breakfast. Rooms cost $108/127 (att); discounts are available for online bookings.

A good choice for those seeking a spot of tranquillity, *Hotel Antigua* (☎ 241 6116, 🖥 www.peru-hotels-inns.com, Av Grau 350) is away from the tourist strip. Try the rocking chairs on the black and white tiled veranda for size. This is an elegant colonial mansion inside and out. Good breakfast, excellent service. Rooms cost $79-109/94-129/129-154 (att).

Or why not splurge on a suite at *José Antonio* (☎ 445 7743, 🖥 www.hotelesjoseantonio.com, Av 28 de Julio 398)? It has very big, very beige rooms, all mod-cons and a swimming pool. After conquering the

Inca Trail your body deserves the massaging jets of a Jacuzzi bath. Rooms cost from $154/176/198 (att).

Barranco [see map p127]

Budget *The Point* (☎ 628 7952 or 247 7709, 🖳 www.thepointhostels.com, Malecón Junín 300) is the place for those who like to party. Meet at the hostel bar and then hit Lima's nightspots together as a group. Guests are given a bracelet and wearers are given free entry to nightclubs like Gótica (see p139). It also happens to be a good place to stay with a cosy lounge, garden with hammocks, laundry service, kitchen, airport pick-up (s/45) and free breakfast and internet use. Opened in 2002 in an old colonial mansion with high ceilings and wide corridors there is a light, spacious feel to the place and rooms are well maintained. Dorm beds are s/26-34 depending on the number of beds in the room and rooms are s/50/68 (com).

Although only two blocks from the main plaza, *Barranco's Backpackers Inn* (☎ 247 1326, Malecón Castilla 260) is on a quiet road with great views of the ocean from some of its rooms. Staff are friendly and helpful and will organize an airport pickup and tickets for onward travel. There is a kitchen, free breakfast and internet. The beds have cheery, colourful covers and in a dorm cost $10. A double is $30 (att).

Kaminu (☎ 252 8680, 🖳 www.kaminu.com, Bajada de Baños 342), opened in 2007, is a tiny hostel with hugely enthusiastic staff. It is located under Puente de los Suspiros, one of Barranco's most notable landmarks. There's a roof terrace where you can barbecue and a small kitchen and lounge with large ceilings and artwork. Dorm beds cost $8 and a double $20 (com).

Mid range There is street noise but you will avoid backpacker noise at *La Quinta de Allison* (☎ 247 1515, 28 de Julio 281), which has modest rooms off hospital-white

corridors. Rooms cost s/50/70 (att) and a continental breakfast an extra s/6.

Expensive For those seeking tranquillity or a treat, the Pacific views from the gardens and terrace of *Second Home Peru* (☎ 247 5522, 🖳 www.secondhomeperu.com, Domeyer 366) will impress. A Tudor style mansion, it has five spacious guest rooms with polished wooden floors, crisp white bed linen, queen-/king-sized beds, and free-standing bath tubs; great to soak those sore limbs in after the Inca Trek. It was once the home of Peruvian sculptor Victor Delfín and his work is on show throughout. Rooms cost from $85/95 (att) and a continental breakfast is included.

Lima Centro [see map pp120-1]

Budget *Hostal España* (☎ 428 5546 or 427 9196, 🖳 www.hotelespanaperu.com, Jr Azangaro 105) may look like a stately home with its gilded mirrors, chandeliers, religious paintings and Greek statues but it's actually a budget backpackers with chintzy flowery bed covers. This is a popular choice, which may have something to do with the roof-top terrace and café which afford views across the roof line of San Francisco monastery. This is a great spot to escape from the heat and chaos below. A dorm bed costs s/14, rooms cost s/28/40/51 (com) and s/40/50/60 (att). Breakfast is available for s/4 and internet use for s/2/hour.

Two blocks from Plaza de Armas, *Inka Path* (☎ 426 1919, 🖳 www.inkapath.com, Jr de la Unión 654) is good value. Rooms are clean, well furnished and lead off a lobby with orange and lime walls, cream sofas and a small bar. Breakfast is included, and internet and a laundry service are available. Rooms cost s/70/90-110/140 (att) and s/50/60-70/100 (com).

Hostal Roma (☎ 427 7576, 🖳 www.hostalroma.8m.com, Jr Ica 326) is an old colonial mansion, a two-block walk from Plaza de Armas and with a hotch-potch of

LIMA

Lima area code: ☎ 01. If phoning from outside Peru dial ☎ +51-1.

basic but clean rooms. There is a café. Rooms cost $13/20/28 (com), $16/25/35 (att) and include breakfast.

Lima Centro [see map p120-1]
Mid range *Hotel Maury* (☎ 428 8188, Jr Ucayali 201) boasts two restaurants and a magnificent dark wood bar in which to enjoy a Pisco Sour; both the Maury and the Bolivar (below) were important in popularizing the Pisco Sour.

The hotel was renovated in 2000 and offers all the services you'd expect of an upscale hotel. Rooms cost from $55/65 (att).

The bathroom suites and heavy bedroom furniture at *Gran Hotel Bolivar* (☎ 619 7171, Jr de la Unión 958) may remind you of a rich great aunt but there is a certain charm to the place. Presidents have stayed here and you too can book a suite (from $92), recline on a peacock-blue settee beneath a twinkling chandelier and look out over Plaza Martín. Stay a night here and step back in time. Rooms cost from $65/75/85 (att).

WHERE TO EAT
If you want a quick bite at a cheap and familiar food chain then head to **Parque Kennedy** in Miraflores where McDonald's (and Bembos, the Peruvian equivalent), Pizza Hut, Burger King, KFC and Starbucks are easy to spot. It's also hard to miss 'Pizza Alley', just follow the food smells or the cries of the waiters hoping to entice you in with their picture menus.

If you have a craving for roast chicken (*pollo a la brasa*) and chips walk up **Jirón de la Unión** in Lima Centro and take your pick of *pollerias* (chicken restaurants). Domino's pizza and Rocky's chicken are

near **Parque Municipal** in Barranco. **Larcomar** in Miraflores has a food court with ocean views.

To limit yourself to what you know, however, would be to deny yourself the wonderful experience of dining in world-class restaurants (modestly priced if you're a tourist), savouring Peruvian flavours (tipped to be the next big cuisine) and understanding why Limeños are so passionate about and proud of their food. A short taxi ride will bring you to the door of some fabulous places to eat.

Miraflores [see map p125]
Cafés For great coffee, juices, a wide selection of freshly prepared sandwiches and salads (around s/12) head to *San Antonio* (Av Vasco Nuñez de Balboa 770; 7am-11pm daily).

T'anta (Av 28 de Julio 888; Mon-Fri 10am-midnight, Sat 9am-midnight, Sun 9am-10pm) also has great coffee and a feast of cakes and desserts that are temptingly wheeled past your table on a hostess trolley. It is good for breakfast, lunch, or a light supper. Try the empanadas with imaginative fillings (s/7) or the traditional favourite *rocoto rellano* (stuffed 'hot' pepper). Main courses are around s/30.

Il Cappuccino (🖳 www.cafe-ilcappu ccino.com, Calle Manuel Bonilla 103; daily 8am-10pm) offers customers wi-fi and comfy couches to flop in after a day's shopping as well as coffee and light bites.

While *Mangos* (🖳 www.mangosperu .com, Larcomar, Malécon de la Reserva 610; Mon-Fri 8-1am, Sat-Sun 7.30-2am) is perfectly perched on the cliff to offer diners a Pacific panorama with their order. Drop by for a drink or linger longer over a breakfast buffet (Sat/Sun 7.30-11.30am, s/38.50),

---

❏ **Suspiro de Limeña (Lima Sigh)**
This classic Peruvian dessert consists of a thick caramel bottom layer made from condensed milk, vanilla and egg yolks, topped with meringue combined with port syrup and a sprinkle of ground cinnamon as the finishing touch. Legend has it that it was named by the famous writer and poet Jose Galvez Amparo Ayarez, whose wife created it, because it was 'as sweet and soft as the sigh of a young woman from Lima.' First served in 1818, it epitomises the Peruvian love of sweet things.

a lunch-time buffet (daily 12.30-4pm, s/60), or a tea-time buffet (Mon-Sat 4.30-8pm, s/62). There is no limit to how many times you can fill your plate.

Fish and seafood A visit to a *cebicheria* (seafood restaurant) is an absolute must when you're so close to the sea but they open for lunch only. A three-course meal in a top restaurant, with Piscos and a bottle of Chilean wine, will cost about $40 per person and is worth every cent.

La Mar (☎ 421 3365, 🖥 www.lamar cebicheria.com, Av La Mar 770; Mon-Thur noon-5pm, Fri to 5.30pm, Sat/Sun 11.45am-5.30pm) is an ultra-popular lunch spot so get here early to secure a table, although people-watching at the bar with a bucket of vegetable chips and a Pisco Sour is part of the experience. A bamboo roof creates a light and airy dining area. Traditional Peruvian flavours with a twist. Try the *Cebiche Nikei* (s/34) and *Choritos a La Chalaca* (mussels; s/19).

You'll be licking your lips well before your order arrives at *Pescados Capitales* (☎ 4218808, 🖥 www.pescadoscapitales.com, Av La Mar 1337; daily 12.30-5pm & Mon-Sat 7.30-11pm). It's another great choice for lunch with both indoor and outdoor tables; the menu is fun, imaginative and unique. The *pulpitos bebes a la parilla* (grilled baby octopus) is simply divine.

Segundo Muelle (☎ 241 5040, 🖥 www.segundomuelle.com, Malecón Cisneros 156; daily 11.30am-5.30pm) has cheerful and friendly service, excellent food and an ocean view, while *La Red* (☎ 441 1026, Av La Mar 391; daily 10am-6pm) is a more traditional and slightly cheaper *cebicheria* along the La Mar strip. Try *Parihuela* (a spicy seafood soup) in this small nautical-themed restaurant.

Mediterranean *La Trattoria di Mambrino* (☎ 446 7002, Manuel Bonilla 106; Mon-Sat 1-3.30pm & 8-11.30pm, Sun lunch only) has a lively atmosphere and is always busy. It serves great pizza and if you can't quite finish you can ask to have it boxed up for your breakfast. An extensive menu and interesting specials (s/35-45)

make deciding on your choice hard. Homemade truffles are served with coffee.

La Bodega de la Trattoria (☎ 241 6899, Gral Borgoño 784; 8am-midnight daily) is a casual and cosy Italian opposite Huaca Pucllana. Its tables spill out onto a patio area which is lit with tree lanterns at night. Be sure to check out the specials board for mains (around s/30) and desserts.

La Tabla (☎ 243 3088, 🖥 www.restau rantetabla.com.pe, Calle Elías Aguirre 698; Mon-Thur 12.45pm-midnight, Fri/Sat to 1am, Sun 12.45-5pm) and *Antigua Bodega Dalmacia* (☎ 447 8919, Calle San Fernando 401; daily 8am-late) are of a similar style and equally excellent choices.

Splurge You should arrive after 9pm, even later, if you don't want to be the only guests for dinner. Expect to pay around $45 per person for a meal with drinks, which is a bargain since these are the restaurants of Lima's celebrity chefs.

With modern black, white and orange lounge décor, *Rodrigo* (☎ 446 0985, 🖥 www.restauranterodrigo.com, Calle Francisco De Paula Camino 231; Mon-Sat 1-3.30pm & 8pm-12.30am) has creative dishes imaginatively presented. Little touches like a complimentary entrée of an assortment of tastes and sorbet between courses makes you feel as if you're somewhere special. Start the experience at the bar with an Apple Martini.

At longstanding favourite *Astrid and Gaston* (☎ 242 5387 or 444 1496, 🖥 www.astridygaston.com, Cantuarias 175; Mon-Sat 12.30-3.30pm & 7.45-11.45pm) your dining experience will certainly live up to expectations. Enjoy classic Peruvian and modern flavours whilst admiring the high ceilings and huge napkins.

Rafael (☎ 242 4149, 🖥 www.rafael osterling.com, San Martin 300; Mon-Fri 1-4pm & 8pm-midnight, Sat evening only) is located in an old town house and is an excellent choice for an intimate, romantic meal. The dishes are rich and exquisite, the service friendly and attentive and you leave feeling thoroughly spoilt.

See p129 for *Huaca Pucllana Restaurant*.

Barranco   **[see map p127]**
Cafés *K'antu* (Av Grau 323; 10am-10pm
daily) is an art café run by CIAP, *Central
Interregional de Artisanos del Peru,* an
organization of Peruvian craftsmen which
is devoted to the production and the export
of their work and to improving the living
and working conditions of themselves and
their families. Savour a Fair Trade coffee at
a table top decorated with coffee beans and
afterwards do a spot of guilt-free shopping.

Iskay (Pedro de Osma 106; Mon-Sat
9am-11pm) is another art café with a
brightly painted patio offering sandwiches,
snacks (around s/15) and shopping.

Local *Juanito's* (Av Grau 274, on the
plaza from 11am until last-man-standing) is
more than 60 years old and the décor probably is too. Order a ham, pork, beef or olive
roll with onions and chilli (s/5-7), a bottle
of beer, and pull up a chair at a table to
watch local life in this traditional bodega.
There's no sign but it's painted pink.

Canta Rana (Génova 101; Sun-Thu
7.30am-4pm, Fri-Sat 7.30am-11.30pm) is
an informal and relaxed neighbourhood
cebicheria with simple wooden tables and a
tiled floor. The walls are plastered with
football paraphernalia and local photos. It
serves simple, classic Peruvian preparations (around s/30).

In contrast, *La 73* (El Sol Oeste 175;
noon-12.30am daily) has the feel of an
upmarket American diner. Sit inside the
chocolate-brown tiled restaurant at a cream
table and tuck into the *wontons
champignones* (s/16) and a lamburger
(s/24) or relax outside with a glass of wine
(s/14) slouched on the black leather couches, warmed by the glow of a patio heater.

Pizza *Antica Trattoria* (Av San Martín
201; noon-midnight daily) is a rustic style
pizzeria with a firewood oven and choice of
fresh pastas (s/25-35).

Splurge For fusion flavours and perfect
presentation head to *Chala* (☎ 252 8515, 🖳
www.chala.com.pe, Bajada de Baños 343;
Mon-Sat 1-4pm & 8pm-midnight, Sun 1-
4pm). It is in a magical spot and you can

choose to dine out on the wooden veranda
of this old colonial mansion or inside on red
and orange lounge chairs and get a flavour
of the past from the black and white photos
of old Lima which are projected onto a
wall. It has meat, fish and pasta main dishes for around s/40.

Lima Centro   **[see map pp120-1]**
Cafés *T'anta* (Pasaje Nicolas de Rivera
147; daily 9am-8pm). See p136.

**Chinese It is safer to visit China Town
during the day or take a taxi to the door**.
Wa Lok (Jr Paruro 864; daily 9am-
11pm) and *Salón China* (Jr Ucayali; Mon-
Sat 9am-11pm, Sun 9am-8pm) are both
excellent and popular restaurants. Try the
duck at Wa Lok or check out the lunch buffet (s/25) at Salón China.

BARS AND NIGHTLIFE
Many of the city's nightspots are found in
Barranco (see map p127). *Posada del
Angel* (Av Pedro de Osma 164 & San
Martín 157; Mon-Sat, 11am to the wee
small hours) is a cosy pub decorated with
antique furniture and trinkets, including a
number of angels. Make yourself comfortable in one of the velvet parlour chairs and
order a carafe of house wine (s/19). There is
a cover charge (s/3.50) for live music.

Mochileros (Av Pedro de Osma 135)
is a popular choice with backpackers.
Choose the red-brick cellar bar or come up
for some fresh air in the beer garden set in
the grounds of a decorative sage and cream
mansion built in 1903.

Walk down pedestrianized, bar-lined
Sánchez Carrión and you'll be inundated
with offers of free pisco from touts. If you
can avoid the temptation keep walking to
the end where you'll find *La Noche* (🖳
www.lanoche.com.pe, Av Bolognesi 307,
Mon-Sat 7pm-3am). Start your evening in
the lofty bar and then move next door to the
atmospheric three-floored live music venue
(s/5-50 depending on the band).

La Estación (Av Pedro de Osma 112)
is a snug *peña* with *criolla* (folk music)
shows starting around 11pm (s/20-30
daily).

❏ **Record-breaking fountains of delight**
An absolute must after dark is the magnificent **Circuito Mágico del Agua** (Parque de la Reserva, south of Lima Centro, Wed-Sun, 4-10pm, s/4, 💻 www.circuitomagicode lagua.com.pe). Opened in July 2007, the park currently holds the Guinness Record for the largest fountain complex in the world. A short stroll will lead you to 13 fountains including one 80 metres in height, and through a light and water show mixed with music and images. Two particular favourites are *Fuente Tunel de las Sorpresas*, which is like walking through a tunnel of orange Indian candy and *Fuente de los Niños* which invites you to step onto the dance floor and, in time to the disco beats, to sidestep the shoots of water (unless you want a soaking).

The most popular peña, is, however, in **Lima Centro** (see map pp120-1). *Las Brisas de Titicaca* (☎ 715 6960/1, 💻 www.brisasdeltiticaca.com, Jr Héros de Tarapaca 168) is an all-singing, all-dancing spectacular performance, a dazzling display of colourful costumes and traditional musical instruments and a showcase for the culture of Puno and other Peruvian regions. Get a group together and make an occasion of it (lunchtime shows Fri & Sat noon-6pm, s/35 includes lunch, and evening shows Tue 8pm s/21, Wed 8.30pm s/31.50, Thu 9.15pm s/31.50, Fri & Sat 10.15pm s/42). Table reservations are needed and can be made at the venue (☎ 332 1901 Mon-Sat 9am-7pm) or at Teleticket in the supermarkets Metro (Cuzco 245, Central Lima) or Wong (Av Benavides 1475, Miraflores).

There are plenty of bars around Parque Kennedy in **Miraflores** but more stylish drinking dens are found away from here.

Try *Bar Habana* (Manuel Bonilla 107) for excellent mojitos, psychedelic *Bar Bobo* next door, trendy *O Bar* (Calle San Francisco de Paula Camino 298) and a few doors up, *Cocodrilo Verde* café bar and music venue (Thu-Sat from 8pm) or perhaps the scarlet-walled *Jazz Zone* (Av La Paz 656).

Sip maracuya sours and watch the sun go down at the all-white beach bar, *Bar Cala* (Circuito de Playas, Barranco), or join Lima's movers and shakers at the ultra-popular four-floored *Bar Huaringas* (Bolognesi 460, Miraflores) and indulge in the fruit frappes (*limon y sauco* frappe is heaven in a glass).

If there's an important sports event you just have to watch, head to *The Corner* sports bar (Av Larco 1207, Miraflores) which has 26 TV screens, or *Estadio Futbol Bar* on Plaza San Martin (Lima Centro), where waxworks of Maradona and Pelé will join your table (jugs of beer s/16).

Lima's beautiful young things party at *Gótica* (Larcomar, Miraflores, s/40, it's cool to arrive after 1am). *Sargento Pimiento* (Bolognesi 755, Barranco) is a cheaper option for those who want to dance the night away.

For a quieter night there is a **cinema** at Larcomar, Miraflores (s/18, Cine bar s/23, half-price Tue). Look for film titles followed by (S) since this stands for subtitles and means the film will be in English whereas (E) indicates that the film has been dubbed into Spanish.

SHOPPING

If you've forgotten your toothbrush or another essential you'll find Lima's supermarkets surprisingly well stocked with familiar brands, or head to one for snacks before a long bus journey.

In Miraflores there is **Vivanda** (cnr Benavides & Alcanfores) and **Metro** (Schell cuadra 2) which also has a branch in Lima Centro (Cusco 245) and Barranco (Grau cuadra 5).

For those seeking a more adventurous grocery shop, try **Mercado de Surquillo** (just over the bridge crossing the Via Expressa off Av Ricardo Palma). This is, however, not a particularly safe area so be on your guard.

At the **Mercado del Indios** (Petit Thouars cuadra 54, Miraflores; daily) there are enough stalls selling handicrafts and paintings (which can always be rolled up to fit in a rucksack) to keep even the most ardent souvenir shopper happy. Never ever accept the first price you are quoted, as it will be outrageously high because you're a gringo. However, although bargaining is expected and fun, the salesmen need to make a living and will not sell if your price is too low. Try walking away to test this but if you really like something don't quibble over a few dollars. Knocking a third off the price is realistic. There is a good *café* at the entrance of La Portado del Sol (cnr Petit Thouars & Gral Pershing) if you need to regain your momentum for haggling.

If you are looking for more expensive and individual pieces of Peruvian art, ceramics, textiles, and jewellery look no further than **Dédalo** (Paseo Saenz Peña 295, Barranco; Mon-Sat 11am-9pm). Even if you don't have the cash, visit anyhow just to browse through the beautiful handmade designs. If you are tempted to buy, be sure

to take advantage of the free gift-wrapping service and, while you wait, have a coffee and chocolate brownie in the garden.

A similar spot for shopping is **Killaii** (cnr San Martín & Alcanfores, Miraflores, Mon-Sat 11am-8pm, Sun 11am-4pm). Take a walk through this terracotta colonial mansion and enjoy the contemporary crafts. In both galleries prices are marked and fixed.

Less expensive but still nice to potter around are the higgledy-piggledy souvenir shops of **Pasaje el Suche** (Av La Paz 646, Miraflores) and **El Alamo** (cnr Av La Paz & Ernesto Diez Canseco, Miraflores) and in the evenings there are often **craft stalls** at Parque Kennedy (Miraflores) and Parque Muncipal (Barranco).

Alpaca 111 (Larco 671, Larcomar and airport) is the best choice for baby alpaca and pima cotton clothing since the designs and colours are stylish and contemporary. **Larcomar** (🖳 www.larcomar.com, Miraflores) has a selection of souvenir shops but the prices are high so try the Mercado del Indios first. **Tatoo** sells adventure gear if you're looking for a last-minute bit of magic to propel you along day two of the Inca trail. **Q'orazon** (Larco 1180) is worth

❏ **Airline offices in Lima**

Please be aware that although the following information was correct at the time of research, street addresses in particular are inclined to change. If you are planning to visit an airline office it's best to phone before you go.

Domestic airlines LAN Peru (🕿 213 8200, 🖳 www.lan.com), Av Pardo 513, Miraflores; **Star Perú** (🕿 705 9000, 🖳 www.starperu.com), Av Comandante Espinar 331, Miraflores; **TACA** (🕿 511 8222, 🖳 www.taca.com), Av Jose Pardo 811, Miraflores; **Peruvian Airlines** (🕿 716 6000, 🖳 www.peruvianairlines.pe), Av Jose Pardo 495, Miraflores; **LC Busre** (🕿 619 1313, 🖳 www.lcbusre.com.pe), Calle los Tulipanes 218, San Eugenio.

International airlines

Aerolíneas Argentinas (🕿 444 0810, 🖳 www.aerolineas.com.ar), José Pardo 805, 3rd Floor, Miraflores; **Air France** (🕿 444 9285, 🖳 www.airfrance.com), Av José Pardo 601, Miraflores; **Alitalia** (🕿 447 3899, 🖳 www.alitalia.com), Martir Oláya 129 off 1703, Miraflores; **American Airlines** (🕿 422 8595, 🖳 www.aa.com), Canaval y Moreyra 390, San Isidro; **British Airways** (🕿 411 7801, 🖳 www.britishairways.com, Av Camino Real 390, San Isidro; **Continental** (🕿 221 4340, 🖳 www.continental .com), Víctor Andrés Belaúnde 147, San Isidro; **Iberia** (🕿 411 7800, 🖳 www.iberia .com), Av Camino Real 390, San Isidro; **KLM** (🕿 421 9500, 🖳 www.klm.com), Calderón 185, San Isidro.

a look and **Cuy Arts** (Larco 874) has humourous but tasteful souvenir T-shirts.

Av La Paz is lined with shops selling silver wares and more contemporary designs are found at **Claudia Lira** (Larcomar) and **Ilaria** (Larco 1325). **Neo Mutatis** (San Martín 110) and **Floam** (San Martín 247) are two clothing stores in Barranco selling hand made, one-off funky designs.

MOVING ON

You can travel on to Cusco by bus or by plane, direct or via Arequipa. Taking the bus is obviously cheaper and you can watch the landscape change as you climb out of the coastal desert into the Andes. It's a long journey, however, and if you are hit with a dose of *soroche* (altitude sickness) a bus is the last place you want to be. Internal flights are relatively reasonable but there is your carbon footprint to consider and remember if you've travelled from sea level to about 3300m in less than an hour it's wise to take it easy for the next few days.

Bus

There is no central bus terminal. Each company runs its own offices and terminals, of which there may be several so make sure you confirm which one the bus leaves from when you buy your ticket. With a long journey ahead it pays to choose a reliable company. Several of the companies offer different levels of service and thus fares vary.

Cruz del Sur (☎ 311 5050, 🖵 www.cruzdelsur.com.pe) has a good reputation for service and safety. It runs services to Cusco (daily 2pm & 5.30pm; s/182-220; 21 hours) via Nasca from its terminal on Javier Prado Este, La Victoria. An alternative is to break the journey in Arequipa (up to 7/day mostly in the afternoon/evening; s/130-200; 15 hours). The connection to Cusco is at 8.30pm (s/96; 10 hours). Cruz del Sur has a slightly cheaper and more basic service leaving from Jr Quilca, Central Lima.

Ormeño (☎ 472 1710, 🖵 www.grupo-ormeno.com.pe), also on Av Javier Prado Este, is another reputable choice and departs for Cusco at 4pm, for s/160. There are two daily services to Arequipa at 9am and 4pm for s/130 with a connection to Cusco at 9.30am for s/70.

Other options include: **Civa** (☎ 418 1111, 🖵 www.civa.com.pe) or **Flores** (☎ 332 1212, 🖵 www.floreshnos.net), both on the corner of 28 de Julio and Paseo de la República in Lima Centro and offering routes south; **Empresa Molina** (☎ 428 4852), Ayacucho 1141-1145, Lima Centro, has services to Cusco. There are several companies on Paseo de la República, such as **Ittsa** (☎ 233 3612) at No 809 which covers the north coast; **Movil Tours** (☎ 716 8000, 🖵 www.moviltours.com.pe) at No 749 for Huaraz, Chachapoyas, Tarapoto and Caraz; and **Soyuz** (☎ 205 2370 or 226 1515, 🖵 www.perubus.com.pe), on the corner of Paseo de la República and Mexico 333, which runs along the Pan-American Highway to Ica. **Tepsa** (☎ 202 3535, 🖵 www.tepsa.com.pe) offers northern routes and many inland destinations including Arequipa.

Air

See p129 for details about getting to and from the airport.

The main national airline is **LAN** (🖵 www.lan.com); it has frequent flights to Cusco leaving throughout the morning. Flights are from $116 return; if you book online you might sometimes be lucky enough to find fares cheaper than this. See box opposite for contact details for this and other airlines.

The airport has a couple of decent shops if you suddenly remember someone you haven't bought for and you should certainly buy a cup of **Coffee Britt** and fill your pockets with the free tastings of chocolate-covered coffee beans, nuts and fruit for the flight.

7

CUSCO & AROUND

Cusco
(Qosqo, Cuzco)

In the whole of old Peru, there was undoubtably no place that was as deeply revered as the imperial city of Cuzco, which is where all the Inca kings held court and established the seat of government.
Garcilaso Inca de la Vega *The Royal Commentaries of the Incas* (1609)

The cultural and religious centre of the Inca world, Cusco was once a truly awesome city. The seat of the God-king, the Inca, it was built to reflect the might of the Empire. Yet despite its brutal sacking by the Spanish conquistadors, Cusco remains an exciting and vibrant place, much more than just a tourist town. The capital of Cusco Department, it's also the undisputed archaeological capital of South America and a UNESCO World Heritage Site.

Spectacular colonial architecture stands astride monolithic ruined Inca palaces made of perfectly hewn stone, which line atmospheric, scorched cobbled plazas. White-washed alleys and terracotta-tiled roofs house a rich mix of history, lively nightlife and a vast array of museums, sights and scenery. Although it's embraced tourism and developed a sound infrastructure to support the influx of visitors, the city's magnificent historical past still has a powerful hold on its glorious present. The collision and fusion of indigenous Andean and imported colonial cultures is fascinating and always evident, even to those tourists who come to the city only as a staging post for the Inca Trail to Machu Picchu.

The city stands at 3360m (11,000ft) above sea level so the air is thinner here than you might be used to. Upon arrival spend a couple of days acclimatizing before you attempt anything too strenuous.

HISTORY

Origins and early history
Legend states that the city was founded around AD1100 when the original Inca Manco Capac, having descended from the sun and risen from Lake Titicaca, plunged a staff into the soil and declared it fertile enough to support a city, a city he called Cusco (popularly thought to mean 'navel of the earth').

With no written records, the history of Cusco before the arrival of the Spanish is unclear. There is, however, archaeological evidence to suggest that other tribes lived here long before the arrival of the Incas. The Killke were probably the first but they were subjugated by the powerful and successful Huari culture, which came to dominate the area, with the Sacred Valley forming part of their northern highland frontier. Eventually the Huari moved away and the Killke resumed control of the region and secured it with hilltop fortifications. However, they never built in the Cusco valley, leading archaeologists to believe that by the 12th century there were already stable, sizeable settlements there. These weren't strong enough to resist the Incas though, and by the 13th century most had been subdued by the new arrivals, although it wasn't until the early 15th century that Cusco enjoyed its great expansion and rise to prominence.

Inca capital

During its heyday, as the Inca capital, the city must have looked dazzling with gold, silver and precious stones adorning its fine buildings, truly awe-inspiring to the visitor. It was the centre of political power and the cultural and religious heart of the society. All roads led to Cusco: the main roads to each of the four corners of the empire led away from the main plaza, whilst sacred and religious lines from other spiritually significant sites convened on the Coricancha. Built to reflect the enormity of the Incas' achievements and visibly demonstrate their superiority, the city ranked alongside many of the great European buildings when it came to elaborate architecture and sheer opulence.

The city was allegedly constructed on the orders of the Inca Pachacutec, who oversaw the destruction of the original simple structures found there after the conquest and demanded a city of stone be built in their place. Legend tells that Pachacutec went on to design the city in the shape of a puma, one of the Incas' sacred animals: the river Tullumayo forms the spine, the river Huatanay the belly and Sacsayhuaman (see p183) is laid out in the shape of the animal's head. The success of the city was down to Pachacutec's skills as a sophisticated urban planner. The city's superb infrastructure and a series of channels that diverted streams across the city provided fresh drinking water and ferried waste away, making it clean and hospitable.

Sadly the city was gutted in the wake of the Spanish conquest and now appears as a pale imitation of itself. The gold, silver and jewels that adorned the buildings were all looted, whilst the most significant and impressive buildings were all torn down. The infrastructure was damaged and the city allowed to become squalid and dirty. In a final desperate bid to oust the Spanish, the rebel Incas set fire to their own city and torched what was left of their once magnificent capital.

Cusco after the conquest

Once the Spanish had definitively added Peru to the realms of Charles V, they realized that they needed a capital by the sea in order to support their new conquest. Since Cusco was set inland and moreover had strong associations with the past, it wasn't a suitable seat for government. With the transference of power to Lima, Cusco's influence inevitably waned.

The city was rebuilt, using stones pillaged from once great Inca buildings to construct new colonial structures. Often these new buildings rose phoenix-like from the foundations of the Inca buildings, a not-so-subtle visual reminder of the dominance of the Spanish over their subjects. Unfortunately the colonial buildings were less robust than their predecessors and the occasional earthquakes that Peru experiences inevitably reduced them to rubble, leaving the remnants of the Inca architecture still standing.

Despite taking a back seat in determining the country's future and direction, Cusco still enjoyed moments in the headlines. During the 17th and 18th centuries the Cusco School of painting developed here and attracted a worldwide reputation. In 1780 it was the centre for the revolution staged by José Gabriel Condorcanqui, who took on the name Túpac Amaru II. In 1825 Bolívar arrived in the city and later the first royal oath of independence was sworn before the giant blackened crucifix nicknamed *El Señor de los Tremblores*, now kept in the cathedral (see p145).

More recently, with the uncovering and popularization of Machu Picchu and other Inca ruins, the city has developed a role as Peru's most important tourist centre, a fact which has ensured its renaissance and re-emergence as one of the country's most vital, important cities.

❏ Boleto Turístico Unico (BTU) – Visitor's Ticket

Admission to many of Cusco's museums and archaeological sites can only be achieved by using the **Boleto Turístico Unico** (BTU or Visitor's Ticket, 🖳 www.bole toturisticocusco.com or 🖳 http://cosituc.gob.pe), which costs s/130 (US$45) for adults and s/70 for students with a valid ISIC card; it is valid for ten days and is sold at the **Oficina Ejecutiva del Comite** (OFEC; Mon-Sat 8am-4pm, Sun 8am-noon), on the corner of Garcilaso and Plaza Regocijo and at Av El Sol 103 (Mon-Fri 8am-6pm, Sat 8.30am-12.30pm), as well as at most of the sites featured on the ticket.

The ticket allows only one entrance to each of the 16 sites it covers – tiresome if you want to go back – but if you paid entrance fees for all the sites separately it would cost much more than s/130. Note that the ticket does not cover the Coricancha-Santo Domingo complex, merely the small museum in the grounds whose entrance is on Av El Sol. Nor does it include any religious sites.

There is a separate four-site ticket, the **Boleto Partial**, which gives access to either the museums and churches on the list, or the sites of Sacsayhuaman, Qenko, Puca Pucara and Tambo Machay, or Tipón, Pikillacta, Chinchero, Ollantaytambo and Pisac. These tickets are valid for just one day. To further complicate things, there is a **Boleto Religioso** (Religious Sites Ticket) entitling you to entry to the Cathedral, La Compañía, San Blas and the Museo de Arte Religioso that costs s/70 (US$25) and is valid for 10 days.

Tickets are available for the following 'circuits' (all are s/70):
● Sacsayhuaman, Qenko, Puca Pucara and Tambo Machay
● Pachacutec Monument, Municipal Museum of Contemporary Art, Regional History Museum, Popular Art Museum, Coricancha Museum (not the complex) and Centre of Native Dance
● Ollantaytambo, Pisac and Chinchero Ruins
Also available are Tipón, Pikillacta and Santa Catalina Museum

❏ **Casa Concha – new home for Machu Picchu treasures**
As we go to press Yale University has agreed to return everything that was taken from
the ruins between 1911 and 1915 by Hiram Bingham and his team of archaeologists.
It's likely that these will be returned in 2011-2 and housed in a new museum based
in **Casa Concha** (on Santa Catalina de Ancha) in Cusco. It should be widely advertised; enquire at the tourist office if it's not.

WHAT TO SEE

Plaza de Armas

The main square has always been the city's focal point although during the time
of the Incas it was twice as large. Once called Aucaypata ('the square of war or
weeping'), it was a ceremonial site surrounded on three sides by huge Inca mansions. Along one side ran the river Huatanay in a stone ditch. On the far side of
the river stood Cusipata ('the joyful square'), which is where modern-day Plaza
Regocijo now stands. Cusipata was the setting for Inca celebrations and feasts.
Nowadays, colonial arcades full of shops and restaurants line the square, and the
balconies that overlook the original heart of the Inca capital are used by cafés and
restaurants to provide exceptional views. There are usually two flags flying in the
square, the red and white striped Peruvian national flag and the rainbow striped
Quechua flag, which bears a striking resemblance to the gay pride banner, and
from which it can be distinguished by an additional blue line.

The Cathedral

(Mon-Sat 10-11.30am & 2-5.30pm, Sun 2-6pm, entrance through the church of
Jesús María, free with Religious Sites Ticket or s/25) Built between 1556 and
1669 on the site of the Inca Viracocha's palace, the monolithic renaissance-style
cathedral dominates one side of the plaza. The cathedral stands between the
church of Jesús María (to the left as you look at the cathedral) built in 1733, and
Cusco's oldest church, El Triunfo (to the right), which dates from 1536 and is
the resting place of the historian Garcilaso de la Vega. The main doors, which
are discretely marked with a carved puma head, are open first thing in the morning for genuine worshippers. This is an excellent time to slip in and see the
cathedral, and to appreciate the stunning works of art in rather better light than
the gloom that pervades once the doors are shut again.

Full of treasures, the cathedral is one of the city's best repositories of colonial art, particularly from the Cusco School, and a sacristy full of portraits of
priests from the past. There are also carved altars and a very finely carved choir
dating from the 17th century by Martín Torres and Melchor Huamán, as well
as the blackened crucifix, *El Señor de los Tremblores* (the Lord of the
Earthquakes) that was paraded around Cusco in 1650 to stop a giant earthquake
and which now stands in an alcove adjacent to the entrance to El Triunfo. The
parade worked and the event has been commemorated in a giant canvas that
stands facing the entrance of El Triunfo. In the north-east corner of the cathedral there's also a very famous painting of the Last Supper by Marcos Zapata,

with Christ and his disciples feasting on roast *cuy* (guinea pig). Some people hold that the face of Judas is actually a portrait of Pizarro.

The three buildings are periodically restored and worked on, meaning that sections may be shut off or various works of art covered or moved into storage.

La Compañía (Jesuits' Church)

(Mon-Sat 11am-noon & 3-5pm, free with Religious Sites Ticket or s/10) This Jesuit church is the other massive building on Plaza de Armas. Built on the ruins of the palace of the Inca Huayna Capac, described by chronicler Pedro Sancho as the greatest Inca palace, it is a grand building complete with decorative baroque façade and a pair of impressive belfries. Work began in 1578 but a giant earthquake in 1650 practically demolished the building and it wasn't finished until 1668. The Jesuits intended the church to outshine the neighbouring cathedral, but Pope Paul III intervened and declared it must not. Unfortunately by the time the message filtered back to Peru the work had already been completed. The two buildings are quite similar, although some believe that La Compañía eclipses its neighbour.

The interior is cool and dark, the shadows hiding interesting paintings of local weddings that show plenty of period detail, including a representation of the marriage of Martín García de Loyola to the Inca princess Ñusta Beatriz. The catacombs beneath the church are worth exploring and the view from the second floor choir area worth climbing a set of rickety steps to see. Often illuminated at night, the church is visible from many of the hotels and hostels high on the surrounding slopes and can also be seen from the train as it descends into Cusco.

Museo de Historia Natural

(Mon-Fri 9am-noon and 3-6pm, s/2) This motley collection of stuffed local fauna is hidden off Plaza de Armas on the same side as La Compañía. There is also a number of birds, reptiles and snakes from Manu National Park, but the specimens are pretty poor and presentation is disappointing.

Inca walls

The Inca walls that line the north-western side of the plaza are reputed to be part of Pachacutec's palace, whilst those in the northern corner belong to the palace of Sinchi Roca.

Coricancha (Temple of the Sun) and Santo Domingo

(Mon-Sat 8am-5pm, Sun 2-4pm, s/10, s/6 for students, not on the Visitor's Ticket)

> 'All the Incas enriched this city and, among its countless monuments, the Temple of the Sun remained the principal object of their attention. They vied with one another in ornamenting it with incredible wealth, each Inca seeking to surpass his predecessor.' **Garcilaso Inca de la Vega** *The Royal Commentaries of the Incas* (1609)

To the south-east of Plaza de Armas, the Inca Sun Temple, Coricancha, was the centre of the Inca religion, having previously been the site of a Huari sun temple. The building comprised four small sanctuaries set around a central courtyard and was once lavishly decorated with gold plates and precious stones – the name Coricancha is Quechua for 'Golden Enclosure'. Writing 50 years after the conquest, the historian Garcilaso de la Vega described the awe-inspiring magnificence of the main sanctuary, dedicated to the Sun:

> 'The four walls were hung with plaques of gold, from top to bottom, and a likeness of the Sun topped the high altar. This likeness was made from a gold plaque twice as thick as those that paneled the walls, and was composed of a round face, prolonged by rays and flames, the way Spanish painters represent it; the whole thing was so immense that it occupied the entire back of the temple, from one wall to the other.'
>
> **Garcilaso Inca de la Vega** *The Royal Commentaries of the Incas* (1609)

The Spanish Conquistadors pillaged the site and stole the lot.

The other sanctuaries within the temple were dedicated to various deities including the Moon (the bride of the Sun); Venus, the Pleiades and the stars; Thunder and the Rainbow. Garcilaso de la Vega noted that 'They called the rainbow *cuichu* and revered it very specially. When it appeared, they immediately put their hands over their mouths through fear, they said, that it might make their teeth decay. I can't say why'.

The mummies of previous Incas were kept here as were the kidnapped principal idols of tribes that the Incas defeated. 'They were', wrote Garcilaso, 'so well preserved that they seemed to be alive. They were seated on their golden thrones resting on plaques of this same metal, and they looked directly at the visitor.' He went on to describe the astonishing garden outside the temple:

> 'In the time of the Incas, this garden, in which today the convent brothers cultivate their vegetables, was entirely made of gold and silver; and there were similar gardens about all the royal mansions. Here could be seen all sorts of plants, flowers, trees, animals, both small and large, wild and tame, tiny, crawling creatures such as snakes, lizards and snails, as well as butterflies and birds of every size... quinoa as well as other vegetables and fruit trees... very faithfully produced in gold and silver... and large statues of men and women and children made from the same materials.'
>
> **Garcilaso Inca de la Vega** *The Royal Commentaries of the Incas* (1609)

The Spanish looted almost everything from here too.

Conquering Cusco, Juan Pizarro took control of the Coricancha. Fatally wounded at the siege of Sacsayhuaman, he bequeathed the temple to the Dominicans, who built the Monastery of Santo Domingo here. Constructing the monastery on the foundations of the Inca building was meant to demonstrate the superiority of Christianity over the indigenous beliefs. An earthquake in 1950 destroyed the monastery but left the Inca stonework, some of the finest masonry in Peru, undamaged.

The **Chapel of Santo Domingo** also merits a visit, with intricate carvings, the priest's fine clothing and other fabrics on display. The graves of the rebel Incas, Sayuri Túpac and Túpac Amaru, and of the conquistador Juan Pizarro are also contained here. Black and white photographs in the entrance to the complex catalogue the damage sustained by the chapel during the various earthquakes.

Outside the temple is a set of grassy gardens with a pre-Inca spring and bath dating back to the Huari culture. The **Coricancha Site Museum** (Mon-Sat 9am-5pm, Sun 8am-2pm, Visitor's Ticket) is under the gardens and can be accessed by walking downhill from the complex on Avenida El Sol. Although small this archaeological museum boasts some interesting pieces including pre-Inca ceramics and stonework, Inca crafts and carvings, some found in the Coricancha, and a mummy.

West and south of Plaza de Armas

This constitutes the area south of Plateros and north of Avenida El Sol, behind the Portales de Comercio and Confiturías.

● **La Merced** (Mon-Sat 8am-noon & 2-5pm, s/6, s/3 students) Originally built in 1534 this grand church, Cusco's third most important colonial church, was largely reconstructed after the 1650 earthquake in a combination of baroque and renaissance styles. Inside are riches to rival those contained in the Cathedral, with the ornate white-stone cloisters and large collection of Cusco School religious art a special highlight. In a locked cloister is kept the church's most prized possession, a metre-tall solid-gold *monstrance* (vessel) covered in precious stones, diamonds and pearls. Because the church faces on to the market the priests were able to preach directly to the milling crowds of Indians and espouse their message to a large audience. Buried here are the conquistadors Gonzalo Pizarro and Diego de Almagro.

● **Museo y Convento de San Francisco** (Mon-Fri 6.30-8am & 6-8pm, s/5) This forbidding building, dating from the mid-17th century, dominates Plaza San Francisco. Inside are suitably bloodthirsty decorations and paintings by local artists and two crypts piled high with bones.

● **Iglesia de Santa Clara** (Irregular opening hours, free) This 16th-century church is only rarely open, but worth a visit if you are lucky enough to come upon it whilst a service is in progress. If you do go during a service, the nuns sometimes sing from behind a substantial metal grille. Inside the church are huge mirrors; originally intended to lure curious Indians into the building, they now multiply and reflect the candlelight magnificently.

● **Museo Historíco Regional y Casa Garcilaso** (Mon-Sat 8am-5pm, Visitor's Ticket) Originally inhabited by the historian Garcilaso de la Vega, the building was rebuilt by the famous Peruvian architect Víctor Pimentel after the 1986 earthquake reduced it almost to rubble. The museum offers a basic overview of Peruvian history and has a token collection of pre-Inca ceramics, pottery, arrow heads and other Inca weaponry, architectural tools and agricultural implements, a Nazca mummy and some gold jewellery found at Machu Picchu. The main attractions, though, are the colonial furniture and copious examples of the Cusco School of Art, many drawn by Cusquenian artists including Marcos Zapata, Bernando Biti and Antonio Huillca. There are also a number of black and white photographs that capture the aftermath of the 1950 earthquake.

● **Mercado San Pedro** (Daily) An essential stop on any tour of the city, the central market is opposite San Pedro train station. Everything is for sale, from fruit and veg to meats you recognize and some you won't. Noisy, busy, smelly and something of a sensory overload, it's a great place to people-watch. Keep an eye on your wallet and bag as pickpockets and bag slashers operate here and prey on the distracted.

North of Plaza de Armas

Takes in the streets beneath Sacsayhuaman, between Plateros and Triunfo.

● **Iglesia de San Cristóbal** (Irregular opening hours, free) Set high above Cusco, this church is thought to have been built on the site of the palace of Manco Capac, the first Inca. Surrounded by a massive Inca stone wall, the church was built by Inca Paullu as a means of demonstrating his new Christian faith.

● **Museo Inka and Admiral's Palace** (Mon-Fri 8am-7pm, Sat 9am-4pm, s/10) This impressive colonial house stands on Inca foundations, on the corner of Ataud and Tucumán. Inside is a massive stairway, guarded by sculptures of mythical creatures, and an attractive courtyard. The building, originally belonging to Admiral Don Francisco Maldonado, was badly damaged by the 1650 earthquake but was rebuilt and is still a striking structure. Most importantly, the museum houses the finest collection of Inca artefacts in the city and the largest collection of Inca objects in the world. Metal- and gold-work, jewellery, pottery, ceramics, textiles and paintings are all on display and laid out in an easy-to-follow and informative fashion although the English-language explanations are a little basic. There is also a reconstructed burial chamber containing several mummies. High quality, expensive weavings are for sale in the courtyard of the house and you can often find craftsmen working here on the beautiful fabrics.

● **House of the Serpents** So called because of the snakes carved into the door lintels, this house on the Plazoleta de las Nazarenas is reputed to have once belonged to the man responsible for stealing the golden disc of the sun from the Coricancha. Garcilaso de la Vega describes how he lost it:

'When the Spaniards entered Cuzco, this likeness of the Sun, as the result of a division of property, fell into the hands of one of the early conquistadors, who was a man of noble birth by the name of Mancio Serra de Leguisamo, whom I knew very well before I came to Spain. He was a great gambler and he had no sooner acquired this treasure than he gambled and lost it in one night; and we might even say, echoing Father Acosta, that this is the origin of the expression "to gamble the Sun before it rises".' **Garcilaso Inca de la Vega** *The Royal Commentaries of the Incas* (1609)

● **Museo de Arte Precolombino/Casa de Cabrera** (daily 9am-10pm, s/20, student s/10) This small yet fascinating museum is set within the grand, spacious confines of the Earl of Cabrera's colonial mansion. Cabrera was responsible for founding Ica on Peru's coast. The museum covers the artistic achievements of the various ancient Peruvian cultures and houses a superb collection of artefacts from the Moche, Chimú, Paracas, Nazca and Inca cultures. Dating from 1250 to 1532, these archaeological treasures include carvings, ceramics, and gold- and silver-work, all of which are superbly lit and well presented with both English and Spanish text explaining what you are looking at.

● **Hotel Monasterio del Cuzco** This hotel (see p168), Cusco's finest, was converted from the elegant old Seminary of San Antonio Abad. Although a very upmarket establishment, it is possible to visit if you drop in for a beer at the bar. Once through the Inca-colonial doorway you look onto a spacious courtyard, which is only slightly spoiled by the glassed-in cloisters surrounding them.

PRACTICAL INFORMATION
Arrival

As a result of its position high in the Andes, you will need to take a couple of days to acclimatize once you have arrived in Cusco. Do not attempt anything too strenuous whilst your body adjusts during this time. Acclimatization is quicker if you do not eat or drink excessively.

By air The airport (information ☎ 222611) lies 5km from the main Plaza de Armas at Quispiquilla. A ten-minute taxi ride will cost about s/10-15 from the airport car park or about half that from the street outside as drivers here don't have to pay the waiting fee levied by the car park. *Colectivos* to the centre cost even less and can be hailed from the street outside the airport. You could walk to the plaza in around an hour but this isn't particularly safe.

By rail   Trains from Juliaca and Puno arrive at **Huanchac station**, at the south-eastern end of Avenida El Sol, about a 20-minute walk from Plaza de Armas. Taxis from outside the station cost s/5 to the centre of town.

Trains to and from Machu Picchu or Ollantaytambo arrive and depart from **San Pedro station**, also sometimes called Machu Picchu station, which is next to the church of San Pedro and opposite the Mercado San Pedro, a gentle 10-minute stroll from the centre of town.

By bus   Long-distance buses arrive and depart from the Terminal Terrestre on Avenida Vallejo Santoni, close to the giant statue of Pachacutec, south-east of the city centre. A taxi from here to Plaza de Armas will cost around s/5-10 whilst a *colectivo* to the centre will charge s/0.60.

Getting around

The centre of Cusco is fairly compact and easy to explore on foot. For trips after dark or longer journeys consider taking a **taxi** though. These can be found throughout the city, particularly around Plaza de Armas. They ought to charge a flat fare of s/2-3, rising to s/3-4 after 9pm, for journeys in the city, but if they suspect you've just arrived or aren't on the ball they may try to charge you extra. For longer journeys always agree a price in advance as the cabs don't have meters. In the past there have been reports of taxi drivers robbing people. If you are uncomfortable flagging one down in the street, ask your hotel to arrange a taxi or call one of the licensed operators. Aló Cusco (☎ 222222) and Radio Taxi (☎ 222000) are both reliable and have good reputations. Alternatively, catch a communal **colectivo**, which will inevitably be cheaper but less comfortable, and which aren't allowed within two blocks of Plaza de Armas.

There is also a hop-on, hop-off tourist **tram** service, Tranvia (☎ 224377) which operates a 2hr city circuit beginning and ending in Plaza de Armas. Fares cost s/15.

Those on a larger budget may choose to **hire a car**. Avis (🖳 www.avisperu.com) have an office at Av El Sol 808 and cars for US$65 per day, and Localiza (☎ 242285/263448) can be found at Av El Sol 1089.

Orientation

Cusco divides into five districts, each centred on a square or temple. At the heart of the city lies Plaza de Armas. The majority of sights are within easy walking distance of here. South of the Plaza, Avenida El Sol runs past Coricancha. Heading uphill and south-west from Avenida El Sol there are Plaza San Francisco, the central market and

---

❏ Word of warning

Cusco has a deservedly poor reputation for robbery. The areas around the markets and the main San Pedro train station are notorious. San Blas at night is also potentially dangerous. Take care when walking after dark, or hail a taxi.

Iglesia de Santa Clara. One block west of Plaza de Armas is Plaza Regocijo which has Inca origins and contains some of the city's finest mansions and municipal palaces.

From the north-east corner of Plaza de Armas, Calle Triunfo climbs steeply through a stunning Inca-walled street to the artisan quarter of San Blas, centred on an attractive church. Uphill and north-west from Plaza de Armas, Calle Plateros climbs towards the Inca fortress Sacsayhuaman and the giant statue of Christ that overlooks the city.

Banks and cambios

Most of the **banks** are strung out along Avenida El Sol. These all have ATMs with 24-hr access and security protection, from which you can withdraw US$ and soles. Queues are common and service can be slow. Banks typically shut 1-3pm.

Banco de Credito (Av El Sol 189) and **Interbanc** (Av El Sol 380) both have Visa ATMs, handle Amex and can convert travellers' cheques. **Banco Continental** (Av El Sol 366) also has a Visa ATM and changes travellers' cheques but charges commission. **Banco Latino** (Av El Sol 395) has ATMs for Mastercard. **Scotiabank**, at Calle Maruri 315, is a good alternative if you aren't on Av El Sol.

In addition to the ATMs found at the banks, there are also machines in Plaza de Armas, at the entrance to the Inka Grill restaurant, Portal de Panes, Portal Belén, by the entrance to the Cross Keys pub and in the jewellers in the southern corner of the plaza. Machines are also beginning to crop up in the San Blas district.

There are **cambios** all over Cusco, especially on the western side of Plaza de Armas, and it's difficult to pick out any one over the other. These tend to charge slightly higher commission than those on Av El Sol, the best of which is **LAC Dólar** at Av El Sol 150. The street changers tend to congregate outside the major banks, particularly at the top end of Av El Sol. **DHL/Western Union** (☎ 224167) is at Av El Sol 627A and at Maruri 310 (☎ 248028).

Try to save your small change and lower denomination bills as you will need these once outside Cusco, since there is usually a shortage of change in the smaller villages and people will not be able to break a large note for you.

Bookshops

There are a number of places to pick up English-language books around Plaza de Armas on Portal de Comercio and Portal de Confiturías. Elsewhere, try **Jerusalén** at Heladeros 143 (south-west of Plaza de Armas) for guidebooks, postcards and music CDs, or **Librería CBC** (💻 www.cbc.org.pe) at Avenida Tullumayo 465 for material on Peru's history, local anthropology and archaeology. There is a decent book exchange at **The Sun Café** on Plazoleta Limacpampa Chico 471.

Communications

● **Telephone and fax** There are public pay phones everywhere, and it's easy to ring abroad with a Telefonica phonecard that can be bought from almost any of the small shops lining Plaza de Armas. Alternatively, you can get someone else to do it for you in one of the numerous internet cafés, where you can usually also send and receive faxes.

● **Post** For letters, the **correo** (post office; Mon-Sat 7.30am-8pm, Sun 8am-2pm) is on the west side of Av El Sol, No 800, on the fifth block downhill from Plaza de Armas. Poste Restante services are free. DHL have an office at Av El Sol 627A if you want to send packages overseas.

● **Email** Internet cafés open and close around Cusco with alarming regularity. There are a great many to choose from, the main difference being the speed of connection and other facilities on offer: the best places will also have scanners, webcams, CD burners and knowledgeable staff. Rates are fairly standard, costing s/1.50-2 per hour. Worth trying are **Mundo Net** (Santa Theresa 344), which has reliable, fast machines; **Telser** (Calle del Medio 117), which is also reliable; and **Trotamundos** (Portal Comercio 177) set adjacent to the very pleasant café here.

CUSCO & AROUND

Emergencies and medical services

Fire ☎ 103; **Police:** ☎ 105; **Tourist Police**: ☎ 249654 or ☎ free 0800 4 2579 (24 hours), Saphi 510, and an office on Plaza de Armas at Portal Carrizos 250, near the Compañía (9am-6pm); **Hospitals:** Regional ☎ 227661 or 223691 in emergencies, Av de la Cultura; **Tourist Medical Assistance** ☎ 222644/ 621838 (24 hours). **Pharmacy** Millenium (☎ 241784), Calle Santa Catalina Angosta 163 and Inka Farma (☎ 240167), Av El Sol 210 (24 hours).

Equipment rental

Equipment and trekking gear can be hired from the travel agencies along Procuradores or from a number of shops on Plateros. Make sure you check everything carefully in advance as it has been known for bits to be missing and the standard of stuff available can be pretty poor. Butane and other cooking stove fuel can also be bought from these places. To hire anything you will have to leave a deposit and a copy of your passport.

Soqllaq'asa Camping Services (☎ 252560) at Plateros 365 have down sleeping bags, ThermaRest sleeping mats and gas stoves for hire. Cutlery, pots and pans are usually thrown in free. They will sometimes buy your old kit from you too. **Tatoo** on Calle del Medio 130 has high-quality gear available at appropriately high prices. Big brand-name hiking, climbing and camping gear is on offer alongside the house brand clothing.

Trekking provisions

The market Mercado San Pedro opposite San Pedro station is the best place to stock up on basic supplies. Alternatively there are supermarkets at Avenida La Cultura, including **Supermercado D'Dinos** which is open 24hrs. Alternatively try **Supermercado Gato** at Portal Belén 115.

Film and camera shops

Several of the shops lining Plaza de Armas sell print and slide film. Whilst some of these places will also offer to develop your film, it would be much wiser to bring your films home to be developed. Don't rely on being able to buy memory cards or accessories for digital cameras; it's better to bring these from home.

❏ Festivals

Festivals are an intrinsic part of Peruvian life and take place with alarming regularity. The fiestas themselves are almost all vibrant, lively affairs that make for great spectacle. Hard partying, dancing and drinking disguise the fact that the reason for the frenetic festival is usually a practical one, be it a plea for favourable harvests or the health of livestock. The carousing, eating and drinking are considered to be ways of showing thanks for and celebrating the sun and the rain, which give rise to all life. Try to remember this when you awake after several days celebrating feeling rather the worse for wear. See p81 for a list of annual national holidays and festivals.

20th January	**Procession of saints** in the San Sebastián district of Cusco.
February/March	Cusco hosts a wild and debauched **carnival**, with food and water fights in the streets and vast amounts of *chicha* drunk.
Easter Monday	The blackened crucifix **El Señor de los Tremblores** (Lord of the Earthquakes, see p145) is paraded around the city, starting and finishing in Plaza de Armas where thousands of people gather to celebrate and make merry.
2nd/3rd May	The **Vigil of the Cross** is held on any mountain top with a cross on the summit.
June	**Corpus Christi**, on the Thursday after Trinity Sunday, sees all the statues of saints from Cusco's many churches paraded through the city and brought to the Cathedral, which is packed with revellers.

Laundry

You won't have any trouble finding someone willing to take in your laundry for a small consideration. **Lavaclin** at Suecia 400 and **Splendor** at Suecia 326 both collect and deliver your laundry. Also recommended are **Adonai** and **Lavendería Louis** on Choquechaca and **Easy Wash** and **Inka Laundry** on Calle Ruinas. Otherwise there are a host of *lavandarías* on Procuradores and Plateros. Most places are open 7.30am-8pm.

Language courses

Peru has become an increasingly popular country in which to study Spanish. Most organizations run classes for 20hrs. It is cheaper to study for a longer period of time or in a group though. One-to-one sessions cost US$15-20 whilst group classes cost US$5-10 per hour.

Of all the language schools in Cusco, the best is probably **Academia Latinoamericana de Español** (☎ 243364, 🖳 www.latinoschool.com) at Plaza Limacpampa 565, which can also arrange for you to stay with a host family. Also try: **Amauta**

(☎ 262345, 🖳 www.amautaspanish.com), Suecia 480, 2nd Floor; **Amigos Spanish School** (☎ 242292, 🖳 www.spanishcusco .com), Zaguan del Cielo B-23; **Cusco Spanish School** (☎ 226928, 🖳 www.cusco spanishschool.com), Calle Carcilaso 265, 2nd Floor; **Excel** (☎ 235298, 🖳 www.excel-spanishlanguageprograms-peru.org), Calle Cruz Verde 336, **San Blas Spanish School** (☎ 247898, 🖳 www.spanishschoolperu .com), Carmen Bajo 224.

Tourist information

There is a very helpful **iPeru** tourist office in the arrivals hall of the airport, and a less helpful and reliable one at Portal Mantas 117 in the arcade next to the Merced (☎ 252974 /263176). They both hand out free maps and provide information.

There is also an iPeru office on the ground floor at Av El Sol 103 (☎ 252974, 24hr help line ☎ 01 574 8000, 🖳 www.peru.info; Mon-Sat 8.30am-7.30pm), which provides tourist information and assistance. OFEC (see p144) have an office in the same building on the opposite side of the entrance hall.

June	The festival and pilgrimage of **Qoyllur Rit'i** led by the ukuku bear dancers (see p97), is held on the glaciers north of Ausangate, the mountain 150km south-east of Cusco.
24th June	**Inti Raymi** (the Resurrection of the Sun) is the ancient Inca festival of the winter solstice. Re-enacted at Sacsayhuaman, the lavish festival actually begins at the Coricancha, from where a procession makes its way through Cusco and up to the ruins above the city. The entire spectacle lasts all day and is a great family day out for locals.
16th-18th July	The **fiesta of the Virgen del Carmen** is held in Paucartambo, 80km east of Cusco during the Quechua month of Earthly purification. The statue of the virgin is paraded through the town amidst boisterous dancing, drinking and re-enactments of battles between mythical figures during which good triumphs over evil for another year.
August	On the last Sunday of the month the Inca manhood rite of passage **Huarachicoy** is re-enacted at Sacsayhuaman.
8th September	The **Day of the Virgin** is marked by parades and masked dancers performing in Plaza de San Francisco.
8th December	Everywhere shuts down around noon on the city's **national day**.
24th December	The plaza is packed with stalls and artisans for **Santuranticuy**, the Buying of Saints Festival which is nowadays a celebration of Christmas shopping.

The **South American Explorers Club** (☎ 245484, 🖳 www.saexplorers.org) has a clubhouse at Atoqsaycuchi 670, San Blas (Mon-Fri 9.30am-5pm & Sat 9.30am-1pm). It is a veritable treasure trove of information, and members receive discounts at many of the hotels, sights and entertainments in Cusco.

Entrance tickets for Machu Picchu (see p333) are available from the **Instituto Nacional de Cultura** (☎ 236061, Mon-Fri 9am-1pm & 4-6pm, Sat 9-11am) office on Calle San Bernardo, south west of Plaza de Armas, between Mantas and Almagro.

Tour agencies

Listed here are some of the more established agencies with good reputations and a solid history of delivering services of a high standard, in line with the regulations and requirements to look after porters and crew. Inclusion in the list is no guarantee of quality, though; you should do your own research before settling on a group to guide you.

❑ TOUR AGENCIES, LICENCES AND WHAT THEY REALLY REPRESENT

Background Over the last decade the Peruvian government has introduced a series of rules and regulations designed to control and regulate access to the Inca Trail and so reduce the environmental impact of thousands of trekkers descending on the trail every year. The rules are stringently adhered to, so you must be aware of them (see p206 for a comprehensive list of Inca Trail regulations).

One of the requirements is that for **any trek that uses a stretch of the classic Inca Trail you must have a licensed guide and a trekking permit, both of which must come from a regulated agency**. Consequently this is also a requirement for the short Inca Trail from Km104 and for the Salkantay Trek. At the time of writing this wasn't a requirement for the Santa Teresa, Vilcabamba or Choquequirao treks, but the situation may change and there have been various whispers about proposed alterations to the regulations to include some or all of these routes.

Licence requirements In theory a licence means that the agency has satisfied a series of criteria and been deemed professional and responsible enough to organize treks. They should have good equipment, provide a reasonable standard of food and service and employ properly qualified guides. However, there are still a lot of frankly poor companies in Cusco who have been allowed to operate. The cheaper deals they tend to offer aren't necessarily the best value and almost certainly mean a compromise in standards. These agencies have a reputation for cutting corners, for pairing up groups with others, for failing to provide a Spanish-speaking, let alone English-speaking guide, for being environmentally insensitive and not clearing up after themselves and for failing to look after their porters. On top of this, the food's likely to be pretty grim, the equipment dodgy and there are usually hidden costs that make the whole unpleasant experience more expensive than it was first advertised. Essentially, you get what you pay for.

At the time of writing over 170 agencies licensed to operate Inca Trail treks were competing for business. The list is reviewed every year, with licenses renewed or revoked, so before handing over any money make sure to check carefully that the agency you are considering is still allowed to operate and has the requisite paperwork. Be aware that **licences are only issued to Peruvian companies**, not to overseas outfits or foreign tour operators. For the most comprehensive list of up-to-date licensed agencies check out 🖳 www.andeantravelweb.com where there are links to the Spanish-language only 🖳 www.machupicchu.gob.pe DRCC (Direccion Regional de Cultura Cusco) website showing permit availability.

● **Adventours SAS** (☏ 249194, 💻 www .sastravelperu.com; Calle Garcilaso 270) Large, well-organized agency with a plenty of staff and guides meaning that it is able to offer regular Inca Trail departures as well as treks to Salkantay, Choquequirao and the Lares Valley. Justifiably popular and a little more expensive because of it, especially if you want to travel in a small group. Also offers white-water rafting, mountain-biking and horse-riding expeditions.

● **Amazonas Explorer** (☏ 252846, 💻 www.amazonas-explorer.com; Av Colla-suyo 910, Miravalle) Specialist white-water rafting (see p160) and mountain-biking company owned by British and Swiss expats living in Cusco that is renowned for its adventure tours but which also runs decent, small group, fixed departure Inca Trail trips as well as treks on the Choquequirao to Huancacalle route. Has a good reputation for treating its porters and staff well and paying proper salaries.

Costs and paying There is a wide range of prices quoted for trekking the Inca Trail – from about US$400 to virtually whatever you're prepared to part with. Realistically a classic four-day trek will set you back US$450-550. Although there are deals out there for less than this, simple arithmetic combining all the individual food and transport costs, entrance fees, permits and equipment hire shows that it just isn't possible to run a good-quality trek for less than US$400. Don't allow agencies to fob you off with 'estimates' either, get a definite quote to prevent a nasty surprise later.

At the upper end of the scale, charging upwards of US$600 are the exclusive agencies such as **Condor Travel**, **Explorandes**, **Inka Natura** and **Inca Explorers**. Good quality mid-range outfits selling treks from US$420 to US$550 but still offering a high-level of service and a responsible attitude towards their porters include **Peru Treks**, **Q'ente**, **SAS** and **United Mice**. At the cheaper end of the market but still capable of delivering an all-round good service without compromising standards or porter welfare is **Wayki Trek**.

When it comes to buying a trek, always pay for it at the agency's office and demand a written receipt and contract. There have been various instances where people claiming to be representatives of big agencies have taken money for a place on a trek at a bus station or airport and simply disappeared with the cash.

Arriving in Cusco without a booking It hasn't been possible to just pitch up in Cusco and arrange to walk the Inca Trail for some time now, but still people arrive expecting to do just this. At the very slowest times of year (Dec-Jan) it might be possible to pull something together within a couple of weeks, but usually you have to book a place on a trek at least three months in advance of the departure date. During the high season (Jun-Aug) you should consider signing up five to six months in advance to guarantee availability, especially if you aren't able to be flexible about departure dates.

Should you arrive in Cusco without anything arranged though, don't despair. There are plenty of alternatives to the classic Inca Trail and it is possible to organize a trek on the Santa Teresa route (which actually finishes at Machu Picchu) at shorter notice. However, because this trek isn't regulated there is scope for unlicensed operators and guides to be used, so again, be careful when booking. Other treks that are currently unregulated and so easier to arrange are the Vilcabamba and Choquequirao treks. You might also want to consider the Ausangate Circuit or Lares Valley trek, or multi-day white-water rafting, mountain-biking or jungle trips.

If you are interested in activities other than trekking see box p160.

● **Andina Travel** (☎ 251892, 🖳 www.and inatravel.com; Plazoleta Santa Catalina 219) Recommended American-Peruvian outfit committed to supporting local communities through sustainable development and which runs good quality Inca Trail, Santa Teresa, Salkantay and Choquequirao treks as well as 10-day trips from Choquequirao to Machu Picchu and 6-day treks from Huancacalle to Machu Picchu. They can also arrange jungle trips and bespoke treks. Prices are dependent on group size.

● **Apumayo** (☎ 246018, 🖳 www.apumayo .com; Jr Ricardo Palma Ñ-11, Santa Monica) Professional, high-quality white-water rafting specialist (see p160) with a strong environmental agenda offering excellent, adventurous outings according to a fixed timetable. They are sensitive to the impact they have on the rivers and are heavily involved in programmes to maintain the cleanliness of the Rio Urubamba. Also run trips and tours in the Sacred Valley region as well as Inca Trail, Salkantay and Choquequirao treks.

● **Big Foot** (☎ 238568, 🖳 www.bigfoot cusco.com; Triunfo 392) Tends to focus on tailor-made itineraries but does run a 10-day Vilcabamba trek that isn't readily available elsewhere in addition to the more standard Inca Trail, Salkantay, Santa Teresa and Ausangate Circuit treks.

● **Condor Travel** (☎ 225961, 🖳 www.con dortravel.com; Calle Saphi 848) Expensive, top-end agency offering high-class tours and trips throughout Peru. Slick and professional operation with regular departures on the Inca Trail as well as other treks in the Cusco area. Well-connected and the local representative for a number of international airlines if you are after plane tickets.

● **Ecotrek Peru** (DYF Expediciones; ☎ 247286, 🖳 www.ecotrekperu.com; Carmen Alto 246, San Blas) Decent, porter-friendly outfit run by an ex-manager of the South American Explorers Club that specializes in jungle trips to the Pongo de Mainique but which also arranges single and multi-day mountain-biking tours and cultural trips as well as treks in the Cusco region, including the Inca Trail, Salkantay, Choquequirao and a 9-day Vilcabamba trip.

● **Enigma** (☎ 222155, 🖳 www.enigmaperu .com; Jr Clorinda Matto de Turner 100) Smaller, Peruvian-owned quality operator based away from the city centre in a residential part of town offering reasonably priced mid-range treks supported with good equipment and some knowledgeable guides on the Inca Trail, Salkantay, Santa Teresa and Choquequirao treks as well as the Ausangate Circuit and cultural treks such as the Lares Valley hike.

● **Explorandes** (☎ 238380, 🖳 www.explor andes.com; Av Garcilaso 316-A) Well-established major tour operator at the top-end of the market, with correspondingly high prices, that offers a superb range of treks throughout Peru including the classic Inca Trail, Salkantay, Santa Teresa, Choquequirao and 10-day Choquequirao to Machu Picchu trek in addition to expeditions to the Colca Canyon and Cordilleras Blanca and Huayhuash. Departures are flexible and group sizes are kept small. Also ecologically aware, committed to preserving the environment and conscious of the need for the further development of eco-tourism.

● **Inca Explorers** (☎ 241070, 🖳 www.inca explorers.com; Ruinas 427) Run by the first full-time female Inca Trail guide and known for their ecological and mystical tours, they generally have a good reputation for small group treks. As well as various multi-day tours and treks they also offer longer treks such as the Choquequirao to Machu Picchu trek and a 13-day trip from Choquequirao to Vilcabamba. A small percentage of their profit is reinvested into the porters' communities.

● **Inka Natura** (Lima ☎ 440-2022, 🖳 www .inkanatura.com; Manuel Bañon 461, San Isidro, Lima) Pricey, professional outfit that specializes primarily in jungle trips to Manu where they run excellent natural history and bird-watching treks, but also has various Inca Trail, Salkantay, Choquequirao and Choquequirao to Machu Picchu treks and Cusco regional hikes that are similarly well-supported and similarly expensive.

● **Llama Path** (☎ 240822, 🖳 www.llama path.com; Calle San Juan de Dios 250) Mid-range outfit operated by a Peruvian-English partnership that has a wide range of treks, including the Inca Trail, Santa Teresa, Salkantay and Choquequirao treks, at reasonable rates. They also run a Vilcabamba to Machu Picchu trip. Inclined to try and keep group numbers small they have dependable, fixed departure dates and are committed to sustainable tourism.

● **Machete Tours** (☎ 224829, 🖳 www .machetetours.com; Calle Nueva Alta 432) Budget operator run by a Peruvian-Danish pair that's more often associated with jungle trips to Manu or climbing and hiking expeditions around Huaraz but who also run Inca Trail, Salkantay and Vilcabamba outings as well as regular treks to Choquequirao and nine-day treks between Choquequirao and Machu Picchu.

● **Mayuc** (☎ 232666, 🖳 www.mayuc.com; Portal Confituras 211) White-water-rafting specialist that operates single and multi-day trips to tackle the Urubamba, Apurímac and Tambopata rivers. Also set up to run private and group treks on the Inca Trail, Salkantay/Choquequirao, Choquequirao to Machu Picchu, and Vilcabamba Trail.

● **Mountain Lodges of Peru** (☎ 243636, 🖳 www.mountainlodgesofperu.com; Av El Sol 948, Of 403) This is the only agency offering lodge accommodation on the route to Machu Picchu. Accommodation along the Santa Teresa trail is in a series of private lodges although for the pleasure of not camping you will have to pay a princely sum. The company is environmentally aware and involved in clean-up projects. They are also responsible for founding an artisan association in Mollepata, whose goods are sold at the lodges.

● **PeruTreks and Adventure** (☎ 222722, 🖳 www.perutreks.com; Av Pardo 540) Peruvian-English trekking specialist that focuses on the Inca Trail and which has an excellent reputation for looking after their porters and crew. They are also heavily involved with sustainable tourism, and plough much of their profit into schemes and projects set up to help local people and communities. They also run a **homestay programme** where you can stay with families in Chinchero (see p190) or Amaru (north of Pisac) and experience their way of life and culture.

● **Q'ente** (☎ 222535, 🖳 www.qente.com; Calle Choquechaca 229, 2nd Floor) Upmarket mid-range agency whose name is Quechua for 'hummingbird', with ambitions to be the biggest and best in Cusco. Helpful and accommodating staff, knowledgeable guides and a wide range of treks on offer make them a good bet. Treks include the Inca Trail, Santa Teresa, Salkantay, Choquequirao, Vilcabamba and Ausangate Circuit in addition to a 9-day Choquequirao to Machu Picchu route and a 17-day Choquequirao to Espíritu Pampa trip. They also boast numerous city and Sacred Valley tours.

● **United Mice** (☎ 221139, 🖳 www.united mice.com; Calle Plateros 351) This is the budget outfit with the most memorable name, which offers a range of treks including a number of limited departures on the Inca Trail, Salkantay, Choquequirao and Choquequirao to Machu Picchu treks. Popular and good-value, although the treks aren't as cheap as they once were, the company also offers mountain-biking and rafting trips. A small percentage of their profit is donated to a foundation supporting street kids in Cusco.

● **Wayki Trek** (☎ 224092, 🖳 www.wayki trek.net; Av Pardo 510, Paseos de los Héroes) Small budget agency, whose name is Quechua for 'brother', with a reputation and popularity that belies their size. On offer are good-value Inca Trail treks but also Salkantay, Choquequirao and 9-day Choquequirao to Machu Picchu treks in addition to the Ausangate Circuit, all in groups around half the size of most other operators. The company also offers trekkers the chance to spend a day with a porter prior to their trip, to visit their village and to learn a little more about their lives as a way of showing how closely they work with their teams.

CUSCO & AROUND

❏ AGENCIES SPECIALIZING IN ACTIVITIES OTHER THAN TREKKING

Although synonymous with world-class trekking, there are plenty of other activities on offer around Cusco, and many people take the chance to indulge their passion for adrenalin sports whilst here. Whether you want to ride the rapids through the Sacred Valley, float high over the landscape or crash through it on two wheels, there's something for all levels of ability and experience. Equally if you want to escape the activity and retreat to the forest in search of some of Peru's enormously diverse flora and fauna, there are agencies that are particularly good in putting together jungle itineraries.

For a one-stop adrenalin fix visit **Action Valley** (☎ 240835, 🖳 www.action valleycusco.com; office in Cusco at Calle Santa Teresa 325), 11km outside Cusco on the road to Urubamba and Abancay, where you can try bungee jumping, slingshot (the reverse of a bungee jump), bridge swinging or use their climbing wall.

White-water rafting

White-water rafting is an exhilarating rush, and Cusco boasts access to several rivers with world-class runs and rapids. The sport is inherently dangerous so make sure you check out the company you sign up with carefully and bear in mind that budget outfits may have sub-standard equipment or poorly trained guides. In the Cusco region there are five main options for rafting: the Río Urubamba is a scenic float through the heart of the Sacred Valley with grade 2-3 rapids; the Cusipata is slightly more thrilling with more grade 3 rapids; the Chuquicahuana offers grade 3-4 rapids. Multi-day trips are made on the Río Apurímac, which features some of Peru's finest white water and the Río Tambopata, which allows you to explore the jungle in an unusual way.

● **Amazonas Explorer** (see p157) Professionally run and popular agency headed up by a British-Swiss partnership that specializes in adventure activities but is best known for its exhilarating multi-day white-water rafting expeditions on the Apurímac and Tambopata rivers. Also runs an epic 16-day trip from Lake Titicaca to the Amazon using canoes, rafts and 4x4s as well as standard Inca Trail and Choquequirao treks.

● **Apumayo Expeditions** (see p158) Organizes day trips on the Urubamba and multi-day trips on the Apurímac (4 days), Cotahuasi and Tambopata (12-day safari).

● **Eric Adventures** (☎ 234764, 🖳 www.ericadventures.com; Urb Velasco Astete B-8-B) White-water specialist with a lot of adventure activities such as mountain biking, climbing, paragliding and horse riding on their books.

● **Mayuc** (see p159) Offers day trips on the Urubamba, Cusipata or Chuquicahuana as well as 4-day expeditions on the Apurímac.

Paragliding and ballooning

For an alternative view of the Sacred Valley consider taking to the air and flying or floating across the countryside. The Sacred Valley provides exciting but challenging flying conditions and if the wind isn't just right your trip will, very sensibly, be postponed.

● **Wayra** (see *Sol y Luna*, p191) For a thrilling alternative view of the Sacred Valley consider taking one of the tandem flights offered by this Urubamba-based outfitter. Flights launch from two sites in Chinchero and cost US$100. They also offer three- and eight-day courses for people who want more than a brief introduction to the sport.

● **Globos de los Andes** (☎ 232352, 🖳 www.globosperu.com; Av de la Cultura 220) Less challenging than paragliding but still a great way to get a condor's eye view of the Sacred Valley and Cusco region are the balloon trips organized by this respected outfitter. Multi-day trips using balloons and 4WD vehicles can also be arranged.

● **Eric Adventures** (see above) offer a three-day paragliding course in Chinchero and a 900m tandem jump as a single-day activity.

Mountain biking

Cusco is an excellent base for mountain biking and there are masses of well-used farm roads, single tracks and dirt trails through the surrounding mountains and countryside offering exciting alternatives to trekking. Facilities are pretty basic and hire equipment isn't great so serious cyclists should bring their own bikes. However, a number of agencies in Cusco offer mountain-bike tours in and around the Sacred Valley, the most popular being day trips to Maras, Moray and Salineras (see pp194-5), or to the Inca ruins at Pikillacta and Tipon (see pp203-4). Multi-day tours explore the Lares Valley or even venture into the jungle.
- **Ecotrek Peru** (see p158)
- **Eric Adventures** (see opposite).
- **Adventours SAS Travel** (see p157).

Climbing

The Cordilleras Vilcabamba and Vilcanota provide some challenging routes for mountaineers with experience and their own gear. There are few opportunities for inexperienced climbers though, and hire kit is often barely adequate. There are few guides or companies capable of leading expeditions in Cusco, the majority being based in Huaraz instead.

Eric Adventures (see opposite) offer a half-day rock climbing course near Sacsayhuaman and a full-day canyoning expedition near Pisac.

Jungle trips

The rainforest and jungle within easy reach of Cusco is some of the finest in Peru. Without too much effort it's possible to swap the Andes for the Amazon and immerse yourself in an entirely different landscape.
- **Amazon Trails Peru** (☎ 437499, ⌨ www.amazontrailsperu.com; Calle Tandapata 660) German-Peruvian outfit that runs multi-day tours to Manu and owns their own private nature reserve situated to the south-east of Manu. They also have their own accommodation, Amazonas Hostal, in Cusco (see p167). In addition, they organize a handful of trips and treks in the Cusco and Sacred Valley area including the Inca Trail, Salkantay and Choquequirao to Machu Picchu trek.
- **Inka Natura** (see p158) Offer trips to Manu where you stay either in their own Manu Wildlife Centre or a luxury tented camp alongside Cocha Salvador, one of the area's most stunning oxbow lakes.
- **Manu Expeditions** (☎ 225990 or 224235, ⌨ www.manuexpeditions.com; Calle Clorinda Matto de Turner #330) Brilliant, well-established outfit set-up by self-confessed 'birding bum' Barry Walker that organizes and runs group and tailor-made trips to the Manu biosphere.

Private guides

There's also a handful of private guides registered with Inrena, the government agency committed to managing and conserving the national parks and archaeological sites. It can be difficult to track these people down because they are usually affiliated to a larger agency and don't want to spoil the relationship they have with their employers. However, a list can be obtained from the Asociación de Guías Oficiales de Turismo (☎ 249758, ⌨ www.agoturcusco.org.pe). The website ⌨ www.leaplocal.org also recommends local people qualified to lead treks and tours.

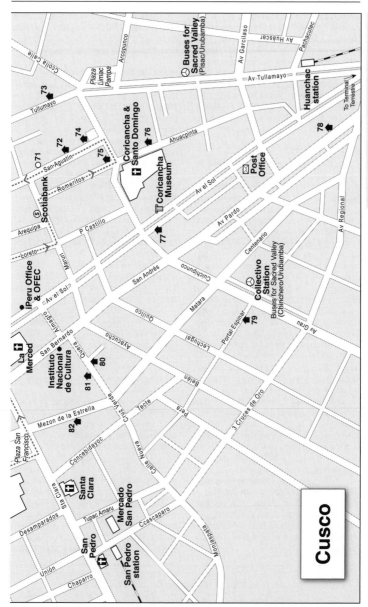

Cusco

Embassies and consulates

Austria (☎ 246595), Confraternidad 434; **Belgium** (☎ 251278), José G Cosio 307; **France** (☎ 233610), Av Micaela Bastidas 101, Diagonal, 4th Floor, Huanchac; **Germany** (☎ 235459), San Agustín 307; **Holland** (☎ 224322), Av El Sol 954; **Ireland** (☎ 243514), Santa Catalina Ancha 360; **Italy** (☎ 224398), Av Garcilaso 700, Huanchac; **UK** (☎ 239974), Barry Walker, Av Pardo 895; **USA** (☎ 231474), Av Pardo 845.

WHERE TO STAY

Cusco is extraordinarily well-equipped for tourists and has an enormous number of places to stay that should suit all tastes and budgets. Whilst rates are proportionally more expensive than elsewhere in Peru, they still tend to represent remarkably good value for money. Quoted prices also tend to be negotiable, as they are seasonally affected and driven by demand. The city gets busiest during July and August, particularly during the run-up to Inti Raymi, when rates rocket by as much as 20%, but outside of peak season you ought to be able to negotiate a good deal. Plaza de Armas is understandably the focus for most people when looking for places to stay, but these tend to be the hotels with the most inflated prices and often represent the worst value for money. Step away from the plaza, though, and there are good deals aplenty, particularly in the hilly streets that lead up to Sacsayhuaman or up towards the San Blas district. Bear in mind that many of the very cheap places to stay are often in the less salubrious, less safe parts of town. Breakfast is not always a given so it is included in the description where it is available. Many of the places below now have wi-fi.

An organization, **Casas de Hospedaje** (Family House Association, ☎ 242710, 🖥 www.cusco.net/familyhouse), has been set up to find accommodation with local families in family-run hostels and provides an alternative, more intimate way of staying in the city.

Note: Abbreviations used below are as follows: **sgl/dbl/tpl** = single/double/triple room, **att** = room with attached bathroom, **com** = room with common bathroom.

Plaza de Armas and around

Budget A good budget bet in a central location is the youth hostel **Albergue Municipal** (☎ 252506, 🖥 albergue@muni cusco.gob.pe), at Kiskapata 240, which is spanking clean, has a café and good views from a sunny concrete balcony. It costs s/15 per person with a discount for members and is a great place to stay if you're in a group. The dorms have bunk beds for four to eight people. Also recommended is **Hostal Resbalosa** (☎ 224839/240461, 🖥 www .hostalresbalosa.com), Calle Resbalosa 494, which has a bright friendly courtyard, beautiful 180° views over the town towards Mount Ausangate, and costs just s/15/23/35 (dorm/sgl/dbl, com). Avoid the rooms around the entrance, which are older and noisier. Taxis can only reach within about 100m of the hostal as it is set on a steep, cobbled, pedestrian-only street.

Another good-value place is **Hostal Rojas** (☎ 228184, 🖥 http://hostalrojas cusco.com), Tigre 129, with a pleasant green courtyard behind enormous front doors; rates are s/25/35/45 (sgl/dbl/tpl, com), s/50/70 (sgl/dbl, att). Try to get the top floor rooms, which have a view and are slightly quieter.

Other places worth looking at in this area include the two Hostals Suecia run by the same friendly people, popular with foreigners. **Hostal Suecia I** (☎ 233282, 🖥 www.hostalsuecia1.com), is at Calle Suecia 332. The plain rooms surrounding the courtyard cost s/60/90/120 (sgl/dbl/tpl all with attached bathroom). **Hostal Suecia II** (☎ 239757), set in a colonial-style building at Tecescocha 465 costs s/20/30 (sgl/dbl, com), and has some rooms with attached bathroom for s/30/50 (sgl/dbl). There's also **Hostal Machu Picchu** (☎ 231111), Calle Quera 282, with its two colonial courtyards,

CUSCO MAP KEY – see previous pages for map

Where to stay
1 Hostal Familiar
2 El Balcón Inn
3 Loki Backpackers Hostel
4 Niños 2
5 Niños
6 Hostal Tumi
7 Hotel Picoaga
8 Hotel Royal Inka II
9 Hotel Royal Inka I
12 Hotel Garcilaso
14 Casa Andina Plaza
15 Hostal San Isidro Labrador
16 Hostal Suecia II
17 Hostal Corihuasi
21 Hostal Rojas
29 Del Prado Inn
30 Hostal Suecia I
31 Hostal Resbalosa
32 Albergue Muncipal
35 Hostal Rumi Punku
36 Hotel Arqueologo
37 Los Apus Hotel y Mirador
39 Casa de Campo Hostal
40 Hospedaje Familiar Kuntur Wasi
41 Hostal Pensión Alemana
42 Hostal El Grial
44 Casona los Pleiades
46 Amazonas Hostal

47 Marani
49 Hospedaje Sambleño
51 Boutique Hotel Casa San Blas
55 Amaru Hostal
58 Hotel Monasterio
62 Casa Andina Catedral
63 Emperador Plaza Hotel
66 Novotel Cusco
67 Albergue Casa Campesina
68 Hotel Ruinas
69 Orquídea Real Hostal
70 Casa Andina San Blas
72 Casa Andina Koricancha
73 Estrellita
74 Casa Andina Private Collection
75 Hotel Libertador Palacio del Inka
76 Hostal Pascana
77 Maison de la Jeunesse
78 La Posada del Abuelo
79 Sonesta Posada del Inca Cusco
80 Los Aticos
81 Hostal Machu Picchu
82 The Point

Where to eat and drink
10 Chi Cha
11 El Truco
13 Kin Taro
18 Los Perros

19 Victor Victoria
20 Big Blue Martini
22 A la Petite France
23 Sumaq Misky
24 The Muse
25 La Tertulia
26 Chez Maggy
27 Kusikuy
28 Mystique
33 Fallen Angel
34 MAP Café
38 La Quinta Eulalia
43 7 Angelitos
45 Km0
48 La Bodega
50 Pachapapa
52 El Buen Pastor
53 Macondo
54 Granja Heidi
56 Café Cultural Ritual
57 Jack's
58 Hotel Monasterio
59 Mandela's Bar
60 Cicciolina
61 Greens
64 Rosy O'Grady's
65 Al Grano
71 Moni

CUSCO & AROUND

tiled floors and flower-filled courtyard, s/40/70/100 (sgl/dbl/tpl, com). *Los Aticos* (☎ 231710, 🖳 www.losaticos.com), Quera 253, is a good bet for longer stays. Small and simple, it has a free self-service laundry room and kitchen facilities. Peruvian cookery classes are also taught here. Rooms cost US$25/35 (sgl/dbl, att).

The Point (☎ 252266, 🖳 www .thepointhostels.com), at Mesón de la Estrella 172, is part of a well-respected small chain that provides secure, clean, comfortable surroundings for backpackers at reasonable rates, although they tend to be raucous, party-fuelled places: the Horny Llama Bar here does little to dispel this reputation. Dorms in the spacious colonial house cost s/24-32 depending on the number of beds, whilst single rooms cost s/40 and doubles s/80. *Hostal Tumi* (☎ 244413), Siete Cuartones 245, s/15/25 (sgl/dbl, com), s/25/30 (sgl/dbl, att) is a real gringo dive in need of a bit of care and attention but is cheap and popular with young travellers because of it.

Mid-range *Loreto Boutique Hotel* (see Cusco centre map p171, ☎ 226352, 🖳 www.loretoboutiquehotel.com; US$75/95 /115 sgl/dbl/tpl, att), Calle Loreto 115, deserves a mention because some of the rather dark rooms have genuine Inca walls; it's right on the plaza, down an alley adjacent to La Compañía.

Much better value is *Hostal Corihuasi* (☎ 232233, 🖳 www.corihuasi.com), Calle Suecia 561, Casilla Postal 157, which charges US$38/49/60 (sgl/dbl/tpl, att, breakfast) during low season and US$6 more for each type of room during the high season. This labyrinthine, larger hotel set on the slopes north of the plaza is favoured by some adventure-tour companies and can get fully booked easily. The good-sized rustic rooms are equipped with alpaca blankets and woven textiles. Try to get the room directly above reception (No 1) which has the best view in all Cusco. Price includes complimentary pick up from the airport. If you fancy something a little more central there's *Emperador Plaza Hotel* (☎ 261733/227412, 🖳 www.emperadorplaza

.com), Santa Catalina Ancha 377. It's clean, has cable TV in the rooms and costs from US$55/58/68 (sgl/dbl/tpl, att, breakfast); the balcony rooms are best.

Another good option is the *Del Prado Inn* (☎ 224442, 🖳 www.delpradoinn.com), Calle Suecia 310, a smart hotel charging US$70-80/102-120/125 (sgl/dbl/tpl, att) depending on whether the room has a balcony or not. At the top end of this price bracket but it's worth the money if you're looking for an efficient, friendly place to stay in a superb central location. Some rooms have balconies although they can be noisy; the dining room boasts original Inca walls.

Expensive *Hotel Ruinas* (☎ 260644, 🖳 www.hotelruinas.com), Calle Ruinas 472, is a well-sited place popular with business travellers and tour groups that has little real character although the rooms are spacious and well-presented. Those with outside views are the best. It is well run but is a little overpriced at US$100/125/155 (sgl/dbl /tpl, att, breakfast). *Hotel Picoaga* (☎ 227691, 🖳 www.picoagahotel.com), Santa Teresa 344, was once the colonial home of the Marques de Picoaga and is now a much better bet as somewhere to stay. Large double rooms around the attractive, shady courtyard of this fine colonial building cost upwards of US$180, whilst suites start at US$300. *Sonesta Posada del Inca Cusco* (☎ 227061, 🖳 www.sonesta.com/CuscoPos adas), one block from the plaza at Portal Espinar 108, is a very accommodating, hospitable place to stay with rooms on the upper floors looking out on to the plaza and its own restaurant. Rack rates start at US$125 /135/160 (sgl/dbl/tpl, att) but good discounts are possible throughout the quieter part of the year and if you book well in advance.

San Blas and around
Budget *Hospedaje Familiar Kuntur Wasi* (☎ 227570), Tandapata 352A, is run by a very considerate, friendly local family. Regular hot water, access to a decent kitchen and the friendly atmosphere make this a good choice, which will only set you back s/25/40 (sgl/dbl, com) or s/40/80

(sgl/dbl, att). The recommended *Hospedaje Sambleño* (☎ 262979), Carmen Alto 114, which is built around a maze of staircases, has cable TV in the lobby and is a bargain at s/20 per person for a room with attached lavatory.

Mid-range There are numerous options in this bracket in this area. *Amaru Hostal* (☎ 225933, 💻 www.cusco.net/amaru), Cuesta San Blas 541, is an old house with a sociable green courtyard filled with geraniums in rusty cans. Some of the rooms off the courtyard boast original Inca walls. It also has a free book exchange, piano and oxygen. They charge US$23/29 (sgl/dbl, com), US$33/43/55 (sgl/dbl/tpl, att). If you're after a pleasant little bed and breakfast joint try *Casona los Pleiades* (☎ 506430, 💻 www.casona-pleiades.com), Tandapata 116, which has compact, tidy rooms in a renovated colonial house overlooking the city and costing US$53/71 (sgl, dbl, att, breakfast). The staff here are helpful, friendly and keen to offer advice.

Amazonas Hostal (☎ 236770, 💻 www .amazonhotelcusco.com), Calle Tandapata 660 is a bright, friendly place run by a trekking and tour agency (Amazon Trails Peru, see p161) that offers reasonable rooms for US$28/40/52 (sgl/dbl/tpl, breakfast) and has a garden and terrace with panoramic views where you can unwind after your trek.

Hostal El Grial (☎ 223012, 💻 www.hotelelgrial.com), Carmen Alto 112, is attached to a neighbouring Spanish school with whom they can arrange lessons at discounted rates. Rooms are modern and well-kept, as is the cosy lounge. Rates are US$30/45/54 (sgl/dbl/tpl, att, breakfast).

Marani (☎ 249462, 💻 www.hostal marani.com), Carmen Alto 194, is full of character and run by a knowledgeable couple who are heavily involved in the local community: in the decade or so they've been in business they've built schools in the surrounding rural areas, trained teachers and helped out at the Cusco hospital. The rooms vary in size and shape but are generally large and high ceilinged; all provide a haven from the hustle and bustle outside. They cost US$32/51/67 (sgl/dbl/tpl, att, breakfast).

Hostal Pensión Alemana (☎ 226861, 💻 www.cuzco.com.pe), Tandapata 260, is a Swiss-German hostel whose clean, European décor looks as if it would be more at home in the Alps. Popular with European travellers, it is a comfortable, attractive place to stay and at US$40/55/70 (sgl/dbl/tpl, att) it won't break the bank either. Cheaper but less atmospheric is *Orquidea Real Hostal* (☎ 221662, 💻 www.orquidea.net), Alabado 520, which is owned and run by a package tour company, but has pleasant rustic rooms with modern amenities that enjoy views across the city. Rates start at US$33/44/55 (sgl/dbl/tpl, att, breakfast). *Hostal Rumi Punku* (☎ 221102, 💻 www.rumipunku.com), Choquechaca 339, is instantly identifiable because of the giant Inca stonework around the main door. This stylish colonial house has good quality but pricey rooms costing US$45-70/50-90/70-115 (sgl/dbl/tpl, att, breakfast) depending on the season. There is also a rooftop terrace as well as attractive gardens and the staff are particularly helpful.

For those who want to get away from it all, *Casa de Campo Hostal* (☎ 244404, 💻 www.hotelcasadecampo.com), at the very northern end of Tandapata in San Blas, at No 298, is just delightful. Built on a slope overlooking the town, the rooms and terrace are simply gorgeous, the location so peaceful, and they'll even throw in an airport pickup if you book in advance. Rooms start at US$45/55/65 (sgl/dbl/tpl), though bargaining is distinctly possible.

Expensive *Hotel Arqueologo* (☎ 232522, 💻 www.hotelarqueologo.com), Pumacurco 408, is named after the Inca stonework in the street leading to the entrance. A favourite with the French, it's pleasant enough and the inner courtyard and fireplace lounge are great places to hang out but at US$97/120/160 (sgl/dbl/tpl, com, breakfast) you can do better for your money. Similarly priced but better value is the *Boutique Hotel Casa San Blas* (☎ 237900, 💻 www.casasanblas.com), Tocuyeros 566, which was Cusco's first boutique hotel. Set in an 18th-century colonial mansion and centred round a courtyard are a number of spacious, simple rooms costing US$110/110/156-192 (sgl/dbl/suite, att, breakfast). Service here is polished and personalized. Also worth a look is *Los Apus Hotel y Mirador* (☎ 264243, 🖳 www.losa pushotel.com) at Atocsaycuchi 515, an atmospheric, airy Swiss-run establishment full of distinctive features, varnished wood and classy furnishings. The best views are from the breakfast lookout on the top floor. All this comes at a price: rooms are expensive at US$114/140 (sgl/dbl, att).

Two of Cusco's finest hotels can be found in this area. *Novotel Cusco* (☎ 228282, 🖳 www.novotel.com), San Agustín 239, has evolved from the earthquake-damaged ruins of the home of the conquistador Miguel Sanchez Ponce and now includes elegant stone archways, a glass-roofed courtyard and a central fountain. Prices vary from US$200-240 (sgl/dbl, att), according to whether the room is in the contemporary or more characterful older, colonial wing. Best of all though is *Hotel Monasterio* (☎ 604000, 🖳 www.monast eriohotel.com), Calle Palacio 136, Plazoleta Nazarenas, a sensitive conversion of the old Seminary of San Antonio Abad that retains a sense of its roots and original purpose. Along with everything you'd expect from an international five-star hotel it also has a gilded baroque chapel, peaceful courtyards, elegant cloisters, a Michelin-starred chef and oxygen-enriched air in the rooms (US$40 additional fee). Cusco's finest hotel is not cheap at US$495 (dbl, att, breakfast, suites US$600-1590), but you may be able to negotiate a better rate.

Plaza Regocijo and around

Budget To the west of the main plaza there are fewer options, but still some gems to be found. *Loki Backpackers Hostel* (☎ 243705, 🖳 www.lokihostel.com/en/cusco), Cuesta Santa Ana 601, is an historic viceroy's residence transformed into a funky backpacker's haven, with mixed or single-sex dorms, a shared kitchen, free internet access, a bar sporting superb views over the city and a lively atmosphere. Dorms cost US$7.50-11 and rooms US$30 (twin or dbl, att).

Mid-range *Hostal San Isidro Labrador* (☎ 226241, 🖳 Labrador@qnet.com.pe), Saphi 440, is an elegant, unpretentious place in a decent location. Simply furnished it has colonial arches, two patios and comfy rooms at US$35/45/55 (sgl/dbl/tpl, att).

One of the most impressive hotels in the category though is *El Balcón Inn* (☎ 236738, 🖳 www.balconcusco.com), Tambo de Montero 222, housed in a restored pre-colonial house dating back to 1630. All 16 rooms are en suite, many with magnificent views of the city, and the staff are incredibly friendly. It's a bit of a climb to get here, but it's worth every step: room prices are US$60/75-80/95 (sgl/dbl/tpl, breakfast).

Expensive *Hotel Royal Inka I* (☎ 222284, 231067, 263276, 🖳 www.royal inkahotel.com), Plaza Regocijo 299, US$68-72/90-95/105-110 (sgl/dbl/tpl, att, breakfast) depending on season, is built on the foundations of Pachacutec's palace and has front rooms with colonial furnishings overlooking the plaza as well as a bar and restaurant. It's slightly better than its similarly priced sister, *Hotel Royal Inka II* (same contact details), which is just up the road at Santa Teresa 335 but which does have a sauna and Jacuzzi. *Casa Andina* (🖳 www.casa-andina.com) is part of an up-market Peruvian chain. There are five hotels in Cusco, with top-end accommodation on offer close to the Cathedral (Santa Catalina Angosta 149, ☎ 233661), between Plaza de Armas and Plaza Regocijo (Portal Espinar 142, ☎ 231733), near to the Coricancha (San Agustín 371, ☎ 252633) and in San Blas (Chihuampata 278, ☎ 252400). The flagship branch, *Casa Andina Private Collection* is at Plazoleta de Limacpampa Chico 473 (☎ 232610). Service is exemplary and rates (including breakfast) for the modern, well-equipped rooms start at US$119 and rise to US$372 for those in the Casa Andina Private Collection. However, discounts are often available.

For the chance to stay in part of Garcilaso de la Vega's own mansion, head to *Hotel Garcilaso* (☎ 233031, 🖳 www.hotelesgarcilaso.com), Garcilaso 233. The mansion also extends into the Museo

Historico Regional (see p148) next door. Rooms cost US$240/240/285 (sgl/dbl/tpl, att, breakfast).

Elsewhere

Budget There are also some good options dotted elsewhere in the city, particularly south of the plaza. One such place is the *Albergue Casa Campesina* (☎ 233466, 🖳 www.cbc.org.pe/casacampesina), Av Tullumayo 274, which supports the work of the Casa Campesina organization that in turn works to promote and help local *campesina* communities. The hostal is tranquil and pleasant with rooms costing US$6/11 (sgl/dbl, com) and money generated going to support the project. The **Store of the Weavers** (see p175) is on the same site.

Estrellita (☎ 234134), Av Tullumayo 445, is a basic option with a compact communal area, simple kitchen and rather rudimentary rooms, but it is clean, handily positioned and excellent value at US$6/11 (dbl, com/dbl, att). *Hostal Familiar* (☎ 239353, 🖳 hostalfamiliar@hotmail.com), Saphi 661, is a well-established rickety old guesthouse away from the centre whose welltended courtyard, rudimentary rooms and family atmosphere are perennially popular. Rates, which start at US$7.50/15 (com) are flexible when the place is quiet. *Maison de la Jeunesse* (☎ 235617, 🖳 hostellingcusco @hotmail.com), is set down a small side street, 5 Pasaje Grace, off Av El Sol, opposite the Coricancha. Affiliated to Hostelling International (🖳 www.hihostels.com) this is a good-quality hostel with kitchen facilities, communal rooms and a balcony. Dorms cost US$12-20 whilst rooms start from US$21/30 (sgl/dbl, com).

Mid-range If you're looking for somewhere south of the plaza *La Posada del Abuelo* (☎ 222646, 🖳 www.laposadadel abuelocusco.com), Av Pardo 869, is a good bet. Rooms are cosy and comfortable and cost US$35/45/55 (sgl/dbl/tpl, att). *Hostal Pascana* (☎ 225771, 🖳 www.hostal pascana.com) is hidden away on a side street, Ahuacpinta (No 539), behind the Coricancha. Well-run and reasonably priced at US$30/40/50 (sgl/dbl/tpl, att) it is

a well-kept secret in this part of town. Another place worth looking at is *Niños* (☎ 231424, 🖳 www.ninoshotel.com), Calle Meloc 442. Run by a Dutch couple, the proceeds are used to fund a charity looking after underprivileged street kids: the couple have adopted a dozen street children themselves. The 17th-century colonial house has been converted into a stylish, spotless place to stay, with gorgeous rooms set around a pretty courtyard. Service is fabulous, although the sumptuous breakfast costs extra. Rooms cost US$22/44/66 (sgl/dbl /tpl, com) or US$48/48/70 (dbl/tpl/tpl, att). There is also a second branch, *Niños 2*, a little further out from the centre on Calle Fierro that follows a similar design.

Expensive *Hotel Libertador Palacio del Inka* (☎ 231961, 🖳 www.libertador.com .pe), Plazoleta Santo Domingo 259, is an enormous converted colonial building, once a palace called Casa de Los Cuatro Bustos. Not quite as luxurious as the Monasterio, this award-winning hotel nonetheless offers the full five-star package and an excellent restaurant but is a little more welcoming to dirty trekkers. It costs US$277/296 (sgl/dbl, att, breakfast) and up to US$365 for a suite.

WHERE TO EAT

There's almost too much choice in Cusco when it comes to picking a place to eat. From cheap steaming *anticucho* barrows on the street to five-star, white-linen restaurants where you have to book in advance there's something for everyone and every budget. If you're just after a drink and a snack wander along Calle Procuradores or Calle Plateros and you'll inevitably stumble on somewhere that takes your fancy. San Blas also has an up-and-coming scene with various cafés and good-quality restaurants now open here.

If you're after very cheap meals there are plenty of fixed menu places offering three courses for s/5 on Pampa del Castillo near the Coricancha or south of Plaza de Armas. Alternatively, **Mercado San Pedro** is a good bet, offering the finest, freshest juices squeezed in front of you, soups and main dishes in the heart of a traditional, boisterous setting. Beware though, your stomach should be attuned to local food before you go and some of the sights and smells in the market might just put you off your meal.

Plaza de Armas   [see map opposite]

There are plenty of places immediately around the plaza where you can hang out and snack throughout the day. *Trotamundos*, Portal de Comercio 177, has a balcony directly opposite the Cathedral that overlooks Plaza de Armas. It has a relaxed atmosphere, board games, good breakfasts and real toast. Larger meals are also available and in the evening it turns into a laid-back bar-cum-café with an open fire. There is also internet access here.

La Tertulia (see map pp162-3), at Procuradores 44, is justifiably popular thanks to the classical music that accompanies every breakfast, the efficient service and the superior quality of its scrambled eggs. There is also a vegetarian buffet and set menu available during the day.

Amaru (see map opposite) on Plateros 325 is very popular, not least because of its balcony seating which catches the sun first thing and the variety of breakfasts on offer. Opposite, *The Real McCoy* at Plateros 326, 2nd Floor, is a stylish yet relaxed place to spend time. They also serve fabulous big breakfasts, toast and marmite, cauliflower cheese, Branston pickle and puddings with custard as well as staples such as sandwiches and salads. They also do a great roast with sage and onion stuffing and gravy, ideal for people missing a taste of home.

Although there are plenty of pretenders, the queen of pizzerias remains *Chez Maggy* (🖳 www.pizzeriachezmaggy .com). With no fewer than three establishments on Procuradores (at Nos 344, 365 and 374), another on Plateros (No 348), and a further outpost in Aguas Calientes, Maggy's has come to dominate the city's pizza industry, producing wood-fired pizzas for every taste. They also run a delivery service (☎ 246316).

Victor Victoria, at Tecsecocha 466, is another perennially popular place offering good-sized portions of cheap vegetarian and Israeli-influenced food as well as some Peruvian staples. *A La Petite France*, at Tecsecocha 429B, is a *creperie* and so much more. In addition to sweet and savoury pancakes there are good-value breakfasts and full meals, both French and Peruvian, in this split-level, atmospheric hangout that has sofas, board games and French tunes playing. *Varayoc*, Espaderos 142, is a Swiss-Peruvian run, relaxed literary-style café where you can feel completely at ease as you enjoy a selection of pastries and a coffee, or come for the fondues and other European-style dishes such as goulash, whilst live harp music plays in the background.

If you're desperate for a plate of reasonably priced fried rice try *Chifa Sipan* in Plateros, on the corner of Plaza de Armas, although there is a second, better branch on Calle Quera 251, on the other side of the road from the Colonial Palace.

Kin Taro, at Heladeros 149, serves delicious sushi, using Peruvian trout, and other Japanese staples such as miso soup and saki.

For traditional Peruvian fare or contemporary *Novo Andino* dishes try *Inka Grill* on Plaza de Armas at Portal de Panes 115; it is more modern and imaginative than its competitors as regards food and is a decent place in which to treat yourself. They try to give Peruvian dishes a contemporary twist, so you could have Novo Andino dishes such as *pollo relleno prosciutto* (chicken stuffed with prosciutto ham), or a good *aji de gallina*.

Mystique, Calle Suecia, is another venue where traditional food is given an interesting twist. The alpaca steak and trout dishes are especially good. There's also a

---

decent bar in the front of the building that makes a mean Pisco Sour. *La Retama*, Portal de Panes 123, is a popular place serving up Novo Andino fusion food. It's often booked up by people who come to enjoy the balcony and lively music and dance performances. On the same stretch is *Pachacutec*, Portal de Panes 105, that serves typical Peruvian fare to packed tables filled with travellers waiting to catch the nightly folk shows. Equally busy is elegant *Tunupa*, Portal Confitura 233, which has panoramic views of Plaza de Armas from a narrow glassed-in balcony and serves first-rate international and traditional food from a menu or buffet. Popular with tour groups, the cavernous interior often reverberates to the sound of live music.

If you're after one of Cusco's most famous dishes and want to try guinea pig (*cuy*), consider *Sumaq Misky* (☐ www .sumaqmisky.com), Plateros 111, 2nd floor, the entrance to which is concealed up an alley of souvenir stalls. Once you've found your way in and upstairs, there is a small bar and a large dining room with an open kitchen serving up traditional Peruvian fare (alpaca steaks, *aji de gallina*, *lomo saltado*) and more adventurous dishes. They specialize in guinea pig though, which is available in a multitude of different ways: buffalo guinea wings, crispy aromatic guinea, tandoori guinea, guinea wellington, etc. They

also hold weekly Sapo tournaments (see box p173). *Kusikuy*, Suecia 339, is reputed to be one of the best places to try cuy, although it also offers other traditional Peruvian dishes on its short menu. The set lunch is remarkably good value too.

San Blas

On the road up to San Blas is the superb *El Buen Pastor*, at 579 Cuesta San Blas, which has everything you could ask from a bakery: great, great bread, fantastic *empanadas*, drool-inducing gateaux and low prices. What's more, this place is a charitable concern, helping to finance a home for girls from disadvantaged backgrounds. Equally good first thing in the morning is *Cicciolina*, Calle Triunfo 393. Set off the main street adjacent to a courtyard this two-storey building caters to different tastes: on the ground floor is a bakery doling out generous breakfasts and fresh, tasty pastries whilst upstairs is a sophisticated tapas bar and Spanish-themed restaurant that fuses Andean and Mediterranean food and styles of cooking with an impressive range of wines available. As befits a bakery, the desserts are also excellent.

La Bodega, 146 Carmen Alto, is another laid-back and friendly place with magazines and they do some great snacks too. *Jack's* on the corner of Choquechaca and Cuesta San Blas is also a good bet for decent coffee, fresh juices and large internationally themed comfort food such as pancake stacks, burgers and enormous breakfasts in a smart venue with friendly staff. Overlooking the plaza itself, *The Muse*, Plateros 316, is a bohemian café on the second floor that serves coffee and snacks as well main meals and some superb cocktails. They also have a range of vegetarian and vegan dishes. For healthy salads, delicious vegetarian dishes and a full menu in atmospheric surroundings head to *Greens*, on the second floor at Santa Catalina Angusta 135.

Café Cultural Ritual has two branches, on Choquechaca 140 and on Plaza San Blas. Both offer a tasty, largely vegetarian menu of Andean specialities such as fried yucca and quinoa pancakes, although there are some meat dishes too. *La Quinta Eulalia,* at Choquechaca 384, is another decent local option at the budget end of the scale. Only open for lunch, its small terrace is an ideal place to enjoy local fare, traditional music and traditionally brewed chichi. *Moni*, San Agustín 311, is a vegetarian place recommended for its innovative takes on Peruvian staples as well as for the chilled ambience in the café-bar and the puddings on offer.

Swiss-run *Granja Heidi*, at Cuesta San Blas 525, serves half-litre jugs of authentic, piping-hot chocolate for just s/2.5. During the day they offer freshly sourced and prepared food, yoghurt and delicious crêpes. The contemporary Peruvian dishes such as *seco de cordero* (lamb in coriander sauce), *carapulcra con pollo* (sun-dried potatoes in a mild chilli sauce) and vegetarian options like *loqro* (mashed pumpkin with fava beans, cheese, potato and rice) and *rocoto relleno* (chillies stuffed with vegetables) that are on offer in the evenings are also well worth trying. For more unusual dishes try *Macondo*, at Cuesta San Blas 571, which is one of the coolest and campest restaurants in Cusco, and run by one of its most flamboyant citizens. Walls are decorated with regularly changing art exhibitions, sofas are made out of bedsteads and cushions litter the surfaces. The food is contemporary Andean and Amazonian, based on local recipes that are given a twist. Desserts are first-rate and the cocktails dangerously good.

The best food though is to be found at *Pachapapa* on Plaza San Blas at No 120. With excellent, classic Peruvian dishes ranging from commonplace roast *cuy* (guinea pig) to the more exotic *alpaca* steaks, a very pleasant evening can be had munching on the native wildlife; the outdoor seating around an open fire pit is a bonus too and there's often live harp music playing.

Elsewhere

El Truco, Plaza Regocijo 261, is stylish and has good service although it is popular with tour groups who come for the nightly folk music shows, so can be very busy. *Chi Cha*, also at Plaza Regocijo 261, is renowned chef Gastón Acurio's first Cusco restaurant and features his take on regional highland cooking. The results are full of bold flavours, although his Lima staples, such as ceviche, are also available.

If you fancy something East Asian, try *Al Grano*, Santa Catalina 398, which serves delicious, reasonably priced Indian, Sri Lankan, Malay and Vietnamese dishes as well as generous breakfasts, as good a coffee as you'll find in the city and home-made pastries. For somewhere truly unique, head to *Fallen Angel* (🖥 www.fallenangel incusco.com), in the corner of Plazoleta de las Nazarenas. Run by the same individual who owns Macondo, it uses aquariumesque Perspex-topped baths full of fish and coral as tables and is crammed full of glitter and kitsch. The food is sumptuous though, especially the steaks, and the cocktails are lethal. Another of Cusco's best restaurants is found next door. *MAP Café* (🖥 www.cuscorestaurants.com) in Casa Cabrera, home to the Museum of Pre-Columbian Art, Plazoleta de las Nazarenas 231, is run by the same people as are in charge of the Inka Grill (see p170). Set in a beautifully sited restaurant in the courtyard of a restored colonial house, it serves a creative menu of excellent Peruvian cuisine including trout with ginger potatoes, Andean pesto-stuffed chicken and guinea pig confit with peanut-tossed potatoes. An excellent range of European and New

World wines are available to wash your meal down with. Quality comes at a price though and it isn't cheap (main course s/27-60, wine s/66-120, cocktails s/10-25). There's live music most evenings to accompany supper.

Cusco's first-ever Michelin-starred chef can be found at *Hotel Monasterio* (see p168). With food this exquisite being served in suitably sumptuous surroundings – the dining room is where monks once sang – you could be in any one of the finer restaurants in Europe, an illusion that the bill will do nothing to dispel.

For those in search of an authentic dining experience, the finest *cevichería* in Cusco is reputed to be *Las Machitas*, found on a dirt street, Av Peru F-9 Urb Progresso, some way from the centre of town. Huge portions of ceviche are reasonably priced and very tempting, although the other Peruvian specialities on offer are also recommended.

WHERE TO DRINK

Other than Lima, no Peruvian city can match Cusco for places to drink and dance. The plaza is a hive of activity from early to late, whilst those in the know head to less obvious parts of the city to find the latest hip hangout.

Plaza de Armas

Cross Keys, Portal Confiturías 233 (see map p171), is a Cusco institution and probably the most established pub in town. Set in a rather rickety building on the plaza, it's virtually a British pub (and is therefore your best bet for watching premier league football), and has a dart board and challenging, unstable pool table. Local beers such as Cusqueña are on offer alongside home favourites including Speckled Hen, IPA and Boddingtons. There's also a short but tasty menu of food. *Norton's Rat Tavern* also overlooks the plaza. It's almost a North American biker bar, and has TVs, darts and pool tables as well as a balcony from which to watch the world go by. The food is simple but filling and wholesome. *Paddy Flaherty's*, at Triunfo 124, is a compact Irish bar, complete with Guinness, that's usually absolutely heaving with travellers, although largely devoid of locals. There are TVs, games and a generous happy hour.

Elsewhere

Los Perros, on Tecsecocha 238, is a very comfortable place to kick back and while away an afternoon or evening. One of Cusco's favourite watering holes, it is renowned for its magnificent salads, wontons to die for, curries, stir fries and puddings such as sticky fig cake. There's also a book exchange, board games and stacks of out-of-date magazines to keep you entertained. *Km0*, Tandapata 100, is a Mediterranean-themed bar set just off Plaza San Blas. An expat favourite, it's a convivial place to spend time, snack on tapas and listen to live jazz or Latin bands. South of Plaza de Armas, *Rosy O'Grady's*, at Santa Catalina Ancha 360, is a vast Irish bar that's

---

❏ **Sapo**

This game of skill involves throwing a disc into a series of holes in the top of a box, worth different amounts of points, with a series of obstacles designed to make these targets more challenging. The most valuable hole is guarded by an ornate metal frog and to score the highest points you must throw the disc into the frog's mouth, at which point the player typically yells 'Sapo!' The game, similar in many ways to the English Pitch Penny, evolved from a game where the Incas would toss a gold coin into a lake in the hope that a frog, which was considered powerful, would take the piece in its mouth. If the frog (El Sapu) took the piece, the player was instantly granted a wish and the frog turned into solid gold. In reality the frog is rarely gold and the wishes made rarely come true, but it is still an exciting, entertaining way to pass the time over a couple of Pisco Sours.

a little less crammed than Paddy Flaherty's. Open late, it has some pretty tasty food and a decent happy hour.

Mandela's Bar, on the third floor of Palacio 121, is a funky hangout with a South African twist that has tempting snacks, good though slightly pricey drinks and live music. There are panoramic views from the roof too. *Big Blue Martini*, at Tecsecocha 148, is a modish sofa bar serving up good cocktails in a comfortable setting with hip tunes to keep you company. A very small haunt set above the city, *7 Angelitos*, Siete Angelitos 638, attracts a young, cool crowd looking for live music, DJ sets, quality mojitos and a funky atmosphere when it all kicks off.

Equally cool and popular is *Fallen Angel* (see p162) which hosts outrageous parties and serves decidedly devilish cocktails, as does its sister bar, *Macondo*, at Cuesta San Blas 571.

Clubs

You will have no trouble finding a club in Cusco; the difficult part is trying to avoid them. Touts swarm around Plaza de Armas handing out flyers and free drink tokens, so it is now possible to spend an entire evening touring the clubs without once paying for your drink; beware though, the rum is cheap and the Cuba Libres handed out are often potent. The clubs themselves tend to be located on the corners of the plaza. Although clubs come and go and the names change, the venues and addresses usually remain the same. The longest-running venue is *Mama Africa*. There are now two branches: *Mama Amerika* stands on the original site, Portal Belen 115, and is decorated in a jungle theme. It serves food, has any number of drink specials (happy hour 3-10pm) and plays an eclectic mix of music. *Mama Africa* itself, Portal Harinas 191, 2nd Floor, plays something for everyone and is usually packed, particularly for its happy hour (8.30-11pm).

On the opposite side of the plaza above the Gatos market on Portal Belén is *Uptown*, which caters to a similar crowd, but which although slightly larger is generally hot and smoky, owing to the lack of

windows or ventilation. *Extreme*, Portal de Cranes 298, is a long-standing Cusco mainstay that's similarly busy and plays contemporary dance music as well as techno and R'n'B (Rhythm and Blues). It also has a big screen for films and sport and a couple of bars that seem to give out an awful lot of free drinks. *Kamikase*, Plaza Regocijo 274, lies in a cavernous basement and plays rock music as well as hosting daily live acts. It has a happy hour (8-10pm) and is frequented by locals as much as tourists. *Mythology*, Portal de Carnes 298, plays '80s and '90s tunes. *Ukuku's*, at Plateros 316, plays the widest selection of music, including reggae, rock, techno, salsa, samba, blues, jazz and Huayno and is consistently popular. It also has live acts every evening and a happy hour (8-10.30pm).

Other entertainment and things to do

Peliclub, at Tecsecocha 458, is a small independent **cinema** that shows some classic old movies (s/5, s/2 students). Just down the road is Indigo – part of Hotel Royal Qosqo (Tecsecocha 2) – which shows four films a day (entrance free but you have to spend s/6 or more on food or drinks), and many of the pubs and nightclubs (Cafetacuba on Portal de Panes 109, Mama Africa's, Ukuku's, Extreme) also show movies in the afternoon. If none of the films on offer grabs you, you can always visit the **video store** at Portal de Panes 123, where you can choose any video you want and watch it in the comfort of one of their private video booths (s/6).

There's a regular, nightly folk music and dance show at **Centro Qosqo de Arte Nativo** (Av El Sol 604), which was founded by a group of artists in 1924. Entrance to the energetic, authentic shows which run from 7-8.30pm is free with a Visitor's Ticket (see p144). There are also nightly dance shows at the **Teatro Municipal**, on Calle Mesón de la Estrella 149, which occasionally hosts plays and dance classes too. The **Teatro Inti Raymi**, at Saphi 605, has one of the best live music shows, every evening from 6.45pm.

If you fancy doing something a little more active, Mama Amerika (see left) has **salsa lessons** starting at 9pm, followed by samba lessons at 10pm. Salsa Perú (☎ 255745) offers group and one-to-one salsa, merengue and cha-cha classes for people of all abilities.

Finally, if you're just back from the trail there's no better way to pamper yourself than to visit Siluet at Calle Quera 253, down an alley by the Chinese restaurant, a health spa with a sauna (s/25), Jacuzzi (s/12) and masseur/se (s/25). It's open every day 10am-10pm. Therapeutic massage is also available at Salon Hampi Wasy (💻 www.incamassage.com) on Choquechaca 136, Yin Yang on Portal Espinar 144, Angel Hands at Heladeros 157, the Aquabella Spa and Sauna at San Agustin 371, the Body Shop Spa at Procuradores 50 and at Healing Hands in Loki Hostel.

SHOPPING

Cusco has some of the finest craft markets and authentic souvenirs anywhere in Peru. Sadly in a bid to clean up Cusco, the authorities have moved on the artisans so often seen in the streets and plazas and relocated them to the giant Centro Artesanal at the end of Av El Sol. Not many tourists actually trek all the way down here, which is very bad for the local craftsmen but very good for those that do make the trip as they can expect a bargain if prepared to haggle. There are however a handful of much smaller markets dotted about and a number of weekend fairs.

San Blas is Cusco's traditional artisan district and there are a number of workshops here worth visiting. Taller Olave, Plaza San Blas 651, Taller Merida, Carmen Alto 133, and Taller Mendivil on the plaza have striking treasures, sculptures, colonial religious images and icons, ceramics and earthenware.

In addition there are the many souvenir shops that line the main streets and tend to feature similar produce, at similar prices.

General souvenirs

There are loads of places to choose from around Plaza de Armas. One of the better, more discerning places is Jatum Maqui, just up from the plaza at Tecsecocha 432, which keeps prices down without compromising the quality of the goods. La Mamita, at Portal de Carnes 244, has a very good collection of pottery, but also sells jewellery, wickerwork, baskets and textiles.

Jewellery

Ilaria, Portal Carrizos 258, is part of a nationwide chain of high-quality jewellers. There are also branches in El Monasterio, the Libertador and at the airport. Aldo is another chain with outlets in Hotel Libertador, Plaza de Armas, and at the airport selling Incan and contemporary designs in addition to watches and porcelain. For more unusual, unique designs in gold, silver or using semi-precious stones check out Calas, at Siete Angelitos 619B, Mullu, at Triunfo 120, and Spondylus at Cuesta San Blas 505. Some of the best stuff can be found at Carlos Chaquiras' shop at Triunfo 375.

Alpaca and llama woollens

Kuna (💻 www.kuna.com.pe), Plaza Regocijo 202, Monasterio Hotel, Libertador Hotel and the Museo de Arte Pre Colombino, has good quality alpaca coats, scarves and other knitwear but note that there's a cheaper branch of the same shop in the departure lounge of the airport. Alpacas Best, Portal Confitura 221 and Plaza Nazarenas 197-199, have a selection of handmade sweaters, jackets, coats and accessories.

The Center for Traditional Textiles of Cusco (💻 www.textilescusco.org), Av El Sol 603A, is a non-profit organization set up to aid the survival of Incan textile traditions and to provide support to those communities with a history of weaving. By researching and documenting complex styles and techniques the Center helps to ensure that 2000-year-old textile traditions will not be lost. Examples of the fine work are available for sale in the Center but bear in mind that work of this quality does not come cheap. They can also arrange tours to workshops in Chinchero and elsewhere in the Sacred Valley. The Store of the Weavers (💻 www.cbc.org.pe), at Av Tullumayo 274, is a local co-operative run by a handful of communities promoting traditional techniques. The superb textiles produced are expensive as you are paying for exquisite craftsmanship, and all the money raised goes to the actual artisans, many of whom can be seen working on site.

T-shirts and clothing

For something a bit different from the common-or-garden Peruvian football shirt, the ubiquitous Cusqueña and Inca Kola shirts ('*La Bebida del Peru!*') or the less appealing 'I love Cusco' numbers, look out for the unique designs in **Andean Expressions** at Choquechaca 210. For more up-market attire, visit **Werner and Ana**, Plaza San Francisco 295A, a top-end showroom offering innovative and unusual alpaca clothing from the chic Dutch-Peruvian duo.

Handmade leather shoes and boots are available from **Away** at Procuadores 361.

Ponchos and textiles

The shop at Portal Comercio 173 on Plaza de Armas has the widest range of antique and new ponchos in Central Cusco. A little expensive but it's worth coming here to see some of the fabulous old blankets, *mantas* (shawls) and ponchos they have in the store even if you don't want to buy. The **Tankar Gallery**, Calle Palacio 121, has a variety of tapestries produced by local artists that are representative of Andean traditions and customs. They also produce handmade ceramics.

Ceramics and pottery

Maky, at Carmen Alto 101, has a fine collection of tea sets, incense holders and other pottery decorated with pre-Hispanic and Inca motifs. Slightly more expensive and better quality are the goods at **La Mamita**, at Portal de Carnes 244.

Instruments and Andean music

Anyone interested in Andean music should head to **Taki Museo de Musica de los Andes** at Hatunrumiyoc 487. The knowledgeable owner runs a workshop and shop here producing and selling typical musical instruments. For Andean CDs try **Flutes of Peru**, at Av El Sol 230, which offers both traditional and more modern Peruvian music.

MOVING ON
Air

The airport is a few kilometres south of Plaza de Armas. It takes five minutes by taxi from there. From here you can fly to most major Peruvian towns. See box p74 for information about departure taxes.

Airlines include: LAN (☎ 255552/3/4, 🖳 www.lan.com, daily flights to Lima), Av El Sol 627B; Star Perú (☎ 234060, 🖳 www.starperu.com), Av El Sol 627; TACA (☎ 249926, 🖳 www.taca.com), Av El Sol 602B.

There are seven flights daily to Lima. The cheapest leaves early in the morning and costs around US$69. Later flights cost US$10-20 more. There are spectacular views of Salkantay out of the right-hand side windows, about 10 minutes after take-off. The flight takes 50 minutes. You should try and catch as early a flight as possible since there is a higher risk of flights being delayed or cancelled later in the day.

Bus

All international and long-distance buses leave from and arrive at the main bus terminal (the Terminal Terrestre) 2km south of Plaza de Armas, near the airport. Agencies on Av El Sol and in Plaza de Armas sell tickets for a healthy commission, but you will get far cheaper tickets at the station itself. It isn't necessary to book far in advance, but if you arrange your tickets the day before you can usually choose your seat. International services operate to La Paz and Copacabana in Boliva, or to Tacna by the Chilean border.

The route to Lima via Abancay and Ayacucho takes 20-25 hours and costs between US$20-37. The alternative is to go via Arequipa, which takes up to 30 hours

---

(Opposite) Spectacular façade of La Compañía Jesuits' church (see p146) in Cusco's Plaza de Armas. (Photo © Alexander Stewart).

and costs US$20-50. Other destinations include: Nazca (US$20); Abancay (US$5, 5hrs); Juliaca (US$3-4, 5-6 hrs); Puno (US$5-10, 6-7hrs); and Arequipa (US$10-25, 10-12hrs).

Local buses leave from a variety of departure points. Buses to Quillabamba leave from the Santiago bus terminal in the west of the city.

Regional services to Pisac (s/2-3, 1hr) and Urubamba (s/3, 2hrs), leave frequently throughout the day from Av Tullumayo. Alternatively try to catch a *colectivo* from Av Grau near Centenario. The furthest destination in the Sacred Valley is Ollantaytambo (s/5, 3hrs).

The cheap way to Machu Picchu In the past you had no choice but to take the train to Aguas Calientes and were at the mercy of the expensive fares levied by the train company. However, there is now an alternative, cheap access route as a result of a new bridge having been built across the Urubamba (see p178).

From Terminal Terrestre catch a bus to Quillabamba (s/20, depart 7pm) but ask to be dropped off at Santa María. Pick up a minibus to Santa Teresa (s/7.50), two hours

away, arriving around sunrise. Here you can now cross the Urubamba on the new bridge. Turn right on the far bank and hike the 6km to La Hidroeléctrica on an even, graded road, although there is a possibility of catching a lift on the back of a passing truck. From the train station at La Hidroeléctrica you can ride to Aguas Calientes (s/30). Alternatively carry on walking along the tracks and after 2-3 hours you will come to the town.

If you start to flag, there is overnight accommodation at *Hospedaje Mandor*, about 2km downstream from the bridge back across the Urubamba that leads to Machu Picchu.

To return to Cusco either retrace your steps via Santa Teresa and catch the 10am bus from here to Santa María, in time to meet the 1pm bus to Cusco which arrives 6-7 hours later. Alternatively catch the train from Aguas Calientes to Ollantaytambo or direct to Cusco.

Rail [see Appendix C p356-8]
Trains for Juliaca and Puno leave from **Estación Huanchac** on Av Pachacutec. Tickets must be bought at the station. Trains for Aguas Calientes (for Machu

---

❏ **Landslides**
In January 2010, days of heavy rain, the worst for 15 years, triggered up to 40 land- and mud-slides in the Machu Picchu region. One of these blocked the railway between Machu Picchu and Cusco, stranding nearly 2000 tourists. A state of emergency was declared and eventually helicopters were used to airlift people out. The rains also ruined crops and destroyed several thousand homes, causing a huge humanitarian effort to be launched. PeruRail worked to clear and repair the rail track but for some considerable time the only artery and access route to Machu Picchu remained at least partially blocked. A provisional service using a combination of bus and train kept a small trickle of people coming but journey times were vastly increased. Machu Picchu itself also remained closed for several months.

Eventually the site reopened in April, with a ceremony that included a blessing of Pachamama (mother earth) several months later. In late June, and following a lot of intense reconstruction, the rail route was reopened and train services completely restored. With Machu Picchu officially declared open and accessible, tourists at once returned to the site.

(Opposite) The popular market held at Pisac (see p187) every Sunday caters to local and tourist needs with everything from multi-coloured corncobs to patterned pottery and traditional textiles on sale. There are also smaller markets here on Tuesday and Thursday. (Photos © Alexander Stewart).

Picchu) leave from **Estación San Pedro** on Calle Ccascaparo. However, tickets for this route must also be bought from Estación Huanchac or online (see below). Pay close attention to timetables, opening hours and ticket prices as these change frequently. To get to Machu Picchu as cheaply as possible see the preceding advice.

Buying tickets   The main office for PeruRail can be contacted on Cusco ☎ 581 414 or via ▢ www.perurail.com. Estación Huanchac is open for ticket sales Mon-Fri 7am-5pm & Sat-Sun 7am-noon. Make sure you have ID, preferably your passport, with you when buying tickets. It is also possible to buy tickets in advance online with a credit card. This generates an e-voucher that is not valid for travel; it must be converted into a proper ticket at least an hour before departure.

❏ A bridge too far

In February 2007 a new bridge was opened that may still have a dramatic impact on Machu Picchu. The 80m/260ft long Carilluchayoc bridge, which crosses the Urubamba River by the town of Santa Teresa, 12 miles from Machu Picchu, offers much reduced access times to the ruins and opens up a much cheaper road route. The project has gone ahead despite being dogged by controversy and prohibited by a court order brought about by concern that the bridge would have a negative impact on the region and open up a smuggling route for drug traffickers.

The former mayor of La Convención province, Fredia Castro, argued vociferously that Santa Teresa needed the bridge, which replaces one washed away in 1998, in order to bring an end to its isolation and encourage commerce and tourism in the region, home to 200,000 people. However, although the bridge hasn't yet resulted in an excessively large influx of tourists to the already overcrowded site, there is still a fear that if tour agencies start to offer organized trips along this route this could happen. This will then potentially further damage the ruins. With more than 2500 visitors a day to the site already, some believe that the fragile ecosystem and the ruins themselves could be further threatened by the flood of tourists that the bridge might allow.

Traditionally the easiest and fastest way to reach Machu Picchu from Cusco is by train, on board the PeruRail service. Fares start at $48 one-way. The opening of the bridge means that there is road access to the site for the first time, with the cost of a bus fare starting from as little as $4 one-way. Although the bus takes 7-8hrs to make the journey, as opposed to the 3½hrs the train currently takes, it will still present an appealing option to those on a tight budget. Should demand increase as the word continues to spread, the construction of an infrastructure to cope with this new demand would present enormous logistical problems and would of course be detrimental to the ecology of the surrounding area.

There is also a real fear that the bridge will provide a new route for cocaine traffickers in La Convención province, which has a history of coca production and instability. Without the bridge though, the villagers had to travel an unacceptably far distance to take their produce to market.

Thus on the one hand there is a poor rural community struggling to develop itself and essentially seeking an easier way of life, and on the other a national treasure that is already seriously under threat. The ideal solution would be a compromise between the two arguments, which saw local people benefit, but which prevented tourists having access to the ruins via the bridge. This, however, could deny those tourists unable to afford the train fare access to Machu Picchu. The fear is that in the time it takes to reach a solution, permanent damage will be done to the region and to Peru's golden goose.

Around Cusco

High on the hill above Plaza de Armas stands **San Cristóbal**, a church built by Cristóbal Paullu Inca and dedicated to his patron saint. The church is open during the day and free to visit. Inside the gloomy interior, it is just about possible to make out the restored atrium. Lining the back wall of the terrace outside the church is an original Inca stone wall featuring 11 large, doorway-sized niches. This wall once belonged to the Palacio de Colcampata, in which Manco Inca lived prior to his rebellion and flight to Vilcabamba.

Further uphill stands the **statue of Christ**, looking out over the city, his arms outstretched. Donated by Palestinian refugees to express their thanks in 1944, the statue is clearly visible from below during the day and at night it is brilliantly illuminated.

RUINS NEAR CUSCO (DAY HIKE)   [see map p181]

The landscape around Cusco is dotted with small, interesting archaeological sites, many within easy walking, horse-riding or mountain-biking distance of the city. Five of the main sites can be visited in the course of a single half-day's trek, which allows you plenty of time at each ruin. A gentle stroll across the rolling grasslands is also an ideal way to acclimatize to the altitude here. Access to four of the five is with the Visitor's Ticket (BTU, see box p144). The fifth, Salapunco, is free anyway. If you do not have a Visitor's Ticket it is possible to buy a separate ticket for just these four sites. The **Boleto Partial** costs s/40.

The 8km route detailed below is the most commonly trekked path in the vicinity of Cusco and gives you access to Tambo Machay, Puca Pucara, Salapunco, Qenko and Sacsayhuaman. The trek can be done in either direction but it is simpler to catch a taxi out to the furthest point and then walk back again. This way each site builds in magnificence too, until you arrive at Sacsayhuaman, one of the most spectacular standing stone sites anywhere in the world. Taxis from Plaza de Armas to Tambo Machay cost around s/20 one way. Alternatively take a bus bound for Pisac and ask to be dropped off at Tambo Machay (about s/2).

In the past there have been robberies and muggings around the ruins close to Cusco, so keep your wits about you, leave all your valuables in your hotel and don't try to visit these places after dusk. It is always much safer to walk in small groups rather than on your own.

Tambo Machay

Tambo Machay is set back from the road from Cusco to the Sacred Valley. From the corner where you are deposited, walk up the gravel track for 200m until you reach the site (7am-5.30pm, Visitor's Ticket). The name Tambo Machay translates as 'Inn Cave', but is more frequently referred to as Los Baños del Inca,

'The Inca's Baths.' The carefully cut stones frame and channel a fresh water spring which issues from high on the slope above the site and is channelled from one terrace to another, vanishes underground and re-emerges in twin cascades. The precise purpose of the site is unknown but it is likely that it was used in the worship of water.

● **Route from Tambo Machay to Puca Pucara** From Tambo Machay walk back down the gravel path to the main road. There is an alternative trail that climbs over the hill above the site, but this is periodically closed to visitors. Cross the road and take a slight dogleg to the right then left to Puca Pucara and begin to walk back towards Cusco, following the signpost to Puca Pucara, which is actually visible ahead of you. About 200m later veer left from the main road and drop to the entrance to Puca Pucara (7am-5.30pm, Visitor's Ticket).

Puca Pucara

This collection of stone buildings perched on a promontory overlooking a deep valley was probably a private hunting lodge connected to one of the Inca's private estates. It has also been suggested that it used to be a military fort or checkpoint along an Inca Road, since the literal translation of the name means 'Red Watchtower' or 'Red Fort'.

● **Route from Puca Pucara to Salapunco** Beyond Puca Pucara walk parallel to the road heading back to Cusco and briefly follow it for 50m before cutting away left. A faint track sets off parallel to the road and descends to a small hamlet with a football field on your right. Descend south beyond the adobe houses for about half an hour, negotiating some boggy patches and marshy depressions as the path traces the route of a seasonal stream. Having curved left then right, the path splits. Two clearer trails stay high on the flanks of the valley that has begun to form, but you want to take the central path which sticks to the valley floor and descends amidst scrub and small trees. As you get lower, keep an eye out for Andean flickers (see p103), a type of woodpecker, which live in the surrounding area.

The path winds between some rocky outcrops and beneath several cliffs pocked with niches and caves. The last of these, on your right as you descend, is a 50m high, split cliff-face, sometimes called Laqo, which conceals two caves. The area has been partially excavated to reveal carvings and engravings in the rock as well as what could be an altar. Following a dog-leg left immediately after this cliff you should be able to see the monolithic rock of Salapunco ahead of you. Walk towards the giant boulder sitting in the centre of a rolling plain. As you approach the site you will start to see carved rocks and carefully flattened surfaces, evidence of Inca activity.

Salapunco

Salapunco (also known as **Cusilluchayoc**, always open, free) is a giant limestone boulder that is riddled with passages and carvings, many representing animals. The Quechua name translates as 'place of the monkeys', from the Quechua *kusillo*, meaning monkey. Cut steps lead to the top of the rock, where

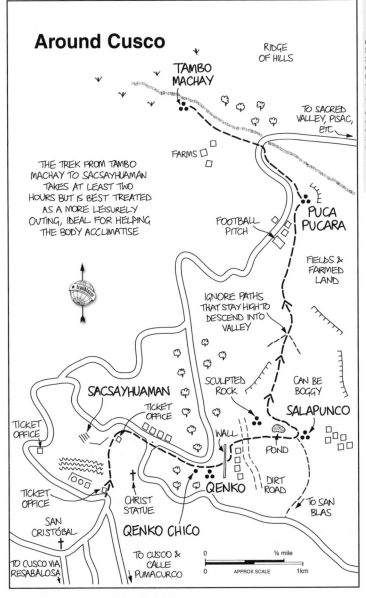

Around Cusco

RIDGE OF HILLS

TAMBO MACHAY

TO SACRED VALLEY, PISAC, ETC

FARMS

THE TREK FROM TAMBO MACHAY TO SACSAYHUAMAN TAKES AT LEAST TWO HOURS BUT IS BEST TREATED AS A MORE LEISURELY OUTING, IDEAL FOR HELPING THE BODY ACCLIMATISE

trailblazer

PUCA PUCARA

FOOTBALL PITCH

FIELDS & FARMED LAND

IGNORE PATHS THAT STAY HIGH TO DESCEND INTO VALLEY

SCULPTED ROCK

CAN BE BOGGY

SACSAYHUAMAN

SALAPUNCO

TICKET OFFICE

WALL

TICKET OFFICE

POND

TICKET OFFICE

DIRT ROAD

QENKO

CHRIST STATUE

TO SAN BLAS

SAN CRISTÓBAL

QENKO CHICO

TO CUSCO VIA RESABALOSA

TO CUSCO & CALLE PUMACURCO

0   ½ mile

0   APPROX SCALE   1km

there are polished surfaces and smoothed seats giving excellent views out over the surrounding countryside. Off the beaten path, the site is usually deserted. There has been a fair amount of excavation here recently and archaeologists have discovered remnants of Inca walls and other structures buried beneath the site. In fact, it appears that there may be several metres of interesting features here below ground level, although nobody knows why this might be the case.

● **Route from Salapunco to Qenko** If you stand on top of Salapunco and look toward Cusco, you can see a faint trail heading diagonally across the grassland towards a cluster of houses, Villa San Blas, backed by a stand of eucalyptus. Follow the diagonal path west across the field. After 100m you drop briefly into a creek bed. Around 400m further on the path passes to the left of a small sculpted outcrop of rock that has finely cut and polished platforms. As you approach the houses, keep them to your left. Turn left (south) when you reach a dirt road and pass in front of the houses, descending into a shallow gully alongside a stone wall. Walk downhill briefly, turn right (west) and cut through a gap in the wall and stroll 50m through a eucalyptus copse before emerging at a car park adjacent to the main road, in front of the next site: Qenko.

Qenko

Qenko (7am-5.30pm, Visitor's Ticket) is a second large limestone outcrop, the name of which translates as 'zigzag' or 'labyrinth'. Smaller than Salapunco, it has far more designs cut into it, many of which are very detailed. The site is a *huaca* (sacred site) and many of the carvings have special significance. A llama, a condor and snakes have all been identified, although unfortunately most of these are on the upper surface of the rock and it is now forbidden to climb on the stone. Channels and rivulets have been cut into the stone and may have been used to course *chicha* during ceremonies. At the front of the site, a standing stone enclosed by a finely sculpted niched wall has also been identified as casting a shadow shaped like a puma's head when the sun rises on the winter solstice (21st June). Inside the huaca is a tunnel that leads to what appears to be a beautifully sculpted altar.

● **Route from Qenko to Sacsayhuaman** From Qenko rejoin the road and turn left towards Cusco. Follow the road as it passes to the right of a mound, **Qenko Chico** (Little Qenko), which is built above a stone wall that includes a fitted block with 21 angles. As the road bends left, veer right and join a dirt track which passes through a scruffy wood. Beyond this it eases past a straggle of souvenir shops and emerges on a wide open plain. Continue towards a hut. Turn left (west) and present your Visitor's Ticket at the ticket office. From here continue downhill gently towards a car park. To your left you'll see the **Christ Statue** (Cristo Blanco) with his arms outstretched. To your right is the awesome ruin of Sacsayhuaman (7am-5.30pm, Visitor's Ticket). To avoid the worst of the crowds, consider getting here early, before the tour buses arrive, or later in the afternoon once they have moved on again.

Sacsayhuaman [see map p184]

The size of the stones here really is incredible and historian Garcilaso de la Vega was massively impressed but quite at a loss for an explanation as to the construction of Sacsayhuaman, preparing the way for theorists such as Eric von Daniken who was convinced that this was the work of visitors from outer space:

> 'A Spanish monk, who recently visited Peru, told me on his return, that he would never have believed what people tell him about this fortress if he hadn't seen it with his own eyes, because it is even more difficult to imagine than one can say; and that, in reality, it seemed hardly possible that such a project could have been successfully carried out without the help of the Evil One. Those were his very words. If we think, too, that this incredible work was accomplished without the help of a single machine, it is too much to say that it represents an even greater enigma than the seven wonders of the world?.. One sees how the Egyptian pyramids were constructed, with the combined forces of time and countless workers... But how may we be explain the fact that these Peruvian Indians were able to split, carve, lift, carry, hoist and lower such enormous blocks of stone, which are more like pieces of a mountain than building stones, without the help of a single machine or instrument. An enigma such as this one cannot be easily solved without seeking the help of magic, particularly when one recalls the great familiarity of these people with devils.'

Garcilaso Inca de la Vega *The Royal Commentaries of the Incas* (1609)

The Spanish nicknamed the site 'the Fortress'. However, current research and the discovery of Inca tombs containing the bodies of priests in the area suggest that it was more likely to have been a temple. The layout of the site makes it likely that it was used as a sanctuary and place to worship the sun. Regardless of its original reason for being built, the massive stone walls were used as a fort by the armies of Manco Inca as he fought to evict the Spanish from Cusco (see p114).

The site itself is one of the most impressive stone monuments left standing in the world and is awe-inspiring in its stature and form. Enormous stone blocks stand solemnly in three tiers of zigzag walls that stretch 360 metres. John Hemming calculated in *Conquest of the Incas* that the largest stone in the structure stands 8.5m high and weighs 361 tons. The massive blocks curve into one another as if squashed together like clay. For structural strength the largest stones are set at the apexes of the zigzags that form the wall. Unfortunately the site has been used as unofficial quarry for cut stones over the years and many of the smaller stones have been pillaged by people for use in construction elsewhere. The structure used to be topped by three giant towers, called Salla Marca, Paunca Marca and Muyu Marca, which were razed to the ground following the defeat of Manco Inca. The foundations and concentric ringed outlines of these three giants are slowly being uncovered and renovated.

Across a broad, flat space known as the Esplanade, stands a giant mound called the Inca Throne, where an altar has been carved out of the rock. It is thought the Inca or other high-ranking individual oversaw ceremonies from here. Nearby are numbers of seats cut into the stone. Nowadays however, the smooth grooves and polished slopes on the far side of the mound are used by children as a slide, giving the mound the nickname *el rodadero*. Beyond the mound is a series of

CUSCO & AROUND

To Tambo
Machay

0   50   100m

Smooth rocks
used as a slide

Tunnel

Amphitheatre

To Qenko &
ticket office/
control post

Inca
throne

Giant
stone walls

Flat
esplanade

Foundation of
Muyu Marca
Tower

Foundation of
Paunca Marca
Tower
(Foundation
barely visible)

Foundation of
Salla Marca
Tower

Dirt
path

Steep
hillsides

Control post
& ticket office

To
Cusco

Sacsayhuaman

small amphitheatres and a section of hill riddled with tunnels. Some of these remain open, but you'll need a torch to make your way through them.

Returning to Cusco

From Sacsayhuaman it takes about 20-30 minutes to stroll gently downhill to Plaza de Armas. Although there are several routes, the simplest is to descend from the car park on the dirt path that drops through a gully to eventually join the tarmac road on a hairpin bend. There is an OFEC ticket office here that checks Visitor Tickets for people walking up to the site. Join the road and follow it carefully around a set of S-bends to reach the church of **San Cristóbal**. Below here there is a set of steep stairs (Resbalosa) that drop rapidly towards Plaza de Armas, emerging on one of the streets by the Cathedral. Turn right from here for the plaza.

If you choose to walk the route in reverse and trek from Sacsayhuaman to Tambo Machay, you will need to retrace your steps, hail a bus or *colectivo* from the main road or try to flag down a taxi.

THE SACRED VALLEY   [see map p186]

The road north from Cusco climbs up to a pass, undulates across the pampa and then descends dramatically into the spectacular, fertile Urubamba Valley, which is also known as the **Valle Sagrado** (Sacred Valley).

The mighty river that flows through the valley was considered sacred by the Incas. The region is dotted with historic sites and archaeological ruins, signifying the importance of the valley to both the Incas and the conquistadors. The Incas built their palaces, religious centres and retreats alongside this giant tributary of the Amazon: highlights include the citadels at Pisac and Ollantaytambo, but less well-known sites such as Salinas and Moray are also here to be discovered. Upstream from Pisac it is known as the Vilcanota, whilst downstream it tends to be referred to as the Urubamba. The region is considered sacred because of its vital importance to Cusco as a source of food and grain. Quechua legend also holds that when the sun sets it slips through the underworld beneath the Urubamba, where it draws deeply from the chill waters and rises the following morning refreshed. A separate legend claims that the earthly Urubamba is a mirror for the celestial river of the Milky Way, and that the two flow into one another.

The area is rich in history and well worth several days exploring. Most of the travel agencies in Cusco offer day or half-day trips to a number of sites and traditional markets in the valley, although you are often better off tackling these places under your own steam and at your own pace. Many of the towns and villages throughout the Sacred Valley are set up to receive visitors and there are plenty of places to stay and linger. There are also a number of Inca trails and more recent paths cut into the flanks of the valley. For inspiration look for Charles Brod's *Apus & Incas* in one of the bookshops in Cusco. In order to access most of the sites though you will need a Visitor's Ticket (see p144).

The Sacred Valley

Pisac

Pisac, which is named after the Quechua for partridge (*pisaca*), lies 32km north-east of Cusco. Built by Viceroy Toledo, the man responsible for crushing the last Incas, on the site of an Inca settlement, the village is split into two parts. On the valley floor sits the colonial village with its traditional Andean market, whilst high above the valley on a spur stands the citadel, a lofty Inca site set above a series of giant sweeping terraces that presides magisterially over the valley.

Pisac village

There are lively, traditional **markets** in Pisac. The most significant one takes place on Sunday, when you can see traditionally dressed locals buying and selling crops, foodstuffs and craftwork, and smaller affairs on Tuesday and Thursday. This is an ideal opportunity to pick up a well-made souvenir; the ceramics and rugs available here are particularly high quality though they're not the cheapest. Locals pack the plaza early on and the chaotic scene unfolds throughout the morning, before easing down around lunchtime.

There is an ATM (cashpoint) on the main Plaza de Armas, close to Ulrike's Café.

Where to stay and eat

There are a few options if you are tempted to stay in Pisac: *Hospedaje Beho* (☎ 203001), 50m north of the plaza, on the path to the ruins, is a small shop offering simple bed and board (US$5/10, sgl/dbl, com); *Hospedaje Familiar Semana Wasi* (☎ 203018) on the eastern edge of the plaza has basic but clean rooms (US$11/15, sgl/dbl); *Pisaq Inn* (formerly Hotel Pisaq; ☎ 203062, 🖳 www.pisacinn.com) in the south-west corner of the square has an attractive courtyard, bright, bold hand-painted murals, a relaxed ambience and renovated rooms (US$40-45/50-65, sgl/dbl, att) as well as a **restaurant** serving light meals and a natural rock-heated sauna.

A little further out are two smarter outfits. *Paz y Luz* (☎ 203204, 🖳 www.pazyluzperu.com, s/90/150/190 sgl/dbl/tpl, suites for s/180, breakfast) is 1km east of the centre, close to the river, with a homely feel, a well-kept garden and impressive views of

the surrounding hills. The expat owner also offers healing courses drawn from Andean and international traditions, meditation classes, Reiki and yoga sessions. A little further out is *Royal Inca Pisac* (☎ 203064, 🖳 www.royalinkahotel.com, US$54/80/100, sgl/dbl/tpl, breakfast) set in a converted

CUSCO & AROUND

Intihuatana

Ritual bath

Sun Temple & Intihuatana Stone

Water channel

0 5 10m

Cliff tombs

Qanchisracay

To Pisac

0 100 200m

Terraces

Hanan Pisac

Rio Quitamayo

Cliff tombs

Tunnel

Viewpoint

Tunnel

Terraces

Intihuatana (see inset map)

Pisaca

Terraces

Qorihuayrachina

Terraces

To ruins

Path to ruins

Church

Plaza

PISAC

To Urubamba

Rio Urubamba

To Cusco

Pisac ruins

hacienda and boasting its own restaurant, bar, swimming pool, sauna and tennis courts. The hotel also has bicycles for rent. The hotel is part of a chain with other branches in Cusco (see p168).

Should you get hungry, there is a giant *Clay Oven Bakery* on Mariscal Castilla that is used to bake traditional flatbreads and empanadas or sometimes to roast guinea pig. Alternatively, there are several decent cafés adjacent to the plaza in which the market is held. Laid-back *Mullu* stands on the second floor of a house opposite the church and has a rickety balcony from which to watch the activity whilst enjoying a selection of juices and smoothies, sandwiches and other Novo Andino cuisine snacks. There's also an **art gallery** downstairs. Close by is the café *Doña Clorinda*, which serves mostly Peruvian staples. *Ulrike's Café* is on the western side of the square and has a decent vegetarian menu as well as some superb cakes and pastries.

Transport

To get to the town from Cusco catch a minibus from Av Tullumayo (buses to Calca) or Calle Puputi (buses to Urubamba). Buses leave roughly every quarter of an hour, the journey takes up to an hour and fares cost s/2-3. A taxi from Cusco to Pisac will set you back about s/30. Buses back to Cusco leave from close to the bridge outside the main centre, up until around 8pm.

Pisac ruins The citadel is open 7am-5.30pm and entry is with a Visitor's Ticket (see p144). Guides charge US$5 for a tour of the ruins. It is a large site and you should allow a couple of hours to explore the terraces, water ducts, ruins and hidden chambers as well as to take in the superb views of the valley, the patchwork of patterned fields, sheer cliffs and jagged ridges.

These ruins, some of the most spectacular in the Sacred Valley, are thought to have been built during the reign of Pachacutec. Narrow paths edge above steep drops and have to pass through **giant stone archways** and a short stretch of **tunnel** to reach the ceremonial centre at the heart of which stands a rare intact **Intihuatana** – a sacred sculpted rock or 'hitching post of the sun', the vast majority of which were decapitated by the conquistadors. A number of tombs have been uncovered in the cliff faces behind the site, on the far side of the Qitamayo Gorge, but have been plundered and are now closed to visitors.

The stiff climb up to the site from the valley floor takes 1-1½hrs. If you aren't already acclimatized to the altitude you will have to take it even more slowly. From the market in the heart of the village pick up the path to the north of the square, which sets off west of the church. After 10 minutes the path forks. The upper branch is a longer, gentler ascent alongside the Rio Quitamayo to **Hanan Pisac**, the northernmost sector of the site. The lower branch crosses the river and climbs more directly and aggressively through a set of terraces to the lookout post above the valley, from where it is a short walk to the heart of the site and the Intihuatana. If you'd rather not walk, a 15-minute taxi ride from the town to the ruins costs s/15-20. Alternatively you can hire horses in the town and ride to the top for s/10 per person.

Chinchero

This small town north-west of Cusco is set amidst the Anta plains, overlooking the Sacred Valley. The village mostly comprises adobe houses, but there is also a split-level plaza at the top of a steep winding street, with an impressive Inca wall inset with large trapezoidal niches separating the two sections. Beyond here there are also **Inca remains and terraces** (7am-5.30pm, Visitor's Ticket). Further down the valley there are also interesting examples of channels and stairs cut into the rocks.

The attractive **colonial church** built on the upper level of the plaza, dating from the early 17th century, was constructed on Inca foundations and has been unusually decorated inside with red and blue floral patterns. It also has paintings from the Cusco School. The colourful **Sunday market** (crafts as well as local produce) is worth coming for as it attracts fewer tourists than the Pisac markets and is considered to be more traditional.

Chinchero – Where to stay and eat

There are few **places to stay** in Chinchero. Your best bet, other than a handful of rather basic hospedajes such as *Hospedaje Mi Piury* (☎ 306029, s/30/50 sgl/dbl, att), on Garcilaso 187, is *La Casa de Barro* (☎ 306031, 🖥 www.lacasadebarro.com; US$40 /55/70, sgl/dbl/tpl, breakfast), a modern hotel with hot water, a bar and its own restaurant.

Peru Treks and Adventure (see p159), in partnership with Andean Travel Web (see p41), have a well-established **homestay** programme in Chinchero, where you can stay with a local family (s/20 per person). Facilities at the house are generally very basic and the family only speak Quechua and Spanish, but you are able to experience a more realistic local way of life and gain a brief insight into the daily lives of the local people. Contact the agency to arrange a visit.

Transport

To get to Chinchero from Cusco catch a bus to Urubamba from Tullumayo (about s/2, 1hr); the bus tends to leave early in the morning. From the Sacred Valley take any bus to Cusco that goes via the village. From Urubamba the journey also costs approximately s/2. To return to Cusco from Chinchero catch the bus from the main road.

Urubamba

This sprawling transport hub at the junction of the roads from Pisac and Chinchero is often a necessary stepping stone to somewhere else in the Sacred Valley. Urubamba's not a particularly attractive town but the setting is magnificent, beneath a set of fine snow-capped peaks.

Many of the **adventure activities** run by agencies in Cusco, such as whitewater rafting, hot air-ballooning and horse riding, begin from Urubamba. It also hosts a local **market** one block west of the plaza and is home to a number of artisans including weavers, ceramicists, potters, sculptors and artists.

It is quite possible to spend half a day wandering about the **studios and workshops** watching the workers create their wares. One of the most interesting is Seminario-Behar Ceramic Studio (☎ 201002, 🖥 www.ceramicaseminario.com, open daily, free), on Calle Berriózabal; it specializes in producing ceramics using pre-Colombian techniques. World renowned, the studio produces exquisite but expensive pieces.

Cusco department area code: ☎ 84. If phoning from outside Peru dial ☎ +51-1.

Urubamba – Where to stay and eat

There are plenty of hotels in Urubamba. *Quinta los Geranios* (☎ 201093), Cabo Conchatupa, has clean rooms (US$15/ 30/45, sgl/dbl/tpl), a garden and an open-air restaurant. There are some cheaper places too, such as *Hostal Urubamba* (☎ 201062; s/15/20 sgl/dbl, com; s/20/30 sgl/dbl, att) on Jirón Bolognesi, one block east of Plaza de Armas.

Many of the hotels are lined up along the main road running along the south-western edge of the town. Most luxurious is the *Tambo del Inka* (☎ 9613316, 🖳 www.libertador.com.pe; US$130, dbl, att), which has large colonial-style rooms in expansive grounds, 12km west of Urubamba.

On the road to Ollantaytambo, 3km from Urubamba, is a handful of colourful, rustic cottages complete with small kitchen, terrace and balcony, to rent at *K'uychi Rumi* (☎ 201169, 🖳 www.urubamba.com; s/460/640/760, sgl and dbl/tpl; cottages that can sleep up to six people cost s/980).

Just west of town is the charming *Sol y Luna Lodge Spa* (☎ 201620, 🖳 www.hotelsolyluna.com; US$235/258/341/ 419, sgl/dbl/tpl/quad, breakfast), which has luxury bungalows set in a pleasant garden full of eucalyptus and cypress trees, its own restaurant that hosts folk shows, tennis courts and a spa. The hotel's activity centre, Wayra (🖳 www.wayrasacredvalley.com) organizes horse-riding with Peruvian Paso ponies, mountain-biking, paragliding and white-water rafting.

San Agustín Urubamba (☎ 201444, 🖳 www.hotelessanagustin.com.pe; US$84/96 /120, sgl/dbl/tpl, breakfast) lies 1km east of town in spacious grounds and with a swimming pool, sauna and Jacuzzi. There is a 15% discount for online booking. On the

(Continued on p194)

❏ **Hugh Thomson describes living in the small market town of Urubamba**

'While writing a book on Peru, I wanted to find a quiet base where I could live with my family. Cuzco itself does not have the healthiest climate for kids, as the high mountain bowl can trap the car pollution and they can find the altitude hard, whereas the town of Urubamba seemed more easy going and had a good school. I remembered the American traveller Ephraim George Squier's comments in the 19th century:

Although only 2500 feet lower than the Cuzco Basin, the Yucay [Urubamba] Valley, protected on all sides, enjoys a much more benign climate, similar to that of Nimes and other parts of the south of France. Both healthy and fertile, easily accessible from the capital, and with a vegetation unrivalled in the Sierra, this sweet and tranquil valley, surrounded by some of the highest mountains of the Continent, quickly became the favourite place of recreation for the Incas. The soil is rich and the climate, in spite of the fact that the Valley is enclosed by high snow-capped mountains, is soft and agreeable. A more beautiful place than this does not exist in all of the Andes...'

We found a house on the outskirts of Urubamba, at a place called K'uychi Rumi which means 'rainbow stone' in Quechua: the houses shared a communal garden, a riot of hibiscus, abutilon, poinsettias and roses, with arum lilies growing alongside the small irrigation ditches that ran through the property; the owners, architect Carlos Rey and his wife, Claudia, had also introduced some pre-Columbian plants – *polylepis* trees and *quinoa*. A line of yellow broom led along paths to a large stand of eucalyptus at the far end of the property where the children would spend many happy hours swinging over the stream; immediately beyond rose the ravine up to Pumahuanca, one of the passes leading to the Amazon.

The rhythm of such small market towns had always appealed to me and I now quickly found it seductive: the Post Office that never seemed to open; the old men moving around the benches in the Plaza to keep getting the sun – I overheard one telling another: 'get it written down on paper because you know that words can be blown away by the wind'; a shoe shine boy playing his Gameboy while he waited for customers; the café on the corner of the square called, with the utmost simplicity, 'The Corner Café'.

But Urubamba was a mountain as well as a market town: like a settlement in the old West where the main drag is only a temporary slowing of a longer route through the wilderness, the high street past the gas station turned into a country lane which led directly up to the Chicón glacier.

We rode up there sometimes from the town, picking our way through the cobbled streets nervously as the odd mototaxi could shoot without warning from an alley and scare the horses, the drivers treating them as if they were errant pedestrians. By riding, we could get glimpses over the high patio walls of hidden courtyards, orchards and market gardens. The surrounding fields were a reminder too that Urubamba was organized not around its streets but around its water supply: there was a complicated series of irrigation canals, which could be diverted at different points during the day under a tightly regulated system. Woe betide the *campesino* who 'forgot' to divert a canal back to his neighbour at the appointed hour – or for that matter the three-year old boy like ours, Leo, who enjoyed damming or diverting them at 'inappropriate' moments.

Within a few weeks of arriving we were invited to a local wedding and realized that we already knew most of the congregation. The bride and groom emerged from the town hall registry office to a full band playing in the town square, a band in which the bridegroom usually played himself.

I had met Joyo several times at the Corner Café, eating empanadas with a saxophone slung over his shoulder. He was an architect who had travelled in France, been an active revolutionary during the 1968 Sorbonne uprising, and had since settled in Urubamba with Lola, his French girlfriend and now bride, to play music; they were getting married to regularize both their own nationalities and those of their adopted children.

Unfortunately, as Joyo had told me, the Peruvian authorities had made a mistake and thought initially they wanted to get divorced, not married. Peruvian bureaucracy, once started, will move in only one direction: Joyo's protests that they could not get divorced because they weren't married had fallen on deaf ears; it had taken six months of bureaucratic confusion before their 'divorce' had come through and they could get 'remarried'.

Joyo unslung his sax and was leading his own wedding procession around the town square and up to their house for a wedding party that would last all day and all of the night. One of his band had played with the Grateful Dead. There were fond memories of the time Keith Richards had passed through with the Stones on one of their Peruvian adventures and busked in the Corner Café (it had been a country that had always appealed to Mick Jagger, not least because when in the Amazon to film *Fitzcarraldo,* no one had recognized him).

Indeed over the months that we lived there, I began to realize that there was a bohemian diaspora around Urubamba of pony-tailed hippies and Peace Corps veterans of a certain age, who had fetched up here in the cheap land and low regulations of the 70s, when dope could be grown in your back garden. The valley had changed considerably since then. In recent years the beginnings of the tourist boom engulfing Peru had spilled over from Cuzco and hotels were being built at an alarming rate, usually with our landlord Carlos Rey as architect. There were also many exiled Limeños, like Carlos, who had moved here for the good life. Some had put Jacuzzis into their haciendas. Even the taxi drivers now had mobile phones.

It intrigued me that the picture I had always had of Urubamba from afar – the small market town in the heart of the Sacred Valley, the grain basket of the Incas – should have such a touch of Laurel Canyon about it. Of course there were still plenty of local villagers still keeping horses, minding their small plots and threatening to shoot the neighbours if the irrigation canal wasn't turned over to them at the appointed hour. But just when you least expected it, with the wood-smoke drifting past the eucalyptus stands and the sun setting on the Chicón glacier, a four-wheel drive would flash past blaring out rap music'.

The book **Hugh Thomson** wrote while based in Urubamba was
Cochineal Red: Travels through Ancient Peru

outskirts of Urubamba at Jirón Recoleta and part of the same chain is **San Agustín Monasterio de la Recoleta** (☎ 201666, 🖥 www.hotelessanagustin.com.pe; US$120 /144/180, sgl/dbl/tpl, breakfast, 15% discount if booked online). Set in a converted 15th-century monastery, this striking hotel offers standard rooms and more luxurious suites (US$198), but also retains the chapel and cloistered courtyards of its original incarnation.

If you're not eating in your hotel and want to head out for food visit the excellent **La Casa de la Abuela**, Bolivar 272, two blocks north from Plaza de Armas, or the more traditional **El Fogon**, Parque Pintacha. Nearby is the rustic **El Maizal** which serves Novo Andino cuisine dishes from an extensive buffet.

There are a few pizza restaurants on Av Mariscal Castilla, the best of which is **Restaurant Pizzonay** which offers lasagne and ravioli in addition to the standard fare.

Alternatively make your way to **Muse Too** on the corner of the plaza, which is run by the same people behind The Muse (see p172) in Cusco and provides the same sort of laid-back comfort, quality coffee and cakes and decent drinks that their reputation has been built on. There's also often live music in the evenings. Some of the best food is at **El Huacatay** (🖥 www.el huacatay.com), Arica 620, a smart atmospheric place that serves great Novo Andino staples with a contemporary flourish.

Transport
Minibuses to Cusco leave throughout the day from Av Grau and buses from Tullumayo, going via Pisac or Chinchero respectively (about s/5, 2 hrs). Quicker *colectivos* depart from Calle Pavitos. Urubamba bus station is just to the west of the town, on the main road. There's also a tourist train service between Urubamba and Aguas Calientes (see p357).

Around Urubamba West of Urubamba, high on the flank of the valley, is the unusual site of **Salinas** (s/5) where mineral-rich, salty water from a hot spring higher up the valley is channelled into thousands of large, flat, shallow pans and allowed to evaporate so that salt is produced. This is then collected intensively by hand, just as it has been for hundreds of years, and continues to provide work for the locals. To get here it's a 45-minute walk from Urubamba, or catch a bus (s/2) back to Chinchero and ask to be dropped off at the junction to Maras (see map p186). You may then be able to pick up a taxi from the junction to the site, otherwise walk west for about 2½ miles and take the right-hand track that cuts north across the pampa for a further three miles to descend to the site (1hr).

Maras is a shabby colonial-era village that once supported a thriving community. Evidence of past glory can be seen in the decorated stone arches and intricate lintels that still adorn some of the run-down houses. When the nearby silver mines ran dry, the town was virtually abandoned and has been allowed to become a poor, rural community. There is very little left here except for a barely standing colonial church, a dusty, empty plaza and a set of market stands with nothing to sell.

If you were to continue west from Maras on an unpaved, dirt track for 9km though, you would come to the unusual, atmospheric site of **Moray** (s/10). Three large concentric depressions in the earth have been cut and shaped into circular terraces of varying sizes. Hidden from sight until you are virtually on top of them, these giant amphitheatres are very striking. If you clamber up the hill behind the deepest depression you get a view of all three amphitheatres and can see the entire site in context. Thought to be an Inca farm, this extraordinary place was used to test the effects of altitude on different plants. The deepest depression is around 30m from rim to floor and temperatures within the bowl can vary by up to 10°C. It is thought that the terraces, built over containing walls filled with fertile earth and watered by complex irrigation systems, each had their own micro-climate enabling the Incas to grow more than 250 species of plants.

If you don't fancy walking all the way up to the site, catch a Chinchero-bound bus, s/2 from Urubamba, and ask to be dropped off at the road to Maras, on the way. It's a 2½-mile walk from here to Maras (1½ hrs) and a further four miles to Moray (2½ hrs), although you may be able to hitch a lift or pick up a taxi from the junction (typically s/5 to Maras and s/20 for a return trip to Moray).

Ollantaytambo [see maps p196, p198]

The historic town of Ollantaytambo stands at the far end of the Urubamba Valley, 68km from Cusco. Here the fertile valley narrows and the river flows into a gorge. In this strategic spot the Inca Pachacutec built the fortress and religious complex of Ollantaytambo having subjugated the valley's former residents. The massive ruins set above a compact town are some of the most striking and impressive in the whole of the Sacred Valley. The town itself is a relaxing, easy-going alternative to Cusco and a good way of escaping some of the bustle associated with the larger city.

The fortress temple The daunting fortress was described by Pedro Pizarro as 'so well fortified that it was a thing of horror'. It was to this mighty castle that Manco Inca retreated following his uprising. Pursued by the Spanish, he holed up in the fortress high above the surrounding plain and faced the conquistadors. After two days of heavy fighting he forced the Spanish to retreat, the first time that the colonial army had been bested in combat by the Incas. Manco realized he wouldn't be able to maintain his superiority so close to Cusco and sadly abandoned the fortress to move over the mountains to Vilcabamba.

The **fortress** (7am-5.30pm, Visitor's Ticket) still looks much as it once did and it's easy to see how the Spanish would have been appalled at the prospect of throwing themselves against the 16 great walled terraces that hug the contours of the hills and bar the route up to the unassailable fortress. More than 200 steps climb steeply through the terraces from the plaza below. Giant walls rise from the almost sheer cliff faces preventing any attacker from flanking the site. At the top of the staircase stands the unfinished **Sun Temple**, which is made up of six enormous, mortarless monoliths cut from pink porphyry and mottled with orange lichen. These upright stones have been carefully fitted together aligned east to west. Double-jambed archways on the approach to this point indicate that this was a very important centre. From the top you can see the quarry Cachicata, 3.5km south-west of the site at the foot of Yana Urco (the Black Mountain), where a huge rockfall provided loose stones of huge size. From the top of the fortress you get a very good impression of the Herculean task required to haul the stones all the way from the quarry to the temple. In order to cross the Urubamba, it is thought that the Incas simply diverted the

Ollantaytambo ruins

Defensive wall

Residential complex

Unfinished Sun Temple

Giant sculpted monoliths

Gateway

Broad terraces

Broad terraces

0   25   50m

Path continues along cliff above terraces. Steps down at several points bring you towards church/corner of plaza

Plaza

Church

Inca Miscana

To main town

To Baño de la Ñusta

river around the blocks positioned on its banks. A handful of giant blocks, known poetically as *piedras cansadas* ('tired stones'), litter the valley floor, lying where they were presumably abandoned whilst being transported from the quarry.

Work your way along the terraces north-east and descend again to a point just behind a church set on the side of the small plaza. There are a few smaller Inca ruins here including a small temple or observatory called **Inca Misanca**, and 200m below, the **Baño de la Ñusta**, a site associated with ritual bathing and the worship of water.

Opposite the main site, on the western edge of Ollantaytambo is a steep cliff known as **Pinkuylluna**. High on this cliff-face are the remnants of a number of *qolqas* (storehouses). There is a faint path that climbs to the storehouses, but you need to be careful and should take a guide rather than set off alone.

The old town The photogenic town set in the shadow of the illustrious ruins is one of the finest examples of Inca town planning. In most towns the original Inca streets and housing have been knocked down and built over, but in Ollantaytambo there are still plenty of original examples of each. The town is laid out on a grid and the corners of the main streets are marked by giant stone blocks. The Incas arranged their towns in communal blocks called *canchas*, which housed a number of families. The double-jamb doorways to these *canchas* indicate that the residents must have been part of the Inca elite. Simpler structures that would have belonged to poorer, less important citizens employed to work for the Incas can be found in the northern part of the town.

El Museo CATCCO (☎ 204204, daily 9am-7pm, entrance by donation) is one block west of Plaza de Armas on Patacalle. Inside this well-kept museum dedicated to ethnography and regional history are superb displays of historical and cultural artefacts. Local artisans, weavers and ceramicists also work on the premises, and their wares are on offer for sale in the museum shop or in the Casa Ecologica shop next door to the restaurant Mayupata. Guides trained by the museum can be hired here, and they can also arrange tours of the surrounding area. For a fascinating, detailed examination of the Inca stonework here, read *Inca Architecture and Construction at Ollantaytambo* by Jean-Pierre Protzen (1993).

Where to stay and eat   [See map overleaf]

Hostal Ollanta (☎ 204116; US$7.50/15, sgl/dbl, com) on the south side of the plaza has a good location and decent-sized rooms, albeit rather rudimentary.

The friendly *Albergue Kapuly* (US$12/24, sgl/dbl, att, breakfast) is immediately on your left as you leave the station.

Hostal Munay Tika (☎ 204111, 🖥 www.munaytika.com) on the road to the station is an attractive guesthouse with a bar, sauna and quiet, spacious rooms (US$30/35, sgl/dbl, breakfast) as well as access to the kitchen for guests.

Nearby, *Las Orquídeas* (☎ 204032) is a reasonably priced hostel with basic rooms (US$20/24, sgl/dbl, breakfast) and a pleasant courtyard in which to lounge.

On the road between the ruins and Plaza de Armas is the excellent *KB Tambo* (☎ 204091, 🖥 www.kbperu.com), which has good-sized comfortable rooms (US$15/30, sgl/dbl, att) and less expensive budget accommodation (US$10) as well as a pretty garden, roof-top deck with views of the ruins and a restaurant.

CUSCO & AROUND

The excellent North American-owned *El Albergue* (☎ 204014, 💻 www.elalbergue .com; US$58/74-95, sgl/dbl, att, breakfast), Casilla 784 Cusco (entrance on the platform of the station), has eight elegant rooms set around a courtyard, a sauna and a shop/gallery selling handicrafts. Good discounts are available here during the low season.

The modern terracotta-coloured *Hotel Pakaritampu* (☎ 204020, 💻 www.pakari tampu.com; US$127/132-150/169, sgl/dbl /tpl, att, buffet breakfast), on the road just up from the station, is comfortable and friendly, has a bar and restaurant as well as internet service for visitors and a TV room.

Hostal Sauce (☎ 204044, 💻 www. hostalsauce.com.pe; US$89/98/145, sgl/ dbl/tpl, att, breakfast) has the best location, over looking the Inca ruins and close to the main plaza. The rooms are comfortable though service is sometimes brusque.

La Fortaleza is a good restaurant serving backpacker staples with branches on both the north side of Plaza de Armas and on Plaza Ruinas. Opposite, on the south side of the plaza is *Camping Café*, which has an extensive menu of local dishes and hosts live music in the evenings. Also on Plaza de Armas is *Heart's Café* (💻 www.heartscafe.org) which opens early for breakfast and specializes in vegetarian and wholefood dishes cooked with a local twist. Run by townsfolk, the proceeds are ploughed back into the community and go towards children's and women's projects in the Sacred Valley. For coffee and breakfasts also try *Il Cappuccino*, just before the bridge, which offers a slightly more up-market service. The same owners run *Kusicoyllor*, on Plaza Ruinas, which dishes up pizza and pasta in generous portions. *Mayupata*, on Jr Convención by the bridge, serves good Peruvian food in addition to international dishes and has an open fireplace and bar overlooking the river.

Transport

There is a tourist train service from Cusco to Ollantaytambo (see p357). The station is about a 10- to 15-minute walk from Plaza de Armas. From Ollantaytambo there is a cheap train to Aguas Calientes. The Backpacker Noche leaves at 8.15pm and arrives at 9.45pm. A return ticket is US$47 and is available in advance from Estación Huanchac in Cusco. Having caught the train back from Aguas Calientes it is very easy to pick up an onward bus to Cusco.

Direct buses to Ollantaytambo leave Cusco four times a day from Av Grau or Tullumayo (about s/5, 2hrs). At other times you will have to catch a bus to Urubamba and get an onward connection from there. Buses for Urubamba also leave from Av Grau (s/5, 2hrs). From Ollantaytambo buses and *colectivos* depart for Urubamba (s/1), Chilca and Km82 from the main plaza and outside the station. Direct buses to Cusco (s/10) depart from outside the station, where they meet the incoming trains. To avoid the scrum you may be better taking a *colectivo* to Urubamba and catching a bus on to Cusco from there.

Cusichaca Valley

Some 26km from Ollantaytambo is the Cusichaca Valley. This area has been at the heart of a series of excavations carried out by the archaeologist Ann Kendall over the last 30 years (🖳 www.cusichaca.org). The organization also pioneers integrated rural development projects in tandem with local communities, promoting the use of local resources, traditional skills and appropriate modern techniques to benefit the communities involved.

The Inca Fort **Huillca Raccay** (see box p226) was uncovered in the late 1970s before work focused on the ruins at **Patallacta** (see p210), at the start of the classic Inca Trail. Current excavation is being done in the Patacancha Valley to the north-east of Ollantaytambo.

Aguas Calientes (Pueblo Machu Picchu)   [see map p201]

Officially known as Pueblo Machu Picchu, this village is very much the end of the line now that the track that used to run on to Quillabamba has been destroyed. Really just a dormitory town for the ruins themselves, it's an ugly rash in the pristine forest of the Sanctuary and has in the past been described as the 'Armpit of Peru'. The town is, however, undergoing something of a renaissance and amidst all the development work there now stands one of the finest hotels in the entire valley and a very good restaurant. Information is available from the iPeru branch (☎ 211104) on Av Pachacutec, in the same building as the Machu Picchu ticket office that sells entrance tickets to the ruins.

For a while regulation changes have meant that you can no longer buy entrance tickets for Machu Picchu upon arrival at the site itself but must buy them in advance in Aguas Calientes. Even if this situation has changed it's far better to **get your ticket in advance in Aguas Calientes** rather than waste precious time in a line at the ruins. If you are travelling with a trekking agency or tour group then they should ensure that you are provided with a ticket. Tickets are available from the INC/Machu Picchu Cultural Centre in Aguas Calientes, which is adjacent to the main plaza in the same building as the iPeru office. The office opens at 5.15am and payment for the ticket must be in exact money only. Buy your ticket the day before – they are valid for three days from the date of purchase, but only for a single entry to the site. If you want to return to Machu Picchu you will have to buy a second ticket. Tickets are also available in Cusco (see p156).

There are plenty of **internet cafés** and **cash machines** on Av Pachacutec, around the plaza and throughout the town.

The **hot springs** after which the town is named comprise a series of rather pungent communal baths several minutes' walk north from town. These are open daily 5am-8.30pm and cost s/11 to visit. If you are tempted, the pools are cleanest and most pleasant first thing in the morning.

On the road to Machu Picchu it's worth visiting **Museo de Sitio Manuel Chávez Ballón – Machu Picchu Museum** (Carreterra Hiram Bingham; 10am-4pm, s/20) a small museum displaying a number of objects uncovered at Machu Picchu. There are interactive displays and a wealth of information on excavations, Inca building methods, cosmology and other cultural bits and pieces. There's also an interesting **botanical garden** here.

The trail up the mountain **Putucusi** also starts here. Follow the railway track 250m west of the small station on Av Imperios (not the main station for Cusco) to pick up a steeply ascending path that climbs for two hours to the top (ask at Gringo Bill's if you're having trouble locating the path). Parts of the trail have ladder rungs fixed in place and in others you may have to scramble. If it has been raining the path can be very slippery and treacherous. The views from the top across to Machu Picchu are stupendous, though.

Where to stay

Cheapest of all is the *municipal campground* about 1km downhill from the centre of town towards Machu Picchu and adjacent to the bridge over the Urubamba; it charges s/15 per person; there are cold water showers. Take great care of your possessions here.

In an alley off Pachacútec, is *Hospedaje Joe*, where rooms can cost as little as s/20/40 (sgl/dbl, com). On the plaza just before Gringo Bill's, *Hospedaje Bromelias* (☎ 211145) is rough and ready but cheap as a result (US$7.50/12, sgl/dbl, att). *Hospedaje los Caminantes*, at Av Imperio de los Incas 140, alongside the railway tracks, is clean and friendly enough to make up for the basic rooms (US$7.50/15, sgl/dbl, att) and noisy location.

For other cheaper accommodation, head up the hill towards the hot springs; this street, Av Pachacútec, is dotted with places to stay including the efficient and comfortable *Ima Sumac* (☎ 232111, US$20/35 sgl/dbl, breakfast).

A mid-range option close to the train tracks is *Machupicchu Hostal* (☎ 211034; US$30/35/45 sgl/dbl/tpl) which is tidy and efficient, boasts a pretty interior courtyard and has rooms which are good value but

with paper-thin walls. The bohemian *Rupa Wasi* (☎ 211101, 🖥 www.rupawasi.net, US$69-99, dbl, breakfast) is a rustic eco-lodge hidden up Huanacare, a small alley off Collasuyo. Ridiculously laid-back it's a haven for those who just want to chill out, although cooking classes, birdwatching trips and other treks can be arranged by the knowledgeable, friendly owners as well.

Hostal Wiracocha Inn (☎ 211088, 🖥 www.wiracochainn.com; US$65/65/85, sgl/dbl/tpl, att), on Calle Wiracocha, is small and helpful. The rooms, with large windows and good views, are smart and well-tended and service is good.

Gringo Bill's (☎ 211046, 🖥 www.gringobills.com), is at Pasaje Colla Raymi 104, just off the plaza. The place is something of an institution in Aguas Calientes and still maintains its high standards, remaining friendly, easy-going and offering reasonable value at US$75/105 (dbl/tpl, att). There's a restaurant, a bar and a rooftop *Terraza Lounge*.

Also recommended are the smart *Hotel Machu Picchu Inn* (☎ 211011, 🖥 mapiinn@terra.com.pe, US$105, sgl & dbl), on Pachacutec 101, amidst the hostels and cheap eateries, and the good-value *Hostal*

Aguas Calientes

To hot springs

Govinda
El Manu
Ima Sumac
Inca Yupanqui
Clave de Sol/Chez Maggy
Wiracocha
Hostal Wiracocha Inn
Av Pachacutec
Football pitch

trailblazer

Waisicha Pub
Indio Feliz
Yupanqui
Hotel Machu Picchu Inn
Hospedaje Joe
Manu Capac
Market
Railway station
Machu Picchu Pueblo Hotel & Café Inkaterra

Rupa Wasi
Gringo Bill's
Hospedaje Bromelias
Av Pachacutec
Centro Cultural Machu Picchu
iPeru & INC office
Pueblo Viejo
Sinchi Roca
Plaza de Armas
Colla Raymi
Collasuyo
Ticket office & buses to Machu Picchu
Toto's House

Police station
Train ticket office
Local railway station
Av Imperio de los Incas
Hostal Presidente

Hospedaje Los Caminantes
Machu Picchu Hostal
Hatuchay Tower
To Municipal Campground & Museo de Sitio Manuel Chávez Ballón
To Putucusi

Rio Urubamba

0   25   50m

Presidente (☎ 211065, 🖳 presidente @terra.com.pe; US$55/60/65, sgl/dbl/tpl, breakfast), situated by the train tracks on Imperio de los Incas.

Hatuchay Tower (☎ 211201, 🖳 www .hatuchaytower.com), at Carreterra Puente Ruinas 4, is a smart, modern place opposite the river and just down from the old station. Although soulless and lacking any real character, the rooms are luxurious and have balconies (US$350/450, dbl/tpl, att). Buffet breakfast, dinner and collection from the station are included in the room rates.

The top hotel is *Machu Picchu Pueblo Hotel* (☎ 211122; reservations in Lima ☎ 01 610 0400, 🖳 www.inkaterra.com), where beautiful colonial-style bungalows are set in 12 acres of exquisite, enclosing forest, five minutes' walk east from the rest of town; to get here follow the basic path next to the railway line. There is also a pool, a sauna, spa and an expensive restaurant. Room rates begin around US$400 and rise sharply depending on the style of room and the season.

There's also an expensive hotel at the ruins themselves (see p336).

Where to eat
The best restaurant is the outstanding French-run *Indio Feliz*, (☎ 211090, 🖳 www.indiofeliz.com), Calle Lloque Yupanqui Lt 4. If you walk up towards the springs it's on the left just after the school on Av Pachacútec. Dishes here include Urubamba trout, ginger chicken, beef skewers and a wide range of delicious desserts. The wine list is well chosen and prices are reasonable.

Café Inkaterra at Machu Picchu Pueblo Hotel (see above) gives Indio Feliz a run for its money with high-class Peruvian fusion food and good views over the river. The vast *Toto's House*, overlooking the river at the south-eastern corner of the village on Imperio de los Incas, offers an 'all-you-can-eat' international and Peruvian buffet for US$12, while *Pueblo*

Viejo on Pachacútec, owned by the same group, serves grilled meats and pizzas from its open wood-fired grill. *Govinda*, on Pachacútec, serves good-value vegetarian food. You can also get decent veggie food at *El Manu*, which is one of the town's best-value eateries. Cusco's Chez Maggy has a branch at Pachacútec 156, called *Clave de Sol*, selling decent oven-baked pizzas and other international fare. For live music in a good atmosphere visit *Waisicha Pub* on Calle Lloque Yupanqui.

Transport
Aguas Calientes boasts two **railway stations**: the modern one, surrounded by wire fencing and policed by armed guards, serves the expensive tourist trains. During 2004 this was damaged twice by landslides and floods ensuring that for a while the platform area and actual station couldn't be accessed as the bridge crossing the river just before the station was destroyed. The ticket office here is open from 6.30am-5.30pm.

Local trains set off from the stretch of tracks running beneath the police station, to the south of the main square. There's no indication that this is a station, for it's little more than a rail track with pizza restaurants either side. All train tickets must be bought from the ticket office (8.30am-6pm) to the east of the police station. See p357 for details and timetables of the train service. This is also where the train from La Hidroeléctrica, at the end of the Santa Teresa trek, stops (see p253).

The **buses for Machu Picchu** leave from the bus 'station', just a patch of concrete where the train tracks pass over a small stream, every 15-30 minutes from 6.30am-1pm. You can buy tickets for the 20-minute journey (US$6 one way) at a concrete house near where the bus leaves.

See p336 for more information on transport from Aguas Calientes and Machu Picchu.

Cusco department area code: ☎ 84. If phoning from outside Peru dial ☎ +51-1.

SOUTH AND EAST OF CUSCO

For many people the focus of a trip to Cusco is the Sacred Valley and Machu Picchu. However, there are also several fascinating ruins to see to the south and east of the city. A paved road runs south-east from Cusco to **Sicuani**, following the upper reaches of the Río Urubamba. There are some ruins scattered across the altiplano here, indicating the spread of the Incas towards Lake Titicaca, where the road eventually arrives at Puno. Just outside Cusco, making it virtually a suburb, stands **San Jerónimo**, which hosts an enormous fruit and veg market on Saturdays. South-east from here the valley narrows as you approach Oropesa, before which lie the ruins of Tipón and after which the ruins of Pikillacta.

Tipón (7am-5.30pm, s/10 or entry with Visitor's Ticket) is 25km from Cusco and 2km before Oropesa, around an hour's walk away from the main road, hidden at the head of a small valley beyond the remains of the hacienda Quispicanchi. The extensive Inca ruins here include a series of agricultural terraces, ceremonial baths, fountains and stone-lined irrigation channels. Above the last terrace a trail leads to a temple complex built around a *huaca*. An enormous reservoir collected water from a spring, which was then distributed to the terraces along a series of channels. Behind and to the left of the main site a faint trail leads to a further series of ruins and well-preserved Inca terraces that are now in use by local people. So extensive are the terraces here that archaeologists have suggested the site may have been an experimental farm, much like Moray (see pp194-5).

Historians counter that Tipón could have been a palace but the accounts left by chroniclers make it difficult to say whose it was. Garcilaso de la Vega believed that it was the royal house of Viracocha whose father, Yáhuar Huácac, was defeated by the Chancas. Viracocha stood up to and later defeated the Chancas, and was subsequently crowned Inca in place of his father. Garcilaso wrote that, 'It was determined that the son, as most of the court decided, would be the head of the kingdom; and to avoid riots and civil wars, they accepted everything the prince wanted. After it was agreed, they obtained a Royal House, between Muyna and Quepicancha, in a pleasant place with all the gifts, fields, gardens and other royal amusements for hunting and fishing.' Other chroniclers such as Pedro Cieza de León and Juan de Betanzos claim that it was actually Viracocha's son Pachacutec who defeated the Chancas after his father and older brother Inca Urcon had fled Cusco.

Further on from Tipón are the villages of Oropesa and Huacarpay; the latter stands on the shores of Laguna Huacarpay. Dotted around the lake are several pre-Columbian sites. Foremost of these is **Pikillacta** (7am-5.30pm, s/10 or entry with Visitor's Ticket), whose name translates rather unfortunately as 'City of Fleas'. The substantial site, 32km from Cusco and 7km from Oropesa, is the largest provincial outpost of the Ayacucho-based Huari (AD600-1000) and is the only major pre-Inca site around Cusco. The large complex, which is surrounded by a defensive wall, is thought to have been a storehouse or centre for collecting tributes and supplies. There were also adobe buildings and *tambos* here, many of them more than one storey tall, and many whose rough walls were treated with lime. Unusually the doors to these buildings appear to be on the first floor and in theory they must have been entered via ladders. Not much is known of the history of the site, but the small turquoise figurines in the Museo Inka (see p151) were found here. The Incas subsequently modified the site and possibly built the aqueduct that links Pikillacta to Rumicolca.

Around 1km beyond Pikillacta stands the beautifully crafted, enormous Inca archway and defensive passage at **Rumicolca** (open all day, entry free). Built on top of an original Huari site, the Inca stonework is vastly superior to the cruder, original construction. The archway itself rears up from the altiplano in a series of four tiers and stands a full 12m/40ft above the plain. During Inca times all traffic on the road to and from Cusco had to pass through the giant, imposing archway, which acted as a checkpoint, regulating the passage of goods and people.

To get to any of these sites catch a bus from Cusco to Urcos, departing from Av de la Cultura. For Tipón ask to be dropped off at Oropesa and then walk back down the Cusco road for 2km, until you come across the signposted path to Tipón and follow this for an hour as it climbs through a gully to the ruins. For Pikillacta or Rumicolca, both of which are on the main road, ask to be dropped by the entrance to the site. Alternatively, you can catch a taxi from Cusco, or take an organized tour run by one of the agencies in town (see pp156-161).

ROUTE GUIDE & MAPS

8

Using this guide

ROUTE DESCRIPTIONS

Directions in the following chapter are shown as an instruction to go left or right and as a compass point. For instance, if the instruction stated 'turn right (west)', it would indicate that west is to your right.

Direction

The trails described in this book are laid out as they are usually walked, from the traditional start point to the typical finish point. In a number of instances it is possible to walk the trail in either direction. The exceptions are that you are not allowed to start at Machu Picchu and hike the Inca Trail in reverse, meaning that you can't finish at Km104, Km88, Km82, Chilca (Km77) or Mollepata. The Choquequirao trek is typically done as a there-and-back hike along the same route, although it is possible to connect it to other treks and complete a linear hike, finishing at Machu Picchu or Vilcabamba.

ROUTE MAPS   [See pp26-7 for route planning map]

Scale and walking times

Most of the trekking maps in this guide are drawn at the same scale, roughly 1:50,000 (20mm = 1km). Many of the trails are uphill and downhill, and the length of a trek is not an accurate reflection of the time it will take you to complete. The times included on the maps are there only as a guideline. They refer to **walking times only** and do not include any stops for breaks or food. To calculate the total time it will take you to complete a section you will need to make allowances for these and add on a few minutes. Overall you may find that you need to **add between 10% and 30% depending your walking speed** and average length of time taken at each break.

Gradient arrows

There are gradient arrows marked on the trekking maps throughout the book. The arrows point uphill; two arrows close together mean that the hill is steep, one on its own means that it is a gentler gradient. If, for example, you are walking between A (at 3100m) and B (at 3300m) and the path between the two is short and steep, it would be illustrated as follows: A - - - >>- - - B.

Place names

The Quechua names for many of the ruins and archaeological sites along the various treks can be spelt in several ways as the original language had no alphabet. The more common Hispanic versions have been used here as they appear on most maps in this form. Where there's the potential for confusion all names are shown so, for instance, Llactapata is also referred to as Paltallacta – but not to be confused with Patallacta (no first 'l') which is an entirely different place.

GETTING TO THE TRAILHEADS

For the Inca Trail you are almost certain to be trekking with an agency, which means that you will be collected in Cusco and taken to the trailhead either by bus or by train. The **trains** to Aguas Calientes, which go via the trailheads at Km77, 82, 88 and 104, leave regularly each day. See p357 for details of times and prices.

It is also possible to catch a ride on a tourist **bus** from Cusco to Chilca (Km77) or Km82. These are cheaper, but usually packed with fellow tourists, meaning that you will inevitably start walking as a group. You are far better off overnighting in Ollantaytambo and catching an early bus from there to the trailhead, to arrive well before the first bus from Cusco.

❏ **Inca Trail regulations explained**

The Inca Trail is governed by a series of complex and convoluted regulations, which are enforced stringently. They also change frequently and prices are hiked from time to time. Before booking check the latest information with Andean Travel Web (🖥 www.andeantravelweb.com/peru) where there are links to the Spanish-language only DRCC (Direccion Regional de Cultura Cusco) website (🖥 www.machupicchu.gob.pe) showing permit availability. South American Explorers (🖥 www.saexplorers.org) also has good information.

The key elements to remember are that **you must have a permit before embarking on the trek to Machu Picchu**. A maximum of 500 people including guides, cooks and porters are allowed to start the trail each day. In reality this means that only around 200 tourists per day can begin the trek. This daily limit covers not only the classic Inca Trail but also the extended routes from Km77 and Km82, the Salkantay Trek that joins the Inca Trail at Huayllabamba and the two shorter routes from Km104. The result is that there is fierce competition for the permits, and in order to secure a preferred departure date you will have to **book well in advance**, especially during high season (Jun-Aug) when you should try to secure your permit up to five months ahead.

To book a **permit** you must use a **licensed agency** based in Peru; they are not issued directly to tourists. In order to obtain a licence, the agency must prove that they provide professional, licensed guides, good-quality camping equipment, radio equipment and first-aid supplies including oxygen. Licences are reviewed annually in February. Agencies can only take groups of up to sixteen people at any one time, and must provide two or more guides for groups of more than eight people (seven on the routes from Km104). See pp156-9 for information on arranging treks in Cusco and for a list of well-established companies with sound reputations. You will need to provide the agency with your name and passport details, and pay the entrance fee in advance. Permits are issued for an individual and are not transferable. Nor are they

Route map key

					♠	Accommodation
	Route		Steep slope	𝚫	Campsite
	Road		Slope	◻	Building
	Track		Water	⁘	Archaeological site
	Railway		River/waterfall	⌘	Trees/forest
	Bridge		Mountain		Grassland/puna
	Pass		Spur/ridge		Viewpoint
	Steps		Cliff/sheer hillside	⑱	Map continuation

refundable. Once issued, it is also impossible to change the start date. Agencies have to make the booking for an entire group in one go and can't make alterations afterwards, so prefer to wait as long as possible to secure as many trekkers as they can before committing themselves to a set of permits as it is more profitable.

The **entrance fee** for the classic Inca Trail is s/251 (around US$90) for adults and half price for children under 15 and students under 28 with a valid International Student Identity Card (ISIC), which must be presented at the time of booking. The fee is payable by anyone trekking to Machu Picchu via Huayllabamba regardless of where their trek started from. There is a fee of s/146 (US$53) per adult and s/83 (US$30) per child or student for people using the Salkantay Trek to simply hike over Salkantay and out via Km88. The entrance fee for the shorter routes from Km104 is s/146/83 (US$53/30) adults/children under 15 and students. The fee does not include the s/126 (around US$45) one-day entrance charge to Machu Picchu (half-price for students with ISIC card). People on the Santa Teresa trek need to pay s/129 (around US$46) for an INC permit when they get to Soray Pampa. For those tackling the Vilcabamba Trail, be aware that there is a s/108 (around US$39) fee that includes access to the ruins themselves. Regulations have also been imposed to try and improve the plight of **porters** working on the Inca Trail, whose permits are paid for by the agency that employs them (see pp18-19).

Whilst on the trail, trekkers must carry their actual **passport** with them; a photocopy is not sufficient. You will be required to present your passport at various checkpoints with your trek permit and, if relevant, your ISIC card.

As part of an attempt to conserve the trail the following are **banned**: plastic bottles (although evidence along the trail suggests that this isn't being enforced properly); pets and pack animals (although llamas are allowed as far as Huayllabamba); and walking poles unless the tips are covered by a rubber bung to minimize damage to the Inca paths.

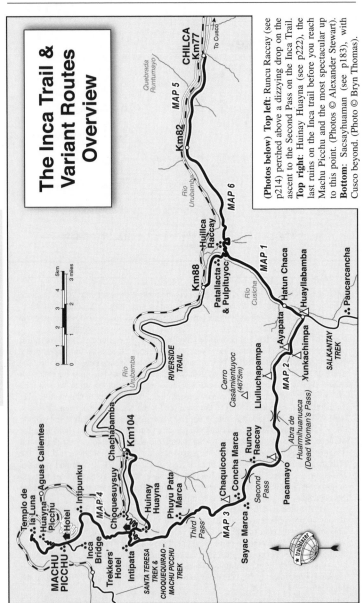

The Inca Trail & Variant Routes Overview

(Photos below) **Top left:** Runcu Raccay (see p214) perched above a dizzying drop on the ascent to the Second Pass on the Inca Trail. **Top right:** Huiñay Huayna (see p222), the last ruins on the Inca trail before you reach Machu Picchu and the most spectacular up to this point. (Photos © Alexander Stewart). **Bottom:** Sacsayhuaman (see p183), with Cusco beyond. (Photo © Bryn Thomas).

Buses from Cusco to Mollepata leave early from Calle Arcopata. Buses to Abancay that also depart from here can drop you off at the road that leads up to Mollepata although it's a long walk from here to the actual trailhead. For information on how to get to Huancacalle for the Vilcabamba Trail see p259; for Cachora for the Choquequirao Trek see p287.

The classic Inca Trail

This is the undisputed draw for most people coming to Cusco and is by far the most popular and over-subscribed trek in the region.

KM88 (QORIHUAYRACHINA) TO HUAYLLABAMBA   [MAP 1, p211]

The train from Cusco only stops briefly at Km88, sometimes also referred to by its Quechua name Qorihuayrachina, so watch the kilometre markers after Km82 and be ready to disembark. Once off the train continue to walk west along the tracks, in the same direction as the train was heading. A path leads away from the tracks and down to the river, where there is a substantial bridge and a warden's hut. A guard here will check your permit and passport before letting you cross the river and begin the trail proper.

Once on the far side of the bridge bear left (east) and climb gently through a stand of eucalyptus trees above the southern bank of the Urubamba.

Three-quarters of an hour after setting off from the bridge you will come to the mouth of the Cusichaca Valley, down which flows a river by the same name.

ROUTE GUIDE & MAPS

The Classic Inca Trail

Elevation (m)

- 4000 — Abra de Huarmihuanusca (Dead Woman's Pass)
- 2nd Pass
- Runcu Raccay
- 3rd Pass
- 3500 — Phuyu Pata Marca
- Pacamayo
- 3000 — Huayllabamba
- Trekkers' Hotel
- 2500 — Km88
- Machu Picchu

Distance (km): 0 5 10 15 20 25 30 35 40

(Opposite) The local people who work as porters and arrieros are the mainstays of every trekking team. **Top**: Approaching Dead Woman's Pass (see p212). (Photo © A Stewart). **Bottom left**: Arriero and his mule on the heavily overgrown trail to Espíritu Pampa. (Photo © H Stedman). **Bottom right**: Taking a break near Choquequirao. (Photo © A Stewart).

At the junction of the two valleys lie the sprawling ruins of **Patallacta** (see box below). A small round tower, **Pulpituyoc**, stands on a ridge by the river. It is possible to *camp* on the banks of the river in the lee of the ruins.

Passing to the east of Patallacta, the trail continues gently gaining height whilst continuing south before crossing over the Cusichaca and climbing steeply up the opposite slope for 10-15mins. It settles on the eastern bank and begins to head upstream towards Huayllabamba. In places the path splits briefly before coming together again. Follow the broader, most obviously used track (usually the lower branch) in these instances.

The path climbs gently but steadily for an hour, passing first beneath cliffs covered in bromeliads and then through gentler terrain. There are a number of terraces visible on the far side of the river. Ignore the lesser tracks leading down to the river, one of which crosses a bridge to a small settlement on the far, western bank. Continue on the eastern bank past a signboard exaggerating the steepness of the route ahead and a hut from which you can buy soft drinks. From this point there are good views back down the Cusichaca valley to Mt Verónica, which is visible as a pyramid in the middle of the valley.

Beyond the huts the path arrives at a second bridge (Puente). Cross the Cusichaca here and climb sharply to a small settlement called **Hatun Chaca**, where you can also buy soft drinks or chicha. Half an hour and 2km after Hatun Chaca cross another bridge over a tributary of the Cusichaca, the Llulluchayoc, at the outskirts of **Huayllabamba**, a sprawling village built above Inca terraces.

Huayllabamba is the largest village on the trail, and it's the last place where you can buy basic food supplies before the Trekkers' Hotel at Huinay Huayna. There are a number of *campsites* here with toilet blocks and cold running water.

❏ Patallacta and Pulpituyoc

Although first uncovered by Hiram Bingham in 1911 and partially excavated by him in 1915, it wasn't until the late 1970s when Ann Kendall and the Cusichaca Trust extensively excavated the site that people realized just how substantial **Patallacta** was. The site is laid out in a typical Inca fashion and dates from the mid-15th century. There are 116 buildings and five baths laid out in a regular pattern. A canal feeds the main baths but appears to have fallen into disuse shortly after the invasion of the Spanish conquistadors, implying that the site was abandoned around 1540. Extensive terraces surround the buildings, suggesting that the site used to be primarily an agricultural station responsible for the production of crops such as maize that would have been used to supply other Inca sites in the region, and a distribution centre for those crops produced higher up the Cusichaca valley such as potatoes. The site probably also had a strategic function as it sits at the junction of a number of Inca paths, and was ideally placed to regulate traffic and monitor who was moving where.

The round tower standing close to the main ruins, **Pulpituyoc**, whose name means 'containing a pulpit', was the religious centre for the site. Here there are eleven buildings, two baths and a carefully sculpted rock. Although the exact purpose and use for the buildings isn't known, the fact that they have curved walls signifies that this was a place of great spiritual importance to the Incas.

MAP 1

RÍO URUBAMBA

KM88

TO CHILCA & KMS 77 & 82

HUILLCA RACCAY

6

Km88

45 MINS

TUNNEL

4

PATALLACTA & PULPITUYOC

RIVERSIDE TRAIL

PATALLACTA

TERRACES

CERRO PATALLACTA

RÍO CUSICHACA

60 MINS

0   ½ mile

0   1km
APPROX SCALE

PUENTE BRIDGE

HATUN CHACA

HATUNCHACA

30 MINS

STEEP STEPPED SECTION THROUGH RARE CLOUD FOREST

Ayapata

QUEBRADA

2

LLULLUCHAYOC

HUAYLLABAMBA

HUAYLLABAMBA

Yunkachimpa

RÍO CHAUPIHUAYJO

SALKANTAY TREK

11

HUAYLLABAMBA

45 MINS

ROUTE GUIDE & MAPS

PAUCARCANCHA (MAP 11)

TO LLULLUCHAPAMPA ◄─ (MAP 2)   YUNKACHIMPA   ◄ 60 MINS   HUAYLLABAMBA

Huayllabamba used to have a reputation for theft but it is much improved and is one of few sites along the trail where you can *camp* within a community, chat with locals and even join a game of football on the local pitch (though it is exhausting work at this altitude). At the top of the village is a warden's office where you must register and where porters have their loads checked and weighed before they can progress.

HUAYLLABAMBA TO PACAMAYO CAMP   [MAP 1, p211; MAP 2, opp]

From the bridge over the Llulluchayoc follow the trail on the river's left-hand (south-west) bank, heading uphill. At a hairpin bend it quickly gets much steeper, and after about an hour of climbing you reach the *Yunkachimpa campsite* alongside the Río Chaupihuayjo (also shown as the Río Huayruro on some maps). Small and set on two tiers, the campsite itself is OK, but the surrounding area is badly littered and has in places been used as an al fresco toilet by inconsiderate trekkers.

Pass through the campsite and over a bridge across the river. Then head steeply uphill through a clearing and small campsite called *Ayapata*, before following the left-hand (south-west) bank of the Llulluchayoc as it veers to the west. Lupins and snapdragons line the path and you soon enter a beautiful cloud forest or *polylepis* woodland, rare in the Andes because it's self-contained. The path climbs through the forest alongside the course of a river, occasionally close to the water and at other times high above it, on a series of steep steps.

As you reach the fringe of the forest there is another *campsite*, but 20mins beyond this, above the treeline, is a better one. *Llulluchapampa* has running water, a toilet block set on the top tier of terraces and exceptional views down the valley. It is exposed though and can get very cold at night, and after torrential rain the ground becomes boggy here.

Beyond Llulluchapampa it is possible to make out the first pass. **Abra de Huarmihuanusca** is more commonly known as **Dead Woman's Pass**. It isn't known who the dead woman was or even if there was actually a dead woman at all, with many putting the name down to the fact that the pass resembles a woman lying on her back as if dead. The ascent to the pass looks deceptively simple and, although it is a gradual, steady climb parallel to the river to its source and then across the puna and over a section of paved path (laid in 1998 to protect the mountain from erosion), it will take $1^{1}/_{2}$-2hrs to reach the high point (4200m/13,775ft).

From the broad saddle that marks the pass, the path descends steeply and swiftly into the neighbouring valley, plummeting 800m/2625ft in the course of

---

❏ **Important note – walking times**
Unless otherwise specified, **all times in this book refer only to the time spent walking**. You will need to add 10-30% to allow for rests, photography, checking the map, drinking water etc. When planning the day's hike count on 5-7 hours' actual walking.

Within the map:

4613M △

4644M △

CERRO
CASÁMIENTUYOC
△ 4675M

4774M △

4539M △   △4531M

Llulluchapampa

RÍO PACAMAYO

Pacamayo

FIRST
PASS

FALSE
SUMMIT

3

ABRA DE
HUARMIHUANUSCA
(DEAD WOMAN'S PASS)
(4200M)

PUNA
GRASSLAND

1

0   ½ mile

0   APPROX SCALE   1km

MAP 2

LAGUNA
SOQTACOCHA

120 MINS FROM
YUNKACHIMPA (MAP 1)

PACAMAYO ◄— 60 MINS   PASS ◄— 90 MINS   LLULLUCHAPAMPA ◄—

just over a mile. At the bottom of this dizzying descent is a vast, sprawling campsite set amidst some scrubby trees, adjacent to the Pacamayo river. The *Pacamayo campsite* is popular with large tour groups and although facilities here are reasonably good, with two toilet blocks, it is often noisy and crowded. Guides have to register at the warden's hut in the centre of the site.

PACAMAYO CAMP TO THIRD PASS   [MAP 2 above; MAP 3, p215]

The path climbs very steeply from the Pacamayo camp up a series of steps, crossing two bridged sections over precipitous drops where the original trail has crumbled away. Take the opportunity during the climb to admire the viewpoints over the valley below whilst pausing for breath on the way up.

After about an hour, you reach the Inca ruins of **Runcu Raccay** (see box p214), a circular structure with a rectangular outbuilding perched precariously on the edge of the valley. This was probably a *tambo*, where chasquis rested, but some think it was a guard post or even, because of the circular walls, a ritual building, although the fairly basic build quality tends to suggest otherwise. The site is best viewed from higher up the path, where you can see both structures together as well as outstanding views back to Dead Woman's Pass. Camping is not permitted around the ruins.

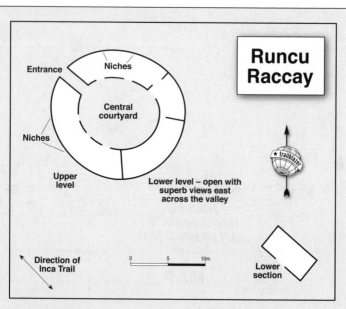

Runcu Raccay

Entrance
Niches
Niches
Central courtyard
Upper level
Lower level – open with superb views east across the valley

★ trailblazer

Direction of Inca Trail

0   5   10m

Lower section

❑ Runcu Raccay

The compact ruins at Runcu Raccay, perched precariously above a vertiginous chasm, were found by Hiram Bingham. Given its location on the Inca Trail and the fact that it had superlative views across the valley to Abra de Huarmihuanusca, Bingham decided that it must have been a fortress or watch tower. The archaeologist Dr Paul Fejos examined it in 1940 and concluded that it was a *tambo* for passing travellers.

The site consists of two structures: a larger, round building with a double skin and walls indented with niches, and a smaller, lower, rectangular structure. Both are completed in fairly basic, rustic style and the stonework is rough and ready in comparison to what the Incas could really do. The popular theory is that the site is a transitional building, taking travellers from the purely practical buildings in the Cusichaca Valley to the far more elaborate, significant structures closer to Machu Picchu.

The **second pass** (3950m/12,955ft), sometimes called Abra de Runcu Raccay, is another hour up, beyond a series of false summits and at the top of a series of steep staircases. Just before the real pass, the path winds between two tarns where Andean gulls sometimes gather. The ground around the tarns is boggy. Don't stray from the dirt-gravel path as you risk damaging this very fragile eco-system. By the tarns there's a sign saying 'Deer Area', but you'll be very lucky to see any. You are no longer allowed to camp alongside the tarns or at the pass itself. The second pass is another broad saddle, boasting exceptional views of Pumasillo (6072m/19,915ft) and the Vilcabamba range. Below it the path

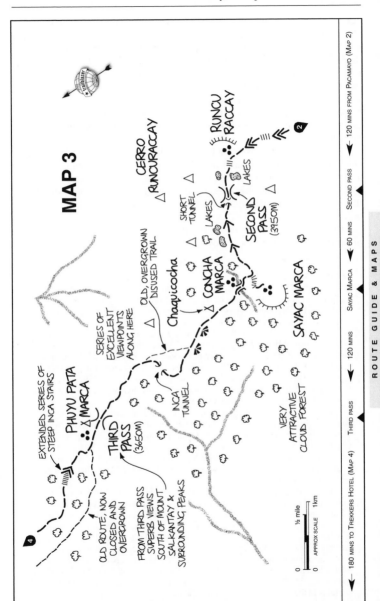

MAP 3

RUNCU RACCAY

CERRO RUNCURACCAY

LAKES

SHORT TUNNEL

LAKES

SECOND PASS (3950M)

Chaquicocha

CONCHA MARCA

SAYAC MARCA

OLD, OVERGROWN DISUSED TRAIL

SERIES OF EXCELLENT VIEWPOINTS ALONG HERE

PHUYU PATA MARCA

EXTENDED SERIES OF STEEP INCA STAIRS

THIRD PASS (3650M)

INCA TUNNEL

VERY ATTRACTIVE CLOUD FOREST

OLD ROUTE, NOW CLOSED AND OVERGROWN

FROM THIRD PASS SUPERB VIEWS SOUTH OF MOUNT SALKANTAY & SURROUNDING PEAKS

0   ½ mile
0   1km
APPROX SCALE

ROUTE GUIDE & MAPS

← 180 MINS TO TREKKERS HOTEL (MAP 4)   THIRD PASS   ← 120 MINS   SAYAC MARCA   ← 60 MINS   SECOND PASS   ← 120 MINS FROM PACAMAYO (MAP 2)

again falls away steeply into an adjoining valley. Having descended through a **short tunnel** the trail begins a series of tight switchbacks, dropping height quickly until it reaches a small viewpoint atop a promontory. Beyond here the descent is more gradual and the path curls and coils across the slopes. To the right (north) of the pass lies a large, algae-covered lake, whilst ahead of you (west) Sayac Marca is visible straddling a rocky spur high above the cloud forest. The path tumbles down a stretch of hillside towards a hairpin bend. Just before this dog-leg right is a staircase that branches left (south-west) and climbs 50m/150ft to the entrance of **Sayac Marca** (see box below). Camping is not permitted here.

Around the hairpin bend and sitting in the shadow of Sayac Marca is the small set of ruins at **Concha Marca**. Tucked in a little valley and perched atop a series of tall, rounded terraces, these ruins were only uncovered in the early 1980s. There is a small stream here that is a good place to fill up with water as there isn't another water source until the third pass. Be careful to purify your water carefully though.

Beyond the ruins lies a stretch of very attractive trail. The path skirts a series of precipices on stone slabs, most of which are of Inca origin and contours

---

❏ Sayac Marca

The dramatically sited ruins of Sayac Marca are protected on three sides by sheer cliffs that fall away to the jungle far below. Hiram Bingham again first found the site, but it was Dr Paul Fejos who gave it the appropriate, descriptive moniker Sayac Marca, meaning 'Inaccessible Town', in the 1940s. The ruins overlook the Aobamba Valley and stand at a fork in the original Inca road. The classic Inca Trail continues on one branch of the fork whilst the other descends through the jungle to the river Aobamba that flows along the bottom of the valley, then climbs steeply up the other side of the valley to the ruins at Llactapata (see box p250), before dropping off the far side of the next ridge and descending to the river Santa Teresa. Fifteen kilometres from Sayac Marca it clambers once more to the ruins at Ochopata before becoming completely subsumed by the jungle.

Bingham believed that the site was a fortress and an outpost for Machu Picchu. Fejos disagreed saying that it wasn't impressive enough to be a fortress. Neither is the stone work of sufficiently high quality for the site to be a religious centre and there aren't enough terraces or agricultural land in the vicinity for it to have been a farming outpost. With the compact **Concha Marca** ruins just below, it is also unlikely to have simply been a *tambo*, meaning that no-one is actually sure what these superb ruins were originally used for.

The building appears to grow organically out of the rocky promontory on which it stands and the entire shape of the structure emphasizes and exaggerates the natural features and shape of the prow that sticks out from the hillside. At the heart of the site is a large, unadorned outcrop of rock that juts up from the foundations. The stonework is more impressive than that at Runcu Raccay, marking the next stage on the pilgrimage to Machu Picchu, but is still quite rustic in appearance. Bingham drew particular attention to the 'eye-bonders', holes drilled in corners of walls, which were used to fasten thatched roofs onto the stone structures. The elaborate layout of the site and the way in which it incorporates the natural terrain has led archaeologists to date the ruins to the second half of the 15th century.

Sayac Marca

Triangular
plaza

Rock

Ritual
bath

Ritual
bath

Ritual
bath

Curved-walled
building

To Inca
Trail

Remains of
aqueduct

Remains of
old Inca Trail

0   5   10m

through some very beautiful cloud forest. If you find yourself tackling this stretch in cloud or mist you would do well to wait it out, itinerary and time allowing, in order to enjoy the drama and beauty around you. Twenty minutes' easy walk from Sayac Marca is an open section of hillside called **Chaquicocha** where you are allowed to pitch *camp*. There are a number of flattened, grassy pitches and a toilet block. If it has been raining the ground can be boggy.

From the campsite the path snakes steeply uphill, past two **viewpoints**. At the second of these the trail forks, with a faint, disused and heavily overgrown side path leading off right (north). This path avoids the Inca tunnel and used to rejoin the main route around a kilometre (half a mile) further along the trail. The main trail continues, rounding a spur and turning from north-west to north-east. A section of intricately laid Inca paving leads down to a **tunnel**. This 16m long corridor exploits a fault in the seemingly sheer cliff that blocks the way ahead. Emerging from the impressive tunnel the path climbs again towards the third pass. Just before it reaches the pass, it narrows and at a point just before the top it is possible to see into the Urubamba and Aobamba valleys simultaneously.

From the large *campsite* set around the **third pass** (3650m/11,970ft) there are also spectacular views. Looking south and left to right are the peaks of Palcay (c5600m/18,370ft) and Salkantay (6270m/20,565ft). Some 35km west lies the high, sharp summit of Pumasillo (6072m/19,915ft) and a string of lesser peaks, whilst 15km north-west is Veronica (5750m/18,860ft).

THIRD PASS TO MACHU PICCHU [MAP 3, p215; MAP 4, opp]

From the stunning eyrie where you camp there are also excellent views of the most impressive Inca site so far encountered along the trail. Just below the lip of the pass lies **Phuyu Pata Marca** (see box p220), christened by Dr Paul Fejos and whose name translates appropriately as 'Cloud Level Town'. With the site prone to swirling Wagnerian mists and often seen shrouded in blankets of white cloud, it is an apt nickname. However, the site still looks spectacular and potentially even more atmospheric this way, and even the presence of the large campsite just above can't spoil it.

A long staircase descends between several tiers of buildings, the stone work of which is much better than that seen previously. To one side are six 'Inca baths' that were probably not actually used to wash in, but are more likely to have been used in conjunction with the ritual worship of water. Similar structures can be seen at Tambo Machay and further along the Inca Trail at Huinay Huayna and at Machu Picchu itself.

From the lowest terrace of the ruins pick up the set of **stairs** heading downhill. These are the most impressive flight of steps on the entire Inca Trail. The Incas turned a 500m (1500ft) hillside into a staircase, etching each step out of the natural shape of the bedrock: one giant boulder has over 30 steps carved into it. The trail coils down into dense cloud forest, one of the most delightful wooded sections on the trek. It's a lovely walk, but be careful of your knees, which will feel the strain by the end of the day. It will take about three hours to reach the Trekkers' Hotel.

MAP 4

❑ Phuyu Pata Marca

This extensive site was first spotted by Hiram Bingham, who discovered the baths and the tops of a couple of walls protruding from the thick jungle. However, he failed to grasp the size or the importance of the site. Paul Fejos did realize what lay below the jungle covering, but after several months' excavation had still only managed to clear a fraction of the site, uncovering two plazas, four groups of houses and a hidden house concealed in a terrace.

The site is thought to date from the late 15th century and is attributed to Pachacutec or his successor Túpac Yupanqui (Topa Inca). It is built in an atypical style, unlike the more structured Inca sites elsewhere. However, the stone work is very good in parts, particularly on the upper terraces. The function of the site is again unclear and the handful of basic Inca ceramics found in the ruins give no clues as to its purpose. The most likely theory states that the site was connected with the ritual worship of water, but other suggestions range from a guard house to a private hunting lodge.

From Phuyu Pata Marca there used to be two trails. The old trail, which everyone took up until the dramatic Inca Staircase was discovered during the early 1980s, left Phuyu Pata Marca from the west and contoured around the valley side, hugging the lie of the land. Although a couple of miles longer it offered excellent views of the Urubamba valley and eventually wound its way to

Intipata. This route has subsequently been closed and the majority of it allowed to become overgrown and virtually impassable.

Having stepped down the Inca staircase for around an hour you will gain the first glimpse of the Trekker's Hotel, its green tin roof visible amongst the trees. It is to this unsightly shambles that the trail is heading. About 2½hrs from Phuyu Pata Marca the path passes to the left of a pylon set just off the trail. Just before the pylon though a narrow trail breaks away right (east) and descends to the hotel within half an hour, losing height rapidly through a series of short, tight switchbacks. However, the shortcut doesn't really save you all that much time and it is in fact far less scenic than the traditional route, which pushes on beneath the pylon cables towards **Intipata** (see box below). As you approach the site you first glimpse it through the trees and can better gauge its enormous size. The path emerges on one of the upper terraces. Descend to the lowest terrace, from where a trail leads to the Trekkers' Hotel.

The *Trekker's Hotel* is a basic, cramped, unruly place to spend your final night on the Inca Trail, but it is the last place where you are allowed to *camp* before Machu Picchu. Because of this it is always full. There are dorm beds (s/20 per night) in the hotel itself, or you can sleep on the floor for s/5, plus there is a series of small tent pitches throughout the immediate vicinity. These get booked up by tour agencies so there is little choice and you are likely to have a crowded, noisy night wherever you end up. There's an overpriced *restaurant* and a small shop in the main building, and a number of toilet blocks in the grounds. If you don't mind standing in a queue there's also a hot shower although the water is unreliable and frequently runs cold. If you've come from Mollepata or Chilca and haven't already bought your permit, you must do so here.

❏ Intipata
The name Intipata literally means 'sunny slope' and is particularly apt for this massed range of terraces that seem to stretch on endlessly. Whilst clearing the huge steps over a period of four months during 1940, Dr Paul Fejos despairingly described in his diary terraces 'extending indefinitely to the south'. In total he cleared and mapped 48 terraces. There are no plazas, houses, ceremonial sites or fortifications to disturb the broad sweeping terraces suggesting that the site was used exclusively as an agricultural outpost. However there are three hidden houses concealed in hollow terraces. Given the broad panoramic views down into the valley to the site of Choquesuysuy and across the mountains to the lookout platform on top of Cerro Machu Picchu, the site probably had some sort of strategic importance as well. By using Intipata as a mid-point, messages could have been transmitted from the valley floor all the way to Machu Picchu.

Despite cutting and removing 40,000 square metres of jungle, Dr Fejos was convinced that there was still more to be uncovered. Although historians are anxious to try and reveal as much as possible, naturalists are concerned that insensitive clearing and blunt restoration techniques have damaged prime habitat favoured by a particular breed of very rare orchid. In order to preserve the habitat and protect the flower, there are frequent rumours that the site will be closed and left uncleared, and that the jungle will simply be allowed to reclaim the ancient stones.

ROUTE GUIDE & MAPS

To Trekkers' Hotel

Huinay Huayna

★ trailblazer

0   25m

Terraces

To 'km 104'

Terraces

Gateway

Upper Level

Terraces

Lower Level

Stone platform

Levels linked by set of stairs and ten ceremonial baths

❏ Huinay Huayna (Wiñay Wayna)

This is the most impressive site on the Inca Trail to date. Dating from the second half of the 15th century, the site shares a number of characteristics with Intipata: both comprise a series of terraces spread across a hillside and both were used to grow crops. However, Huinay Huayna is a much more significant and important site. The stonework is very impressive and of a much higher quality. The sweeping terraces lead round to a series of buildings and a staircase that descends to a second level, alongside a sequence of 10 stone baths. The likelihood is that these were involved in the ritual worship of water and that the site had an important role as a ceremonial or religious centre. The finest examples of Inca stonework can be found in the buildings on the upper level, which are constructed out of some of the largest and most perfectly fitted blocks along the Inca Trail. There are also lots of gables and exterior pegs used to secure thatched roofs.

From the hotel a short 10-minute trek takes you to the ruins of **Huinay Huayna** (the name Huinay Huayna belongs to an attractive orchid that grows in the region, and means 'forever young'), a stunning terraced complex with a flight of 10 baths and some exquisite stonework, 500m and a world away from the modern mess you've just left. The ruins are locked every evening around dusk and you should be careful not to leave valuables lying about your tent whilst visiting. It takes two hours to trek to Intipunku (the gateway to the sun). Machu Picchu is another 45mins further on. Remember to have your torch handy as you'll be packing and starting to walk in the dark.

The gate out of the Trekkers' Hotel opens at 5.30am and closes at 3.30pm. Most trekkers crowd by the gate in the dark, hoping to get the earliest start to Machu Picchu when it opens. The result is a convoy of bobbing headlamps in the mad dash to reach Intipunku by sunrise. You may consider delaying your departure from the Trekkers' Hotel by 15-30mins to enjoy an emptier path, better light and the very attractive final section of the Inca Trail. After all, sunrise over Machu Picchu is often hazy or shrouded in light cloud, so the chances are you won't miss much by arriving a little later, and you'll still get to enjoy the ruins before the tours and trainloads of day-trippers arrive.

The trail to Intipunku is easy and very straightforward to follow. It undulates a little, then passes a couple of steep rock faces, before climbing about 14 very steep steps to what you assume is Intipunku. It's actually the remains of a watchtower commanding superb views south back to Intipata, Huinay Huayna, Phuyu Pata Marca and to Choquesuysuy at the start of the Purification Trail. Intipunku is, in fact, just around the corner, at the top of a short set of rather gentler stairs. This is an awe-inspiring approach, the architecture reinforcing your sense of anticipation. When you finally arrive at **Intipunku**, the view across the wide bend of the Urubamba explodes before you and you can at last see, sheltering under the sugar loaf mountain of Huayna Picchu, your journey's end, **Machu Picchu** (see pp325-48).

Variations on the classic trail

These variations are up to four hours longer than the first day of the classic Inca trail and provide alternative start points. They are particularly popular with trekking agencies, which tend to begin all their trips from Km82. You won't gain much from starting at Chilca instead, although it is a scenic, simple stroll to the main trail that allows you to ease in to the trek proper.

FROM CHILCA [MAP 5, p224]

The small village of Chilca stands at Km77 on the railway. It is also readily accessible by road, and indeed many of the trekking agencies drive here to start their organized hikes. If you're arriving by bus make sure you let the driver

MAP 5

RÍO SILQUE

CHILCA KM77

QUEBRADA RUNTUMAYO

DIRT ROAD

QUEBRADA LOURDES

DRY & ARID

ROCABAMBA

ROCABAMBA

GENTLE CONTOUR ALONGSIDE THE RIVER

SCRUB

END OF DIRT ROAD

KM82

STATION

FOOTBALL PITCH

CEMETERY

RÍO URUBAMBA

TO HUAYLLABAMBA

RÍO URUBAMBA

APPROX SCALE
0   ½ mile
0   1km

★ trailblazer

← 150 MINS TO JUNCTION (MAP 6)   ▲ KM82   ← 90 MINS   ▲ KM77 know that you want to get off here though as they will otherwise assume that you are bound for Km82, the more popular starting point. Although little more than a collection of adobe houses and shacks, the hamlet at Chilca is still more substantial than anything found at Km82 or Km88.

From the train station head south and wind through the houses towards the banks of the Urubamba. Cross the river here and turn right (west). Follow the clearly defined dirt track along the southern bank of the river as it descends towards a stand of eucalyptus trees. Bromeliads, wild pepper trees and chilca bushes, from which the village gets its name, also line the path. Beyond the small copse the path bears north-west and undulates through a patch of dry scrub dotted with cacti to the village of **Rocabamba**, where there is a stream.

Bearing west, the path crosses the stream and weaves through a further patch of scrub to arrive at the Km82 bridge, 1½hrs after leaving Chilca.

FROM KM82   [MAP 5, opp; MAP 6, below]

This is the end of the road for tourist buses and the furthest point along the Urubamba Valley accessible by road. Most tour agencies pull into the car park to the north of the houses here and start the trek from this point. There are precious few amenities here, but a couple of enterprising individuals will sell you last-minute supplies and cold soft drinks. You must present your passport and register at the warden's kiosk. The trail is only fractionally longer than the classic Inca trail as the routes join somewhere approximately mid-way between the two start points.

Head south-west from the houses and walk down towards the river bank. Cross the bridge here and on the south side of the Urubamba turn right (west), ignoring the path left that goes to Chilca. Immediately the path climbs steeply

ROUTE GUIDE & MAPS

MAP 6

PATALLACTA & PULPITUYOC

HUILLCA RACCAY

MISKAY   SCRUB

RÍO URUBAMBA

5

TO CHILCA & KMS 77 & 82

TERRACES

TO HUAYLLABAMBA

0   ½ mile
0   APPROX SCALE   1km

★ trailblazer

1   JUNCTION   ◄— 150 MINS FROM KM82 (MAP 5)

❏ **Huillca Raccay**
It doesn't look like much but this fort is thought to be one of the earliest built in the region. Between 1978 and 1980 it was extensively excavated by Ann Kendall who discovered that people inhabited the area long before the Incas arrived. Once they had subdued the original residents of the valley, the Incas built the fort to maintain control and assert their dominance over the local tribes. The ruins comprise a complicated collection of gate-houses, lofts and what are thought to be barracks. In total there are 37 Inca buildings here and some 70 pre-Inca constructions scattered on the flatter land behind. From this vantage point the Incas commanded exceptional views up and down the Urubamba and managed access to the Cusichaca. Later, once Llactapata had been built, the fort protected and controlled the agrarian settlements further down the valley.

away from the river. It evens out and heads south-west past a **football pitch** and a graveyard before passing through a small village.

As the river curves west, so the path follows it and arrives at the village of **Miskay**. At the far end of the village the path splits. Take the less-substantial left-hand fork (south) and head briefly towards a rocky cliff before veering right (west). Follow the path as it ducks into and scrambles out of a small gully, having crossed a stream. Just beyond here, commanding the mouth of the Cusichaca Valley, stands the Inca hillfort **Huillca Raccay** (see box above).

Further west on the far side of the valley lies the sprawling site of Patallacta (see p210). The path descends in a series of gentle zigzags towards the eastern bank of the Cusichaca river, where it joins the main Inca trail from Km88, some $2^1/_2$hrs after leaving Km82. Lupins and broom overgrow the descent and it is easy to lose the way, but you should have no problem in picking up the trail if you continue westwards and downhill towards the valley bottom. At this point turn left and head up the valley (south) towards the village of Huayllabamba on the broad, well-worn trail.

The shorter trails

For those people who don't have the time or inclination to tackle a four-day walk, there are various alternatives. It's only a half-day hike uphill to the Trekkers' Hotel from Km104 on the railway line (Map 4) and just a couple of hours' gentle stroll along the classic Inca Trail from here to the first glimpse of Machu Picchu and the ruins themselves.

Alternatively, follow the southern bank of the Urubamba downstream for a couple of hours to the ruins at Choquesuysuy and then climb more steeply towards the Trekkers' Hotel, from where you join the Inca Trail for the final push to Machu Picchu. Both of these treks are also ideal for people who have arrived during February when the Inca Trail is shut but who would still rather

ROUTE GUIDE & MAPS

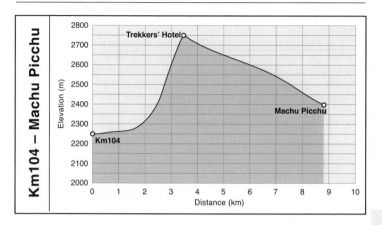

Km104 – Machu Picchu

trek to Machu Picchu than simply catch the train and a bus up to the site, since they are open year-round.

People using these trails used to be allowed to stay at the Trekkers' Hotel, but are no longer able to do so. Instead, they must push on to Machu Picchu and descend to stay overnight in Aguas Calientes, before returning the following day to fully explore the ruins.

KM104 TO THE TREKKERS' HOTEL [MAP 4, p219]

The train takes $3^{1}/_{2}$-4hrs to travel from Cusco to Km104, where it pauses briefly to let people disembark. A warden's kiosk stands adjacent to the bridge across the Urubamba, where you must present your passport and register. On the far side of the river turn right (west) and shortly come to the ruins at **Chachabamba** (see box p228).

From the ruins the path divides: the right-hand path follows the river west towards **Choquesuysuy** (see box p229) before scrambling steeply up to the ruins at Huinay Huayna alongside the Trekkers' Hotel. Picking up on the perceived religious function of the site, the steep track has been dubbed the Purification Trail. It takes 2-3hrs to climb from the valley floor to Huinay Huayna (see p222). Pass through the site on a staircase adjacent to a series of ceremonial baths and pick up the path from the upper level of the site that undulates for a further 15mins to reach the Trekkers' Hotel (see p221).

A slightly gentler alternative is to take the left-hand fork that crosses a stream and passes through a patch of forest and underneath a pair of electricity wires before climbing more evenly across an exposed slope in a westerly direction. This stream is the last water source before the ruins and since the climb is exposed and exhausting in direct sunshine, you should make sure to fill up all water bottles. After a mile you gain your first glimpse of the hotel and the massed terraces of Intipata (see p221) beyond it. A little after this, good views of Huinay Huayna come into focus whilst far below you Choquesuysuy is also visible.

The narrow path continues to climb up and across the mountainside before levelling and finally descending briefly through some woods. Rounding a small spur it passes a waterfall and a number of Inca walls and bits of building still shrouded in vegetation before emerging at the foot of Huinay Huayna. Climb the staircase through the site and then up past the stone baths to the upper level. Turn right (north-west) and exit the site on a well-trodden trail that leads to the Trekkers' Hotel (see p221) after 15mins.

Chachabamba

Baths
Boulder
Terrace
Baths
Baths
Terrace
Baths

0   10m

❏ Chachabamba

Dating from the late 15th century, Chachabamba is a sophisticated site set on an old Inca road. Uncovered in 1940 by Dr Paul Fejos, the site had lain undisturbed despite the construction of the railway on the opposite bank of the river some time earlier. Since then it has been cleared and a number of buildings and a natural shrine uncovered. There are also fourteen ceremonial baths associated with water worship, more than almost anywhere else along the Inca Trail, suggesting that the site must have been an important religious centre. It probably also fulfilled a function as a watchtower, controlling access to Machu Picchu via this particular path.

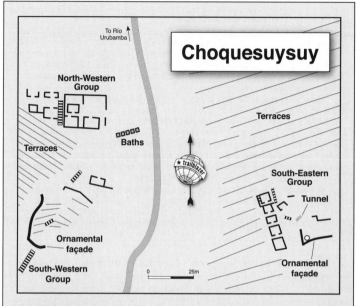

□ Choquesuysuy
Built on either side of a tributary of the Urubamba at Km107, Choquesuysuy comprises six groups of buildings, totalling 18 houses, a series of seven ceremonial baths and a number of well-crafted terraces and walls. The site is ideally placed to oversee traffic along the valley floor and commands the approach to Machu Picchu, although the hydroelectric power station now blocks the path. The quality of the stonework and the presence of the baths suggest it was also a religious centre.

KM88 TO KM104 – RIVERSIDE TRAIL [off MAP 1, p211; MAP 4, p219]

Instead of following the classic Inca Trail from Km88 to Machu Picchu, there is the option to escape the crowds, and the majority of the stiff climbs by following the river as it flows downstream from Km88 to Km104 before ascending to Huinay Huayna and the Trekkers' Hotel. Rarely done and consequently not nearly as well-worn as the classic trail, this gentle riverside stroll is an excellent way of accessing the major ruins at the end of the trek and allows you to explore some interesting sites along the way, including Machu and Huayna Q'ente and the Inca compound Torontoy which boasts a 44-angle stone in one of its walls. The trail typically takes two days to complete. You will need a permit for the trek though and because it overlaps with the final section of the classic Inca Trail the route is subject to the same regulations and restrictions.

❑ **Huayna Q'ente and Machu Q'ente**
Once across the Urubamba, if you turn right (west) instead of left and walk for around 20mins you come to the rarely visited ruins of Huayna Q'ente and Machu Q'ente. These two sites stand on the Inca road to Chachabamba, although the road actually follows the river all the way to the Amazon. Their exact purpose isn't known, but they are thought to have multiple functions, including being resthouses or inns, religious sites and agricultural posts.

Huayna Q'ente is the more impressive structure. Dating from the second half of the 15th century, it is thought to have been built either during the reign of Pachacutec or that of his successor Túpac Yupanqui (Topa Inca). It is an intricately constructed site with plenty of fine stonework on display, suggesting that it was used as a *tambo* (a type of inn) by people making pilgrimages to Machu Picchu. There are two stone baths connected with the worship of water and two sacred rocks thought to be *huacas* (sacred sites). Extensive terraces support the site and a clever canal system supplies the various levels of agricultural land with water.

In contrast, **Machu Q'ente** is plainer, suggesting that it had a primarily agricultural function, although there are also the remnants of a large building thought to have perhaps been a barracks. Close by is a large, peculiarly carved stone that looks similar to Ñusta España (see p262), the sculpted boulder close to Huancacalle.

Having registered at the warden's kiosk before the bridge at Km88, cross the Urubamba but instead of turning left for the classic Inca trail, turn right instead and having headed south for 50m bear west along the southern bank of the river in the lee of several sheer cliffs. The 16km path is clear and reasonably well-maintained, but as a result of the reduced traffic it receives can occasionally be overgrown. There are *campsites* just two hours down from Km88 and at Chachabamba, five hours from Km88. From Chachabamba you then have the option of ascending to Huinay Huayna via the standard route (see p227) or via Choquesuysuy and the Purification Trail (see pp227-8).

The Salkantay Trek

This is essentially an extension of the Inca Trail that allows you to experience a fantastic section of wilderness free from most of the crowds before committing to the final three days of the classic Inca Trail culminating at Machu Picchu. The 6- to 7-day trek from the watershed of the Apurímac to the Urubamba is quite arduous, as you must cross a high pass at almost 5000m/16,400ft. The views of the Vilcabamba range and the proximity to the bulk of Mt Salkantay more than compensate for the effort required. This trek is advertised under various names, and although you may see it listed as the Mollepata Trek, the most common moniker and spelling is the one used here.

❏ Mollepata

The village of Mollepata lies four hours drive to the west of Cusco, at the end of a dirt track off the main Cusco to Abancay road. Described by E G Squier as, 'a collection of wretched huts on a high shelf of the mountain with a tumbledown church, a drunken governor... a place unsurpassed in evil repute by any in Peru', it has fortunately evolved since 1877 into a pleasant mountain town perched on a hillside overlooking the deep citrus-producing valley of the Apurímac. This small huddle of houses is the start point for two increasingly popular treks, the Salkantay trek and the Santa Teresa trek, each of which pass beneath the imposing glaciated peak of Mount Salkantay (6271m/20,569ft).

The early **bus** from Cusco (5am and 1pm from opposite the western end of Calle Arcopata, s/8-15, takes 2¹/₂ -3hrs) will take you all the way to the plaza in the village, but some of the later ones drop you only at the bottom of the dirt track, down by the Apurímac river. Alternatively take the bus from Cusco to Abancay, departing from the Terminal Terrestre, and get off at the road junction for Mollepata. From the main road to the village is a fair walk, which whilst feasible over the course of several hours isn't very interesting or scenic. It's usually possible to hitch a lift from the junction to the village though.

There are a couple of **hostals**, the better one, *Hospedaje Mollepata* (☎ 832103, s/15 per night) being one block to the west of the main plaza, behind the church. Breakfast in the attached restaurant costs s/2.5 and a simple *cafecito* will set you back just s/1.5. *Restaurant Salkantay* on the same street is very popular with locals and the food is fresh. It is also reasonably priced – dinner will cost s/3.

There are a few small **stores** where you can buy some basic last-minute provisions. There are also **arrieros** for hire. In addition to the wages and the hire of the mules, you are responsible for paying for the arrieros' return trip, which from Huayllabamba should only be one day, whilst from Santa Teresa or La Hidroeléctrica takes two days.

MOLLEPATA TO SORAY [MAPS 7-8, pp234-5]

See box above for details about Mollepata. The trail leaves from Mollepata's Plaza de Armas and follows the dirt road that winds all the way to Soray via the small settlement of Marcocasa (also known as Cruzpata). Most of the agencies now drive at least as far as Marcocasa to begin the trek, with some continuing all the way to Soray. There is no public transport along this stretch of road, which is quiet and rarely travelled but not particularly exciting or interesting to trek along.

Take the concrete road that leaves from the plaza's north-west corner and follow it as it snakes through the houses. Ignore the dirt track branching left and continue until the concrete runs out at a T-junction after 200m. Turn right (north-east) onto a dirt and cobble road before veering round to the left (north-west) through a **grove of eucalyptus**.

The road from the village eases along the left (west) side of a valley that's heading roughly north-west. Should you wish to avoid this rather tedious section of the trail there is a faint track that drops into the Pumachupán valley to

Salkantay Trek Overview

To Inca Trail
Huayllabamba

Paucarcancha

MAP 11

Quebrada
Churomayo

Pampa
Cahuana

Rio
Cusichaca

Salkantay
6264m

To Coolpapampa
& Machu Picchu

Inca
Chiriasqa
Pass

MAP 10

SANTA
TERESA
TREK

Quera
Machay

Salkantay
Pampa

Quebrada
Sisay Pampa

MAP 9

Soray

Soray Pampa

0 1 2 3 4 5km

MAP 8

Challacancha

Rio Blanco

Marcocasa
(Cruzpata)

MAP 7

MOLLEPATA

ROUTE GUIDE & MAPS

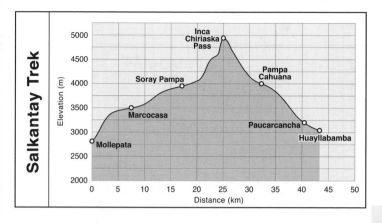

the right of the road, contours roughly north towards the head of the valley and climbs to Marcocasa, cutting between the bends and switchbacks of the road until it reaches the hamlet. It is difficult to pinpoint exactly where the track branches right, so check with your arriero. Don't drop too low into the valley as a number of trails simply lead to cultivated farm plots further below.

The road leads towards the head of the valley, gaining height gently. It curves left and steepens before crossing a **bridge** and coming to a pleasant glade. After the glade the road bends right and climbs past a farm and some cultivated plots of land before beginning a series of long switchbacks. A concrete **irrigation channel** carrying snowmelt from Salkantay bisects the road. Having crossed this irrigation channel on a bridge the road arrives on the crest of a ridge at the small settlement of **Marcocasa** (3500m/11,480ft). It takes 2¹/₂-3hrs to reach the village from Mollepata. Two large blue crosses, often swaddled in different coloured cloths, stand to the left of the road and there is a cleared level patch of ground 100m to the right where you can *camp*. Fill up your water bottles at a spring behind some houses at the back of the cleared area (where the power lines lead to), because the streams are unreliable on the way to Soray. From Marcocasa there are some superb, expansive views of the snow-capped Huarohuirani (to the north behind the hill), the village of Qurawasi away in the distance to the west, and Mollepata off to the south.

Beyond Marcocasa the directions are simple – follow the road all the way to Soray Pampa (Map 8). It takes 3-4hrs to get there. Two hours after leaving Marcocasa the road passes **Challacancha**, which consists of two huts with thatch and tin roofs and a small *campsite* to the right-hand side of the road. There are plenty of water sources nearby.

From Challacancha it is around a further two hours to Soray; after 1-1¹/₂hrs the path passes through a **gate**, and after another 30mins or so it arrives on some high puna fields – Soray Pampa. By now you will have excellent views of the

ROUTE GUIDE & MAPS

HUT →

45 MINS →

MARCOCASA

3 HRS →

MOLLEPATA

HUT

PUITACHUPÁN VALLEY

RÍO BLANCO

POWER LINE

MARCOCASA

TWO BLUE CROSSES

IRRIGATION CHANNEL

ALTERNATIVE ROUTE THAT AVOIDS ROAD BY DROPPING INTO VALLEY & THEN CLIMBING TO MARCOCASA

FOLLOW BROAD DIRT ROAD

★ trailblazer

EUCALYPTUS GROVE

MAP 7

MOLLEPATA

MARKET

POLICE

PLAZA DE ARMAS

TO CUSCO

0   ½ mile

0   APPROX SCALE   1km

SORAY

Salkantay Lodge & Adventure Resort

SORAY PAMPA

ROAD RUNS OUT & TRACK CONTINUES ACROSS PUNA & GRASSLANDS

WATERFALL

GATE

RÍO BLANCO

SEASONAL STREAMS MAY APPEAR ACROSS ROAD

LOOSE HILLSIDE PRONE TO LANDSLIPS

CHALLACANCHA

AS YOU PROGRESS UP DIRT ROAD THE VALLEY NARROWS

MAP 8

0   ½ mile
0   APPROX SCALE   1km

HAVING ENTERED VALLEY GET FIRST VIEWS OF MT HUMANTAY TO THE NORTH-WEST

SORAY

120 MINS

CHALLACANCHA

60 MINS FROM HUT (MAP 7)

ROUTE GUIDE & MAPS

bulk of Humantay and to its right as you look at it the sheer pyramid of Salkantay (6264m/20,551ft), whose name means 'Savage Mountain'.

The pampa is latticed with small concrete drainage canals and streams that you'll have to cross (though these disappear in dry years). Keep to the left (west) side of the pampa, close to the rock wall if you want to remain dry footed. At the far (north) end of the pampa stands **Soray** itself, on the far (north) side of a stream – often there's a simple bridge of tree trunks but you might have to use stepping-stones if this has been washed away. This is a good place to *camp*. The lodge here, ***Salkantay Lodge and Adventure Resort***, is run by Mountain Lodges of Peru but is only for people on their tour so there is no public access. This quality lodge has hot showers and a decent restaurant. Rooms are a mix of Andean and colonial architectural styles and have views of Mt Salkantay, as does the outdoor hot tub.

SORAY TO PAUCARCANCHA
[MAP 9, opp; MAPS 10-11, pp238-9]

Soray to Sisay Pampa The trail heads up the valley to the north-east (right). The path starts on the left-hand side of the valley and crosses the **Río Salkantay**, a tributary of the Río Blanco, before climbing uphill on the other side of the valley. Pass through a **gate** in a stone wall and begin a series of zig-zags that ascend the side of the valley. Direct shortcuts between switchbacks are easy to follow, although steep and occasionally muddy.

Half an hour after Soray Pampa you pass through a second rudimentary **gate** set in another stone wall in order to enter **Salkantay Pampa**. Mt Salkantay, the sacred mountain of the Incas, is ahead of you. Descend to a stream and cross a number of branches to the left-hand side of the pampa, where the path becomes boggy and the track indistinct. As long as you continue following the stream north-east, however, you'll be fine.

At the head of the valley is a massive wall of scree – the terminal moraine (end debris) of a glacier. The flat ground before the moraine is a great place to *camp*. The path splits here; the left-hand fork bearing north-west around the moraine towards a V-shaped valley is the way for the Santa Teresa Trek (see p245). To continue on the Salkantay Trek take the right-hand fork (east), crossing back over the stream, towards the pass at Inka Chiriasqa.

A series of steep switchbacks climbs sharply up the eastern shoulder of Mt Salkantay. A short distance into the climb the path passes a flat patch of hillside called **Quera Machay** which makes for a decent *campsite*. Beyond here the path heads north and then east, continuing to climb all the while. Alternative trails branch off and descend to the lateral moraine of the glacier. Ignore these and keep the river between you and the glacier.

As you gain height the valley narrows dramatically. From the high point there are good views back over the wall of lateral moraine to a pair of lakes. At this point the ridge is visible ahead and the pass can be made out above a very steep slope. It is tempting to cut out the last climb and nip over the watershed by the glacier instead, but this is potentially very dangerous. **Inka Chiriasqa**

MAP 9

90 MINS FROM SORAY (MAP 8) →   ← JUNCTION   ← 3 HRS →   PASS →

MOUNT △ HUMANTAY 5910M

JUMBLED TERMINAL MORAINE MASSED AROUND LOWER SLOPES

SANTA TERESA TREK

MT SALKANTAY 6264M

TERMINAL MORAINE

CAN BE WET & BOGGY

SALKANTAY △ PAMPA

GATE

GATE

RIO SALKANTAY

GLACIER BELOW MT SALKANTAY

GIANT BOULDER

QUERA MACHAY

PAMPA JAPONÉS

STEEP DESCENT

STEEP CLIMB TO KNIFE-LIKE PASS

INKA CHIRIASQA PASS 4950M

POTENTIAL CAMPSITES

NOTE: TERMINAL MORAINE AT SNOUT OF GLACIER COMPLETELY BLOCKS VALLEY

APPROX SCALE
0 — ½ mile
0 — 1km

ROUTE GUIDE & MAPS

150 MINS FROM INCA CHIRIASQA PASS (MAP 9) → START OF PUNA   60 MINS TO PAMPA CAHUANA (MAP 11) →

MAP 10

DEEP GULLIES

SCRUB/PUNA

POTENTIAL CAMPSITE

CAN BE BOGGY

QUEBRADA SISAY PAMPA

FALLEN DOWN BROKEN BUILDINGS

★ trailblazer

0   ½ mile
0   APPROX SCALE   1km

(aka Chiriaska/ca/q'ua; 4950m/16,235ft) itself, which translates as 'the place where the Inca cools down', is a narrow (barely a metre wide), knife-like pass.

From the pass there are stunning views of both the valley behind you and the one that lies ahead. The path drops quickly from the high point, descending swiftly into the adjoining valley. The path is clear and easy to make out – it simply follows the valley down. Initially it crosses puna heading south-east but soon bends north-east and becomes increasingly steep. There is a *campsite* 1½hrs beyond Inka Chiriasqa, just before a ridge, but it is popular with tour agencies and frequently fully occupied.

A little further on, beyond the ridge, the path tracks across a patch of glacial outwash and begins to follow the northern bank of the river. This is **Quebrada Sisay Pampa** (Map 10) and is also used as an overnight stop.

Sisay Pampa to Paucarcancha From Sisay Pampa follow the left-hand (north) bank of the river and continue downstream. The path skirts around two valleys that have seasonal streams flowing through them and continues to descend whilst the surrounding hillsides become increasingly steep. A broad river joins from the south.

Almost immediately after this the valley turns north-east. From here you can make out an Inca canal below you. This area, 3½hrs from the pass, is **Pampa Cahuana** (Map 11). The path meanders between a clutch of houses, farms and a football pitch before crossing a bridge to the eastern (right-hand) bank of the Inca canal. Built to drain the flat upper valley and prevent the river meandering lazily here, the well-engineered canal was used to irrigate this section of the basin and still carries melt water into the valley bottom. At the far

MAP 11

THE INCA TRAIL

HUAYLLABAMBA

PAUCARCANCHA

ATTRACTIVE VALLEY FULL OF VARIED FLORA BACKED BY SHEER CLIFFS

QUEBRADA CHUROMAYO

RÍO CUSICHACA

LONG, STEADY DESCENT ALONGSIDE RIVER – LOTS OF GOOD CAMPSITES TO CHOOSE FROM

FARMS & FIELDS

SEVERAL GOOD CAMPSITES ON FLAT, EVEN GROUND

PAMPA CAHUANA

FOOTBALL PITCH

INCA-BUILT CANAL

APPROX SCALE
0 ½ mile
0 1km

| PAUCARCANCHA | ◄ 45 MINS ► | HUAYLLABAMBA |

ROUTE GUIDE & MAPS

To Huayllabamba & Inca Trail

Terraces

Paucarcancha

Gabled house

Trapezoidal windows

Trapezoidal windows

Reconstructed section

Reconstructed section

0   5   10m

Grassy area

Terraces

To Mollepata

ROUTE GUIDE & MAPS

❏ Paucarcancha

This partially renovated ruin, also sometimes referred to as Incarajay, stands guard over the Cusichaca river, dominating the valley and protecting an approach to Machu Picchu from the Apurímac to the south. The Incas were not native to this valley, but this imposing fort built following the submission of the indigenous tribes sometime in the second half of the 15th century, would have served as a potent reminder of the new rulers of the region. It would also have served as a strategically sited tambo.

The fort contains sixteen buildings, some of which are thought to be barracks. Trapezoidal windows look out over the surrounding countryside, and large sets of terraces adorn the surrounding hillsides, presumably providing crops and foodstuffs for the inhabitants.

❏ Important note – walking times

All times in this book refer only to the time spent walking. You will need to add 10-30% to allow for rests, photography, checking the map, drinking water etc.

end of a narrow gorge the valley and canal turn north, and continue to descend through changing vegetation until, 1 1/2hrs from the bridge, the path arrives at the small hamlet and ruins of **Paucarcancha**.

Beyond the ruins and the small village here there are essentially two ways ahead: trek to Huayllabamba (45mins, see p210) and join the classic Inca Trail; or walk down the Cusichaca Valley, then you could either catch a train back to Cusco from Km82, walk to Chilca or trek along the river to Machu Picchu.

The Santa Teresa trek

This increasingly popular route is the only 'back door' approach to Machu Picchu (see overview map p243). It currently bypasses all the checkpoints and regulations associated with the Inca Trail although you do need to purchase an INC permit (see p207) at Soray Pampa (s/129, approximately US$46) for the section from Soray Pampa to Lucmabamba. If you are trekking with an agency check to make sure that this fee is included in the price of the trek. If going independently make sure you have the correct money in soles – the wardens at the check point will not change dollars and do not carry change.

Closed for a number of years in the wake of the massive landslide in 1998 that wiped out the village of Santa Teresa (see box p248) and the nearby railway line, it was only re-opened by the authorities to ease the pressure on the Inca Trail and provide an alternative for those short of time, money or simply caught out by the complex regulations. However, its growing popularity and the increase in numbers of trekkers now tackling it mean that it is only a matter of time before the government imposes a set of rules in line with those already in place on the classic Inca Trail. Check with South American Explorers (💻 www.saexplorers.org) or Andean Travel Web (💻 www.andeantravelweb.com /peru) for the latest status. All this means that it is no longer the deserted, remote route it once was, and since there are no regulations on the number of people beginning the route each day it can get relatively busy during the peak season.

Although the routes finish at the same point, this is a very different type of trek to the Inca Trail. There no Inca ruins on this trek, except for one when you are in sight of Machu Picchu, which is still being uncovered and its significance and status assessed. However, the scenery is stunning and the varied range of landscapes that you pass through make the Santa Teresa route an excellent outing in its own right. You'll explore a wider range of landscapes, climb closer to the snow line and descend further into the subtropical forest than you would on the Inca Trail, meaning that you'll have a much better chance of seeing a wider range of birdlife and flora.

The route is currently much less well-travelled than its more famous counterpart so it still has fewer people on it: rather than camp amidst crowds of other trekkers, you'll actually have the opportunity to interact with the locals who live

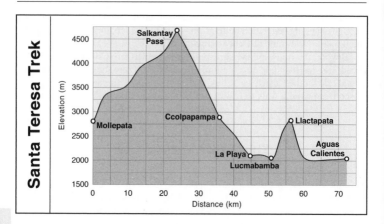

close by. Consequently, it's a pretty good alternative to the Inca Trail and a route worth considering regardless of the regulations issue.

Most agencies now offer the Santa Teresa trek although they may occasionally and confusingly refer to it as the Salkantay trek. At the time of writing it was still possible to attempt it independently or with your own arrieros. This may not be the case for much longer and the first regulation imposed is more than likely going to be the requirement to take a licensed guide. The best time to tackle the trek is during the dry season (May to September), as the high pass can be blocked by snow during the wet season.

The trek begins from Mollepata and traditionally takes four days. You should factor in a fifth to explore Machu Picchu properly. The trek is relatively strenuous since it climbs from the watershed of the Apurímac (2800m/9185ft) to cross a 4700m/15,415ft pass below Mt Salkantay, tumbles back down into the thickly forested Santa Teresa valley (2300m/7545ft), breaches another pass as 2850m/9350ft and descends 600m/1970ft into the Aobamba valley to finish at Aguas Calientes, at the foot of Machu Picchu mountain.

For those who aren't inclined to rough it or don't want to camp, there is now a series of strategically sited lodges strung along the route that belong to a company called Mountain Lodges of Peru (see p159). In order to make use of the lodges though you will have to take one of the company's fully guided tours.

MOLLEPATA TO SALKANTAY PAMPA
[MAP 7, p234; MAP 8, p235; MAP 9, p237]

For information on getting to the trailhead at Mollepata see box p231. For details about the first stage of the trek follow the directions from Mollepata on the Salkantay Trek (see pp231-6).

Aguas Calientes

MACHU PICCHU

Llactapata (Paltallacta)

MAP 16

RIVERSIDE TRAIL

Lucmabamba

Lucma Lodge

MAP 15

Río Santa Teresa

La Playa

INCA TRAIL

Hatun Poccos

0 1 2 3 4 5km

MAP 14

Río Humantay

Rayampata

Ccolpapampa

Salkantay 6264m

Colpa Lodge

Chaullay

Huayraqumachay

MAP 13

Wayra Lodge

SALKANTAY TREK

Salkantay Pass

MAP 12

Salkantay Pampa

MAP 9

Soray

Soray Pampa

MAP 8

Challacancha

Río Blanco

ALSO SALKANTAY TREK

Marcocasa

Santa Teresa Trek Overview

MAP 7

MOLLEPATA

trailblazer

ROUTE GUIDE & MAPS

SALKANTAY PAMPA TO RAYAMPATA
[MAP 9, p237; MAP 12, opp; MAP 13, p247]

At Salkantay Pampa, the trail divides. The Salkantay trail branches right (north-east) around the moraine at the foot of Salkantay towards the Inka Chiriasqa pass and Huayllabamba. For the Santa Teresa trek, you want to bear left (north-west) around the left-hand side of the moraine towards the Salkantay Pass.

The path begins to climb steeply up seven tight switchbacks (Map 12), known as **Siete Culebras** (the Seven Serpents), and crests a small knoll after which it undulates north, parallel to the moraine, gradually gaining height.

Having scrambled through a boulder field, you snake across a level pampa and arrive at a small lake, **Salkantaycocha**, at its northern end. The track passes to the left (south) of the lake and climbs above it for a further 20-25mins, during which time you cross a series of ridges and pass a large boulder daubed with a red 'X'.

A further 5-10mins easy scrambling brings you to **Salkantay pass** (4700m/15,415ft), which is variously known by a handful of other names as well. The pass is marked by a series of cairns (*apachetas*) up to 6ft tall, built to honour the *apus*, the more ghoulish of which include bones and skulls. It takes 3-3¹/₂hrs to get to the pass from Soray Pampa.

The pass is part of the shoulder of Salkantay, which rises to the east. If it is clear you should be able to see across the south face of the mountain to the high pass Inka Chiriasqa in the distance. To the south stands Tucarhuay whilst to the north-west lie the glaciated twin peaks of Humantay.

Beyond the Salkantay pass the path descends steadily west, dropping past a small tarn and through a **boulder field** that chokes the narrow valley. As the valley broadens, the track frequently vanishes in muddy mires where a number of small streams cross the route. Stick to the left-hand (west) side of the valley and you will pick up the path further down. In places simple stone walls span the width of the valley, but there are gaps or gates along them allowing you to pass through. The bogs and streams eventually give rise to the **Río Humantay**, which you follow on its left (west) bank, crossing small tributaries as you go.

About two hours from the pass on the left bank (west) of the river, you'll reach **Huayraqumachay** or 'Eye of the Wind', a couple of farm huts and a flat, raised patch of ground which makes a good *campsite*. **Wayra Lodge**, part of Mountain Lodges of Peru (see p159), also stands close to here, perched above a cliff with spectacular views down the valley.

After Huayraqumachay the path is fairly imprecise, but keep to the left (west) of the river and remain fairly high on the valley. You'll pass a number of simple farm plots amidst some giant boulders. Below these the valley sides steepen and the puna gives way to scrub and then cloud forest draped with moss and lichen. Although frequently muddy and often churned up by mules, the main path can be found quite easily.

This track continues to descend gently through the cloud forest and around an hour and a half after Huayraqumachay, you'll pass some gravestones marking the fringes of **Rayampata** (Map 13), which is also shown as Arayan Niyoc

MAP 12

MORAINE SNOUT

← 60–90 MINS →

PASS

← 3–4 HRS →

HUMANTAY
5217M

HUAYRAQUMACHAY

← 120 MINS FROM RAYAMPATA (MAP 13)

SALKANTAY
6264M

SALKANTAY TREK

TERMINAL MORAINE

LAGUNA SALKANTAYCOCHA

ROCK DAUBED WITH RED 'X'

SMALL LAKE

SALKANTAY PASS
4700M – BROAD PASS MARKED BY CAIRNS

BOULDER FIELD

SMALL STREAMS

Wayra Lodge

Río Humantay

HUAYRAQUMACHAY

PATH OFTEN INDISTINCT. STICK TO LEFT SIDE OF RIVER AND REMAIN FAIRLY HIGH TO PICK UP PATH BEFORE START OF CLOUD FOREST

PAMPA

BOULDER FIELD

SIETE CULEBRAS
SERIES OF STEEP, TIGHT SWITCHBACKS

JUNCTION

← 90–120 MINS →

PASS

← 120–150 MINS →

HUAYRAQUMACHAY

← 90 MINS TO RAYAMPATA (MAP 13)

90 MINS FROM SORAY (MAP 8) →

½ mile
APPROX SCALE 1km

ROUTE GUIDE & MAPS

on some maps. There are several huts adjacent to the track and a few small terraces where you can *camp*. Water can be collected from the river below the huts. The families occasionally have soft drinks for sale. The views from the huts down the valley, of the snow-capped range ahead, are excellent.

RAYAMPATA TO CCOLPAPAMPA [MAP 13, opp]

From Rayampata you descend through thickly forested slopes. The skies are often clear first thing in the morning and an early start means that you'll be able to enjoy outstanding views. You'll also be able to hear the spectacular dawn chorus, as there is a wealth of birdlife in the upper reaches of the cloud forest.

After an hour the path passes a pair of small earthen cliffs or *collpas*, clay licks used by parakeets, and a further half hour later you reach the village of **Chaullay** (not to be confused with the ruins of the same name on the Vilcabamba Trail). This is a very attractive settlement at the junction of two valleys with a handful of rudimentary stores selling basic provisions. Greener and cleaner than Rayampata, it would make an excellent campsite were it not for the clouds of mosquitoes. If the pests are out in force there are a couple of good alternative campsites a further 15mins along the path.

Pass through the village and cross the Río Chaullay on the concrete suspension bridge and turn right (north) on the far bank, ignoring the well-trodden trail that zigzags west up the side of the valley. Head downstream along the left (west) bank of the river to **Ccolpapampa**, a slightly larger community than Chaullay where there are a number of level pitches on which to *camp*. *Colpa Lodge*, owned by Mountain Lodges of Peru (see p159), is perched high above on a panoramic viewpoint.

CCOLPAPAMPA TO LA PLAYA [MAP 13, opp; MAP 14, p249]

The onward path can be picked up on the far side of the grassy central square and continues down the valley. The path soon bends left (west) into the **Quebrada Totora**. At a fork below the lip of the valley, turn right and double back on yourself before weaving a steep descent down to the wooden bridge over the Totora River. The onward path from the junction actually leads to Choquequirao (see p309) and is part of the route that links Choquequirao to Machu Picchu. Adjacent to the wooden bridge are a pair of cement baths that have hot spring water channelled into them from a little higher up the valley.

On the far side of the bridge the trail leads along the left (west) side of the river, now the Río Santa Teresa, in a north-easterly direction. Where the path divides take the lower (right-hand) branch to make a slow descent through the cloud forest. Half an hour before entering the Santa Teresa Valley the path reaches a tributary. Head upstream here along the tributary for about 8m before crossing it in order to pick up the path on the far side. A little further on the path crosses beneath the thundering course of a 300m waterfall, which plunges from the cliff tops through the forest, crashing into the river below in six great bounds. Cross the falls on a series of stepping stones, watching your footing.

RAYAMPATA

MAP 13

RÍO SANTA TERESA

WOODEN BRIDGE OVER QUEBRADA TOTORA

HOT SPRING POOLS TO EAST OF BRIDGE

CCOLPAPAMPA

CHAULLAY

RÍO HUMANTAY

FORESTED SLOPES

½ mile   1km
0
0
APPROX SCALE

HOT SPRING ON SOUTH SIDE OF RIVER

Colpa Lodge

CHOQUEQUIRAO-MACHU PICCHU TREK

IGNORE PATH THAT CARRIES STRAIGHT ON UP HILL

SUSPENSION BRIDGE

RÍO CHAULLAY

About 2km further on, you'll have to scramble over a landslide that has devastated the path and scarred the hillside. Cross a second stream on stepping stones and pass through a gate before descending to **Hatun Poccos**, a village of a few simple houses and some strips of farmed land. You can *camp* in a grassy clearing beside a small hut and thatched shelter.

The path continues down the valley, and about 1¹/₂hrs from Hatun Poccos you'll get your first brief glimpse of Machu Picchu mountain before it is obscured by an intervening ridge as you continue to descend.

About 2¹/₂hrs after Hatun Poccos the path develops into a dirt road and meanders into **La Playa**, a relatively large community of farmers and arrieros that is embracing the numbers of trekkers now taking this route. As you enter the village there's a series of shacks selling drinks and snacks and some tent pitches. At the far end of the village, beyond the football pitch and school, are several houses that allow *camping* in their grounds. There are also a couple of **bars/restaurants**, including *Samana Wasi*, and small kiosks selling soft drinks here as well as a cold water shower.

The main square used to be on the far side of the river that divides the town in two, connected by a makeshift bridge. However, with the increased number of visitors, the bridge across the river has been improved and the road extended, meaning that the town has been able to develop quite considerably.

This is also where transport to the village of **Santa Teresa** (see below), an hour away by bus (s/3), departs from. Some agencies will now pick you up here and shuttle you to the hot springs at Santa Teresa, before leading you across the bridge that now crosses the Urubamba and taking you the final stretch to Aguas Calientes. This option prevents you from completing the trek on foot, and actually deprives you of the bulk of the final stage, a stage that includes the recently rediscovered and partially uncovered ruins of Llactapata (see box pp250-1).

❑ **Santa Teresa**
Santa Teresa used to be a small, subtropical village connected to Aguas Calientes, and therefore Machu Picchu, by a short train ride. The railway represented the main link between the town and the outside world. In spring 1998 both the village and the railway line were destroyed by an enormous landslide that swept down from the surrounding mountains.

Torrential El Niño rainstorms loosened the soil on the mountainside, releasing a colossal landslip into the Río Urubamba, sweeping over the town and crashing into the railway line. Around 15 people died and over 350 families were affected. Almost 80% of the buildings in the old part of Santa Teresa were destroyed or partly damaged. The railway line was mangled beyond use and hasn't been fixed since the disaster. The power station, La Hidroeléctrica, was also badly damaged.

The reconstruction and regeneration of Santa Teresa is taking place slowly, with the 'back door' route to Machu Picchu and the recently opened bridge across the Urubamba (see p178) bringing more people into the valley, but it remains a fairly basic settlement, of little real interest to the casual visitor.

POSSIBLE TO CAMP AT
FAR END OF VILLAGE,
BEYOND FOOTBALL
PITCH, SCHOOL & HANDFUL
OF BAR/RESTAURANTS

LA PLAYA

15

BRIEF VIEW OF
MACHU PICCHU
MOUNTAIN

DRINK & SNACK
STANDS
INTERMITTENTLY
LINE LAST STRETCH
BEFORE LA PLAYA

HATUN
POCCOS

GATE

GIANT
LANDSLIDE
SITE

300M
WATERFALL

RIO SANTA TERESA

MAP 14

13

0   ½ mile
0   APPROX SCALE   1km

La Playa 90 MINS ▲ View of Machu Picchu 90 MINS ▲ Hatun Poccos 120 MINS ▲ River 30 MINS FROM Ccolpapampa (Map 13)

La Playa 60 MINS View of Machu Picchu 120 MINS Hatun Poccos 150 MINS River 30 MINS FROM Ccolpapampa (Map 13)

ROUTE GUIDE & MAPS

❏ Llactapata (Paltallacta)

Despite their proximity to Machu Picchu, the ruins of Llactapata (also known as Paltallacta) have been little investigated since they were initially uncovered by Hiram Bingham in 1912. The site, situated on and below a long ridge, had in fact lain hidden for more than 70 years since this discovery, until being 'rediscovered' in the early 1980s. Since then, studies have shown the site to be far larger and more significant than previously imagined.

The first account of the ruins was published by Bingham. An initial foray into the Aobamba Valley by Bingham's assistant had met with 'almost insuperable difficulty' as a result of the dense, impenetrable forest that clad the hillsides. Bingham himself explored the region ten days later and recorded that he '… found some interesting ruins … The end of that day found us on top of a ridge between the valleys of the Aobamba and the Salcantay.' The small collection of structures he then loosely described is part of Llactapata, which, owing to its strategic location overlooking Machu Picchu's western flank, and the clear and unrivalled view of the city from here, he decided was 'the ruins of an Inca castle'. He went on to attribute its construction to one of Manco Inca's captains.

In total, Bingham spent just five daylight hours at the site and failed to properly explore or map the ruins. His expedition was sorely handicapped by an unhelpful team of *arrieros* who had been press-ganged into service; his account of the trip in fact spends more time lamenting the deficiencies of his team than describing the ruins. The *arrieros* later abandoned him.

Unfortunately Bingham's imprecise notes regarding the location were too vague for anyone to be able to retrace his steps, and slowly the forest closed back over the ruins. In truth his descriptions of the ruins, published alongside news of the uncovering of Machu Picchu, Vitcos and Espíritu Pampa, failed to inspire people to follow in his footsteps. It wasn't until the early 1980s that Hugh Thomson rediscovered them, and not until the early part of the 21st century that any serious archaeological investigation was carried out here, with extensive excavation and mapping undertaken by Thomson.

The site, whose name means 'High Town' in Quechua, is considerably larger than first thought, although it is still hard to tell where the ruins begin and the cloud forest ends. The complex faces Machu Picchu, which lies five kilometres to the east, on the far side of the Aobamba valley. The sacred peaks of Veronica and Salkantay are also visible from here.

The site consists of several interrelated high-status building groups including a feature thought to be a sun temple, which has uncanny similarities in terms of structure, size and alignment to the Coricancha (see pp146-8) in Cusco. There are also residential sectors here that might have served as high-status *tambos*, and agricultural areas thought to have been used to grow crops to supplement food production at Machu Picchu. Although the stonework is generally less impressive than at Machu Picchu because of the metamorphic rocks available, the solid buildings, multiple niches, shaped corner stones and double-jamb doorways are indicative of a place of great importance. Evidence shows that the crude walls were in fact coated with light-coloured clay that would have concealed the rough stonework beneath a smooth, striking façade. An Inca path uncovered by Hugh Thomson and Gary Ziegler leads from the site towards Vilcabamba and Vitcos, whilst the Inca path that starts at the Inca drawbridge behind Machu Picchu and runs across the head of the valley to Llactapata would have provided a suitably elaborate and spectacular entrance to the site. This would have allowed the Inca to visit the site for particular ceremonial occasions, such as the June solstice.

A unique feature is a 45m/145ft long sunken corridor set 1.8m/6ft into the earth and aligned so as to point directly at Machu Picchu. During the summer solstice, the sun rises over the Torreón in Machu Picchu, and falls directly along this channel. The building thought to be a sun temple and various viewing platforms throughout the site lend further weight to the ritual significance of Llactapata.

In his report on the site, Hugh Thomson suggests that the careful alignment (see box p252) of the key buildings and features in relationship to Machu Picchu indicate that Llactapata was 'part of a carefully designed network of interrelated administrative and ceremonial sites supporting the regional administrative and ceremonial centre at Machu Picchu'. Underlining the importance of the site and its ritual significance are the facts that a number of key buildings in Machu Picchu are set to look over the Aobamba valley towards Llactapata. The Intihuatana and the small structure at the summit of Huayna Picchu are both aligned to look east across the valley. The house on Huayna Picchu also contains a *huaca* that replicates the Llactapata ridge.

So far much of the site is off-limits to the public whilst investigations and excavations are carried out. Just a handful of buildings have been restored, but with a little imagination it is easy to visualize the grandeur of the sprawling site and imagine the significance of the spectacular view of Machu Picchu spread out across the horizon to the west.

Llactapata – Machu Picchu alignment

LA PLAYA TO AGUAS CALIENTES
[MAPS 15-16, pp254-5; MAP 4, p219]

On the far side of the **bridge** that bisects the village, join the gravel road that runs above the river towards Santa Teresa. After 3km there is a large faded blue 'INC' sign on the right-hand side (east) of the road, next to the small community of **Lucmabamba**. Turn right (east) here on to a grassy track and a short section of restored, broad Inca steps, which climb past coffee plantations and plots of lemon and passion-fruit trees. Thirty minutes from the junction, on the right-hand side of the track, stands the thatched, modern *Lucma Lodge* belonging to Mountain Lodges of Peru (see p159). Continue ascending for 2-2^{1}/2hrs on a wide, even path, around a series of spurs before entering dense, virgin cloud forest and arriving at a ridge-pass (2850m/9350ft).

Ignore a wide, newly laid path heading east and instead follow the narrower, muddier track that branches left (north) and runs along the ridge for 5-10mins, before it begins to descend into the Aobamba Valley. There are now tantalizing glimpses of Machu Picchu sprawled across the ridgeline 5km ahead of you, shadowed by the unmistakable shape of Huayna Picchu.

The path runs down the hillside past the partially cleared ruins of **Llactapata** (Paltallacta), which remain largely hidden under moss and leaves, and weighed down by a dense tangle of twisted tree roots.

Immediately below the ruins is a clearing boasting exceptional views of Machu Picchu sprawled across a ridge, where it is possible to *camp* (Map 16). There are some makeshift shelters here and a local farmer who sometimes has soft drinks or water for sale. The next accommodation is in Aguas Calientes.

From the campsite, the descent begins in earnest for 1^{1}/2hrs, plunging 600m down a remorseless series of switchbacks to enter a **coffee plantation** and emerge at a suspension bridge across the Aobamba River. On the far side of the river turn left (north) and follow the right-hand side (east) of the valley downstream towards the confluence of the Aobamba and Urubamba rivers. To your right and high on the cliff above a huge stream of water spews from a hole in the cliff; it's part of the hydroelectric project (La Hidroeléctrica).

Cut over a low hillock and enter the Urubamba valley. Join the broad gravel road running adjacent to the river and head upstream towards La Hidroeléctrica and the small **railway station** next to it. Ignore the bridge over the Urubamba and push on to the station, which is signposted below some power station buildings. The platform, up a series of steps to the left of the road, is lined with makeshift stalls and shabby cantinas selling drinks and snacks. The ticket building is one of the last buildings on the right; it opens around 3pm and the train to Aguas Calientes departs around 4pm. Tickets cost s/20. If you find you have plenty of time to kill at the station, there is a small but interesting set of sculpted stones at **Sector Intihuatana**, a short walk along the line. Head down the tracks towards Machu Picchu, and take the unmarked track that climbs briefly between two shacks. Cross the railway line as it doubles back on itself and climb a further short slope into a patch of forest. Scattered here, surrounded by banana and avocado trees, is a series of terraces, walls, archways, foun-

ROUTE GUIDE & MAPS

TO SANTA
TERESA

LLACTAPATA
(PALTALLACTA) **16**

TURN LEFT ON
RIDGE AND FOLLOW
FOR 5-10MINS TO
RUINS THEN
DESCEND

PASS
2850M

IGNORE
THIS
PATH!

GRADED
TRACK
CLIMBS
STEADILY

Río Santa Teresa

Lucma Lodge

LUCMABAMBA

FRUIT & COFFEE
PLANTATIONS

BLUE 'INC' SIGN. TURN RIGHT
HERE AND JOIN RESTORED,
STEPPED INCA PATH

MAP 15

★ trailblazer

RAMSHACKLE TOWN SQUARE.
CAN CATCH A BUS OR HITCH
FROM HERE

BRIDGE

14

0 ½ mile

0 APPROX SCALE 1km

LLACTAPATA — 105-135 MINS — TURN-OFF — 45 MINS — SQUARE — 10 MINS TO LA PLAYA (MAP 14)

LLACTAPATA — 160-190 MINS — TURN-OFF — 45 MINS — SQUARE — 10 MINS FROM LA PLAYA (MAP 14)

tains, scooped stones and carefully sculpted boulders, all within site of Machu Picchu and the Inca drawbridge. There are no signs and there has been no restoration here, meaning that it is rarely visited. The site lies on the site line between Llactapata and Machu Picchu, suggesting that the various ruins are interlinked and shared ceremonial roles, particularly during the summer and winter solstices.

It takes almost an hour for the train to trundle across the Urubamba, clatter past **Puente Ruinas** at the foot of Machu Picchu and wheeze to a stop in Aguas Calientes (see p199) at the old station on Avenida Imperio de los Incas. Alternatively, you can walk the 10km to Aguas Calientes in about 2-3hrs by simply following the railway tracks. Along the way there are several places where enterprising locals have set up stalls to sell soft drinks and snacks, and you are treated to great views of the newly uncovered lower terraces at Machu Picchu. As you near Aguas Calientes, the tracks pass through two tunnels and a path that climbs left to **Putucusi** (see p200), before arriving in the lower part of the town.

From **Aguas Calientes** you can catch a shuttle bus up to Machu Picchu, something you'll most likely want to do first thing the following morning to get a full day exploring the site. For details on moving on from Aguas Calientes and Machu Picchu see p202.

The Vilcabamba Trail
Alexander Stewart & Henry Stedman

INTRODUCTION

This is an exceptional, rarely tackled trek through the forest between the remote villages of Huancacalle and Chaunquiri, via the ruins of Espíritu Pampa, which is thought to be the remains of Vilcabamba, the last city and capital of the Incas.

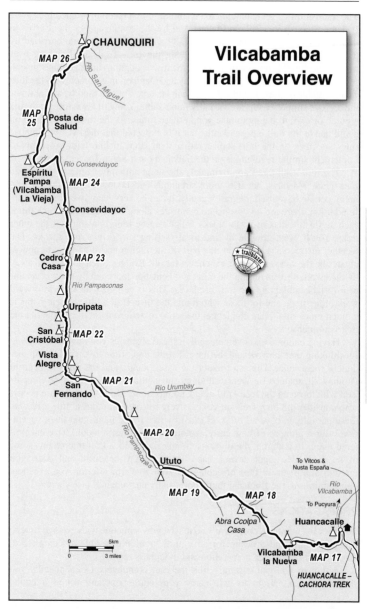

Vilcabamba
Trail Overview

CHAUNQUIRI

MAP 26

Río San Miguel

MAP 25 — Posta de Salud

Río Consevidayoc

Espíritu Pampa (Vilcabamba La Vieja)

MAP 24

Consevidayoc

Cedro Casa — MAP 23

Río Pampaconas

Urpipata

San Cristóbal — MAP 22

Vista Alegre

San Fernando — MAP 21

Río Urumbay

MAP 20

Río Pampaconas

Ututo

MAP 19 — MAP 18

Abra Ccolpa Casa

To Vitcos & Nusta España

Río Vilcabamba

To Pucyura

Huancacalle

Vilcabamba la Nueva — MAP 17

HUANCACALLE – CACHORA TREK

0   5km
0   3 miles

ROUTE GUIDE & MAPS

The trail follows a route thought to be similar to that taken by Manco Inca as he fled the Spanish in 1537, and later taken by the conquistadors themselves in their two invasions of Vilcabamba in 1539 and 1572. For anyone horrified by the tidal wave of humanity surging along the Inca Trail and breaking over Machu Picchu, this remote trek free from crowds ought to have genuine appeal.

The trek is best tackled between May and October, in common with the Inca Trail. Outside of these months the trail can be very wet and muddy, and at times the narrow, slippery paths are virtually impassable. You will also struggle to find a guide or *arriero* happy to take you at these times. At the time of writing you could tackle the trail independently, but it is expected that the INC will impose rules and fees on the trail sooner rather than later, in line with proposals to implement similar regulations on the Salkantay and Santa Teresa treks.

The trek itself takes approximately the same amount of time as the classic Inca Trail, 3-4 days, but it is more strenuous and taxing. Depending on how many people have used the trail recently, it can be very heavily overgrown too. In addition, there are no designated campsites along its length and no facilities such as flush toilets or wash blocks which can be found on some of the other treks. You'll even struggle to find locals selling soft drinks and snacks. The weather also wreaks havoc on this part of the region and it appears to almost always be the wet season with rain never far off. Bridges often get washed away by the swollen rivers during the rains and landslips loosened by the wet weather invariably obliterate the trail in places. This is certainly no straightforward walk in the park, and for those who found the Inca Trail a little too easy, this is a much more significant challenge: the sense of achievement in completing the trek is immense.

Having endured and overcome all of these obstacles you might be forgiven for thinking that the goal and the reward at the end of the trek would be immediately spectacular. This isn't really the case though, and the ruins at Espíritu Pampa (Vilcabamba La Vieja), although substantial, do not bear close comparison with those on the Inca Trail or at Choquequirao. However, for those people who consider the Inca Trail sites excessively restored and thus a little artificial, these partially uncovered ruins, cloaked by tree roots, lianas and thick vegetation offer a glimpse of how early explorers and pioneers would have encountered them. In addition, the route itself, an original Inca trail that retains some of its distinctive giant paving slabs, is stunningly beautiful and takes you through almost every type of ecological zone in Peru, offering you excellent opportunities to see flora and fauna not usually encountered elsewhere.

PREPARATIONS

This trek is fairly tough but there's no reason why someone with average fitness, decent stamina and a desire for adventure shouldn't be able to complete it, though a bit of advance preparation and thought is required.

Although you can currently trek the trail completely independently, you should hire an *arriero* to help carry your equipment and act as a guide.

ROUTE GUIDE & MAPS

Experienced *arrieros* can be engaged in Huancacalle (see p261). Before you begin the trek ensure that you have agreed an exact itinerary and price and be aware that you may need to provide food and shelter for your guide. In addition to the fee you should tip the team if they did a good job. Alternatively, there are a handful of agencies that run treks on this trail, who will supply guides and mules as part of the package you sign up for (see pp156-9).

There is no accommodation or opportunity to resupply along the trail so all equipment and food must be brought from Huancacalle. You will need a tent and camping gear, although if you are trekking with an agency they will usually be obliged to provide these – check that they do. No special equipment is required, although a machete might come in handy if the trail is overgrown: your *arriero* ought to have one of these. Make sure that you have plenty of wet-weather gear and that your kit is stored in waterproof bags, as there is a higher than usual chance of it getting soaked in this part of the region. Insect repellent is also essential as the trail can be plagued by mosquitoes, and you must have some sort of anti-malarial medication.

To get the most out of your trek and fully appreciate the history and significance of the region and the ruins, you should also read up about the Vilcabamba district (see p40).

GETTING TO THE TRAILHEAD

The trek begins in Huancacalle, which can be reached by bus from Cusco, via Quillabamba. It takes 7-9hrs to drive from Cusco to Quillabamba and a further 4-5hrs from here to Huancacalle. Onward transport from Chaunquiri is rather erratic, so to maximize your chances of picking up a bus aim to reach the village in time for the weekend markets, after which you should be able to find a ride.

When considering timings for the trek, remember it takes a long time to travel to the Vilcabamba region and that you may want to spend a day in and around Huancacalle, exploring the nearby ruins and archaeological sites. Bearing this in mind, you should allow at least a week for the entire trip and possibly as many as nine days to complete everything you might want to do here.

Cusco to Quillabamba

Since the suspension of the railway line from Aguas Calientes to Quillabamba many years ago, the only way to reach the town is by road. From Cusco buses run via Ollantaytambo. They leave throughout the day from the Terminal Terrestre. The road trip is spectacular and takes you across the Abra de Malaga, which affords you outstanding views of the Veronica Range. If you take the overnight bus you will of course miss these. Beyond here the tarmac runs out. The journey, pot-holes, punctures and traffic permitting takes 7-9hrs and costs around s/20. There are a handful of bus companies plying this route, the best of which are Ampay (☎ 245734) and Selva Sur (☎ 247975).

ROUTE GUIDE & MAPS

❏ **Chaullay**
Chaullay, not to be confused with the settlement of the same name on the Santa Teresa Trek, was once the site of the strategically important Inca rope bridge Choquichaca, which provided access to the Vilcabamba valley. If the Incas anticipated an invasion they simply cut the bridge and withdrew into the protected valley, safe in the knowledge that the gorge was too precipitous to cross any other way. It was here that Inca warriors fatefully killed the Spanish envoy Atilana de Anayo, an atrocity that sparked the final invasion of the region in 1572.

Around 1¹/₂hrs before Quillabamba is **Chaullay**, where the historic Choquichaca Bridge, built on Inca foundations, crosses a gorge. Here the road continues parallel to the Río Urubamba until it reaches Quillabamba.

Quillabamba
Set at the confluence of the Chuyapi and Urubamba rivers, Quillabamba is the most important town in the region. Known as La Ciudad de Eterno Verano (the City of Eternal Summer), Quillabamba was a thriving jungle town with a decent food market at its centre, whose prosperity derived from the coffee industry.

ROUTE GUIDE & MAPS

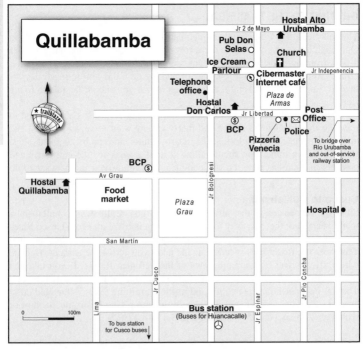

Quillabamba

Hostal Alto Urubamba
Jr 2 de Mayo
Pub Don Selas
Ice Cream Parlour
Church
Cibermaster Internet café
Jr Independencia
Telephone office
Plaza de Armas
Hostal Don Carlos
Jr Libertad
Post Office
BCP
Police
Pizzería Venecia
To bridge over Rio Urubamba and out-of-service railway station
BCP
Av Grau
Jr Bolognesi
Hostal Quillabamba
Food market
Plaza Grau
Hospital
San Martín
Jr Cusco
Jr Lima
Jr Espinar
Jr Pio Concha
Bus station
(Buses for Huancacalle)
0   100m
To bus station for Cusco buses
★ trailblazer

Goods such as fruit and coffee are still shipped to Cusco, but the town is now better known as a stepping stone on the way to Vilcabamba, or the Pongo de Mainique (canyon) and beyond that the Amazon.

The **bus stations** for Huancacalle and Cusco are several blocks south of Plaza Grau. There is an **internet café**, Cibermaster, on the plaza on Jr Espinar and **banks** can be found on Jr Libertad and Jr Bolognesi. The cheaper **accommodation** options are around the main market. Alternatively, try the clean, friendly *Hostal Alto Urubamba* (☎ 281131, s/20/25/35 sgl/dbl/tpl, com, or s/40/50/60, att) at Jr 2 de Mayo 333 which has a pleasant courtyard and a small restaurant attached. Well worth considering is the spotless but simple *Hostal Don Carlos* (☎ 281150, s/45/65/75 sgl/dbl/tpl, att) to the west of the plaza on Jr Libertad 566; it has hot water showers, a bar and restaurant. A little more expensive is the smarter *Hostal Quillabamba* (☎ 281369, s/50/70/80 sgl/dbl/tpl, att) on the corner of Prolongación and Av Grau, just behind the main market. Large, kitsch and a little out of place, the rooms all have private bathrooms and there is a swimming pool that just occasionally has water in it. There are also parking spaces and a restaurant here.

For fast, wholesome **food** try one of the chicken restaurants strung out along Av San Martín. *El Gordito* on Jr Espinar is also a good place for chicken whilst *Pub Don Selas* at Jr Espinar 235 serves sandwiches and other snacks. *Pizzeria Venecia* on the plaza serves just what the name implies. On the west side of the plaza are also several decent ice-cream parlours. For local fare and superb, freshly squeezed juices try the main **market**.

Quillabamba to Huancacalle

Combis depart from Quillabamba for Huancacalle at 9am and at noon. The bumpy journey takes 4-5hrs and costs around s/10. You may be able to find a service that goes all the way through to Vilcabamba La Nueva, although these are infrequent and, despite saving you time on the trek, would mean you miss the fascinating ruins around Huancacalle. Just before Huancacalle is the larger village of **Pucyura**; this was the location of the first church built in the valley. Constructed by Friar Diego Ortiz in the wake of the peace treaty between the conquistadors and Titu Cusi in 1568, the original has long since been torn down, and a modern church now stands on the same site.

Huancacalle   [see map p263]

Huancacalle is a simple, typical Andean town set in a very pleasant part of the Vilcabamba valley. It essentially comprises a single street, along which all life is visible, with pigs, chicken and donkeys roaming loose and locals sat watching the world go by. The traditional start point for people trekking to Espíritu Pampa, and nowadays for those tackling the route that links Huancacalle to Choquequirao or even Machu Picchu, the town is used to trekkers, even though there are very few facilities to support them. There are just a couple of places to stay, although you can *camp* by the road opposite the abandoned visitor's centre, and there aren't really any restaurants to speak of. You can hire *arrieros* and guides here though, and pick up a smattering of last-minute provisions.

The best accommodation, **Sixpac Manco Hostal** (☎ 812714) at the far end of the village, is run by the Cobos family. This family are also the best-known and most reliable guides in the region. Beds in this tranquil, pleasant hostal cost s/15/20 and the owners will also prepare meals (s/3-5). The only alternative is the simple but functional **Hospedaje los Koyas** on the main street, which has dorm beds for s/10.

Side trip to Vitcos [see map opposite]

On the prow of a promontory poised between the Río Vilcabamba and Las Andenes stream stand the ruins of Vitcos (see box p264), Manco Inca's first capital in Vilcabamba and another of Hiram Bingham's discoveries. Easily accessible from Huancacalle, you can make a very pleasant half-day round trip to the ruins and surrounding sites. The paths are clearly defined and you should have no problem following the broad tracks. Alternatively, you can hire a guide in Huancacalle for a small fee.

Opposite Sixpac Manco Hostal on Huancacalle's main street is a trail that crosses two rivers. Just after the second river the trail splits. Take the left-hand fork and begin to climb north along the flank of a hill known as **Rosaspata** (3050m/10,004ft), passing the remains of an old Spanish mill as it goes. The entire hill is dotted with the remains of Inca structures, though most remain covered in scrub and unrestored. On the crest of the hill, surrounded on three sides by sheer cliffs and overlooking the valleys below and the town of Pucyura to the north-west, is Vitcos, the centre of operations for the Incas whilst in exile. Unlike the other ruins, the complex here has been partially restored. On one side of a plaza stands a series of finely crafted ashlars and gateways some 250ft long, the double-jamb entrances of which open onto large rooms filled with niches. This structure is backed by an upper level that comprises residential buildings and storage facilities. There are superb panoramic views from here of not only the valley but also the passes that lead into it. On the lower level, on the far side of the plaza is a finely carved stone throne.

A second path descends the eastern side of Rosaspata, heading south and losing height as it passes through a light **eucalyptus forest**. The valley floor is marked by a series of broad agricultural terraces, or *andenes*, atop which stand a number of sculpted **boulders**. From the valley floor the path begins to climb again and after 10-15mins, at the southern end of Rosaspata, comes to the site known variously as **Ñusta España**, Yurac Rumi (White Stone) or Chuquipalta. Sculpted boulders, carved stone seats, water channels and baths surround an enormous granite boulder more than seven metres tall and fifteen metres wide. The smallness of this sheltered side valley exaggerates and draws attention to the size of the rock. This giant *huaca*, the spiritual centre of the exiled Inca state, is carved with a series of bosses, steps, protrusions and other decorations. Under the stone is a spring, the waters from which are carefully channelled through a small ceremonial bath before being carried away. The stone work is outstanding and the various features are illuminated as the sun tracks over the sacred site. A Spanish priest, Antonio de la Calancha, described the site as 'the principal *mochadero* – the common Indian word for their shrines – in these *montañas*'. He also recorded that a devil 'captain of a legion of devils' used to inhabit the rock. Such was the fear of this creature and the dislike of the Inca habit of worshipping natural objects such as stone that in 1570 two

Side trip to Vitcos

TERRACES

STEEP BLUFF

PLAZA

VITCOS

PUCYURA

NARROW NECK APPROACHES SITE

STEEP BLUFF

VITCOS

ROSASPATA

NOTE: COMPLETE CIRCUIT TAKES 2-4 HRS

EUCALYPTUS GROVE

CARVED BOULDERS & TERRACES ON VALLEY FLOOR

HUANCACALLE

Hospedaje Los Koyas

Sixpac Manco Hostal

COLONIAL RUINS

ÑUSTA ESPAÑA

TO VILCABAMBA LA NUEVA

17

RÍO VILCABAMBA

TO CHUPANI & CHOQUEQUIRAO

35

0   ½ mile
0   APPROX SCALE   1km

❏ Vitcos

Constructed by Manco Inca in 1537 following the Incas' retreat from Cusco, the new capital was only briefly occupied before a raid by the conquistador Orgóñez caught the Incas unaware. Routed, Manco was forced to quit the site and flee further into the jungle. Orgóñez was subsequently summoned to Cusco and forced to abandon the pursuit, meaning that Manco was able to return from the jungle to reclaim Vitcos. A further attack by Gonzalo Pizarro meant the Inca once again had to temporarily quit his capital before returning when the Spanish returned to Cusco. From here Manco went on to mount raids and guerrilla attacks on the Spanish, who were now embroiled in a civil war between those who supported Almagro and those who backed Pizarro. Gonzalo Pizarro was eventually executed and his brother Francisco assassinated. Manco welcomed the seven Spanish renegades responsible for the assassination on the basis that any enemy of Pizarro was a friend of his and gave them shelter at Vitcos. Manco's friendship was to be his undoing and after several years, in 1544, the Spanish murdered him in a final act of treachery. The soldiers, supporters of Almagro's cause, thought that by slaying the Inca they could curry favour with the victorious Pizarrists and earn their right to return. Manco's son, Titu Cusi, witnessed the attack and recorded it in his chronicles: 'One day with much good fellowship they were playing at quoits with him: only them, my father, and me, who was then a little boy ... Then just as my father was raising the quoit to throw, they all rushed upon him with knives, daggers and some swords ... he fell to the ground covered with wounds, and they left him for dead. I being a little boy, and seeing my father treated in this manner, wanted to rush up to help him. But they turned furiously on me and threw a lance which only just failed to kill me too.'

The assassins made their escape, but were tracked down, caught and burnt to death by Manco's supporters. The Inca himself survived for a further three days, long enough to learn that his attackers had all been killed. The assailants' severed heads were paraded at Vitcos and staked there for more than 20 years as a gruesome reminder of their fate.

Titu Cusi went on to become Inca in his turn and later also died at Vitcos, following a severe illness.

Augustinian friars exorcized the rock and had it burnt. They also destroyed as much of the surrounding temples and structures as they could. The toppled stones and razed walls are the result of this assault, although they were of course unable to do anything much to the rock itself. Legend also records that during Inca times a girl could prove her virginity by urinating at the top of the rock: if the urine precisely followed the grooved channel across the surface she was deemed to be chaste.

From here the path climbs westwards before eventually dropping back down, past the junction with the trail you initially took, to cross the river below Huancacalle. The complete circuit takes around two hours to trek, but you should factor in a couple of hours exploring the various sites along the route too.

❏ Important note – walking times

All times in this book refer only to the time spent walking. You will need to add 10-30% to allow for rests, photography, checking the map, drinking water etc.

HUANCACALLE TO UTUTO   [MAPS 17-18, pp266-7; MAP 19, p269]

Overview
From the centre of Huancacalle a dirt road coils and snakes westwards across the hillside beyond the village, gaining height steadily but evenly in the course of 2¹/₂hrs to arrive at the Abra Ccolpa Casa, which marks the boundary between the Andes and the Amazon basin.

Route
At the far end of the village look for the fork in the road and take the right-hand branch. Rather than follow the road all the way to the pass, which would be time consuming and tedious, look for the path that cuts between the loops and climbs the hill in a more direct fashion. Having joined the path just outside the village, it zigzags and then rejoins the road before leaving it again immediately before a bridge, close to the **VIIth Station of the Cross**, one of fourteen crucifixes lining the roadside. Cross the subsequent bridge and forge ahead, keeping the Río Vilcabamba on your right. Cutting between the next set of switchbacks, you pass the VIIIth and IXth Stations of the Cross. Rejoin the road close to the XIth Station of the Cross, where the gradient eases and the land begins to resemble farmland, and pass through the village of San Francisco de la Vitoria de Vilcabamba, more often simply referred to as Vilcabamba or **Vilcabamba La Nueva** in order to distinguish it from the Inca's final capital city.

Originally built in the 16th century adjacent to Vitcos by the first Spanish settlers in the region, the town was moved up the valley to its current exposed location by the source of the Río Vilcabamba to support a silver mine nearby and became the capital of the region. The Spanish were never fully able to settle this region though as it was too high and too remote to appeal to many of the new arrivals. The settlers quickly exhausted the land, and once the mine ran dry in the late 18th century, they abandoned it. Once intended to be a symbol of Spanish success, Vilcabamba La Nueva once again became a backwater. Straggling along the road, the modern town is centred on the remains of a 16th-century chapel, whose ancient **bell tower** is all that still stands, and a large modern Catholic mission and its church which now stands where the original once did. The town is not geared up for visitors and there is nowhere to stay here although you should be able to *camp* nearby. Ask permission first though. Nor are there many shops or places to pick up anything more than the most basic supplies.

Beyond the town enter the wide valley to your right and follow the road which struggles on northwards across small-holdings and arable land dotted over the mountainside before petering out (Map 18) just before the **Abra Ccolpa Casa** (3900m/12,792ft). A shrine to Santa Rosa de Lima stands here close to the remains of an Inca plaza, in the south-eastern corner of which are heaped the remains of an Inca shrine. The views of the surrounding peaks are spectacular from here in clear weather; Bingham described the view as he came over the pass as 'a great wilderness of deep green valleys and forest-clad slopes'.

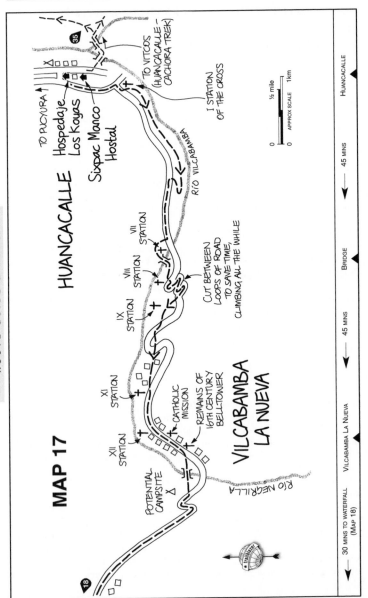

MAP 17

HUANCACALLE

TO PUCYURA

Hospedaje Los Kogas

Sixpac Manco Hostal

TO VITCOS (HUANCACALLE–CACHORA TREK)

I STATION OF THE CROSS

RIO VILCABAMBA

VII STATION

VIII STATION

IX STATION

CUT BETWEEN LOOPS OF ROAD TO SAVE TIME, CLIMBING ALL THE WHILE

XI STATION

XII STATION

CATHOLIC MISSION

REMAINS OF 16TH CENTURY BELLTOWER

VILCABAMBA LA NUEVA

RIO NEGRILLA

POTENTIAL CAMPSITE

30 MINS TO WATERFALL (MAP 18)

0   ½ mile
0   APPROX SCALE   1km

HUANCACALLE   ◀   45 MINS   ◀   BRIDGE   ◀   45 MINS   ◀   VILCABAMBA LA NUEVA   ◀   30 MINS TO WATERFALL (MAP 18)

MAP 18

SECTION OF INCA PAVED PATH

STEADY DESCENT ACROSS PUNA & GRASSLANDS – CAN BE BOGGY AFTER HEAVY RAIN

MOLLIPUNKU

GATE

TO CHALCA

USUAL ROUTE

BOULDER

RÍO CHALCA

PUENTE ANTIGUO

TO PAMPA-CONAS

19

FOOTBALL PITCH

CATHOLIC SHRINE TO SANTA ROSA DE LIMA

INCA PLAZA

REMNANTS OF INCA SHRINE

ABRA CCOLPA CASA (PASS, 3900M)

ROAD PETERS OUT

RÍO MINASNAYU

17

WATERFALL

APPROX SCALE

0   ½ mile

0   1km

PUENTE ANTIGUO — 30 MINS — MOLLIPUNKU — 60 MINS — ABRA CCOLPA CASA — 30 MINS — WATERFALL

On the far side of the pass descend gently north-west, sticking to the left-hand side of the long valley. There is evidence of a road being built here, and the path cuts between the wide bends. The path passes a football pitch and undulates across the puna to the crossroads at **Mollipunku**. Great slabs of Inca paving and original steps descend from here towards the Río Chalca and the bottom of the valley, which you reach within half an hour.

Cross the river on the **Puente Antiguo**, after which the trail forks. Both branches lead to Ututo in roughly the same amount of time although the lower one is the simpler, gentler path. The lower path descends from the bridge to the left bank of the river and follows it, passing a number of scenic spots that would make attractive campsites. As the trail progresses the vegetation becomes increasingly wild and dense. Small plots of farmland stand partially hidden amongst the tangle. As you near the small hamlet of **Ututo** the ground becomes increasingly boggy, with small streams, some of which aren't bridged, flowing off the hillside and across the path to join the main river. However, the dry patches of ground that can be found around the collection of rudimentary houses here also make excellent *campsites*.

The higher path goes via the village of Pampaconas (Map 19), which lies on the far side of a large, deep bog known as **Oncoy Cacha**. **Pampaconas** (3340m/10,955ft) is an exposed, fairly inhospitable place, but there are the remnants of an Inca plaza and platform here that were used by the Incas for ceremonial sun worship. Eventually Titu Cusi gave permission for the first Christian cross in the region to be erected here.

Beyond the village the countryside used to be heavily forested, so much so that the Spanish invaders in 1539 and 1572 were forced to leave their horses at Pampaconas and progress on foot. Bingham suffered the same misfortune in 1911 whilst exploring the region. Nowadays the way is clear though and descends evenly along stretches of Inca staircase and original path to reach Ututo.

UTUTO TO VISTA ALEGRE
[MAP 19, opp; MAP 20, p271; MAP 21, p273]

Overview
This gentle, wonderfully scenic section of the trail makes for an excellent day's walking, with plenty of flora and birdlife to keep you enthralled as you amble largely downhill through increasingly verdant cloud forest.

Route
Cross the large **orange bridge** at the western end of the village and begin to walk on the right-hand (eastern) bank of the river. Fields and tended pastures give way quickly to **forest** (Map 20). The path rises and falls above the river, occasionally climbing or descending on original Inca steps. Vincent Lee has suggested that the Spaniards were oblivious to the Inca trail here and tried to hack out another trail on the far side of the river, which explains how it took them eight days to march to Vilcabamba, whilst modern trekkers complete the same route in just two.

MAP 19

60 MINS FROM PUENTE ANTIGUO (MAP 18)

USUAL (LOWER) ROUTE

GATE

ALTERNATIVE (HIGHER) ROUTE

RÍO KOLPACÁSA

RÍO PAMPACONAS

STICK TO LEFT BANK OF RIVER – DO NOT CROSS AT THIS STAGE

SCRUB

ONCOY CACHA VERY BOGGY

REMNANTS OF INCA PLAZA

ORANGE CONCRETE SUSPENSION BRIDGE

WET & BOGGY

INCA STAIRS

PAMPACONAS

SECTION OF PAVED INCA PATH

UTUTO

PAMPACONAS

75 MINS

UTUTO

½ mile   1km

0

0   APPROX SCALE

20

18

❏ **Huayna Pucará**

The narrow ridge of Huayna Pucará dominates this section of trail. The Spanish friar Martín de Murúa, who chronicled the conquest of Vilcabamba, described the ridge as 'a knife edge which two men could not walk along side by side'. The name of this strategic spot literally translates as New Fort.

Unfortunately the site didn't really live up to its name. As the Spanish pushed into the region during 1572, the Incas planned to stage an ambush here, using the vertiginous ridge as the ideal place from which to launch an attack on the troops below. The plan was to hurl enormous boulders down on the enemy, whilst archers picked off any survivors. The surprise was lost though when a defector betrayed the position of the fort and warned the Spanish of the trap.

During the night the Spanish scaled the hillside to higher ground, outflanking the fort and turning the tables to give themselves the advantage. Realizing the hopelessness of the situation, the Incas fought a determined rearguard action as they retreated, before fleeing into the forest below. The Incas had lost their last effective chance to defeat the Spanish and subsequently they offered little further resistance. It is not known what eventually happened to the Inca traitor.

As you descend, the trail crosses several small streams issuing into the river to your left, which steadily grows in size. Following a particularly scenic stretch of cloud forest the path reaches an **orange suspension bridge**, the Puente de Cedro or Cedrochaca. It is possible to pitch a tent on the bank adjacent to the bridge.

Cross the bridge and begin to climb on the left-hand bank of the river, gaining height briefly through a further forested stretch. Having lost the accumulated height slowly and evenly the path bends north-west and enters the clearing of **Tambocarahuina** (Map 21). Bingham noted that in this part of Peru 'any little natural breathing space at the bottom of a canyon is a *pampa*'. The clearing itself is pretty unremarkable, except that it has views of the narrow ridge above, upon which Vincent Lee identified the Inca fort **Huayna Pucará** (see box above) in 1984.

Beyond the clearing, pass through a gate and cross a small stream before working your way through a small settlement, past patches of hillside that have been slashed and burnt, and converted into homestays and small holdings. A series of zigzags bring you down to the Río Zapatero and the single house here.

A second series of switchbacks climbs away from the river before the gradient lessens and the path climbs more gently towards the village of **San Fernando**, where it is possible to pitch a tent. Shortly beyond here are two streams in quick succession. The Sucsu Chincana is crossed via a **blue suspension bridge** whilst the Ounay has to be breached using a rickety wooden bridge. If you're not confident on the slippery, makeshift bridge and the stream isn't too high or fast, simply ford it. On the far side of the bridge stands **Vista Alegre** (Happy View), which comprises a scattering of houses and a football pitch, on which it is possible to *camp*.

RÍO URUMBAY

MAP 20

45 MINS TO TAMBOCARAHUINA (MAP 21)

CEDROCHACA / PUENTE DE CEDRO

75 MINS FROM UTUTO (MAP 19)

21

CEDROCHACA/
PUENTE DE CEDRO
(ORANGE SUSPENSION
BRIDGE)

SET OF
INCA STAIRS

STEADY, GENTLE
DESCENT THROUGH
BEAUTIFUL STRETCH
OF CLOUD FOREST

ATTRACTIVE
CLOUD FOREST

RÍO PAMPACONAS

ROCKY
CLEARING

0   ½ mile
0   APPROX SCALE   1km

19

VISTA ALEGRE TO CONSEVIDAYOC
[MAP 21, opp; MAP 22-23, pp274-5; MAP 24, p277]

Overview
This section begins much as the previous one finished, with a walk across small streams and through scenic forest as you hug the western flank of the valley, descending all the while.

Route
The narrow path beyond Vista Alegre crosses the Río Vista Alegre on an unstable wooden bridge and begins to undulate in a northerly direction, hugging the flank of the valley and climbing into and out of the folds in the hillsides (Map 22). The vegetation here is potentially very thick and the trail can be overgrown in places. Rainfall also loosens the steep-sided slopes and landslides are frequent, so you may have to improvise a path or climb further up the hillside to pick your way carefully across the scar before rejoining the main path.

Just over an hour beyond Vista Alegre is the farm of **San Cristóbal**, where a small grassy clearing doubles as a *campsite*. Another hour's walk through thick forest, past occasional farms and along the steep-sided valley flank high above the river, lies the village of **Urpipata**. Set beneath the crest of the hill, this is a good spot to *camp*. Vincent Lee has also identified the site as the location of Machu Pucará (the Old Fort), although all that remains are a handful of tumbledown walls, which may or may not be part of the original structure. The Incas fought a highly successful battle here in 1539, killing a number of conquistadors in an ambush. Their victory was short lived though as Pedro Pizarro returned within ten days of the attack with reinforcements and seized the hill. By the time of the second invasion in 1572 the site had been abandoned and offered no resistance to the invading army. Descending from the hill top the path weaves through a stretch of farmland and crosses a slippery log path before dropping steeply to the Río Tunqul Mayu (Map 23) and the wooden bridge that crosses it. There are limited camping opportunities here, although the pools in the river are good for dunking yourself in. Cross a boggy patch of ground on the far side of the stream and climb sharply to a small clearing in the forest before dropping back down to cross the Río Luca Mayu.

A series of steep switchbacks ascend to a handful of farmed plots at **Cedro Casa**. At this point the path begins to follow a pattern, descending steeply west towards the river before climbing aggressively east away from it again. An hour further on is a vast, bare rock outcrop known as **La Roca**, from where you can catch the first tantalizing glimpses of Consevidayoc, another hour to the north. The intervening countryside is scarred with farmed plots and slash-and-burn clearances as well as by the landslips.

The scattered settlement of **Consevidayoc** (Map 24) is thought by Vincent Lee to be the site of Marcanay, where Friar Diego Ortiz was martyred for failing to cure the Inca Titu Cusi with medicine he gave him. You can *camp* in the school compound here if you get permission from the school director, who lives on site. Pitches cost s/10-15 depending on group size and the number of mules you have.

MAP 21

Broad, Stony Riverbed
Río Vista Alegre
Rickety Wooden Bridge
Blue Suspension Bridge
Football Pitch

VISTA ALEGRE

Río Oñay
Río Sucsu Chincana

NOTE
Don't cross Río Pampaconas – stick to left bank

SAN FERNANDO

Waterfall

Steep descent on set of switchbacks

Río Zapatero

Huayna Pucará

Gate Tambo

Cultivated Plots

Gate

Río Pampaconas

TAMBOCARAHUINA
Clearing with good views of ridge of Huayna Pucará

½ mile 1km
0 Approx Scale

23

LOGS LAID ACROSS MUDDY, BOGGY SECTION - SLIPPERY

FENCES & CULTIVATED PLOTS ADJACENT TO PATH

URPIPATA

RÍO URPIPATA

GATE

COFFEE PLANTATION

PATH UNDULATES THROUGH DENSE FOREST; BEWARE OF LANDSLIP SCARS THAT HAVE ALTERED HILLSIDE THE AND DAMAGED THE TRAIL

MANY STREAMS ARE UNBRIDGED OR ONLY HAVE BASIC LOG CROSSINGS

SAN CRISTÓBAL

MAP 22

RÍO PAMPACONAS

45 MINS TO RÍO TUNGAL MAYU (MAP 23)

URPIPATA

60 MINS

SAN CRISTÓBAL

60 MINS FROM VISTA ALEGRE (MAP 21)

0   ½ mile
0   APPROX SCALE   1km

21

24

FIELDS EITHER SIDE OF PATH & SIGNS OF CLEARING

FIRST SIGHTING OF CONSEVIDAYOC FURTHER NORTH

ROCKY OUTCROP OF LA ROCA

0   ½ mile
0   APPROX SCALE   1km

SMALL WATERFALL

STREAMS FREQUENTLY UNBRIDGED OR ONLY BASIC CROSSING ON LOGS AVAILABLE

RÍO DIABLO

CEDRO CASA

STEEP CLIMB ON SET OF SWITCHBACKS

THIS SECTION PRONE TO LANDSLIPS

RÍO LUCA MAYU

HUAYNAPATA
(SMALL CLEARING)

CAN BE VERY BOGGY

RÍO TUNQUL MAYU

MAP 23

RÍO PAMPACONAS

CAMPSITE IN CLEARING

trailblazer

22

ROUTE GUIDE & MAPS

CONSEVIDAYOC TO ESPÍRITU PAMPA [MAP 24, opp]

From Consevidayoc the path climbs through yet more plantations and farm plots to a junction. Ignore the right-hand fork that descends to the river as it goes directly to Chuntabamba, avoiding the ruins at Espíritu Pampa completely.

Instead, take the left-hand fork and climb again for almost an hour to reach the top of a forested hill. Here there are the remnants of a small Inca building thought to have been a **watch tower** looking out over the broad, restored Inca steps that sweep down towards Vilcabamba La Vieja – the Incas always knew how to make an entrance.

Descend the wide, **ceremonial staircase** into the lush valley for 15-20mins to reach a small settlement centred on a church-cum-school. There's also a farm here and some houses, as well as a small shop and some decent tent pitches. The ruins themselves are a further 10mins walk through the forest.

Espíritu Pampa

The Plain of the Spirits, the evocative literal translation of the name Espíritu Pampa, is a large densely forested region where some 400 ruins lie concealed by jungle and vegetation. Bingham gave a good indication of the thickness of the vegetation and the challenge in spotting, let alone uncovering the ruins when he wrote that: 'Nothing gives a better idea of the density of the jungle than the fact that the savages themselves have been within five feet of these fine walls without being aware of their existence'.

It also explains why he himself failed to uncover the extent of the city or recognize its true scale and importance. Gene Savoy, fifty years after Bingham, is in fact responsible for the early work and revised view of the ruins. Only a handful of the most important structures have been uncovered, with very little reconstruction having taken place.

The rest of this considerable city is subsumed by the jungle, and awaits discovery by you; be careful moving vegetation though so as to not disturb any of the stones. Although the structures and the site in general aren't immediately impressive, with a bit of effort and imagination you can fully appreciate the scale of this spectacular abandoned city. For those who find the overly reconstructed ruins at Machu Picchu a little fake, these structures, found just as early explorers would have uncovered them, offer an atmospheric alternative. Stones are held in the muscular embrace of vines and creepers whilst roots burst through the walls like buttresses. Moss and lichen mottle the masonry and the whole lot is stained green. It's a charming, moody place to spend time and even basic exploration of the site is immensely rewarding.

The city was built according to an Inca template and the layout is reminiscent of other sites. The central section where you first arrive is the most carefully cleared and exposed part of the site. The trail to the impressively large central plaza passes several carefully carved **baths** and crosses a **bridge** over an Inca canal. The **plaza** is backed by a long *kallanka* and terraces surround it.

In the north-east corner of the plaza stands a *huaca*; the **Vilca stone** is a giant, uncarved boulder leaning slightly on its side, and described as looking

MAP 24

Espíritu Pampa

90 MINS

Consevidayoc

25

UNNAMED
REMNANTS OF
WATCHTOWER

RÍO CONSEVIDAYOC

TO
RUINS

GRAND
CEREMONIAL
STAIRCASE

ESPÍRITU
PAMPA
(VILCABAMBA
LA VIEJA)

RUINS ARE
ONLY JUST
OFF MAP

STEADY ASCENT
ON BROAD TRAIL

SET OF
STEPS

WATERFALL

FORK TO
CHUNTABAMBA — GATE

PLENTY OF FARM
ACTIVITY AND
EVIDENCE OF SLASH
& BURN CLEARING
FOR CULTIVATION

SCHOOL –
POSSIBLE TO CAMP
WITHIN SCHOOL
COMPOUND

CONSEVIDAYOC

FIELDS & CULTIVATED
PLOTS ON BOTH SIDES
OF THE PATH

23

0   ½ mile
0   APPROX SCALE   1km

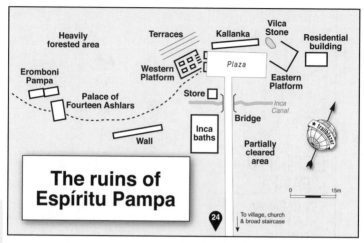

The ruins of Espíritu Pampa

'like a great egg' by Gene Savoy. A couple of minutes to the south of the plaza is a lengthy striking stone wall now covered in moss. Beyond this lies the section originally uncovered by Bingham, called **Eromboni Pampa**, where the **Palace of the Fourteen Ashlars** stands. Bingham describes being guided to them in 1914:

> While we were wondering whether the Incas themselves ever lived here, there suddenly appeared the naked figure of a sturdy young savage, armed with a stout bow and long arrows, and wearing a fillet of bamboo. He had been hunting and showed us a bird he had shot. Soon afterwards there came the two adult savages we had met at Saavedra's, accompanied by a cross-eyed friend, all wearing long tunics. They offered to guide us to other ruins. It was very difficult for us to follow their rapid pace. Half an hour's scramble through the jungle brought us to a pampa or natural terrace on the banks of a little tributary of the Pampaconas. They called it Eromboni. Here we found several old artificial terraces and the rough foundations of a long, rectangular building 192 feet by 24 feet. It might have had twenty-four doors, twelve in front and twelve in back, each three and a half feet wide. No lintels were in evidence. The walls were only a foot high. There was very little building material in sight. Apparently the structure had never been completed. Near by was a typical Inca fountain with three stone spouts, or conduits. Two hundred yards beyond the water-carrier's rendezvous, hidden behind a curtain of hanging vines and thickets so dense we could not see more than a few feet in any direction, the savages showed us the ruins of a group of stone houses whose walls were still standing in fine condition.
>
> **Hiram Bingham** *Inca Land – Explorations in the Highlands of Peru* (1922)

There are few terraces as the uneven terrain was difficult to farm, and yet according to various chroniclers the Incas wanted for very little. The Spanish friar Martín de Murúa recorded that: 'The Incas enjoyed scarcely less of the luxuries, greatness and splendour of Cusco in that distant land of exile. For the Indians brought with them whatever they could get from outside for their contentment and pleasure. And so for that time they enjoyed the good life there'.

The jungle also gave up fruits, coca, sugar, honey and various fowl on which the Inca dined. The reality of course was that Manco retreated to the jungle as a last resort, because it was militarily expedient to do so and because, following his last stand at Ollantaytambo he had nowhere else to go. The Incas consequently had little choice but to endure the humidity, insects, snakes and

---

❑ Manco's capital?

There have been very few excavations of note at Vilcabamba despite the ruins being uncovered by **Hiram Bingham** in 1914. Bingham in fact refused to believe that the small collection of buildings he found was the last capital of the Incas and got himself into all sorts of intellectual knots arguing, against all the evidence, that Machu Picchu must have been the last city of the Incas simply because it looked more suitable and spectacular. He also argued that the Incas 'would not have cared to live in this hot valley'. In fact, it wasn't until 1964 that **Gene Savoy** realized the extent of the ruins and exposed the true scale of the site.

The limited archaeological research that has been conducted, whilst only having just scratched the surface of this giant site, has proved conclusively that the ruins are of Inca origin. Less spectacular or well-crafted than other major Inca sites, they can appear rather mundane and uninspiring to the casual visitor, hence Bingham's belief that the site couldn't possibly be the last capital. However, the distinctive layout, style of craftsmanship and stonework coupled with the features found at the site including canals, baths, ashlars and sacred rocks are all indicative of Inca architecture and conclusively prove that Espíritu Pampa is of Inca origin.

Debate has raged as to whether the site constituted Manco's final capital, though. The sheer scale of the site means that it must have been of some importance. Even in exile, the Incas created a number of extravagant signature pieces. The giant sweeping staircase that descends to the site is one such feature. The Vilca stone, positioned to dominate the plaza and eerily reminiscent of the celebrated *huaca* Ñusta España (see p262), lends weight to the theory that the site also had a special ceremonial significance.

The key discovery when it came to dating the site was the uncovering of a number of terracotta roof tiles. These imitations of Spanish roof tiles can only have been seen by the Incas in Cusco, and then copied. Prior to the conquest, the Incas only used straw or turf to roof their houses. Therefore the site must have been built after the arrival of the Spanish conquistadors. The most likely architect is therefore thought to be Manco Inca. The type of structures built, allied to the date when they would most likely have been constructed, suggests that the site is indeed the last Inca capital, Vilcabamba.

There is, however, no absolute proof that this is the case and some doubts do still remain. Evidence to support descriptions in some of the chronicles of the time is inconclusive; although modern-day Pampaconas still bears the same name as that used by the conquistadors, Marcanay may or may not be the modern village of Consevidayoc; Huayna Pucará is more than likely the site of the Inca ambush that went horribly wrong, but Machu Pucará may or may not be the actual site of the Inca Old Fort. As John Hemming wrote in *Conquest of the Incas*, 'Unless someone can discover another ruin that so exactly fulfils the geographical and topographical details known about Vilcabamba, and that also contains imitation Spanish roofing tiles, the lost city of Vilcabamba has finally been located as Espíritu Pampa'.

diseases rife in the jungle, as well as the constant threat posed by the conquistadors, who were never more than a couple of days' march away from the exiles.

For a fuller picture of the site and for a more comprehensive layout and description of the buildings, check out Vincent Lee's book *Forgotten Vilcabamba*, which contains maps and drawings of the ruins.

ESPÍRITU PAMPA TO CHAUNQIRI
[MAP 24, p277; MAP 25, opp; MAP 26, p282]
Overview
The final stage of the trek is the shortest, but also one of the most taxing, as the combination of exertion and heat can be debilitating.

Route
A path leads away from the church, over a sturdy **orange suspension bridge** (Map 25) and heads north-east down the left bank of the river. Within half an hour it reaches the confluence of two rivers at Chuntabamba, and the junction with the path from Consevidayoc. A short, sharp climb takes you into an area of well-tended fields and farmland, past a concrete house and a health station (Posta de Salud). Coffee, orange and maize plantations line the path as you descend evenly along the flank of the valley for almost an hour, crossing a suspension bridge over a tributary as it goes (Map 26).

The path then drops quickly to the river and crosses it on a suspension bridge. A set of **switchbacks** carry you quickly back up the far side of the river before a long looping bend brings you back on yourself. The path begins to gain height as it follows the river in a north-east direction, before becoming much steeper and tougher to ascend.

At the highest point on the trail there is a view of Chaunquiri, before the path starts to go back down equally steeply in order to cross the Río San Miguel on a robust bridge. From here it's a further 45mins, much of it uphill, to the dirt road that eventually leads to Chaunquiri.

Chaunquiri
Untidy, shabby and centred round a football pitch, Chaunquiri is not the sort of place that you'd usually seek out. It is however, the only way out of the area. There is no accommodation here although you can *camp* in the centre and you may be able to persuade a local family to let you stay in their house for a fee. A couple of cheap, basic **cafés** set around the plaza sell drinks and simple fare.

The way out is to catch a bus from Chaunqiri to **Kiteni**, 34km and two hours away. (It is possible to walk there, but this is a long, dry, full-day's trek.) Buses don't go all that regularly so you are best off targeting the trucks going to market there on Wednesday and Sunday. From Kiteni you can pick up a bus or truck to Quillabamba, which is 7-9hrs away (s/10-15). If you are lucky you may even find a direct truck from Chaunquiri to Quillabamba, particularly if you are trying to travel on Sunday.

Kiteni, which is rumoured to be where Túpac Amaru was captured, is little more than a jungle town, but does at least have a couple of places to stay in the centre and southern section of town. Basic *hospedajes* here cost s/10-15.

MAP 25

26

GATE

GATE

LOTS OF FARMS
AND SECTIONS OF
HILLSIDE CLEARED
FOR CROPS &
PLANTATIONS

RÍO CONSEVIDAYOC

POSTA DE
SALUD

GATE

RÍO CHUNTABAMBA

PATH FROM
CONSEVIDAYOC
(BYPASSES ESPÍRITU
PAMPA COMPLETELY)

RÍO ESPÍRITU PAMPA

ORANGE
SUSPENSION
BRIDGE

24

0   ½ mile

0   APPROX SCALE   1km

ROUTE GUIDE & MAPS

30 MINS FROM ESPÍRITU PAMPA (MAP 24) — BRIDGE OVER RÍO CHUNTABAMBA — 30 MINS — POSTA DE SALUD — 60 MINS TO BRIDGE OVER RÍO CONSEVIDAYOC (MAP 26)

MAP 26

CHAUNQUIRI

SERIES OF STEEP DESCENTS & CLIMBS TO CROSS RIVERS

FOOTBALL PITCH

VIEW TO CHAUNQUIRI

Río Consevidayoc

ALTERNATIVE, MORE DANGEROUS, LESS-USED ROUTE TO CHAUNQUIRI

GATE

Río San Miguel

BROAD, WELL-USED TRAIL FOR FINAL SECTION

STEEP DESCENT ON TIGHT SWITCHBACKS TO BRIDGE

0   ½ mile
0   APPROX SCALE   1km

25

CHAUNQUIRI

45 MINS

BRIDGE OVER RÍO SAN MIGUEL

105 MINS

BRIDGE OVER RÍO CONSEVIDAYOC

The Choquequirao trek

INTRODUCTION

Regarded by many as the original 'lost city' of the Incas, Choquequirao was the first fabled set of ruins to be uncovered. People had been aware of its existence from at least the 18th century but it was rarely visited and despite several acclaimed 'rediscoveries' over the years, it wasn't until Hiram Bingham arrived here in 1909 that it really came to people's attention. For Bingham, it was the discovery that fired his passion to uncover Machu Picchu and Espíritu Pampa.

Set high on a ridge spur around 1750m/5740ft above the Apurímac River and surrounded by sheer, snow-capped peaks, it is an awe-inspiring destination that requires a degree of effort to reach. The final site itself is a pretty good substitute for Machu Picchu, which it resembles in many respects. Perched on a high ridge, above a deep canyon through which one of the Inca's sacred rivers rages, in a remote part of wilderness, the ruins look out imperiously over the surrounding landscape. As its importance to the Incas is increasingly recognized by archaeologists, and awareness of the ruins grows, Choquequirao has gained in popularity as a trekking destination. A donation by the French government has also meant that further archaeological work at the site has been undertaken and further discoveries made that simply enhance the appeal of these ruins.

As the stringent rules on the classic Inca Trail are enforced more rigorously it looks set to continue to offer a genuine alternative to the traditional Inca Trail for trekkers wanting to escape the crowds and explore an outstanding area full of mystery and romance. Although the authorities have moved to simplify

CHOQUEQUIRAO

HUANCACALLE –
CACHORA TREK

Sunchumayo River

Marampata

MAP 29

Santa Rosa

Apurímac River

Apurímac River

Playa
Rosalina

Chiquisca

Cocamasana

MAP 28

Capuliyoc
Pass

★ trailblazer

0   1   2   3km

Pucaira

MAP 27

Choquequirao
Trek Overview

Colmena

Rio Cachora

CACHORA

To Cusco

the trek and increase its appeal, the drama of the region's uncompromising wild landscape remains undiminished and Bingham's classic descriptions of the rigours and scenic attractions of the approach remain true to this day. Despite the increase in popularity and attention that Choquequirao has enjoyed, you are still unlikely to encounter many other people on the trek.

The standard trek takes four days to complete; it's a two-day trek from Cachora to the Choquequirao ruins, and two days back again. The entire trek is slightly tougher than the Inca Trail because it comprises a series of very stiff descents and gruelling climbs, but can be tackled for much of the year although it is best during the dry season (May to September). The route is easy to follow and the trek can be undertaken independently although you may want to consider hiring an arriero to help lighten your load.

The route can also be incorporated into two longer, more arduous treks: one that links Choquequirao to Huancacalle and Vilcabamba and the other that links the site to Machu Picchu. For more information see pp298-324.

BACKGROUND

Little is known about the origin of Choquequirao, not even its original Inca name. Its Quechua name translates as 'Cradle of Gold'. Only marginally more is known about those early explorers who uncovered the ruins, in search of the gold of its name, which they believed the Incas had buried there rather than allow it to fall into the hands of the grasping Spanish conquistadors.

The earliest report of the site is to be found in the writings of the prospector Juan Arias Diaz Topete who recorded the location of an uninhabited town, 'Chuquiquirao', during one of three expeditions to the region that he mounted in 1710. Over a century later, in 1834, the French explorer and treasure-seeker Eugene, Comte de Sartiges, approached the site. A village headman issued a warning to the Comte, declaring, 'Tell the white men that to get where we live, the roads are so bad that they will die on the journey, and that we have no chicken eggs to give them.' Undeterred, the Comte de Sartiges employed a team of porters to hack and burn their way across the mountains from Mollepata via an incredibly long and circuitous route. He endured great hardships on the expedition, lost a man and mules over a cliff and resorted to drinking rum all day to stave off the cold. He described the scenery as some of the finest in the Americas, but cursed the path and conditions, declaring 'I do not believe that man could ever live in this valley, however fertile it is, because of the voracious mosquitoes that have taken possession of it. It was impossible to breathe, drink or eat without absorbing large quantities of these insufferable creatures.'

Although he reached Choquequirao, the Comte de Sartiges' expedition produced neither detailed documentation of the site nor any gold. But this failed foray didn't deter the many treasure seekers that subsequently visited Choquequirao. None of them ever found any gold either.

The first-known drawings of the site were produced in 1847 by the French Consul in Peru, Léonce Angrand, although the originals of these maps languished in the vaults of the Bibliothèque Nationale in Paris until eventually being published in 1972. For a long time academics wrongly declared Choquequirao to be the site of Manco Inca's final capital, Vilcabamba.

Paramount in perpetuating this idea was the Peruvian naturalist and cartographer Antonio Raimondi, who spent the late 1860s scouring the upper

Vilcabamba valley for the ruins of the capital. Upon finding nothing, Raimondi lent his prestige and academic weight to the theory that the site had already been found at Choquequirao, the only major Inca ruin known in the area at that time.

Hiram Bingham forged a path to the site in 1909, an experience that inspired his search for Machu Picchu. Although largely uninterested in the accounts of the ruins hidden in the mountains, Bingham allowed himself to be persuaded by a local official, the prefect of the Province of Apurímac, to mount an expedition to the site and there undertake some serious documentation of the ruins. Bingham pioneered a new and much more direct approach to the site from the south, which avoided the mountain ranges but did involve crossing the Apurímac river on an 80m wide wire bridge: 'The bridge was less than 3 feet wide but 273 feet long. It swayed in the wind on its six strands of telegraph wire. To cross it seemed like tempting fate. So close to death did the narrow cat-walk of the bridge appear to be, and so high did the rapids throw the icy spray, that our Indian bearers crept across one at a time, on all fours and obviously wishing they had never been ordered by the prefect to carry our luggage... It must have seemed to them the height of folly for any one voluntarily to use this bridge' *(The Lost City of the Incas)*.

His route reduced to a matter of days an approach that had previously taken weeks to accomplish and has been used as the way to Choquequirao ever since. To further simplify the trek, the authorities replaced the old cable bridge with a concrete and steel suspension bridge in 1994. Recent exploration and excavation has resulted in the site being opened up. In 2003 the French government donated €5 million (US$5.7 million) to Peru's government to fund the study of the ruins and the development of tourist facilities at the site.

PREPARATIONS

The trek can be undertaken through an agency or done independently. Either way, you'll need a tent and adequate food as there are no stores or huts along the length of the route. Campsites are shown on the maps in this section. If you undertake the trek independently you should consider hiring an arriero and mules to accompany you since climbing the sheer valley sides in the dry heat is tough enough without being laden down with equipment and food. Arrieros can be hired in Cachora (see p287-8) or Colmena (see pp288-90).

Although the trek to Choquequirao is marginally harder than the classic Inca Trail, most averagely fit individuals with a degree of experience and a little preparation should be able to reach the ruins with nothing more than a dull ache in their calves. The trek requires no special equipment. You should, however, make sure that you have the capacity to carry several litres of water since the points at which you can refill bottles are far apart and the heat and humidity of the Apurímac valley will cause you to dehydrate very quickly once you begin to exert yourself. You should also carry sufficient insect repellent, since large sections of the track are plagued by sand-flies and mosquitoes.

The fee for visiting the ruins, s/36 per adult, will be included in the price you pay your agency if trekking with a guided group, but you will have to pay that yourself if undertaking the trek independently.

As a final piece of preparation, read about the ruins in advance to get the most from your visit. Vincent Lee's excellent *Forgotten Vilcabamba* and Hugh Thomson's *The White Rock* are good places to start.

TIMING AND GETTING TO THE TRAILHEAD

This trek takes four days, two to the ruins and two back to the start at Cachora. There is more than enough of interest at Choquequirao to justify spending a day exploring the site. This would entail incorporating an extra day into your schedule, but would enable you to see the site at sunrise and watch as the light shifted and illuminated different aspects of the ruins throughout the day.

To reach Cachora, catch an early morning bus from Cusco to Abancay and ask to be dropped off at the Cachora turn-off. Buses leave throughout the early morning until around 7am. The drive takes $3^1/2$-4hrs and follows the Apurímac river through a spectacular, sheer-sided gorge. Two hours from Cusco the road crosses the Cunyac bridge over the Apurímac, the border between the departments of Cusco and Abancay. The road climbs up and away from the river, passing Sayhuite (see box below) to arrive at the signposted junction for Cachora. None arrive later than 11am.

There is a large sign for Choquequirao at the junction. Occasionally there are taxis waiting to ferry people (30-45mins) along the winding dirt track to Cachora (s/5 fare), 4km away. Alternatively, it's a two-hour walk downhill through eucalyptus groves dotted with cacti, or an hour if you cut across the bends in the road.

Cachora [see Map 27, p289]

Cachora sits in an idyllic spot cupped on three sides by steep sloping ridges at the head of the Cachora valley. It is a picturesque Andean town that enjoys fertile soils, a reliable water supply, reasonably temperate weather and stunning views north of the snow-capped peaks of the Vilcabamba range on the far side of the Apurímac river, including the imposing Padrayoc (5482m/17,990ft).

❑ **Sayhuite**
Some 45km east of Abancay, set back from the road opposite the junction for Cachora, lies the community of Concachaca. In the midst of this hamlet is the enigmatic Sayhuite monolith. This sizeable, elaborately carved boulder is approximately 4m/13ft in diameter and stands over 2m/6½ft high. The delicate reliefs represent aspects of Andean culture and appear to show a complex map of some kind: some rumours allege that it represents the construction plans for Tahuantinsuyo, the Inca Empire. Elaborately carved buildings, animals and geometrical patterns can be made out amidst the intricate sculpture, which has unfortunately been damaged by exposure to the elements and by souvenir hunters and vandals. It costs s/5 to visit the stone.

ROUTE GUIDE & MAPS

On the southern edge of the plaza is the Comisaria PNP building, where you should consider registering if trekking alone or without the back up of an agency (although it is not obligatory to do so). You can hire arrieros from around the central plaza and buy a small quantity of basic provisions from the handful of hole-in-the-wall shops on the main street.

There are a few hospedajes with hot water and double rooms in which to stay cheaply, including *Hospedaje La Ponderosa* (☎ 23546 in Cusco) adjacent to the church and plaza. A little more expensive but better equipped is *Hospedaje La Casona de Ocampo* (s/15/30 sgl/dbl, breakfast), at Jr San Martín 122, which has bed-and-breakfast-style deals as well as places to pitch tents. In addition they have basic tourist information, a restaurant, mini market and an equipment-hire service. They can also arrange tour guides and horses. Best though is the charming, rustic *Los Tres Balcones* (🖳 www.choquequirau.com, s/40/80 sgl/dbl, breakfast) on Jr Abancay whose name comes from the three balconies set above an intricately carved front door. It is possible to *camp* here; otherwise there are good-value double rooms with hot showers on offer. There is also a restaurant serving pizzas, parrilladas and other traditional dishes. The owners can also arrange guides and mules on your behalf. Also worth considering is the small, friendly, family-run *Casa de Salkantay* (☎ 830402, 🖳 www.salcantay.com, s/100/200 sgl/dbl, breakfast), situated just outside the main village, which is run by a Dutchman with a wide experience of mountaineering in Peru. He also organizes horse rides and hires out mules.

A number of small hole-in-the-wall cafés serve simple meals. Try *Bar Restaurant La Terraza* for hearty breakfasts, typical lunches and a range of beers and fresh juices. *Multiservicios Joel* on the main street is an internet café that also operates as a bureau de change, basic tourist information office and snack stop.

CACHORA TO CHIQUISCA [MAP 27, opp; MAP 28, p291]

In the north-western corner of the plaza a small road heads down the valley, directly towards the snow-capped peak of Padrayoc on the far side of the Apurímac valley. After the last house branch left and follow a small track as it descends for 10-15mins towards a **blue 'INC' sign**. Turn left here and descend on a series of tight, dusty loops, crossing an irrigation channel as you lose height. Carry straight on and climb gently through stands of eucalyptus to get up onto the left-hand side (west) of the valley, crossing a stream as you do. This track is narrow and often muddy, and may be impassable to small minibuses or 4WD vehicles after heavy rain.

Shortly after a gate the track divides. The lower branch descends for 1km to **Colmena**, several ranch-style farmhouses where a collection of families live

---

❏ **Important note – walking times**
All times in this book refer only to the time spent walking. You will need to add 10-30% to allow for rests, photography, checking the map, drinking water etc.

MAP 27

GATE

28

APURÍMAC RIVER

PUCAIRA
LAST WATER
UNTIL CHIQUISCA

'LIMITE S.H.N.
CHOQUEQUIRAO'
SIGN

trailblazer

RÍO CACHORA

0   ½ mile
0   APPROX SCALE   1km

COLMENA

GATE

CACHORA

BLUE INC SIGN
AT JUNCTION

CACHORA

HEALTH
CENTRE

TREK
START

CHURCH †

SCHOOL

PLAZA

HOSPEDAJE
LA PONDEROSA

MAIN ST

TO LOS TRES
BALCONES

TO HOSPEDAJE
LA CASONA DE
OCAMPO

TO MULTISERVICIOS JOEL, BAR/REST
LA TERRAZA & CASA DE SALKANTAY

PUCAIRA

PUCAIRA

75 MINS

75 MINS

CACHORA

CACHORA

ROUTE GUIDE & MAPS

with a number of horses. You can hire arrieros and horses from here. From Colmena, you can cross the Cachora river and climb up the western side of the valley to rejoin the original road heading north. Eventually it will be extended all the way to Capuliyoc, but at the time of writing it peters out beside the lone hut at **Pucaira**, 8km from Cachora, beyond the giant boulder marking the start of the Choquequirao National Park.

The stream in a deep U-shaped hollow shortly after Pucaira is the last place to refill water bottles until Chiquisca, at least four hours away. The track then passes through a **gate** and curves around a rocky promontory which gives outstanding views of the surrounding valleys and ridges (Map 28). A battered sign warns of rock fall here, so take care. From this point it is also possible to make out Capuliyoc pass ahead, around half an hour away at the top of a sharp final push. Sometimes you can buy soft drinks and water at a shack up here.

Capuliyoc pass (2800m/9185ft) itself is a narrow wind-beaten arête, whipped by clouds which frequently shroud the vertiginous cliffs and jagged peaks nearby. On clear days, however, you can just make out with binoculars the hazy outline of Choquequirao, perched high atop a forested ridge away to the west, but with the naked eye you can also feast on dramatic views of the canyon-like Apurímac valley, one of the deepest ravines in the Americas.

From the pass at Capuliyoc, the path drops steeply into the Apurímac valley on a series of **switchbacks**, descending amidst tough grasses and cutting across the remnants of a large rock fall. About 2km after the pass the path edges around a rocky prow and across a concrete ledge with handrail to a spectacular viewpoint at **Cocamasana**. From here you can make out the campsite at Chiquisca and the suspension bridge that spans the Apurímac river beyond. Rather depressingly, you can also pick out the steep zigzags up the apparently sheer valley opposite – part of the route ahead.

Just beyond the viewpoint, on a narrow terrace below a hillside of blue agave cacti, is the Cocamasana *campsite*, which has a flimsy thatched shelter

---

❏ The Apurímac

'The sound of the Apurímac rises faintly from the gorge, like a murmur from outer space...

'Apurímac River! Apurímac River!' the Runa children repeat with tenderness and a touch of fear.'   **José María Arguedas**, *Los Ríos Profundos*

The Apurímac river rises near Arequipa and eventually flows into the Amazon as a raging torrent 250ft wide and 80ft deep. The rapids and churning water along its length led to the Indians giving it its Quechua name, Apu-rimac, which literally translates as 'The God Who Speaks', or 'Great Speaker'.

During Inca times a famous rope bridge spanned the canyon where an Inca road crossed from one bank to the other. When threatened, the Incas simply cut the bridge, knowing the river was usually too violent to risk crossing any other way. Unfortunately, when the conquistadors marched on Cusco and the Incas cut the bridge, the invading Spanish were able to ford the river as the usually torrential Apurímac was particularly low.

and room for a handful of tents that are treated to spectacular views straight down the valley.

As the path descends for the next 4km you'll notice changes in vegetation, as trees festooned with bromeliads replace scrub and cacti, and a rise in temperature. Passing a rock indicating the 16km mark, the path curves right and goes by a thatched shack on a small knoll, adjacent to which you could *camp*, although there's no water supply. A much better bet is **Chiquisca**, in the wooded area just below where a local family will let you *camp* (for free) beneath cherimoya, lemon and papaya trees in a clearing adjacent to their house or on a series of terraces behind the house. There's running water, toilets and even a cold shower (s/1); the family sells soft drinks and bottled water and can rustle up a cooked meal for a small charge. There is a second, more spacious *campsite* about 50m further down the track, where the tour groups tend to stay. There is water here too.

CHIQUISCA TO CHOQUEQUIRAO [MAP 28, p291; MAP 29, opp]

An early start will give you the most of the shade and morning cool; the valley bottom becomes unbearably hot later and the ascent of the far side of the valley can be exhausting in direct sun.

Beyond Chiquisca the path descends steeply for half an hour in a series of hairpin bends for 2km to the riverside and **Playa Rosalina** (45mins from Chiquisca), where a *lodge* with dorm rooms, toilets, showers and a restaurant stands amidst boulders and stubby trees. You can also *camp* here but the place is infested with sand-flies. The **Apurímac** is very strong, but you can get water and wash in the sheltered spots. Nearby there is a **checkpoint** where you must sign in and an orange concrete suspension bridge that spans the Apurímac and links the departments of Abancay to the south and Cusco to the north. This is the lowest point on the trek and you must now begin the long climb to Choquequirao.

On the north side of the Apurímac, the ascent begins gently before succumbing to a series of sweeping **switchbacks** (Map 29). These become progressively shorter and tighter as they weave beneath a cliff, and climb swiftly past slopes scarred by recent rock fall.

About two hours beyond the bridge the path climbs above a crop of bright green sugar cane cultivated for the production of *cañazo*, the lethal spirit beloved by the local people. There is a traditional sugar cane press just below the main terrace here. Above this field is **Santa Rosa**, a cleared area and settlement that overlooks the valley. The land belongs to a local family but it is possible to *camp* here; there's a water source nearby, but the pitch is sometimes plagued by sand-flies. Push on for 10mins beyond the small shrine on the other side of Santa Rosa to a second slightly larger, more pleasant *campsite*, **Santa Rosa Alta**, next to a narrow stream and free from sand-flies, which boasts sumptuous views of the valley and the previous day's walk. At the farm here, you may be able to hire mules if you haven't already done so, but they are more expensive than at the trailhead and you'll probably be too exhausted to haggle.

MAP 29

60 MINS TO PLAYA ROSALINA (MAP 28) →

SANTA ROSA ▶

60 MINS →

MARAMPATA ▶

90 MINS →

CHOQUEQUIRAO ▶

SANTA ROSA ALTA

SHRINE

STEEP SWITCHBACKS

23.5KM MARKER

SHELTER

SANTA ROSA

SUGAR CANE

STEEP SWITCHBACKS

28

27.5KM MARKER

CHECKPOINT

GATE

MARAMPATA (2850M)

SUNCHUMAYO RIVER

TO HUANCACALLE, YANAMA & MACHU PICCHU

CHOQUEQUIRAO

30

APURIMAC RIVER

½ mile

APPROX SCALE   1km

0

90–120 MINS FROM PLAYA ROSALINA (MAP 28) →

◀ SANTA ROSA

120–150 MINS →

◀ MARAMPATA

90 MINS →

◀ CHOQUEQUIRAO

ROUTE GUIDE & MAPS

The long, strenuous climb continues past the **23.5km rock**, where the track crosses a stream and zigzags up a forested ridge that rises ahead of you. This lengthy ascent can seem endless in the absence of landmarks or features by which to gauge your progress. After 2-2$\frac{1}{2}$hrs of toil from Santa Rosa the path passes through a rustic gate and rounds the wooded prow to emerge at **Marampata** (2850m/9350ft), a village on a steep hillside that is home to two families. You can *camp* on the terraces by the houses for free and enjoy the exceptional, panoramic views. By now the valley is too steep to see the Apurímac at its foot. A series of hanging valleys block out each succeeding drop from sight, hiding the true extent of the chasm. You can, however, see the outline of Choquequirao on an adjacent ridge top.

From Marampata the path undulates westwards for 45mins before turning into a subsidiary valley. Here you'll find the **Choquequirao checkpoint**, although it's still 1.5km to the ruins where the warden is likely to be; he'll soon find you when you pitch *camp*. The ruins themselves are clearly visible from this point across the gorge. The Upper and Lower Plaza straddle a ridge about 500m above a number of recently uncovered terraces that merge into thick forest; they seem to be clinging to a sheer slope that disappears into a bottomless ravine.

Skirt around the side-valley and at its head pick your way across the Sunchumayo River, which tumbles down in a series of giant shelves, on the boulders acting as giant stepping stones. After heavy rainfall this section can be very precarious and the river can rise significantly making the crossing complicated. Beyond the waterfall the path climbs briefly before splitting. The right-hand fork continues to climb through cloud forest to the ruins, whilst the left-hand branch descends gently for 500m to a pair of long, narrow terraces on which you can *camp*. There are toilets and cold showers here too. It currently costs s/11.50 per person and s/3 per arriero or porter to camp here, but it will inevitably go up as visitor numbers rise.

From the junction the path climbs evenly through the thick forest for 15mins before emerging from the trees on to the north-eastern end of the long curved terraces beneath the Lower Plaza. A 2m-wide stone road runs along the base of these terraces to a rough path leading up to the Lower Plaza.

CHOQUEQUIRAO   [see map p296]

Although about only a third of the site at Choquequirao has been cleared, there is still plenty to see. The site is potentially larger than Machu Picchu, but has fewer buildings. Despite the degree to which the area is still overgrown, or perhaps even because of it, the site itself is utterly spectacular and reinforces the belief that the Incas chose locations in part for their aesthetic value.

The **terraces** you could see on the way from Marampata are the lowest feature at the site. **Paqchayoc** lies about 350m below the Ridge Group of ruins, on a steep slope of between 35 and 45 degrees. Only recently uncovered, ongoing restoration work has revealed sweeping terraces over 450m wide and 250m high.

The tumbledown walls have been cleared and repaired, and the single building at the heart of them restored. The **Casa de la Caida de Agua** (the House of the Waterfall) has several small rooms marked with niches and double-jamb doorways, leading archaeologists to suggest that it was connected in some way to religious ceremonies or the worship of water. There are superb views from here of the Sunchumayo River cascading down the head of the valley, and a broad, smoothed ceremonial rock just below the building. The terraces are well irrigated and it is likely that the Incas grew crops on them to support the main site.

Above the terraces and beyond a stretch of forest are the subtly **curved terraces** beneath the Lower Plaza where you first entered the site. A similarly gently curved **stone road**, known as The Avenue of the Cedars, runs the length of the 350m long terraces. The slight degree of curvature accommodates the contour of the slope and draws the eye left towards the Truncated Hilltop, the focal point of the site, set to the south of the Lower Plaza.

Four sets of stairs link the three broad, high terraces although there is no apparent stairway connecting either the stone road or the terraces to the **Lower Plaza** itself, where the majority of the high-status ceremonial and residential buildings are located. A great hall looking out over the Apurímac valley, a lesser hall and three double-sided two-storey buildings stand at the northern end of the plaza. High status is conveyed by the extensive use of double-jamb doorways on these principal buildings. The stonework is inferior to some of that found at Machu Picchu, something US explorer Gary Ziegler attributes to the frangible metamorphic rock found at Choquequirao, which is an inferior building material to the granite and andesite of Machu Picchu.

An intricate **water channel** runs along the western edge of the ridge to a 'fountain', probably the site's water supply, on the Upper Plaza. From the Lower Plaza a rough path climbs alongside the channel 50m north-west to the **Upper Plaza**. Rustic structures at the southern end of the plaza face an array of terraces and niched retaining walls. Their lesser stonework and the absence of any double-jamb doorways implies that they are less significant than those found around the Lower Plaza.

On the western edge of the Upper Plaza stands an impressive retaining wall above a terrifying cliff-drop that plummets over 1750m/5740ft to the Apurímac river. At the south-western end of this group is the structure called **The Giant Stairway**. This peculiar set of eight small terraces is built around a large outcrop of bedrock and a number of big boulders. Like many of the features at Choquequirao its purpose remains unknown.

A path on the western edge of the Lower Plaza descends through the forested slope below the site to some of the most unusual discoveries at Choquequirao. A frighteningly steep Inca staircase drops off the plaza and plummets down the hillside to a set of terraces. Uniquely, these terraces are decorated with patterns. The first you encounter have white zigzags set amidst the dark stones, whilst a little lower down are the **llama terraces**. Images of 22 llamas, both adult and young, have been uncovered here, either singly or in pairs.

To campsite

CHOQUEQUIRAO

Heavily overgrown
path that climbs
ridge

Upper
plaza

Terraces

Stone road/Avenue
of the Cedars

Giant
stairway

Water
channel

0   50   100m

Steep
steps

Casa de la
Caida de Agua

Lower
plaza

PAQCHAYOC

Viewing
platform

Smoothed
ceremonial
rock

Arch entrance
to truncated
hilltop

Llama
terraces

Truncated
hilltop/Usnu

PIKIWASI
(Ridge group)

PARAQTEPATA

Outlier

Choquequirao Ruins

Unusually, the terraces were built using vertical rather than horizontal stones, so that craftsmen were more easily able to insert shapes and patterns into them. The white rocks used for the patterns clearly stand out and the result is a striking visual celebration of one of the Inca's most prized animals. Quite what the true purpose of this decoration was though, no-one is entirely sure. A rough track leads from the far side of one of the upper terraces to a makeshift viewing platform that gives the best views of the uncovered stretch of hillside.

Back at the southern end of the Lower Plaza is a collection of what appear to be small shrines featuring double-jamb niches. Next to these is a sizeable double-jamb doorway through which a path climbs to the top of what Bingham described as the **Truncated Hilltop**. This ceremonial square, or *usno*, was undoubtedly the focus of the site, as demonstrated by its elaborate entrance and the ring of stones around it. The platform has stunning panoramic views of the surrounding ridges and peaks. Its use is unknown although people have speculated that it may have been a celestial observation platform or a place from which to communicate with other sites.

To the south-west of the Truncated Hilltop is a narrow ridge. A faint track leads south-west of the Truncated Hilltop along the ridge, above vertiginous drops on either side, to the **Outlier**, where two well-crafted oblong buildings stand opposite each other across a small courtyard. The purpose of these buildings is also unknown, although the higher-quality stonework suggests that they were important.

Below the Truncated Hilltop, 50-100m to the south-east, is the **Ridge Group**. This large collection of buildings and terraces, also known as **Pikiwasi**, was only explored and mapped in 1996 by Vincent Lee and still remains uncleared. Below here, and currently accessible only from Paqchayoc is

---

❑ So whose was it?

Unfortunately this enigmatic site is yet to give up all of its secrets and until the material gathered by the current archaeologists is analysed fully there is no conclusive evidence suggesting who may have built Choquequirao or why. To further complicate things there appears to be no reference to the site in any of the Spanish chronicles.

The site most closely resembles Inca country estates and ceremonial centres such as Pisac and more pertinently, Machu Picchu. There are plenty of comparisons to be made between the two sites. Vincent Lee points to the ridge-top location and the way that the Apurímac relates to Choquequirao in the same way as the Urubamba does to Machu Picchu. He observes that although the setting of Choquequirao is probably more spectacular, being three times as far above the Apurímac as Machu Picchu is above the Urubamba, the latter remains the finer site by virtue of its superior architecture. Nonetheless, Choquequirao does exhibit high-status architecture designed for royal occupation, as evidenced by the large number of double-jamb doorways here.

If, as is widely thought, Pachacutec built Machu Picchu, it's fair to surmise that Choquequirao was either also built during his reign or by someone powerful who admired his work. Based on the architectural style and the prevalence of double-jamb doorways, Lee himself concluded in his report into recent work at the site that Topa Inca, who succeeded Pachacutec, was 'the probable suspect' responsible for the site.

Paraqtepata, a further set of steep terraces poised above a sheer cliff. These terraces are the steepest on the site, and have poor irrigation, suggesting that their main purpose may have been to reduce erosion. The surrounding slopes are still heavily forested but outlines of dilapidated structures and further terraces are clearly visible, hinting at what might lie beneath.

OPTIONS FROM CHOQUEQUIRAO

From Choquequirao you essentially have three options. The first and most common is to retrace your steps to Cachora. Back at the main road, you can catch a bus (departs around 5.30am and 11.00am) or flag down a *colectivo* or taxi to Cusco, four hours away.

Alternatively, you have a choice of two trek extensions: to Huancacalle and Vilcabamba following the route described on pp311-24; or to Machu Picchu via the Santa Teresa valley, which is described below. Both routes are very beautiful, but they're also strenuous and isolated, and should only be undertaken by more experienced trekkers after thorough preparation.

Choquequirao to Machu Picchu

INTRODUCTION

The trail from Choquequirao to Machu Picchu connects two of the most impressive archaeological sites in the Cusco region. For people with time, this is one of the finest outings in the Cusco region and a superb way of combining two Inca sites with a genuine wilderness experience. Traversing the entire Vilcabamba range from the Río Apurímac to the Río Urubamba, the path is strenuous and spectacular.

Steep ascents and equally punishing descents quickly follow one another as you trek across the grain of the land and are forced to climb and fall from pass to pass. Extraordinary vistas await you at the top of each crossing and you are constantly aware of the great peaks that line the path; Choquetecarpo, Chaupimayo, Sacsarayoc, Padrayoc and Salkantay are all clearly visible in the course of the trek. The trail follows an original Inca road, which in parts is still visible and well preserved. There are also a handful of colonial-era sites along the route such as the mines at La Victoria, and a number of contemporary hamlets where you can **camp**.

The trek essentially links the Choquequirao Trek to the Santa Teresa trek via a section of very scenic, secluded countryside. The route is tougher than the Inca Trail owing to the terrain but walkers with a reasonable degree of stamina and fitness shouldn't find it unduly taxing. Although it links the major ruins which can be busy, the vast majority of the trek is spent in rarely visited stretches of remote, unconnected countryside and you will see precious few other

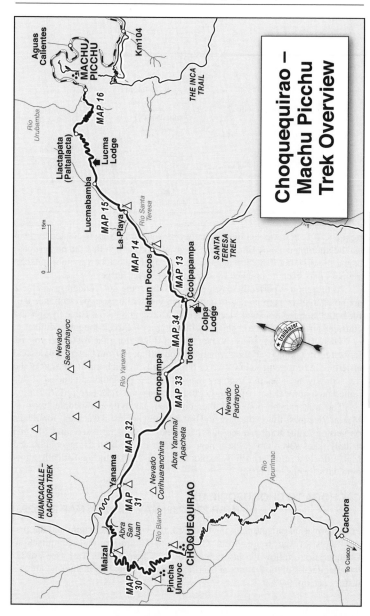

Choquequirao – Machu Picchu Trek Overview

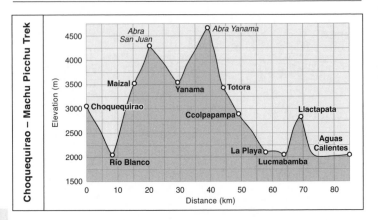

trekkers. It is best tackled during the dry season, from May to September, but can be attempted at any time of year. Bear in mind though that the highest pass is just shy of 4800m/15,750ft and the weather up there can be very inhospitable: the pass may even be blocked by snow at some times of year.

At present it is perfectly feasible to tackle the route independently and there are no charges or permits required, although you will have to pay entrance fees for both Choquequirao and Machu Picchu. You should take a guide though and consider hiring *arrieros* to help carry the weight of a week-long expedition.

There are very few places to buy food or drink along the route and you are far better off taking everything you think you will need from Cusco. Guides and arrieros can be organized in Cusco or hired locally in Cachora, at the start of the trek. Slowly agencies in Cusco are recognizing the potential and appeal of this route and a number now offer fully guided, organized treks (see pp156-9).

The trek can be done in either direction, but typically people finish at Machu Picchu. If this is the case, the trek actually begins in Cachora (for details on getting to the trailhead see p287, for details on Cachora see pp287-8) and usually takes seven days; you'll need a further day at both Choquequirao and Machu Picchu in order to fully explore the ruins, so should realistically allow nine days for the entire trip.

CACHORA TO CHOQUEQUIRAO
[MAP 27, p289; MAP 28, p291; MAP 29, p293]

For information on getting to the trailhead, the village of Cachora and the first two days of the route, from Cachora to Chiquisca and Chiquisca to Choquequirao, follow the instructions for the Choquequirao Trek (see pp287-94). For details of the features at the ruins and an explanation of Choquequirao's history see pp294-8.

CHOQUEQUIRAO TO MAIZAL   [MAP 30, p303]

Overview

Following a day exploring the ruins at Choquequirao and relaxing after the haul there from Chiquisca the previous day, the trail resumes with a long, tiring day. This is potentially the toughest day of the entire trek if completed in one go, as you are required to descend very steeply into the Quebrada Victoria, past the partially restored ruins at Pincha Unuyoc, then climb equally aggressively up the far side of the valley to regain all the lost height and arrive at the following evening's campsite. One alternative and a way to reduce the total trekking time for this section is to quit Choquequirao late on the previous afternoon and hike to Pincha Unuyoc, around two hours away, where it is possible to camp. This will save you time the following day, but could curtail your time spent exploring the ruins at Choquequirao.

Route

From the campsite at Choquequirao, follow the trail that ascends through the forest towards the ruins. Just above the campsite it branches. Take the right-hand fork and follow a series of steep switchbacks as they clamber through the dense vegetation towards the ridge ahead. An alternative is to begin from the Upper Plaza of the ruins themselves. Pick up a heavily overgrown trail that heads straight up the ridge behind the ruins. The path here is steep and poorly marked and you must clamber over roots and push through the vegetation to make headway. As you climb there are several stone walls, channels and outlines of structures hidden tantalizingly in the jungle. After 10-15mins the path joins the main route ascending from the campsite and the two continue to climb gently through the cloud forest, switching from the right to left-hand side of the ridge.

The path crosses the ridge one more time and then contours around 50m across the forested face of the mountain above a precipitous drop. From here you have your final view of Choquequirao, as well as an impressive plunging view into the Apurímac gorge, before crossing a further ridge and dropping below it to lose sight of the ruins. As you briefly descend steeply you leave the cloud forest and emerge onto a hillside swathed in high puna grasses. The views ahead are breathtaking; the Río Yanama plunges through a gorge straight ahead of you, whilst the Río Blanco, which is also sometimes shown as the Río Victoria on maps, courses through the steep-sided valley that you are now standing directly above.

Having contoured across the grasslands, a series of long switchbacks bring you swiftly off the mountainside and lead towards the corrugated roofs of the **archaeologists' huts** visible far below, adjacent to Pincha Unuyoc. Just above the camp and the ruins is a flat, clear shelf that looks over the surrounding valleys. This makes a decent *campsite*, but very little water is available here.

A further 10-15mins descent on a gentler dirt track through scrub and matted vegetation brings you to the massed terraces of **Pincha Unuyoc** (2470m/8100ft; see box p302).

Below the terraces the path continues its long, hot, exposed descent on a series of increasingly loose and sandy switchbacks towards the valley bottom. In direct sunshine this can be a very tiring section of track to tackle.

The river at the bottom of the valley issues from the upper slopes of Corihuaynachina (5404m/17,725ft) at the head of the valley and has gouged out a trench in the soft soil here. The path tumbles into this to finally emerge on the broad flood plain. The width of the flood plain is indicative of just how much water pours off the surrounding glacier-capped mountains during the wet season, and at this time of year or during flash floods, the river can be impassable. Head downstream on the rocky, boulder-strewn banks briefly and look for the makeshift log bridges that act as crossing points. Cross to the right-hand side of the river and continue downstream for a further 200m. Although plagued by sandflies, this area makes an excellent rest stop, and gives you the opportunity to take a deserved dip in the icy meltwater.

❏ **Pincha Unuyoc**
Etched into the broad hillside above the Quebrada Victoria is a mass of more than 50 terraces that spill down the forested slopes. Pincha Unuyoc (sometimes shown as Pinchiunuyoc or Espa Unuyoc) means 'Water bursting forth' and is a reference to a natural spring (now a silted-up cave) which once provided the site's water via a canal. Uncovered by Hugh Thomson in 1982, the site was later detailed and described by Gary Ziegler and Vincent Lee. In size and scale, Pincha Unuyoc resembles Intipata on the Inca Trail. Although only around 15 terraces are currently cleared, work is continuing at the site, with more terraces being uncovered and restored; the suggestion is that at one time much of this vast hillside was actually terraced and used to cultivate crops. Only one structure has been uncovered on the site so far, a small building of unknown function in the centre of one of the upper terraces, set on a giant boulder. The building has a recessed double-jamb doorway, but it is unclear if the structure had any ceremonial function. Above the site on a section of hillside unsuitable for agriculture there are a number of uncleared, unrestored basic buildings thought to be storehouses or rudimentary accommodation. The site itself clearly has an agricultural function, and the advanced Inca irrigation system meant that the flow of water was controlled and directed to each of the terraces. However, the site isn't thought to be originally of Inca origin, and is believed to predate the Incas and the construction of Choquequirao.

A number of the architectural details are clearly not Inca, but are reminiscent of sites attributed to the Chacapoyas. For instance, the stones are laid at geometric angles rather than standing upright. This technique of 'weaving with stone', *tejando con piedra*, is indicative of Chacapoyan buildings. The theory is that the Incas colonized the region and took control of existing structures before improving them and bringing the skills of their engineers to bear on the sites. When Choquequirao was built it would have required a support site to house the workers and to cultivate the crops for the Incas. The Chacapoyas would have been used to serve the Inca nobility, but kept at a discreet distance from the priests and dignitaries at Choquequirao.

It is believed that an Inca trail linked the two sites. Although this hasn't been properly uncovered or traced all the way between Pincha Unuyoc and Choquequirao yet, it is thought to contour round the hill above, cross the ridge under an archway and access Choquequirao via the Llama terraces (see p295).

MAP 30

ABRA SAN JUAN

MINE ENTRANCE

CLOUD FOREST

2ND CAMP

MAIZAL

LA VICTORIA MINE ENTRANCE

GOOD VIEWS EAST OF CORIHUAYNACHINA

LONG STEADY CLIMB THROUGH SCRUB

MAKESHIFT BRIDGE SOMETIMES MISSING

SOMETIMES SHOWN AS RÍO VICTORIA

RÍO BLANCO

PINCHA UNUYOC

ARCHAEOLOGISTS HUTS & FOOTBALL PITCH

LONG STEADY DESCENT ACROSS PUNA & GRASSLAND

CONTOUR ACROSS FACE BETWEEN TWO RIDGES— GOOD VIEWS

CHOQUEQUIRAO TREK

CHOQUEQUIRAO

TO CACHORA

27.5KM MARKER

CHECKPOINT

★ trailblazer

0   ½ mile
0   1km
APPROX SCALE

**Left-hand margin (bottom to top):**

CHOQUEQUIRAO

45–60 MINS — START DESCENT

90–120 MINS — PINCHA UNUYOC

90–120MINS — RIO BLANCO

210–240 MINS

120–150 MINS — MAIZAL

20 MINS — 2ND CAMP

90 MINS — LA VICTORIA

ABRA SAN JUAN

**Right-hand margin (top to bottom):**

ABRA SAN JUAN

30 MINS — LA VICTORIA

120–150 MINS — 2ND CAMP

10 MINS — MAIZAL

90–120 MINS — RIO BLANCO

135–165 MINS — PINCHA UNUYOC

120–150 MINS — TOP OF ASCENT

45–60 MINS — CHOQUEQUIRAO

ROUTE GUIDE & MAPS

Pick up the path that climbs away from the river and edges into the forest to begin to scale the flank of the valley. The gradient is relentless and you climb steeply for the next 3¹/₂-4hrs. The path is clear and relatively even, so not too taxing. Gaps in the increasingly tall and dense vegetation reveal stunning views, giving you reason to pause and draw breath. The path gains around 1300m/4275ft in the course of the climb and eventually brings you to a small ledge, **Maizal**, where a local family has a rudimentary farm. It is possible to *camp* on a small terrace here and the family may be able to sell you soft drinks. Alternatively, there is a second *campsite* 20mins further on. There are a number of paths cut into the forest here, so consider asking for onward directions. Pass behind the small holding and hut perched precariously above the gorge and contour towards the head of the valley before continuing to climb on a narrow track until you arrive at a smaller ledge, where another farmer has a house. It is possible to *camp* on a pair of terraces beneath the basic hut, terraces that boast spectacular views of the valley and snow-capped peak, Corihuaynachina at its head. There are also good views back across the *quebrada* to Pincha Unuyoc.

MAIZAL TO YANAMA   [MAP 30, p303; MAP 31, p306]

Overview
This is a far simpler, but no less spectacular day. From the campsite on the edge of one precipitous valley you climb to the vertiginous Abra San Juan and descend beyond the pass into a second steep valley to reach the traditional Andean hamlet of Yanama, lost in the mountains and unconnected to the outside world by anything more sophisticated than a mule track.

Route
From Maizal take the path that contours through the heavily vegetated slopes towards the head of the valley. Climb gently and after 20mins arrive at a second campsite (see above). Pass below this and continue towards the head of the valley, gaining height as you go. There is evidence here of slash-and-burn farming, with locals desperately cutting back the jungle to create small plots of land on which to grow maize and other crops.

The path hugs the hillside and follows it into a large bowl, climbing in zigzags to gain height. The vegetation is lush and there is a lot of birdlife here. The trail itself is clear, but can be very muddy. If it has been raining the mules will cut up the track quickly and turn it into a quagmire, so take care. Ninety minutes from the campsites the path undulates past the entrance to a mine. It continues to rise and fall across the valley side until a series of switchbacks takes you rapidly up through a very attractive stretch of cloud forest. Around 2-2¹/₂hrs from the campsites the path has gained sufficient height to emerge above the treeline. As it passes through small stands of scrub and tussocks of ichu grass it climbs a mound of red-orange rubble to reach the entrance to **La Victoria mine**,

---

(**Opposite**) **Top**: The imposing peak of Mt Salkantay (6264m/20,551ft), seen from the Salkantay Trek (pp230-241). **Bottom**: A paved Inca trail descending through high alpine puna on the early stages of the Huancacalle to Cachora trek. (Photos © Alexander Stewart).

an 18th-century silver mine that has long since been worked dry. The mine entrance is open and it is possible to creep inside. Take a torch and mind your head. By creeping along the shaft for 50m you can access a central junction where it is possible to stand upright. Three further tunnels descend into the darkness from here. Iron rails dug into the floor of the left-hand tunnel were designed for trolleys carrying rock to be pushed along.

Back outside the path coils across the puna, in places following original Inca paving. The hillside is now exposed and if the weather is clear, you are treated to panoramic views. The path continues to climb gently towards the broad saddle ahead. Around 4-4¹/₂hrs from Maizal you reach a slight notch in the saddle, the **Abra San Juan** (4170m/13,680ft). The far side of the pass is much steeper than the one you have just climbed up, and the sheer drop that greets you at the top is breathtaking. Looking back there are good views of Corihuaynachina and Padrayoc. Ahead stand a number of massed mountains, most prominent of which are Choquetecarpo and Sacsarayoc (sometimes referred to as Pumasillo). In the lee of these giants lies the Yanama valley, along the bottom of which flows the Río Yanama. Machu Picchu lies in a roughly easterly direction, whilst the faint path seen heading north-west on the far side of the valley eventually leads to Huancacalle and the start of the Vilcabamba Trail. Keep an eye out for condors, often spotted surfing the thermals rising up the cliff faces here.

The path edges around a precipitous promontory and clings to the cliff side (Map 31). Just beyond here is a larger mine entrance and a short tunnel that burrows under the mountain. By now the trail is well-graded and relatively gentle. A series of long switchbacks brings you down from the pass and beneath a cliff face. Three smaller mine entrances are cut into this section of the mountain. The trail inches round an exposed spur on a narrow balcony path set above a sheer drop before the switchbacks begin again. Follow these across puna and pasture, amidst wild flowers and clumps of grasses, keeping an eye ahead for the hamlet of Yanama, now visible on the valley floor. Meander down the hillside between stone-walled corrals and fields until, 2¹/₂hrs from the pass, you reach the hamlet.

Set above the Río Yanama, the small rural community of **Yanama** is home to around 20 families. The well-tended village is centred on a school and a football pitch, whilst houses and farms growing potatoes, quinoa and okra are scattered along the valley floor. Some families will let you *camp* by their houses, and some may be able to sell you soft drinks, beer or occasionally basic supplies; if you are lucky the family may lay on a *pachamanca*, the traditional feast cooked in an earth oven beneath hot stones. You may also be able to hire guides and arrieros here. Fields are farmed in the traditional manner and the only concession to modernity is a solar-powered satellite phone, which works irregularly; the connection is best earlier in the day. You can buy phone cards for it from the family whose house it is in for s/1 more than the value printed on the card.

ROUTE GUIDE & MAPS

(Opposite) Top: Choquequirao (see pp294-8) straddles a ridge surrounded by forest, with terraces clinging to the sheer slopes. (Photo © Alexander Stewart). **Bottom**: The ruins of Espíritu Pampa (see pp276-280) subsumed by roots and vegetation, still much as Bingham might have seen them in 1914. (Photo © Henry Stedman).

YANAMA

TO HUANCACALLE
& VILCABAMBA

CAMPSITE BY
EDGE OF
VILLAGE

FOOTBALL
PITCH

YANAMA

RÍO YANAMA

MAP 31

MINE ENTRANCES
CUT INTO CLIFF

STEEP CLIFF
BEYOND PASS

MINE ENTRANCE

150 MINS FROM ABRA SAN JUAN (MAP 30)

150 MINS TO ABRA SAN JUAN (MAP 30)

YANAMA

YANAMA

0   ½ mile
0   APPROX SCALE   1km

ROUTE GUIDE & MAPS

YANAMA TO TOTORA
[MAP 31, above; MAP 32, opp; MAP 33, p308]

Overview
This is a long but stunning day that sees you traverse a section of attractive, windswept puna before crossing the route's highest pass, beneath the imposing snow-fields of Padrayoc. Beyond here you descend into the verdant Quebrada Totora and work your way downhill past a handful of scattered hamlets to arrive at the settlement of Totora.

Route
From Yanama, ignore the trail heading north-west towards Choquetecarpo and ultimately to Huancacalle, and instead pick up the path heading east, which climbs alongside the Río Yanama towards the head of the valley. Stick to the right-hand (southern) bank of the river as the path climbs evenly above it through pasture and farmland. Cross two tributaries issuing from higher on your

right (Map 32), using logs and strategically placed stones to reach the far side. As you gain height the valley starts to broaden and the 'V' shape gives way to a flat bottomed 'U' shaped valley, with waterfalls springing from the cliffs. High above you are the glacier-topped peaks of Sacsarayoc (to the north) and Padrayoc (to the south-east), the mountain so clearly visible from Cachora, where it is seen looming over the Río Apurímac.

Cross a third stream and pass through a gate in a rustic stone wall before continuing to climb. After two hours you arrive at a fork in the landscape, where two valleys come together (Map 33). Continue straight on, ignoring the left-hand branch which leads the eye up to the massed snows and glaciers higher on the mountain. The path now enters a bowl full of rolling hillocks and grassy knolls. The path is indistinct here and there are no obvious landmarks, but if you stick to the right-hand side of the bowl and the stream that flows through it, you should be fine.

At the head of the bowl stands a rock wall with a waterfall cascading down it. Cross the stream flowing through the bowl and aim at the wall, but look for a path that bears left and climbs up the narrow valley to the left (east). A series of easy switchbacks gain height quickly and the glacier hanging from the upper slopes of Padrayoc rapidly comes into view. Cross a stream issuing from the snout of the glacier and follow the zigzagging path as it climbs, occasionally ducking behind a ridge or moraine wall before re-emerging beneath the glacier. An hour after you began climbing, the path scrambles up a final steep section and arrives at a small, narrow saddle between two rocky points,

ROUTE GUIDE & MAPS

120 MINS TO FORK IN VALLEY (MAP 33) FROM YANAMA (MAP 31) ⟶

VIEWS NORTH TO CERRO YANAMA & SACSARAYOC

CROSS STREAMS ON LOGS & STEPPING STONES

31

STEADY GENTLE CLIMB ABOVE RIVER, THROUGH PUNA & FARMLAND

33

MAP 32

0   ½ mile
0   APPROX SCALE   1km

trailblazer

VIEWS SOUTH TO CORIHUAYNACHINA & SOUTH-EAST TO PADRAYOC

MAP 33

Fork in valley — 30 MINS — Start of climb — 60 MINS — PASS — 3–4 HRS — TOTORA

RÍO TOTORA

COMMUNITY CENTRE/CLINIC & FOOTBALL PITCH

HORNOPAMPA - FLAT GRASSY AREA

WALL & EUCALYPTUS TREES

TOTORA

½ mile 1km
APPROX SCALE

LOOSE SCREE THEN BOULDER FIELD AS YOU DESCEND INTO BOWL

ABRA YANAMA/APACHETA
LOWER SLOPES & GLACIER ON PADRAYOC CLEARLY VISIBLE AT PASS

FORK AT HEAD OF VALLEY- IGNORE LEFT-HAND BRANCH

ROCK WALL WITH WATERFALL

RÍO YANAMA

PATH CLIMBS TOWARDS FORK IN VALLEY

LARGE GRASSY BOWL - PATH INDISTINCT HERE

MAP 34

90 MINS FROM TOTORA (MAP 33) ⟶

BEND OPPOSITE LANDSLIP

15 MINS

CCOLPAPAMPA

0   ½ mile
0   APPROX SCALE   1km

VALLEY GRADUALLY DEEPENS INTO A 'V' AS YOU DESCEND

LARGE LANDSLIP

POOL FOR HOT SPRING WATER

POOL FOR HOT SPRING WATER

SANTA TERESA TREK TO MACHU PICCHU

RÍO CHAULLAY

13

Colpa Lodge

CCOLPAPAMPA

SANTA TERESA TREK TO MOLLEPATA

13

GRADUAL DESCENT ON BROAD PATH

RÍO TOTORA

UNBRIDGED STREAMS

SEVERAL LANDSLIP SCARS

33

TRAILBLAZER

the **Abra Yanama** (4700m/15,750ft), which is also sometimes referred to as the Apacheta Pass. From here there are exceptional views of Padrayoc to the south and Salkantay and Humantay to the east.

On the far side of the pass the path drops steeply into another bowl, where loose scree quickly gives way to a boulder field. Stick to the right-hand side of the corrie initially, before following the path as it cuts back towards the centre of the bowl and begins to descend a ridge, the right-hand side of which falls away sharply. Looping switchbacks bring you off the ridge and as you lose height the path gradually broadens and begins to weave through scrub and low vegetation. It crosses to the right-hand side of a river issuing from higher in the valley and descends alongside it until just before two small huts, where it crosses back to the left bank and enters an attractive swathe of cloud forest.

The river quickly swells in size and volume as you follow it downstream towards a small huddle of houses at **Hornopampa**. Just before the houses, cross the river on a makeshift wooden bridge and continue downstream on the right-hand side of the river, passing a couple of small homesteads and farmed plots as you go. Totora comes into view further down the valley, straggled across the hillside. The path undulates past scattered houses, then meanders through a stand of eucalyptus trees and breaches two stone walls before crossing a football pitch and climbing a short way to arrive in Totora 3-4hrs after dropping off the pass.

Totora is a larger village than Yanama, but is still cut off from the rest of the world. Centred on a ratty blue and white building that doubles as a community centre and sometime clinic, it is spread across the valley above the Río Totora. Adjacent to the community centre-clinic is a broad flat area where you can *camp*. There is also a very basic toilet block here.

TOTORA TO LA PLAYA
[MAPS 33-34, pp308-9; MAP 13, p247; MAP 14, p249]

Overview
This section of the trail links the remote wilderness section of the route with the second half of the Santa Teresa trek. From Totora the path follows the Río Totora through an impressive, ravaged valley before reaching Ccolpapampa, where it joins the onward route down the Santa Teresa valley, to arrive at La Playa.

Route
Head downstream from Totora and immediately make your way across two unbridged streams before easing along the hillside high above the Río Totora and crossing a small landslip. The steep soil slopes are particularly prone to landslips here, and there are several sections where the eroded cliffs have collapsed, making the path rather precarious in places. As you progress downstream the valley deepens into a 'V'. Cross a second and then a third deep, plunging landslip, taking the time to gawp at the views of the river far below.

Contour along an attractive balcony path, which loses height gradually and affords you good views of Humantay away to the east. Around 1½hrs from Totora and opposite a giant landslip, a series of switchbacks drop you towards the river. The path then curves round to the right and follows the river around a bend, from where you can see the confluence of the Río Totora and the Río Chaullay, which combine and flow onward as the Río Santa Teresa. A right-hand fork climbs to **Ccolpapampa** (see p246) where it is possible to *camp* and buy soft drinks. *Colpa Lodge* owned by Mountain Lodges of Peru (see p159) also stands here. The main trail drops towards the rivers and crosses the Río Totora on a wooden bridge around two hours after leaving Totora. A pair of concrete pools has been built just beyond the bridge into which water from a hot spring higher up the Quebrada Totora is piped. On the far side of the bridge is a small shelf on which it is possible to *camp*.

Beyond here the path joins the route of the Santa Teresa trek (see Map 13, p247) and follows a gently descending trail down the Santa Teresa valley, through cloud forest. The path passes under a large waterfall and then through the small village of Hatun Poccos (see Map 14, p249). Around 2¾hrs beyond here and some 5hrs from Ccolpapampa the path enters **La Playa** (see p248).

LA PLAYA TO AGUAS CALIENTES
[MAP 14, p249; MAP 15, p254; MAP 16, p255]

For information on the final day of trekking and the partially uncovered but nonetheless spectacular and interesting ruins at Llactapata see the route description and details under the Santa Teresa Trek (see pp248-56). For details about the village of Aguas Calientes see pp199-202.

Huancacalle to Cachora

INTRODUCTION

This relatively new route traverses a huge section of the Vilcabamba range and links Vitcos, Manco Inca's temporary palace whilst in exile, to Choquequirao. The path follows an old, original Inca trail that is still evident in many places. It is a wild and scenic trek for those looking for a little more adventure than the classic Inca Trail can offer. The new route has been opened up and is being promoted in response to the pressures currently on the classic routes. It is also a response to the number of people leaving the countryside, and is designed to generate employment and income in these poor, remote rural parts of the region. The hope is that the advent of tourism will persuade people to stay in their traditional farming communities rather than settle for a slum on the outskirts of Cusco and the prospect of working in the city as a menial labourer or taxi driver.

The route is an excellent way of linking two historically important sites and exploring a stretch of undamaged wilderness. It also means that you can trek to and from Choquequirao without having to retrace your steps, as you do on the standard approach to the ruins. However, the trek is quite taxing; you are crossing the entire Vilcabamba range and it is impossible to exaggerate the amount of ascending and descending involved. Typically it takes seven or eight days to complete. In addition you should spare an additional day to fully explore the ruins at Choquequirao.

Currently the route can be done independently, and there are no fees payable, other than to access Choquequirao, or permits applicable. You should hire a guide though as the route is arduous and in parts fairly indistinct. Arrieros and mules are also a good idea so that you aren't shouldering all the equipment and gear yourself. A number of agencies are now offering variations of this route, so it is possible to sign up for a fully guided, kitted trip (see pp157-9). The route can be done in either direction, but is normally tackled, and described here, from Huancacalle to Cachora, via Choquequirao. The exception is if you are planning on combining the route with the Vilcabamba Trail for one great, epic adventure, in which case you would begin at Cachora, trek to Choquequirao and then on to Huancacalle before joining the trail to Vilcabamba La Vieja and the ruins at Espíritu Pampa.

GETTING TO HUANCACALLE

The trek starts from Huancacalle. For information on accessing the trailhead from Cusco and details of the village itself see p259. For information on the nearby ruins of Vitcos and the half-day walk that allows you to explore these and the *huaca* at Ñusta España see p262.

Huancacalle – Cachora Trek Overview

VILCABAMBA TRAIL

HUANCACALLE

To Espiritu Pampa

MAP 35

Chupani

MAP 36

Abra de Choquetecarpo

MAP 37

Nevado Choquetecarpo

Cerro Layco

Nevado Sacrachayoc

Chichicarayoc

MAP 38

Yanama

CHOQUEQUIRAO – MACHU PICCHU TREK

MAP 31

Maizal

Abra San Juan

Abra Yanama/ Apacheta

Rio Blanco

Nevado Corihuaranchina

MAP 30

Pincha Unuyoc

Choquequirao

Santa Rosa

Marampata

MAP 29

Playa Rosalina

Rio Apurímac

Chiquisca Cocamasana

Capuliyoc Pass

MAP 28

Pucaira

MAP 27

Colmena

CACHORA

To Cusco

0 1 2 3 4 5km

trailblazer

HUANCACALLE TO CHUPANI [MAP 35, opp]

Overview

This is a gentle, fairly short first day's walk that sees you head up valley and ease into the mountains in preparation for the longer days ahead. Given the short trekking time, you could easily combine the day's endeavour with a trip to Vitcos (see p262).

Route

From the main street in Huancacalle, walk downhill until you come to Sixpac Manco Hostal at the southern end of the village. Bear left (east) and cross a pair of rivers here. Ignore the path that branches left and climbs north along the flank of Rosaspata towards Vitcos, unless you wish to explore the ruins, and instead continue roughly east. The path climbs stiffly along a section of Inca stairway and rounds the southern end of Rosaspata. In an open clearing there is a second fork. The left-hand branch drops down the eastern flank of Rosaspata to Ñusta España. Ignore this and instead take the right-hand fork, heading south-east, which begins to climb gently through a small copse.

After five minutes the path emerges from the trees and approaches a stretch of cultivated hillside, the farmed plots of which are marked out with stone walls. The path is vague and unclear for this early stage, but if you bear in mind that you are basically heading in a south-easterly direction and aiming for the adjacent valley you ought to be able to make your way there. Climb between a pair of farm buildings and push on alongside a rustic wall, climbing evenly. Pass between two walls and bend round to the right to follow the original wall as it contours across the hillside. A scrubby hedge also stands to your right at this point. Keep the wall on your right as you climb above a lone building and pass a small clutch of houses with thatched and corrugated iron roofs. As the wall bends round to the right cut away from it and continue straight on through a patch of low scrub. Bear left towards the mouth of the adjoining valley but watch out for boggy ground here. Pass to the left of a further pair of buildings and 15mins after the junction beyond Rosaspata enter the broad U-shaped valley.

Traverse the left (east) flank of the valley, pushing through scrub. The path is clear but can be very muddy. Head up the valley for around half an hour then follow the path as it drops across marshy ground towards the river running through the bottom of the valley. Ignore a trail heading south-east on the same side of the river and instead cross over to the far bank (west) on a rustic log bridge at a point where the river boils through a narrow cataract. On the far side of the river follow a set of zigzags that climb steeply west, away from the river towards a stretch of scrub and other vegetation. Upon entering the scrub pass under and just to the left of an electricity pylon and emerge onto a dirt road which actually comes from Huancacalle. Turn left along the road and head up the valley. At a hairpin bend pick up a trail that cuts between loops in the road, and rejoin the road slightly higher, turning left and continuing to head south-east, up the valley.

PUCYURA

VITCOS

HUANCACALLE

ROSASPATA

Hospedaje
Los
Koyas

ÑUSTA ESPAÑA

MAP 35

0   ½ mile
0   APPROX SCALE   1km

PASS BETWEEN
WALLS, HEAD SOUTH
AND ENTER PATCH
OF SCRUB AT
MOUTH OF VALLEY

17

TO VILCABAMBA

Sixpac Manco
Hostal

CLIMB STEEPLY UP FROM
RIVER THROUGH SCRUB, PASS
TO LEFT OF PYLON AND UNDER
WIRE TO JOIN DIRT ROAD

STONE PAVED
SECTION ACROSS
BOGGY GROUND

DIRT
ROAD

PASS THROUGH HEDGE
AND CLIMB ALONGSIDE
TRIBUTARY IGNORING
TRAILS BRANCHING
LEFT TO CROSS RIVER

LONE
BUILDING

HEDGE

FOOTBALL
PITCH

JOIN ROAD AND
FOLLOW IT UP
THE VALLEY

36

CHURCH †

SCHOOL □

CHUPANI

ROUTE GUIDE & MAPS

HUANCACALLE
30MINS ↓
JUNCTION
30 MINS ↓
RIVER
60 MINS ↓
CHUPANI
30 MINS ↓
ROAD
↓

After 50m, at another hairpin bend, leave the road as it prepares to double back on itself and instead join a path that heads straight on. Contour along the western side of the valley. Just above a small farm the path divides. Take the lower, left-hand fork and cross a section of farmland to join a stone-paved avenue that crosses a boggy bit of ground. The path now descends gently and evenly towards the river and the far end of the valley, which forks. The small village of Chupani is now visible on a raised shelf to the left, at the point where the valley splits, with good views of the countryside behind you.

Cross a river issuing from the right-hand valley, the Quebrada Cayco, on a solid wooden bridge and, two hours after leaving Huancacalle, bear left to meander between a school, small chapel and football pitch to reach the centre of the village, where it is possible to *camp*. There are no amenities or facilities here, but the site does have very good views back down the valley you have just climbed up; Rosaspata can be seen to the north-west, although Vitcos and Huancacalle are both out of sight.

CHUPANI TO CHICHICARAYOC
[MAP 35, p315; MAP 36, opp; MAP 37, p319]

Overview
This is a long, tough day that involves you climbing steadily across the puna to finally cross the Abra de Choquetecarpo, the highest point on the trek. From here you descend quickly into the cloud forest to reach a campsite set in an attractive grove.

Route
From the previous night's campsite retrace your steps and cross back over the river before turning left (south) this time and continuing up the valley. The way ahead is wild looking and the ring of peaks that tower above are daunting and at this point appear inviolable. Having climbed up the valley for around 10mins on a broad track, there is a lone building to your right. Just after the building break away from the broad path that turns right, onto a smaller trail that bears left, ducks through a hedge and cuts away towards a tributary feeding the river below. Follow the path as it then bears right and begins to ascend alongside the tributary, gaining your first proper views of the snow-capped peaks and glaciers at the head of the valley.

Ignore trails branching left, which cross the stream to reach farms on the far side, and instead zigzag up the nearside of the stream until you emerge onto a dirt road half an hour after striking camp. Turn left and walk along the road as it makes its way gently up the valley.

❏ **Important note – walking times**
All times in this book refer only to the time spent walking. You will need to add 10-30% to allow for rests, photography, checking the map, drinking water etc.

MAP 36

0 ½ mile
0   APPROX SCALE   1km

STONE
STAIRCASE

ORIGINAL
INCA PAVING
EVIDENT ON
ASCENT

VIEW AHEAD OF
IMPRESSIVE RING
OF PEAKS

35

37

120 MINS FROM ROAD (MAP 35)

STAIRCASE

90–105 MINS TO 2ND LIP (MAP 37)

ROUTE GUIDE & MAPS

Follow the road for around two hours, as it climbs up the valley (Map 36). As the road shapes up to curve left and descend to cross the river below, look on the right-hand side of the road for a **stone staircase** that climbs a small bluff steeply. Above the bluff there is a path that winds through scrub and then contours up the side of the valley towards a bowl at its head ringed with an impressive selection of peaks. The path at this point is part of an old Inca trail and the original paved stones are still visible in places. Follow them as they climb gently, crossing a stream issuing from your right on a wooden bridge as you do (Map 37).

The path gains height and edges round a spur angling from the right before climbing a flight of steps to breach the lip of a vast deeply scooped bowl. The path continues to hug the right-hand side of this basin, the bottom of which is laced with streams and waterways. It then gains height as it climbs towards the head of the valley. A short section of downhill path leads to a water channel and is quickly replaced by a series of enervating stairs that climb steeply. A little over four hours after leaving Chupani you crest a second lip and enter a much smaller bowl set beneath a craggy ring of peaks.

There is a further lip to attain. The path that climbs to this is particularly fine and has been built up on one side to provide a level, even staircase on which to ascend. Around 30mins of steep ascent bring you to the third lip, where just to the left of the path lie the **ruins** of an old *tambo*. Enter a third bowl, where once again the path sticks to the right-hand wall.

The final climb to the pass, which isn't visible from this point, is long and steep. The steps that have been created are again ingeniously built and initially provide a broad, even staircase on which to climb. As you get to the head of the valley the gradient increases and the steps become narrower and steeper. As you push on up through increasingly rocky surrounds the stairs become especially steep. Eventually the path levels out though and you can make out the cairns and apachetas that decorate the pass, which you gain 5-6hrs after setting out.

The **Abra de Choquetecarpo** (4550m/14,925ft) itself is very dramatic and divides the Urubamba and Apurímac watersheds. The pass, a narrow notch in a stony ridge, is quite slight and the ground falls away on both sides. The view ahead of the sheer-sided U-shaped valley is breathtaking and full of drama. It is into this valley that you are about to plummet.

From the pass an initially steep, tight set of switchbacks plunges into the valley and you lose height rapidly. A long traverse right (west) brings you beneath a set of crags before you continue to descend on an evenly angled path. The path then bears left and passes beneath a rocky bluff before joining a paved stretch of Inca trail, half an hour and several hundred metres below the pass.

The road ahead is an excellent, broad Inca trail that has weathered remarkably well. The going underfoot is solid and straightforward and you are able to take in the views along the length of the valley of which you now find yourself at the bottom. After 15mins you head down a series of steps to cross a stream on a wooden bridge. Beyond here the paving deteriorates and eventually gives way entirely to a grass track.

This path descends the right-hand (west) side of the valley, whilst waterfalls cascade down the left-hand (east) flank and glaciers are visible above the dark, sheer walls and impressive granite spires that line the way. The going is easy, and you can relax as you pass through a stand of trees and then a large boulder field to arrive adjacent to the river. Follow the river downstream. The path braids here, but stick to the stream. All the threads eventually come together in order to cross the stream on a simple bridge before pushing on downstream on the left-hand (east) bank.

As you descend the valley sides steepen and the vegetation begins to grow in height. The humidity also increases and you enter some attractive cloud forest. The path then crosses to the right-hand (west) bank of the river briefly where a stretch of particularly muddy track brings you to a bridge that crosses back over to the left-hand (east) bank. A couple of tributaries issue from high above you to the left and have to be forded or crossed on rudimentary log bridges. Eventually, three hours below the pass and some 8-9hrs since you first set off, you arrive in an attractive clearing adjacent to the river, where it is possible to *camp*. This area is known as **Chichicarayoc** or Quelqamachay depend-

MAP 37

36

4457M △

SPUR

FLIGHT OF STEPS

LIP OF BOWL

2ND LIP

WATER CHANNEL

4719M △

3RD LIP

REMAINS OF TAMBO

△ 5037M

ABRA DE CHOQUETECARPO

CRAGS

5049M △

STRETCH OF PAVED INCA PATH

0   ½ mile
0   APPROX SCALE   1km

PATH BRAIDS BUT ALL STRANDS JOIN

IMPRESSIVE GRANITE SPIRES LINE VALLEY

△ 4935M

OFTEN MUDDY

38   △ CHICHICARAYOC

ROUTE GUIDE & MAPS

90–105 MINS FROM STAIRCASE (MAP 36) ▸ 2ND LIP ▸ 30 MINS ▸ 3RD LIP ▸ 45 MINS ▸ PASS ▸ 30 MINS ▸ INCA PATH ▸ 15 MINS ▸ RIVER ▸ 120–135 MINS ▸ CHICHICARAYOC ing on who you talk to and makes for an appealing place to pass the night although there are no amenities or facilities here.

CHICHICARAYOC TO YANAMA   [MAP 37, p319; MAP 38, opp]

Overview
The onward section is a very pleasant walk through attractive cloud forest. The path clings to the hillside and is very spectacular, yet even and relatively straightforward to follow. A final stiff ascent brings you to the small village of Yanama, from where an Inca trail strikes off east towards Machu Picchu (see p306) and the continuing path to Choquequirao sets off south.

Route
From the campsite you start by heading downstream through lush cloud forest. The valley, the Quebrada Otiyoc (also sometimes referred to locally as the Quebrada de Quelqamachay), steepens and the river below falls away as the gorge narrows. Having undulated through the forest for 15mins follow a set of long switchbacks that strike off up the left-hand (east) flank of the valley before contouring evenly along it. After ducking into a gully to pass beneath a waterfall, a pattern develops whereby the path alternatively contours and climbs. There are several good viewpoints from spurs overlooking the valley and the forested ridges on the far side. The forest itself is thick and full of birdlife.

As you progress down the valley the path drops gently into gullies and then climbs out of them to round a spur and ease into the next ripple in the hillside. Around two hours after setting out a steep climb brings you to a level patch of ground from where you can see a T-junction ahead where the Quebrada Otiyoc intersects with the Río Yanama. The flat ground here would make a scenic *campsite*, although there are meagre water supplies in the vicinity.

A steep climb above this plateau gives way to a long diagonal haul across an exposed area of puna during which time you gain height steadily on a superb balcony path with outstanding views. The path crosses a broad, barely discernable ridge and begins to lose height on the far side. A short switchback leads to a path heading almost due south that descends past a small farm and then bends left to enter the Yanama valley. From high on the hillside here there are further exceptional views of the wild landscape ahead of you.

Dropping below the treeline, you lose height steadily as the path descends towards the Río Yanama, which gets louder as you get closer. Passing a couple of farms and walled plots set aside for cultivation, the path continues to work its way off the mountain, until after an hour you reach the river. Turn left (east) and walk upstream on the left-hand (north) bank for 15mins. Cross the river adjacent to a series of rapids and a small cascade, on a wooden bridge, before beginning a final gruelling climb. For 30-60mins ascend a series of switchbacks that carry you away from the river. Once at the top roughly contour along the valley, heading east and gaining height slowly. Rounding a bend you lose sight of the way you've just come and enter a cluster of eucalyptus trees. Scattered amongst the trees are a number of farm buildings and houses.

MAP 38

PATH GENTLY GAINS
HEIGHT WHILST CLIMBING
INTO & OUT OF GULLIES.
GOOD VIEWS FROM SPURS
AS YOU PROGRESS SOUTH

WATERFALL

POTENTIAL CAMPSITE
BUT NO WATER

BROAD RIDGE

QUEBRADA OTIYOC

ISOLATED FARM

CLEARED &
FARMED PLOTS
ON DESCENT

QUEBRADA MAYOC

YANAMA

CAMPSITE BY
EDGE OF VILLAGE

FOOTBALL PITCH

TO MACHU PICCHU

TO CHOQUE-QUIRAO

37

31

0   ½ mile

0   APPROX SCALE   1km

30 MINS FROM CHICHICARAYOC (MAP 37)   SWITCHBACKS   90 MINS   POTENTIAL CAMP   30 MINS   RIDGE   105 MINS   BRIDGE   90 MINS   YANAMA

ROUTE GUIDE & MAPS

Continue to ease across the hillside and 6hrs after setting out arrive in the small village of **Yanama** (see p305) where it is possible to *camp* adjacent to some of the local houses.

YANAMA TO MAIZAL [MAP 38, p321; MAP 31, p306; MAP 30, p303]

Overview
The next section, from Yanama to Choquequirao is detailed in the description of the Choquequirao to Machu Picchu trek (see pp298-311). Essentially you are following this route, but in the opposite direction. The first stage, from Yanama to Maizal involves climbing from the valley floor to the Abra San Juan and crossing into the adjoining valley to descend back into the cloud forest to reach the campsite at Maizal.

Route
From Yanama look for the path that zigzags south-west through the outskirts of the village and then climbs the hill to the south, passing through scrub and small trees (Map 31). After an hour the gradient eases and you contour across the hillside towards a sheer cliff. Pass below this, above an airy drop, and climb a set of steps worn into the rock. The first of a series of entrance tunnels to disused mine shafts appears on your left. After the third tunnel the path cuts away from the cliff but continues to wind up the hillside in a roughly south-westerly direction.

Having passed a larger mine entrance where it is possible to walk in upright, the path struggles up a last short section and rounds a rocky, precipitous promontory to reach the pass (Map 30). The narrow, steep-sided Abra San Juan (4170m/13,680ft) is 2½hrs from Yanama.

Drop off the far side of the pass and ease across an exposed section of puna to pick up an old paved Inca path. Half an hour's descent brings you to La Victoria mine entrance marked by an enormous slagheap of red-orange scree and rubble dug out from underground. Drop below this and descend into the cloud forest on a muddy, rutted stretch of path that has been badly dug up by mules. A number of zigzags and long diagonals lead you downhill through the trees. Follow the path as it hugs the contours and creases in the hillside, and ducks into and out of gullies, crosses exposed sections of landslip-damaged hillside and explores the dense jungle. Finally, three hours from the pass you reach the first of two *campsites* at Maizal. The second is a further 15mins downhill. Both are adjacent to farmer's houses and both have superb panoramic views but no other facilities. The lower site has a small shack that occasionally sells soft drinks though.

MAIZAL TO PINCHA UNUYOC [MAP 30, p303]

Overview
This is a very straightforward but tiring day that sees you cover an enormous distance but make very little progress as the crow flies, since you are simply descending all the way into the plunging valley below you in order to scale the far side again and reach the campsite you can see from the start point, adjacent to the partially restored ruins at Pincha Unuyoc.

Route

Initially, descend through the cloud forest on a clear, even path for 1¹/₂-2hrs, losing height as the track zigzags downhill. A final switchback brings you to the Río Blanco, sometimes referred to as the Río Victoria, at the bottom of the Quebrada Victoria. Walk upstream briefly. You can plunge into several pools along this stretch but beware, the meltwater is icy cold.

Cross the river on an unstable wooden bridge and begin to regain all the height you've just lost via a punishing collection of long diagonal sections of track that weave uphill through dry scrub. In direct sunshine this can be a very tiring, dusty exercise although the views of the valley and surrounding mountains make up for the effort. After 2-2¹/₂hrs you arrive at the massed terraces of Pincha Unuyoc (see box p302), where it is possible to *camp*. If the site here is busy, there is another *campsite* a little further up, on a broad shelf above the ruins, overlooking the valley.

PINCHA UNUYOC TO CHOQUEQUIRAO   [MAP 30, p303]

This short stretch takes you from the terraces at Pincha Unuyoc to the ruins at Choquequirao, which are set several hundred metres higher, overlooking the neighbouring Apurímac valley.

The path climbs above the site of all the excavation and restoration at Pincha Unuyoc and passes by the archaeologists' hut and temporary residence. It then zigzags through scrub and crosses a football pitch overlooking the valley; woe betide anyone who kicks the ball too far into touch here. The ascent takes 2-2¹/₂hrs after which you arrive at a stunning *mirador* with views along the Río Apurímac to the west and Río Yanama to the north-west. Around 10-15mins contouring across the face of the mountain between two sharp ridges gives you the first tantalizing glimpses of Choquequirao just below you and strung out along a knife-like ridge. Having crossed the second ridge the path descends through dense cloud forest for 10mins to reach a junction adjacent to a tumbledown stone building. The faint, heavily overgrown trail to the right descends to the Upper Plaza of the ruins themselves. The more usually used left-hand fork continues downhill gently and easily for a further 20-30mins. Follow the signposts and arrows that indicate the way to the official *campsite* for Choquequirao (see p294), which you reach 3-3¹/₂hrs after leaving Pincha Unuyoc.

For full descriptions of the ruins and the various features of the site see pp294-8.

CHOQUEQUIRAO TO CHIQUISCA   [MAP 29, p293; MAP 28, p291]

Overview

From here until the end of the trek you are retracing the route described in more detail in the Choquequirao trek (see pp283-98). The first section is seemingly straightforward and almost all downhill, but the descent into the Apurímac canyon is long and strenuous, and your knees will take a pounding as you drop into one of the deepest gorges anywhere in the world. Having reached the bottom and crossed the river, you are faced with the onerous task of having to climb out of the valley again, and must trek uphill until you reach the *campsite* at Chiquisca.

Route

From Choquequirao (Map 29) head into a deep gully and cross the Sunchumayo river as it tumbles down the hillside. Climb back out of the gully and ascend to the **old checkpoint** at Sunchupata, from where there are exceptional views of the terraces far below the main ruins strung out along the ridge. Beyond here the path contours around the hill and arrows across the high puna to reach **Marampata** 1¹/2hrs after leaving Choquequirao. There is a small store selling soft drinks here as well as basic snacks, a toilet block and an area to *camp*.

After Marampata the descent begins in earnest and a long section of dusty, exposed switchbacks takes you across the cliff face and down into the valley. The path is steep and the descent is surprisingly taxing. After an hour you reach the small farm at **Santa Rosa** where you can draw breath and buy soft drinks or water. A further 30-60mins steep climb down brings you to the large suspension bridge that now crosses the Río Apurímac. On the far (southern) bank stands Playa Rosalina (see p292 and Map 28), where you can *camp*. There is also a *lodge* here.

Having reached the lowest point of the trek, you are now faced with the unenviable task of climbing out of the valley. The path begins by contouring upstream briefly, then launches into a sequence of switchbacks, alternatively long and short, that carry you up the flank of the valley. After an hour of continual ascent you reach Chiquisca (see p292), where there are two *campsites*, the first lower and larger than the second, a toilet block and the opportunity to buy soft drinks, water and beer from the accommodating family that lives here.

CHIQUISCA TO CACHORA   [MAP 28, p291; MAP 27, p289]

Overview

The final days trekking takes you out of the Apurímac valley, across the pass at Capuliyoc and brings you to the village of Cachora, from where you can pick up a bus back to Cusco.

Route

From Chiquisca continue climbing the side of the valley on a broad, level path that gains height remorselessly. After 1-1¹/2hrs you arrive at **Cocamasana**, a narrow ledge facing directly down the valley with superb views, where it is possible to *camp*. Two hours further climbing on long zigzags brings you to **Capuliyoc**, a dramatic, narrow pass with breathtaking views of Padrayoc and its neighbouring peaks towering above the valley that you've just emerged from. You are now into the home straight, and an easy, essentially downhill trudge that begins on a narrow balcony path and develops into a broad dust road brings you to the farm at **Colmena** in 1-1¹/2hrs (Map 27), and then takes you through a section of eucalyptus forest towards the head of the valley, where you finally climb briefly to enter Cachora, some 2hrs after leaving the pass.

For information on the town, its services and how best to continue on to Cusco, see pp142-178.

MACHU PICCHU

Sophie Campbell & Bryn Thomas

In the variety of its charms and the power of its spell, I know of no place in the world which can compare with it. Not only has it great snow peaks looming above the clouds more than two miles overhead; gigantic precipices of many-colored granite rising sheer for thousands of feet above the foaming, glistening, roaring rapids; it has also, in striking contrast, orchids and tree ferns, the delectable beauty of luxurious vegetation, and the mysterious witchery of the jungle.
Hiram Bingham *Inca Land – Explorations in the Highlands of Peru* (1922)

Romance swirls about Machu Picchu like the mists that suddenly roll in from the mountains, bringing with it an equal degree of obfuscation. Why are these majestic ruins perched on a saddle ridge high above the Urubamba Valley? Who lived in them and what did they do? The briefest of visits to the site shows that the one thing everyone agrees on is that nobody knows for sure. That doesn't stop them having theories. From the most learned of academics to the youngest of guides, everybody has a hypothesis; just stop and listen to passing tours and you will hear the same place described in a dozen different ways. It adds greatly to the charm of the place – and it is unlikely that we will ever know the truth.

The fame that the 20th century brought to Machu Picchu has been a mixed blessing. It has fascinated the world since its rediscovery in 1911; tourism figures have risen steadily – 860,000 visitors in 2008, according to the latest data – and in 1983 it achieved international cultural status by joining the list of UNESCO World Heritage Sites. In 2007 it was chosen, by online public vote, as one of the world's 'New Seven Wonders'.

A dispute over the ownership of the land rumbles on. Two brothers, Edgar and Adolfo Abrill, are seeking compensation from the Peruvian government, claiming that the land was expropriated from their grandparents in 1935. Other issues include erosion of the Inca Trail and ruins from sheer numbers of enthusiastic visitors, and some controversial restoration programmes. However, a long-running dispute about the return of Machu Picchu artefacts from Yale University has at last been settled. In late 2010 the university agreed to return all 'goods, pieces and parts' that were taken from the ruins between 1911 and 1915 by Hiram Bingham and his team of archaeologists.

But flawed beauty or not, whether it is your first time or your fifth, and whether you come by train, bus or on foot, you cannot fail to be amazed by the sheer, glorious improbability of Machu Picchu.

Historical background

Whoever they were, whatever name be finally assigned to this site by future historians, of this I feel sure – that few romances can ever surpass that of the granite citadel on top of the beetling precipices of Machu Picchu, the crown of Inca Land.
Hiram Bingham *Inca Land – Explorations in the Highlands of Peru* (1922)

WHO BUILT MACHU PICCHU?

Myths aside, the Inca Empire evolved over a period of around 300 years, from modest tribal beginnings in a village to the south of modern Cusco, sometime early in the 12th century, to its demise at the hands of the Conquistadors. When the ninth Inca, Pachacutec (also known as Pachacuti Inca Yupanqui), usurped

Statue of Pachacutec
Aguas Calientes

his brother and took the throne in 1438, he began the great expansion which continued under his son Topa Inca, or Túpac Inca Yupanqui. It saw Inca territory at its peak stretch from Quito in today's Ecuador, down to the north of Argentina and east to Lake Titicaca. It had 12 million inhabitants, many of them Quechua-speaking, as the majority of Andean people are today. It was called Tahuantinsuyu, or the 'Centre of the Four Quarters', and revolved around the city of Cusco. A 16th-century document found by the archaeologists Luis Miguel Glave, María Remy and JH Rowe seems to confirm that it was Pachacutec who rebuilt Cusco, in a manner befitting an imperial capital. He probably built Machu Picchu, as well, in the mid 15th century. Pachacutec died in 1471.

A CITY ABANDONED

Sometime early in the Spanish Conquest, however, it was abandoned for reasons we do not know. This did at least protect it from the Spanish who clearly knew nothing about it. Had they done so there would be far less to see today. This mysterious withdrawal from public life was probably caused by a combination of disease and vicious factional fighting amongst Inca clans. Whatever the reason, the collection of pale granite buildings on its ridge – a masterpiece in architecture and setting by any standards – was left to succumb to the encroaching foliage, much in the manner of Cambodia's Angkor Wat.

It is interesting that Machu Picchu's superbly constructed agricultural terraces, too good to abandon, were used for centuries by local farmers, who always knew about the ruins.

THE GREAT REDISCOVERY – 24TH JULY 1911

It was one of these farmers who in 1911 led the ambitious young explorer Hiram Bingham up the densely overgrown, snake and insect infested path to the ruins. Funded by Yale University, he was actually searching for Vilcabamba, or 'The Lost City of the Incas', which he believed had been built by the penultimate Inca after his defeat at the hands of the Spanish.

In *Inca Land – Explorations in the Highlands of Peru* (1922) he recounts the events of that historic day, 24th July 1911:

'We had camped at a place near the river, called Mandor Pampa. Melchor Arteaga, proprietor of the neighboring farm, had told us of ruins at Machu Picchu... The morning of July 24th dawned in a cold drizzle. Arteaga shivered and seemed inclined to stay in his hut. I offered to pay him well if he would show me the ruins. He demurred and said it was too hard a climb for such a wet day. When he found that we were willing to pay him a sol, three or four times the ordinary daily wage in this vicinity, he finally agreed to guide us to the ruins. No one supposed that they would be particularly interesting'.

Indeed, the other members of his team, naturalist Harry Foote and team doctor William Erving, declined to go. Foote set off to catch butterflies and Erving's excuse was that he had to 'wash his clothes'. Bingham left accompanied by the police sergeant who'd been allotted to them and the farmer, Melchor Arteaga. They followed the Urubamba upstream for 45 minutes and then crossed the 'foaming rapids' on some slender logs.

'Leaving the stream, we struggled up the bank through a dense jungle, and in a few minutes reached the bottom of a precipitous slope. For an hour and twenty minutes we had a hard climb. A good part of the distance we went on all fours, sometimes hanging on by the tips of our fingers. Here and there, a primitive ladder made from the roughly hewn trunk of a small tree was placed in such a way as to help one over what might otherwise have proved to be an impassable cliff. In another place the slope was covered with slippery grass where it was hard to find either handholds or footholds. The guide said that there were lots of snakes here. The humidity was great, the heat was excessive, and we were not in training'.

They reached a hut where 'two pleasant farmers, Richarte and Alvarez', gave them gourds of cool water. As they rested the farmers said they had come up here to use the old terraces and had been living here for about four years. They added that there were many more terraces and even some ruins nearby. Hot and exhausted by the climb Bingham was in no hurry to move on...

'Furthermore, the view was simply enchanting. Tremendous green precipices fell away to the white rapids of the Urubamba below. Immediately in front, on the north side of the valley, was a great granite cliff rising 2000 feet sheer. To the left was the solitary peak of Huayna Picchu, surrounded by seemingly inaccessible precipices. On all sides were rocky cliffs. Beyond them cloud-capped mountains rose thousands of feet above us'.

The farmers said that soon after they had come up here they had cleared off some of the ruins and rethatched some of the houses to live in but they were too far from the water sources. The aqueduct which had brought water into the buildings was blocked with earth from the terraces so they had abandoned the Inca houses and built their own. They continued to farm the old terraces, growing maize, potatoes, sugar cane, beans, peppers, tree tomatoes and gooseberries. When Bingham finally left the cool of the hut to investigate further, a small boy was sent with him as a guide.

'Hardly had we rounded the promontory when the character of the stonework began to improve. A flight of beautifully constructed terraces, each two hundred yards long and ten feet high, had been recently rescued from the jungle by the Indians. A forest of large trees had been chopped down and burned over to make a clearing for agricultural purposes. Crossing these terraces, I entered the untouched forest beyond, and suddenly found myself in a maze of beautiful granite houses! They were covered with trees and moss and the growth of centuries, but in the dense shadow, hiding in bamboo thickets and tangled vines, could be seen, here and there, walls of white granite ashlars most carefully cut and exquisitely fitted together. Buildings with windows were frequent'.

❏ Who really discovered Machu Picchu?

You'll hear various claims that it wasn't Hiram Bingham but a Peruvian landowner, an English missionary or a German entrepreneur who was the true discoverer of Machu Picchu.

Although the Conquistadors certainly didn't get here, Bingham soon realized he wasn't the first outsider to see Machu Picchu. Amongst the ruins he found graffiti left by Peruvians Enrique Palma, Gabino Sánchez, and Agustín Lizárraga that they had made on their visit on 14th July 1901. Other visitors may have been Thomas Payne and Stuart McNairn, English missionaries whose descendants claim they visited the ruins in 1906, having been informed about them by an engineer named Franklin.

From the middle of the 19th century, as the South American rubber boom got under way, the whole area began to be opened up. Gold miners and prospectors also came searching this way. In the 1860s the land around Aguas Calientes was bought by Augusto Berns, originally from Germany, who set up a sawmill to make railway sleepers. Indeed, in 1911 Bingham noted this rusting machinery mistakenly identifying it as a press for sugar cane. It is claimed that in the 1880s Berns tried to get investors interested in an excavation business to search for gold and other treasures on Inca sites in the area. Although Machu Picchu isn't mentioned as one of them, 'Picchu' mountain is actually marked on a map dating from 1874.

In the 1890s the Peruvian government pushed a road up the Urubamba right below Machu Picchu, bringing more people into the area. It was this road that Bingham followed in 1911.

So Bingham was not the first person to see Machu Picchu but what he did after seeing it was very different from what everyone else did: he recorded his visit scientifically and organized expeditions to study the site. As historian Daniel Buck says in an article published in *La Republica* (31 Aug 2008): 'There can be no doubt that Bingham is the site's "scientific discoverer," an honorific bestowed on the Yale professor by José Gabriel Cosío, a Cuzco academic and official delegate to Bingham's second expedition. It is also true that others had known of the ruins long before Bingham. One can make the case that Machu Picchu was never totally lost. It was periodically known and unknown, there and not there — visited, lived in, farmed, and even bought and sold – from the 16th century until Bingham permanently removed it from obscurity.'

Amazed at the quality of the masonry Bingham soon began to realize the significance of the ruins. Seeing the structures that became known as the Torréon and the Temple of Three Windows he wrote:

'To my astonishment I saw that this wall and its adjoining semicircular temple over the cave were as fine as the finest stonework in the far-famed Temple of the Sun in Cuzco.

One of Hiram Bingham's photographs of Machu Picchu in 1911 before excavations began. (From *Inca Land – Explorations in the Highlands of Peru* (1922)

Surprise followed surprise in bewildering succession. I climbed a marvelous great stairway of large granite blocks, walked along a pampa where the Indians had a small vegetable garden, and came into a little clearing. Here were the ruins of two of the finest structures I have ever seen in Peru. Not only were they made of selected blocks of beautifully grained white granite; their walls contained ashlars of Cyclopean size, ten feet in length, and higher than a man. The sight held me spellbound.'

'It did not take an expert to realize, from the glimpse of Machu Picchu on that rainy day in July, 1911, when Sergeant Carrasco and I first saw it, that here were most extraordinary and interesting ruins. Although the ridge had been partly cleared by the Indians for their fields of maize, so much of it was still underneath a thick jungle growth – some walls were actually supporting trees ten and twelve inches in diameter – that it was impossible to determine just what would be found here'.

He returned to his university, Yale, raised funds and came back in 1912 with several projects in mind, including a more extensive investigation of Machu Picchu. He transported many of his finds – not gold, as is widely believed, but mainly potsherds and stone fragments – back to America, with the permission of the then government of Peru. It is now fashionable to disapprove of Bingham, who was one in a long line of post-colonial explorers discovering, or plundering, the world at the time – but nothing can take away from him what he must have seen that first time, peering beneath the undergrowth and realizing the extent and quality of the ruins and their extraordinary position.

And it is Bingham who is responsible, for good or bad, for the second age of the Incas, the tourism age, which has brought so many people to Peru.

THE RE-BIRTH OF A LEGEND – BINGHAM'S THEORIES

Unfortunately he was also, often unwittingly, responsible for some of the myths and misunderstandings that have grown up around the site. He was, after all, not a trained archaeologist (though he was a history lecturer at Yale) but an explorer and treasure hunter, and one should not forget that he did go on to become a politician, elected as a US senator in 1922.

He was also a talented photographer, and when the National Geographic Society devoted an entire issue to the story it ignited world interest. It was sheer romance: the geographical setting, the sun worship, the mythical gold of the Incas, the brutal Conquistadors. Reading the article you can quite see why it's said that the character *Indiana Jones* is based on Bingham:

'There was nothing for us but to run, and we did that, tearing through the jungle down hill in an effort to get around the side of the fire... the grass and soil under my feet let go, and I dropped. For about 20 feet there was a slope of about 70 degrees, and then a jump of about 200 feet, after which it would be bump and repeat down to the river. As I shot down the sloping surface I reached out and with my right hand grasped a mesquite bush that was growing in a crack about 5 feet above the jump-off'. *In the Wonderland of Peru* **Hiram Bingham**, **National Geographic Society** (April 1913).

He wrote several books about Machu Picchu and the Incas, the best known being *Inca Land – Explorations in the Highlands of Peru* (1922) and, in 1948, the best-selling *Lost City of the Incas* (he simply transferred the label from Vilcabamba; it was too good a title to lose). The three conclusions that he reaches in the first book and develops in the second are certainly sensational but have lost their credibility over the last hundred years.

Bingham was most excited to find a fine building with windows at Machu Picchu, the building he called the Temple of Three Windows, as he considered that it fitted a description of the temple at Tampu-tocco, **the birthplace of the first Inca, Manco Capac**, who lived around 1200AD. There are, however, several other more likely contenders for the site of Tampu-tocco, Chokepukio near Cusco among them. Furthermore, in the historical description of the site it's difficult to separate myth from reality.

In his mind this was not just a lost city of the first Inca but **the** Lost City, the final refuge of the Incas who had fled in the path of the Conquistadors. This was also **Vilcabamba**, the city of gold that the Spanish had been looking for. It was the position of Machu Picchu, on a promontory that afforded such good protection from attack and was easily defensible, that made him

Detail of exterior of Temple of the Three Windows. (Hiram Bingham, from *Inca Land – Explorations in the Highlands of Peru* (1922).

believe that it was their final stronghold. Actually Bingham did discover the true lost city when he found the ruins at Espíritu Pampa but the setting of Machu Picchu made it infinitely more romantic cast as a final refuge for this doomed civilization. He ends the books with his most fanciful theory:

'In its last state it became the home and refuge of the Virgins of the Sun, priestesses of the most humane cult of aboriginal America. Here, concealed in a canyon of remarkable grandeur, protected by art and nature, these consecrated women gradually passed away, leaving no known descendants, nor any records other than the masonry walls and artifacts...'

Early excavations revealed that over 80% of the skeletons discovered in Machu

Picchu were female. The Incas dedicated their most beautiful daughters to the service of the sun god and Bingham suggested that these skeletons might be **Virgins of the Sun**, the chosen women who had escaped from Cusco when the Spanish arrived. Indy would certainly have found Virgins of the Sun here but, of course, miraculously still alive. Hiding from the evil Conquistadors they'd have discovered the secret of eternal life from the seeds of a vine found only on the top of Huayna Picchu. Disappointingly, more recent studies have shown that male and female remains were found in almost equal numbers.

SO WHY WAS MACCHU PICCHU BUILT?

In the century that has elapsed since Bingham's rediscovery of Machu Picchu the body of knowledge about the Incas has grown considerably as this and other sites have been more thoroughly excavated, the study of archaeology has evolved and more credible theories have emerged.

It was clearly not a conventional city. Built between 1450 and 1470, during the reign of Pachacutec, it's thought that Machu Picchu would have accommodated only 750-1000 people so it was actually quite small. It was certainly at least agriculturally self-sufficient; the Incas had long since mastered the art of making a little land go a very long way and the ruins are skirted by steep terraces with stone holding walls and efficient drainage systems. In fact, the area occupied by terraces should have been able to produce a surplus of foodstuffs.

Bingham emphasised Machu Picchu's military characteristics, keen to make it fit as the last citadel of the Incas. He identified some of the buildings as barracks, but also recognized distinct areas that he labelled agricultural, spiritual or residential (for nobility or priests, and more humbly, for artisans, farmers or servants). Those divisions, loosely speaking, still hold today. It is certainly true that Machu Picchu's position on the promontory in a bend in the Urubamba would have made it easy to defend. It would have made an excellent lookout station but the quality of the buildings suggest it was very much more than this.

Near one of the trade routes out of the lowland forests to Cusco, could Machu Picchu have been an administrative centre? The Incas kept tabs on their sprawling empire by constant stock- and census-taking. The tallies were knotted into strings (*quipu*) and carried along the trails by swift-footed relay runners (*chasquis*). There could have been a way station here but the buildings seem too grand for it to have been an administrative centre. It's certainly not like any others the Incas built specifically for this purpose.

The setting is important: Machu Picchu is laid out roughly on a north-south axis, which means that it gets the full benefit of sunrise on its main flank and a clear view both of significant peaks around it and the moon, stars and planets in the sky above. There is also the sacred river far below. For the Inca and his people, animists and sun-god worshippers, such a position would not have been a coincidence.

MACHU PICCHU

Machu Picchu as a spiritual centre?

To a Western eye, the ruins bring to mind a mediaeval monastic complex, combining spiritual, ceremonial and agricultural elements with a degree of fortification. Some of the most significant buildings are obviously for religious use.

In Machu Picchu: The Sacred Center, Johan Reinhard examines the sacred and symbolic aspects of the landscape archaeology of the region. The site is spread across a saddle between the two peaks, Machu Picchu and Huayna (Wayna) Picchu. Huayna Picchu is the furthest point of a long spur running north from the snow-capped sacred mountain of Salkantay. In Reinhard's words: 'At Machu Picchu we find a unique combination of landscape and cosmological beliefs which together formed a powerful sacred center which united religion, economics and politics. These factors led to the construction of one of the most impressive ceremonial sites of the ancient world'. He suggests, furthermore, that Machu Picchu would have been an important place of pilgrimage.

While it's undeniable that the sacred buildings of Machu Picchu are carefully aligned and of a high quality suggesting their importance, surely a place of pilgrimage would not have been so quickly forgotten.

The most credible theory – a royal retreat

Imagine that you're standing on the top of Machu Picchu peak looking down on the view as shown in Hiram Bingham's photograph on p329, but that the overgrown terraces that can just be discerned in the picture do not exist. There's nothing here but virgin jungle and you have all the money in the world to build your dream retreat. Where's the perfect site? You wouldn't put it down in the deep dark valley but on that saddle between the two peaks, just where Machu Picchu is now. Richard L Burger and Lucy Salazar-Burger (just as Bingham, both from Yale) have put forward the theory that Machu Picchu was just that: a royal retreat and hunting lodge.

They noted that the site does not resemble any of the five main types of Inca settlement. It's far too small to have been a provincial capital; also too small and lacking the adequate proportion of types of building to have been an administrative centre; unlikely to have been built as a way station or *tambo* or rest stop along the Inca road network because of the fine religious buildings; not a government-established agricultural settlement and obviously not a non-Inca village that paid tribute to the empire. Within the 1% of other known Inca settlements is that of the royal estate, and some of the characteristics and features of these can also be found at Machu Picchu.

Royal estates were outside the state administrative system and owned and operated by *panacas* (royal corporations) for a particular Inca king and used by him as a country getaway for relaxing and entertaining.

The relatively small size of the settlement at Machu Picchu, the high quality of the stonework and the fact that its location and extent indicate it wasn't built for economic reasons together suggest that it probably was a royal estate. The archaeological evidence is backed up by a historical reference. In a document written in 1568, historian John Howland Rowe found a reference to a site named Picchu that was within Pachacutec's estate.

Examined as a royal retreat, the type and style of the buildings of Machu Picchu seem to make much more sense. There are groups of buildings obviously designed for high-status households and others which must have housed their retainers. The fact that there were fine religious buildings of particular significance here is not surprising since the royal retinue would have required rituals, sacrifices and astronomical observations needing numerous priests and attendants. The location is idyllic but also safe, defensible and very private – the perfect royal hideaway.

Practical information

OPENING TIMES & TICKETS

The site is open daily from just before dawn (around 6am) until 5pm but last entry at 4pm. It is sometimes also possible to visit at night (6pm-1am) but only on a 'spiritual tour' organized through the travel agents in Aguas Calientes.

You'll find the ruins slightly less crowded on Sunday when package tourists head off to the market at Pisac; Tuesday and Thursday are also less busy. Very early in the morning and late afternoon is the quietest time of day to be here.

If you're walking the Inca Trail your permit should include entry into the ruins and if you don't want to look round Machu Picchu on the day you arrive it may be possible to do so the next day. Check when you arrive that this still applies.

For several years tickets for Machu Picchu couldn't be bought at the ruins and even if the situation has finally changed you should nevertheless **buy your ticket in advance** from the Instituto National de Cultura (INC cultur-

---

❑ **Top tips for making the most of your visit to Machu Picchu**

1. Get here as early as possible in the morning. If you're staying in Aguas Calientes make sure you get your entry ticket the day before (see above), check the time the first bus leaves and get there early to get a bus ticket. At the height of the season it might also be worth buying your bus ticket the day before.

2. You're allowed to take only **a small 20-litre day-pack** into the ruins. Make sure you have adequate water (in a metal or camping type bottle, not in a disposable plastic bottle); sunblock, suncream and a hat; a waterproof jacket and sweater in case it turns wet or cold; and a torch/flashlight can be useful. Officially food isn't allowed but some people try to sneak in a snack for lunch, given the prices in the café and restaurant. You may be made to leave this in a locker at the entrance.

3. Once in the ruins make sure you **go to the entry gate to Huayna Picchu well before 7am** when it opens (see p338). Only 400 people a day are allowed to climb this peak which rises 350m above Machu Picchu and it's well worth the effort.

4. Maximize your time up here and stay as long as you can; it quietens down in the late afternoon. Avoid the bus and walk back down to Aguas Calientes.

MACHU PICCHU

Inca Trail to Intipunku

Trail to Machu Picchu Mountain

Machu Picchu
Viewed from Huayna Picchu

N

Hotel & Entrance

Start

21

3

8

9

20

19

Eastern Terraces

MACHU PICCHU

Inca Trail to Drawbridge

1 Viewpoint & Guardhouse
2 Kallanka
3 Agricultural Sector
4 Dry Moat
5 City Gate
6 Quarry
7 Fountains Street
8 Temple of the Sun
9 Tomb of the Princess
10 Royal Quarter
11 Western Terraces
12 Principal Temple
13 Temple of Three Windows
14 Intihuatana
15 Central Plaza
16 Plant Collection
17 Sacred Rock
18 Group of Three Doorways
19 Industrial District
20 Temple of the Condor
21 Storage Huts

Entry to Huayna/Wayna Picchu hike

al centre/Machu Picchu Ticket Office, open 5am-10pm daily) in **Aguas Calientes** or the INC in **Cusco**, so as not to waste valuable time queuing at the site entrance. Tickets cost s/126 or s/63 for students with an ISIC card. You'll need to have your passport with you and pay with the exact money in soles as they usually run out of change. They didn't used to take credit cards or foreign currency but this may change. Online bookings (Visa only) should be available soon at 🖳 **www.machupicchu.gob.pe**.

As no backpacks larger than 20 litres (a small daypack) are allowed into the ruins you must leave them at one of the two **left luggage offices**. The one inside the entrance is the cheaper (s/3). Also forbidden are food, disposable plastic drink bottles and walking sticks. You'll need a metal or durable plastic water bottle (not a disposable plastic bottle) so that you can have water with you as you look round.

GETTING THERE
On foot
On the **Inca Trail** trek you reach Machu Picchu via **Intipunku**, the Sun Gate. From here it's a walk of less than 30 minutes, gently down hill.

Walking from **Aguas Calientes** takes 1-1³/4 hours depending on your fitness. Turn right over the bridge and follow the road. When it begins to zig-zag up the hill you'll find the path that shortcuts straight up. The first 15 minutes are along the flat then it's steeply uphill. Coming back down takes only around 50 minutes.

By bus from Aguas Calientes
A large fleet of modern buses ferries day-trippers up to the ruins for US$7/14 single/return; 50% student discount. The first buses leave half an hour before dawn and then every 20 minutes. Don't buy a return ticket unless you're positive you're going to take the bus back as it's a pleasant walk down along the trail through the trees.

WHERE TO STAY
The only accommodation here is at *Machu Picchu Sanctuary Lodge* (☎ +51 16 10 8300, 🖳 www.sanctuarylodgehotel.com), scandalously close to the ruins. It's the kind of place which these days they'd never allow to be built in such an environmentally and archaeologically sensitive position. Full board accommodation costs from over US$850 for two people in a twin or double room, only a few of which actually have views of the ruins. If you can afford to stay here you may as well go the whole way and book a wedding package – US$2200 all in, including the services of a shaman to officiate as you take your vows before an undeniably spectacular backdrop.

Most people stay in **Aguas Calientes** (see p201).

(Opposite): The Intihuatana, the 'hitching post of the sun' (see p345), before being damaged during the filming of a beer commercial. (Photo © Bryn Thomas).
(Overleaf): Machu Picchu revealed, with Huayna Picchu rising in the background. (Photo © Alexander Stewart).

WHERE TO EAT

Food isn't allowed in the ruins and if the snack lunch in your daypack is discovered they'll probably make you leave it in a locker at the entrance. The restaurant at the *Machu Picchu Sanctuary Lodge* serves a buffet breakfast (US$15) and buffet lunch (US$23).

There's also an overpriced *snack bar* by the entrance to the ruins. They sell hamburgers, hot dogs, pizzas, empanadas, sandwiches, beer, Red Bull, Gatorade, water, tea and coffee. A hamburguesa macchupicchu is US$10.

Guide to Machu Picchu

Above all, there is the fascination of finding here and there under the swaying vines, or perched on top of a beetling crag, the rugged masonry of a bygone race; and of trying to understand the bewildering romance of the ancient builders who ages ago sought refuge in a region which appears to have been expressly designed by Nature as a sanctuary for the oppressed, a place where they might fearlessly and patiently give expression to their passion for walls of enduring beauty.

Hiram Bingham *Inca Land – Explorations in the Highlands of Peru* (1922)

In the 21st century the ruins absorb visitors in numbers that would, no doubt, amaze the Incas. Until now, incredibly, you can still wander freely within many of the buildings here – quite aside from potential damage to the ruins, it is surprising that there aren't more accidents, especially when it rains – and the site swarms with people photographing both the ruins and the picturesque llamas that have been re-imported for the purpose. It remains to be seen what restrictions the future holds for visitors; in the meantime, enjoy the freedom.

ORIENTATION

Machu Picchu is at 2350m/7708ft (main plaza) and most of the buildings are spread across a saddle between two mountains, Machu Picchu ('Old Peak', 3060m/10,040ft) and the soaring sugarloaf of Huayna/Wayna Picchu ('New Peak', 2700m/8860ft) – with the Urubamba river and Aguas Calientes far below at 2000m/6560ft.

You can climb **Huayna Picchu** and visit the Temple of the Moon below it but since only 400 people per day are allowed to do so (see p338) you should make your way there soon after arriving. Other excursions include the **Inca drawbridge** (20 minutes each way, see p348) and the climb up **Machu Picchu peak** (about 90 minutes to the top, see p348).

In the guide to the ruins, below, sites are keyed to the overview on p334-5.

(Opposite) **Top**: The Temple of the Sun. As the sun rises on 21 June each year the rays it casts through this window align perfectly with the rock on the floor inside. (Photo © Bryn Thomas). **Bottom**: Passengers boarding the PeruRail train, near Machu Picchu. See pp356-8 for rail information. (Photo © Alexander Stewart).

❏ CLIMBING HUAYNA PICCHU (WAYNA PICCHU)

[Entry for the climb between 7am and 1pm; limited to 400 people] To sit on the 2700m/8860ft shaggy crest of Huayna Picchu on a clear morning, with the ruins laid out below you and the sun sliding up behind the mountains like a new *centavo*, is probably the most magnificent experience that Machu Picchu can offer. But it takes planning to reach the top in some peace – and shouldn't be attempted if you are unfit, struggling with the altitude or suffer from vertigo. A certain amount of scrambling is involved and you'll need good shoes. The numbers are strictly limited (400 per day), enforced by a separate entry kiosk, and you have to sign in and out. By 10am the queue can have reached that number already. The solution is to get into Machu Picchu right at the start of the day. If you're coming from Aguas Calientes on the bus make sure you're on the first bus (5.30am). Once inside the main gate, ignore the ruins, make your way to the northern corner, get in the Huayna Picchu queue and wait until the gate opens at 7am. The gate closes at 1pm or after 400 people have been let in (whichever comes sooner) but once inside you can stay until 4pm.

Huayna Picchu stairway.
Slip here and you could land
up in the Urubamba River.

On the steep route from the
summit of Huayna Picchu to
the Temple of the Moon.

Huayna Picchu summit

The vertiginous walk up takes anything from 40 minutes to 1½ hours depending on how busy it is and your state of fitness. The path zig-zags relentlessly upwards; after 15-20 minutes there's a junction: **take the right path for the top**; the left path is the Gran Caverna Trail to other side of the peak. Near the top and some narrow terraces, there's **another fork**: to the right leads up eventually through a short tunnel to the summit and to the left also leads to the summit but via terraces and some small ruins including an intact, though roofless, building which catches the morning sun on its impossibly steep crag. No doubt offerings to the sun god would have been made from up here and the building may have been a **temple**. The **terraces** up here are really too small for growing anything useful and it has been suggested that they may have been planted with bright flowers to provide a splash of colour that could be seen from the royal estate below. It's also likely that some royal guards would have been posted up here as it would make the perfect lookout station. This area is sometimes roped off, particularly after wet weather when the stairs are treacherous. The **summit** is surprisingly roomy and the views from up here are truly spectacular.

Temple of the Moon & Gran Caverna Trail

From the top you can take the fantastically steep trail, some parts of it by makeshift ladder, down the far side, amongst birds, butterflies and beetles. After

VIEWPOINT & GUARDHOUSE [1]

That first sight, so familiar from a thousand posters and brochures, of the whole of Machu Picchu spread out before you has all the more impact if you come upon it suddenly as you do when approaching on the Inca Trail. To get something of this effect if you've come up by bus from Aguas Calientes, after passing through the checkpoint and walking 100m, don't continue into the ruins but take the path to the left that climbs steeply through the trees and brings you out at the top of the agricultural zone by the guardhouse. It not only starts your heart racing as you scramble up the steps, it also rewards you with a magnificent view of the ruins, Huayna Picchu and the spinach-green peaks beyond. This is a good place to come to watch the sunrise or take that classic picture. If you're planning on climbing Huayna Picchu, however, don't spend too long here but get to the entry kiosk as early in the day as possible.

a 30-40 minute descent to a point lower than Machu Picchu itself, you reach a clearing and a fine double wall of masonry appears, with alternating windows and niches.

The cave behind contains the **Temple of the Moon**: a beautiful double-lintel door fits into the cave, along with walls, niches and a fine throne or platform of white granite. This is some of the finest Inca stonework in Machu Picchu; obviously an important ceremonial building, it may have contained mummies. It's unlikely to have had anything to do with the observation of the moon, though; it faces the star cluster known as the Pleiades. About 50m below is **another group** of caves and buildings. The stonework is less impressive and in places defaced with graffiti.

The Temple of the Moon

To return, walk anti-clockwise along what is known as the **Gran Caverna Trail** around the mountain for 40-60 minutes to rejoin the trail at the junction 15-20 minutes from the entry kiosk. This can also be done in reverse but the climb up from the Temple of the Moon to the summit is very steep: it's easier to approach the summit the normal way.

Inkaraqay Archaeologists are currently clearing these ruins, lower down the steep north face of Huayna Picchu. Covering about 4500 square metres mainly of ter-

Lower buildings, Gran Caverna

races, it appears that Inkaraqay was mainly agricultural in nature, supplying food for Machu Picchu. It is hoped that it will eventually be opened to visitors. A near vertical, snake-infested trail is said to lead from Inkaraqay to the summit of Huayna Picchu.

Guardhouse (aka Watchman's Post) with the kallanka at the back (right)

Funerary Rock: a mortician's slab?

The **Guardhouse [1]** (*Recinto del guardian*) looks too grand to be a restored thatched sentry box, but its position overlooking the entire site suggests some sort of surveillance role.

Above it is a low, carved boulder known as the **Funerary Rock**. Since human bones were found in this area Bingham assumed it was a cemetery and suggested that the rock may have been used for some related purpose. Perhaps it was a mortician's table for the evisceration of bodies during the process of mummification. It's also been suggested that this might have been a sacrificial altar and that the hole on the side of the rock could have been for tying up the llama that was waiting to be sacrificed.

Across the open area here at the southernmost extent of Machu Picchu is a large unremarkable building (actually the largest building on the site) with eight openings in its walls. This is probably a **kallanka [2]**, a hall which provided lodgings for a large number of people. As it is right beside the Inca Trail which runs in here from Intipunku and out to the Inca Drawbridge it may also have been used a rest stop.

Below the Guardhouse are the extensive terraces of the **agricultural sector [3]** (*zona agricola*). These had to be very carefully constructed to allow adequate drainage given the very high rainfall in this region. Each terrace had a base layer of stones followed by gravel sand and then topsoil. Given the number of terraces at Machu Picchu, which is increasing as more are uncovered (4500 square metres recently at Inkaraqay, see p339), it's clear that they could

The Dry Moat divides the agricultural sector from the urban sector.

have produced far more food than would have been needed by the city's population of around 750 people. It's been suggested that some of the terraces may have been given over to the cultivation of the sacred coca leaf, which flourishes in this climate and altitude. It would have been in high demand in Cusco.

At the northern side of the agricultural sector and across the **Dry Moat [4]** you reach the main buildings of the city. As well as providing an obstacle that could have provided some defence if Machu Picchu were under attack it also served as the main drain for the city's carefully constructed drainage network.

CITY GATE [5]

There's usually a bottleneck at this handsome trapezoid entryway, partly because people want to admire the fine stonework with its lintel of one hefty stone slab, and partly because it's instinctive to want to stop on stepping through and absorb the view. Look back as you do so to see the stone eyelet that probably served as some sort of lock for a door hinged into the stone. The sturdy construction, widening towards the base, is classic Inca design; beautifully-fitted stones, no mortar and a form that is said to weather earthquakes. Its size is interesting; this is a doorway, not a magnificent entry to a city – it appears deliberately discreet and low key.

City gate

QUARRY [6]

The source for Machu Picchu's stone is within the city itself: you pass the large area of boulders shortly after going through the city gate. To carve their building blocks without iron tools the Inca masons probably employed the labour-intensive neolithic technique known as flaking, using a hammer stone. They may have split stones using wooden wedges hammered into natural cracks. Bingham attempted to show that the Incas used boiling water to split stones but the experiment was unsuccessful.

Work in progress at
the quarry.

The whackiest suggestion is that the Incas cut the rocks using solar power reflected off large parabolic reflectors made of gold and it's certainly true that such objects were found by the Conquistadors who promptly melted them down into ingots.

Some rocks have clearly been worked on although it's said that the one that's usually pointed out by the guides (photo opposite) was actually a modern experiment by the archaeologist Manuel Chavez Ballón.

This is a good place to come back to when you want a place to sit and rest; you'll find lots of viscachas, rabbit-like rodents, sunning themselves on the rocks.

Viscacha

MACHU PICCHU

Machu Picchu's water
supply still functions

FOUNTAINS STREET [7]

Follow the steps down Fountains Street (*Fuentes*), so named for the 16 watercourses (not actually fountains) that flow along it. Water from the main spring runs for 750m to feed into the topmost of these square cisterns, which descend the hill in a series, getting progressively less fancy as they go. The highest and grandest tank was no doubt reserved for the Inca himself so he would get the cleanest water.

Near the bottom of the street is an open-fronted building, known as a *wayrana*, with its thatched roof restored so you can get an idea of how all the buildings would have looked. It shows how the stone pegs protruding at the top of many of the walls were used to secure the roof struts. This wayrana may have been the focus of ceremonial activities involving worship of the water that flowed past it.

THE TEMPLE OF THE SUN [8]

This tower (*El Torréon*), which curves inwards like a snail shell and encloses a mysterious, tomb-like rock, is surely the most beautiful structure here. Currently roped off, you may only be able to view it from above or below. Bingham went into raptures when he first glimpsed it:

'Owing to the absence of mortar, there are no ugly spaces between the rocks. They might have grown together... The elusive beauty of this chaste, undecorated surface seems to me to be due to the fact that the wall was built under the eye of a master mason who knew not the straight edge, plumb rule, or the square. He had no instruments of precision, so he had to depend on his eye. He had a good eye, an artistic eye, an eye for symmetry and beauty of form'.

Perfect stonework on the tower
of the Temple of the Sun

Palace of the Princess, to the left
of the tower.

Its stonework is darker and finer than that of the surrounding buildings, it has narrow windows towards the top of the wall and one larger window has holes drilled around the edges, though nobody can be sure of their exact function. It may have been that astronomical instruments were attached to them as this temple was used as an astronomical observatory. At the winter solstice (21 June), the rays of the sun as it rises align perfectly with the rock on the floor of the temple. Niches around the walls of the temple would have held offerings and idols. Animal sacrifices may have taken place on the carved central rock.

Stairs lead from the temple down to the fine two-storey building which Bingham fancifully misnamed as the **Palace of the Princess** (*Ñusta*). Its position suggests that it was a kind of sacristy used by the high priest presiding over ceremonies in this temple.

The entrance to this area is through one of finest examples of an Inca gate.

Entrance gate to the Palace of the Princess and Temple of the Sun

THE TOMB OF THE PRINCESS [9]

Right underneath the Temple of the Sun is a striking triangular cave, formed by the hewn edge of the massive supporting boulder and carefully fitted masonry. Inside, a set of steps carved into the natural rock and markedly pale against the darkness, ascend to nowhere. This classic step symbol is often found at Inca sites. It's said to represent the three levels of the world: heaven, earth and the underworld. Again, the 'Princess' title is not based on fact and Bingham found no evidence of bodies buried here and probably didn't expect to as burial was only for the masses; nobles were mummified. It may, however, have been used as a temporary mausoleum for the mummies of important ancestors of the Inca king, which he would have brought with him when he was staying here.

You may overhear guides telling their tour groups that the four sites above (the fountains, the wayrana, the Temple of the Sun and this tomb, symbolize the four elements of water, air (the wayrana being open on one side), fire and earth. The Incas certainly worshipped the elements but whether they identified these particular four sites as a symbolic group is debatable.

Directly beneath the Temple of the Sun is the Tomb of the Princess

THE ROYAL QUARTER [10]

The Inca class system was clearly expressed in stone – the better the dressing, the grander you were – as well as in the distinct division between *hanan* (upper class) and *hurin* (lower class) districts.

Apartments in the Royal Quarter

MACHU PICCHU

The fine ashlars used in these buildings, their size and finesse, show that they belonged to the elite. The Royal Apartments here are laid out as a classic *kancha* (group of rooms for an extended family), with two large rooms and two wayranas around a central patio. One of the open-sided wayranas would have been used as a kitchen. Attached to one of the large rooms is an addition known as the 'Inca's bathroom' which has a drain in the corner.

WESTERN TERRACES [11]

Walk back up the hill, over and around the quarry, to peer over the back wall at the precipitous terraces. Recent research has shown that in Inca times more varieties of maize and potatoes could be cultivated at altitude than today. Whatever they grew, the engineering is impressive: few slopes are so steep that they have not been terraced. Along the top of the terraces runs the path leading to what was once an Inca bridge, probably made of timber and vines, which crossed a sickening drop and continued down the mountain.

THE PRINCIPAL TEMPLE AND SACRED PLAZA [12]

The Sacred Plaza and the Principal Temple

The small open patch of ground often referred to as the Sacred Plaza (*Sector de los Templos*) is surrounded by buildings which, from their elevated position and sophisticated stonework, were obviously religiously significant. The **Principal Temple** is in the wayrana style (open on one side) and has an impressive row of niches all along the back wall. In front is a huge block of stone, rising altar-like out of the ground; this may have been a roof support. There is much speculation about the building; certainly the sun does enter during the winter solstice along an identifiable course and broken pottery remains have been found in the plaza, suggesting some sort of ritual involving the breaking of vessels. Just outside the temple, on the ground, is a kite-shaped rock which is said to be a representation of the stars of the Southern Cross, astronomically important to the Incas. It does, indeed, point south.

Behind the Principal Temple is a separate structure which may have had a priestly function – Bingham named it the **Sacristy** and it's also known as the Ornaments Chamber; it contains a famously elaborate stone, with 32 edges carved into the raw rock, to the left of the doorway. The one on the right has 28 corners.

Rock in the shape of
The Southern Cross

Just below the Principal Temple is the **Temple of Three Windows [13]** (*Templo de las Tres Ventanas*), with a wall of perfectly-finished masonry pierced by three trapezoid windows, overlooking the ruins below. It was this building that convinced Bingham that he'd located Tampu-tocco, the birthplace of the first Inca, Manco Capac (see p330). The temple actually has five windows, two of which have been blocked up.

Temple of Three Windows
(viewed from outside)

Opposite the wall of windows and the remains of the roof pillar is a rock carved with the step symbol representing heaven, earth and the underworld.

INTIHUATANA – THE HITCHING POST OF THE SUN [14]

Steps lead up to this startling carved stone, carved in situ into a wide step and squared-off post aiming skywards, the focus of the highest and perhaps the most significant part of this religious section of Machu Picchu. Similar stones were found at many of the Inca ruins and early archaeologists called them *intihuatana* meaning 'place where the sun is tied'. In winter, with the sun furthest from the earth, the Incas believed they needed to ritually secure it to hitching posts such as this one lest the life-giving sun desert them. The festival of Inti Raymi was (and still is) held at the winter solstice (21 June). Realizing their importance to Inca culture, the Spanish settlers damaged every intihuatana they found by breaking off the post; this is the sole complete survivor.

Visitors under the guidance of a local shaman offer prayers to the setting sun, beside the Intihuatana

The archaeologist Johan Reinhard has shown that Machu Picchu was carefully aligned with sacred peaks, the intihuatana being at its very centre. The top of Huayna Picchu, for example, is due north. The position of the sun and stars was important to the Incas both for religious reasons and, more prosaically, in order to chart the progress of the seasons which was important to farmers so that seeds were planted at the right time to allow for the best harvest. At the equinoxes the sun rises behind the summit of Veronica. The careful alignment of the intihuatana means that it was probably used as an observatory. It has also been suggested that the stone was a sundial but this is unlikely as the Incas had no concept of time in terms of hours and minutes.

Reinhard has also done some fascinating work on structures built to replicate significant mountains. From the south of the stone, look north towards

Huayna Picchu and the shape of the intihuatana does appear to be a conscious imitation of the mountain behind it.

If ever there was a stone with presence, however, this is it – which only added to the national fury when it was damaged during a beer commercial shoot in the year 2000.

THE CENTRAL PLAZA [15]

This huge rectangle of flat green grass is a welcome breathing space amongst all the steep steps and stones and is generally grazed by a llama or two. It must have been significant with so little space available and was probably used for commerce and wider ceremonial purposes. Anyone who has seen the (now colossal) Inti Raymi celebrations in Cusco or at Tiahuanaco at the winter solstice can imagine a smaller version of the event happening here.

In the south of this plaza, near the Temple of Three Windows, is a small collection of **plants [16]** that would have grown here in Inca times. As well as various orchids, *yuca* (the cassava root and foodstuff, not yucca the decorative plant), strawberries and moonflower there are some coca plants, all helpfully labelled.

The Sacred Rock

THE SACRED ROCK [17]

Beside the entry gate to Huayna Picchu this large rock faces a small open square with two thatched wayrana on opposite sides of it. The rock itself is a huge slab, again made significant by its enclosure by its neighbouring buildings and the plaza. Its very position shows it was an object of veneration and its surface may well originally have been polished like the sacred rocks found at Ollantaytambo. Its shape seems to mimic the mountains behind it.

GROUP OF THE THREE DOORWAYS [18]

We are now in the residential area to the north east of the site that was probably occupied by less elevated inhabitants – perhaps the people who did the work, fed and looked after the nobility, maintained the terraces and harvested the crops. It is so called because there are three fine doorways to be seen. Below it is another cemetery area, east facing, and outside the Machu Picchu equivalent of the city limits.

EASTERN TERRACES

Covering an area of four hectares, this is the most extensive set of terraces at Machu Picchu. Not quite as steep as their western counterparts but impressive nonetheless, there are two sections: a smaller run set below the lower residential area and a whole hillside of them, facing due east below. The terraces were constructed between 1470 and 1530 and include ceremonial watercourses.

Part of the newly excavated and restored section that lies between Machu Picchu and Aguas Calientes will be opened to visitors in 2011. Entry to the lower terraces will probably be from the road leading up from Aguas Calientes.

INDUSTRIAL OR MORTAR SECTOR [19]

Bingham quite understandably believed, when he saw that one of the buildings in this more crowded, commercial zone had mysterious, crater-like protrusions on the floor of its courtyard, that they were mortars for grinding corn. It is now thought that the surfaces are too flat for the purpose. It is possible that they may have had some sort of astronomical function; water may have been poured into them, for example, and celestial events such as eclipses observed in reflection.

TEMPLE OF THE CONDOR [20]

This is one of most mysterious structures at Machu Picchu. On the ground is a piece of dark granite, unmistakably polished and wrought into the shape of a condor seen from above, with its distinctive head and white collar formed by a separate piece of stone. If you have a very vivid imagination you may be able to identify the swoops of natural rock behind as wings. The Incas worshipped the *Apu Kuntur* (Condor God) and even today some Andean villages such as Cotabambas celebrate the Yawar Fiesta. In this a captured condor, the spirit of the Incas, is tied to the back of a bull symbolizing the Spanish Conquistadors. The condor overpowers the bull, lashing at it with its beak, drawing blood and gouging out the bull's eyes. The bull dies and the condor is released, the Inca god triumphing over the Spanish to bring good fortune to the village.

Temple of the Condor
(white lines showing how the rocks behind may be seen as the wings)

The rock beneath the natural rock has been hollowed into small vaults, sometimes referred to, with wistful relish, as 'jails'. This idea was first suggested by Bingham who referred to these buildings as the Prison Group. Some guides will tell you that prisoners may have been held here and in the buildings behind. In the so-called **jail** there are human-sized niches with holes in the stones halfway up each side to which the arms of the

The Jail

prisoners could have been bound. This is unlikely as it's believed that the Incas didn't have prisons; wrongdoers were dealt with immediately: either by being put to death or by losing their privileges. It's nevertheless a popular photo opportunity (when this section is not closed off).

Agricultural sector and storage huts

Inca drawbridge

STORAGE HUTS [21]

Cross the terraces of the agricultural sector again to return to the entrance. Bingham referred to these huts as barracks, but being located conveniently at the end of the agricultural terraces, it is likely that they functioned either as housing for farmers or storage huts for tools and supplies, or both. Some have been rethatched.

SIDE TRIPS

The best of the side trips is the climb up **Huayna/Wayna Picchu** (2700m/8860ft, see p338). As an alternative, however, you can climb **Machu Picchu peak** (3060m/10,040ft), the peak opposite. The trail begins off the path to Intipunku (see below) via stairs through the terraces. It's a stiff climb and you should allow 2¹/2-3 hours for the return trip with some time to enjoy the breathtaking panorama from the top.

The Inca Trail skirts through the southern end of the ruins via the guardhouse and the kallanka to reach a **drawbridge**, a considerable feat of Inca engineering. A stone wall has been built against the cliff face with planks to cross the gap in the middle. These could have been withdrawn to close this entrance to the city. Since a visitor plunged to his death from the bridge the path has been closed a short distance before it but you can get a good view of the drawbridge from the viewpoint. It takes about 20 minutes each way from the guardhouse; the path climbs steeply for the first five minutes and then levels out, clinging to the cliff edge with superb views across the valley. The trail may be closed in the afternoon.

If you didn't reach Machu Picchu by following the main Inca Trail it's well worth walking up it to **Intipunku**, (**The Sun Gate**). The robust stone paving on the path is still intact after all these years. Allow 1-1¹/2 hours to walk there and back, with some time at the gate to sit and enjoy the superb views back over the ruins.

APPENDIX A: QUECHUA & SPANISH

Although Spanish is the main language of Peru, you will find that Quechua, also known as *Runasimi*, is widely spoken in the Andes. Although spoken by a number of Andean tribes prior to the spread of the Inca empire, the language was adopted by the Incas to unify their multilingual subjects and consolidate their empire.

After the Spanish conquest, Quechua continued to be used largely as the general language and main means of communication between the Spanish and indigenous people, so continued to expand its range, but all administrative use of the language was banned in the late eighteenth century in the wake of the Túpac Amaru II revolution. Despite a brief revival post-independence the language has generally declined and is increasingly restricted to rural areas but it is still one of the most widespread indigenous languages in the Americas. It remains a largely oral language as there is a lack of written material available. There is, though, a realization of Quechua's value as a national symbol and vehicle for promoting native culture.

QUECHUA

Quechua and Spanish have become intermixed over the years and there are lots of Spanish loan words in Quechua. There are also a number of Quechua loan words in English, via Spanish. These include ayahuasca, coca, condor, llama, puma, quinoa and vicuna.

Until the twentieth century Quechua was written using Spanish spelling, (eg Inca, huayna, collasuyu, quipu, condor), making it more familiar to Spanish speakers and also easier to use for borrowings into English. In 1975 the Peruvian government adopted a new orthography, (eg Inka, wayna, Qollasuyu, khipu, kuntur). The different spellings are still highly controversial in Peru. The Spanish system, which is largely used in this book, is more readable, makes Quechua easier to learn, and is how place names are usually depicted on maps. The newer form is however thought to be a better phonology of Quechua.

The only readily available book is *Quechua Phrasebook*, published by Lonely Planet.

SPANISH

The conquistadors brought their language with them to South America. Over time Castillian Spanish evolved into Latin American Spanish, an arbitrary name for the idiomatic and native expressions and specific vocabulary of Spanish spoken in Latin America. The version of the language spoken here is a dialect of Castillian Spanish as opposed to a distinct language, even though it contains various features that distinguish it from European Spanish. The differences are akin to those between British English and US English. Apart from slang or extreme colloquialisms, the main differences are in pronunciation, rhythm, grammar and unique vocabulary.

Particular pitfalls are 'll', pronounced 'y', 'hu' pronounced 'w', 'q' pronounced 'k' and 'ce' or 'ci' pronounced 's' rather than with the 'th' lisp and 'v' as in English rather than as 'b'.

Stress goes on the penultimate syllable unless there's an accent to indicate alternative stress.

ENGLISH	QUECHUA	SPANISH
General phrases		
Hello/Good day	*¡Napaikulyaiki!*	*¡Buenos días!*
Excuse me	*Munayniykimanta*	*Con permiso*
Mr/Sir	*tayta*	*señor*
Madam	*mama*	*señora*

ENGLISH	QUECHUA	SPANISH
How are you?	*¿Allillanchu?*	*¿Cómo está usted?*
What's your name?	*¿Iman sutiyki?*	*Cómo se llama?*
I'm...	*...-n sutiy*	*Me llamo...*
Please	*Allichu*	*Por favor*
Thank you	*Sulpayki*	*Gracias*
Sorry (apologies)	*Pampachayuay*	*Disculpe*
Where are you going?	*¿Maytataq rishanki?*	*¿Adónde vas?*
What's this called?	*¿Imatataq kaypa sutin?*	*Qué es esto?*
Can I stay here?	*¿Puñupayukuykimanchu?*	*¿Puedo pasar la noche aquí?*
Yes	*Arí*	*Sí*
No	*Mana*	*No*
impossible	*mana atina*	*imposible*
good	*allinmi*	*está bien*
bad	*manan allinchu*	*no está bien*
beautiful	*añañá*	*bonito*
hot	*ruphay*	*calor*
rain	*para*	*lluvia*
wind	*wayra*	*viento*
snow	*rit'i*	*nieve*
Goodbye	*Hokhkootikama*	*Adiós*
See you	*Ratukama*	*Hasta luego*

Directions

left	*lloq'e*	*izquierda*
right	*paña*	*derecho*
here	*kaypi*	*aquí*
there	*chaypi*	*allí, allá*
over there	*haqay*	*por ahí*
up/down	*wichay/uray*	*arriba/abajo*
near	*sispa*	*cerca*
far (far off)	*karu*	*lejos*
straight ahead	*dirichu*	*derecho*
everywhere	*maypipas*	*en todos partes*
Where is...?	*¿Maypin ...?*	*¿Dónde está...?*
...the bus/truck	*...omnibus/karro*	*...el bus/el camión*
...the hotel	*...qorpa wasi*	*...el hotel*
...the house	*...wasi*	*...la casa*
...the pass	*...q'asa*	*...la abra*
...the path	*...ñan*	*...el camino, el sendero*
...the railway	*...ferrocarril*	*...el ferrocarril*
...the river	*...mayu*	*...el río*
...the toilet	*...bañu*	*...los baños*
...the village	*...llaqta, marka*	*...el pueblo*
...water/...food	*...unu/...mikuna*	*...agua/...la comida*

When?

When?	*¿Hayk'aq?*	*¿Cuándo?*
soon	*kunan*	*pronto*
right now	*kunallan, kunanpacha!*	*ahora mismo*
later	*qhepata*	*más tarde*
never	*manan hayk'aqpas*	*nunca*

ENGLISH	QUECHUA	SPANISH

Numerals

1	*u'/ huk*	*uno*
2	*iskay*	*dos*
3	*kinsa*	*tres*
4	*tawa*	*cuartro*
5	*pisqa*	*cinco*
6	*suqta*	*seis*
7	*qanchis*	*siete*
8	*pusaq*	*ocho*
9	*iskun*	*nueve*
10	*chunka*	*diez*
11	*chunka hukniyuq*	*once*
12	*chunka iskayniyuq*	*doce*
13	*chunka kinsayuq*	*trece*
14	*chunka tawayuq*	*catorce*
15	*chunka pisqayuq*	*quince*
16	*chunka suqtayuq*	*dieciséis*
17	*chunka qanchisniyuq*	*diecisiete*
18	*chunka pusaqniyuq*	*dieciocho*
19	*chunka isqunniyuq*	*diecinueve*
20	*iskay chunka*	*viente*
21	*iskay chunka hukniyuq*	*vientiuno*
30	*kinsa chunka*	*trienta*
40	*tawa chunka*	*cuarenta*
50	*pisqa chunka*	*cincuenta*
60	*suqta chunka*	*sesenta*
70	*qanchis chunka*	*setenta*
80	*pusaq chunka*	*ochenta*
90	*iskun chunka*	*noventa*
100	*pachak*	*cien*
101	*pachak hukniyuq*	*ciento uno*
200	*iskay pachak*	*doscientos*
1000	*waranqa*	*mil*
2000	*iskay waranqa*	*dos mil*
1,000,000	*hunu*	*un millón*

Shopping

money	*qolqe*	*dinero*
How much is...?	*¿Maik'ata'g...?*	*¿Cuánto cuesta...?*
...that one	*...haqay, chay*	*...eso/a*
more	*aswan*	*más*
less	*aswan pisi*	*menos*
a little	*chika, pisi*	*un poco, poquito*
big, large	*hatun*	*grande*
small, little	*huch'uy*	*pequeño/a*
How does it cost to...?	*¿Maik'ata'g...?*	*¿Cuánto cuesta...?*
...hire a guide	*...pusawasqaykimanta*	*...arrendar un guía?*
...hire a horse	*...caballoykikunamanta*	*...arrendar un caballo?*
...hire a llama	*...llamaykikunamanta*	*...arrendar una llama?*
...for a week/day	*...sapa semanan/p'unchay*	*...por semana/día*
Do you sell...?	*¿Icha ... ta bendiwankiman?*	*¿Me vende ...?*

ENGLISH	QUECHUA	SPANISH
Food and drink (see pp76-80)		
beer	*sirwisa*	*cerveza*
bread	*t'anta*	*pan*
chicken	*wallpa*	*pollo*
coca	*kuka*	*coca*
egg	*runtu*	*huevo*
fish	*challwa*	*pescado*
fruit	*ruru, añawi*	*fruta*
maize (corn)	*choqllo (sara)*	*maíz (choclo)*
meat (dried)	*aycha (ch'arki)*	*carne (charqui)*
potato	*papa*	*papa*
soup	*chupi*	*sopa*
roast	*kanka*	*asado*
boil	*t'impuy*	*hervir*
fry	*theqtichiy*	*freír*
raw	*hanku*	*crudo*
cooked	*chayasqa*	*cocido*
fizzy drink/pop	*bebida gaseosa*	*bebida gaseosa*
hot (temperature)	*q'oñi*	*caliente*
spicy	*haya*	*picante*
cold	*chiri, khutu*	*frío*
cold food	*kharmu*	*comida fría*

Help!		
Help me!	*!Yanapaway!*	*¡Socorro!*
Take me to a hospital	*Uspitalman pusaway*	*Lévame al hospital*
It hurts	*Nanan*	*Me duele*
I'm cold	*Chiriwashan*	*Tengo frío*
I'm hungry	*Yarqawashan*	*Tengo hambre*
I'm thirsty	*Ch'akiwashan*	*Tengo sed*
I'm tired	*Sayk'usqa kan*	*Estoy cansado*

APPENDIX B: GLOSSARY

AMS	acute mountain sickness
abra	high mountain pass
aclla	a 'chosen woman' of the Inca, an Inca nun
acllahuasi	convent or nunnery
aji	hot pepper from which a spicy sauce is made
alpaca	type of domesticated camelid resembling a small llama, bred for its wool
altiplano	literally 'high place', an area of high altitude plateau
amauta	Inca oral historian who cultivated their myths and legends
andene	terrace
andesite	igneous volcanic rock common in mountains of North and South America, including the Andes, after which it is named
anticucho	beef heart kebabs
Antis	collective term for tribes living in Antisuyu and the rainforest
Antisuyu	the eastern part of Inca empire, bordering the upper Amazon
apacheta	cairn; pile of stones
apu	gods or spirits of the mountains that protect local people in high areas
arriero	muleteer, wrangler of pack animals
ashlar	sculpted square blocks of stone or any dressed stonework
audiencia	a seat of government of Spanish South America
awaska	type of daily cloth garment worn by ordinary people
ayllu	Inca kinship group
Aymara	ethnic group living to south and east of Lake Titicaca and their language
baño	(when used archaeologically), a ceremonial bath
barranca	ravine
bodega	wine shop or bar that also serves snacks
cabildos	town councils
cacique	leader of indigenous tribe
calle	street
cambista	money-changer
cambio	place to exchange money (*bureau de change*)
campesino	Peruvian peasant or worker of the land
cancha	small plot of land or block of houses in an Inca town
cañaso	strong alcoholic spirit distilled from sugar cane
caudillos	the military leaders at the time of Peruvian independence
cejas de la selva	literally 'eyebrows of the jungle' (the eastern slopes of the Andes, fringed with forest)
ceques	sacred lines radiating from the centre of the Sun Temple in Cusco and passing through a set of huacas or shrines
cerro	mountain
ceviche	raw fish marinated in citrus juice and spiced with chilli
cevicherías	seafood restaurants specializing in traditional Peruvian ceviche
chacos	royal hunts
chasqui	messenger or courier usually operating as part of a relay
chicha	fermented maize drink, often homemade, popular with campesions
chicharrones	deep-fried pork
Chinchaysuyu	the northern quarter of the Inca Empire
chullo	type of traditional woolly hat
chullpa	tomb or burial chamber
chuño	type of traditional freeze-dried potato

ciudadela	high-walled enclosure housing a series of storage rooms, a large platform cum burial place and a number of *audiencias* or audience rooms
coca	plant used by Peruvians to ease altitude sickness and for stamina and health; the basic ingredient of cocaine
colectivo	type of public transport that is part bus, part taxi
Collasuyu	south-eastern province of the Inca Empire
Condesuyu	the south-western quarter of the Inca Empire
Convención (La)	the district to the east of Machu Picchu
conquistadors	Spanish explorer soldiers who conquered South Ameica in the 15th and 16th centuries
Coricancha	Inca Sun Temple
Corregidores	local, administrative and judicial position
correo	post office
Coya	the Inca's sister, his official wife and high priestess
Creole	Peruvian-born person of European descent. Criolla music and cooking are predominately found along the coast.
Curaca	Inca name for local noble
cuy	guinea pig
encomendero	name given to the owner of an *encomienda*
encomienda	plot of land governed by a Spaniard whose native inhabitants paid tribute to an *encomendero*
eye bonder	archaeological term for the pierced stones found in Inca buildings, often round or protruding from walls or gables; probably used for securing thatched roofs and hanging doors
guanaco	type of wild camelid related to the llama and alpaca
HACO/HAPO	rare condition of high altitude sickness caused by ascending too quickly, which can be fatal
Hanan	Inca clan division, also a part of an Inca town, the opposite of Hurin
huaca	sacred spot, usually a sculpted stone or feature in the landscape
huaqueros	tomb-robbers or treasure-hunters
huayna	small or young, opposite of machu
huayno	form of Peruvian Andean music with high pitched vocals
Hurin	an Inca clan division, also a part of an Inca town, the opposite of Hanan
INC	Instituto Nacional de Cultura, the government department responsible for managing and preserving archaeological sites
Inca	(see Sapa Inca)
Inti	the sun, and the name of the Sun God
Intihuatana	ritual stone, literally the 'hitching post of the sun'
Inti Raymi	Inca religious festival to observe the winter solstice and honour the god Inti; now recreated and a major toursit attraction
jirón	street
kallanka	Inca meeting hall
llama	a South American camelid (relative of the camel), used in Andean countries as a pack and food animal
llipta	a mixture of lime or quinoa and potash taken with a plug of coca leaves and chewed together to release the active ingredients in the leaves
machay	cave
machu	old, big, opposite of huayna
mamacona	mother superior in an Inca convent, dedicated to serving the Inca
mercado	market
mestizo	person of mixed Indian and European blood
mit'a	Inca tax, often paid in compulsory community labour

mitimaes	Inca settlers transplanted to perform mit'a in another part of the country
moraya	freeze-dried potato
nevado	mountain peak, usually snow-covered
orejones	literally 'big-ears', slang term used to refer to Hispanics and by the Inca to refer to conquistadors
Pachamama	goddess revered by Andean Indians, literally Earth Mother
pampa	plain, or occasionally any small, flat area
panaca	the tradition of preserving the estate of a dead person
parillada	BBQ/grill method of cooking, also a plate of grilled meat
picka	basic method of Inca construction
pisco sour	drink made from pisco (Peruvian spirit), lemon and egg white
posta de salud	health station
pucará	Inca fort
pueblos jóvenes	shanty town or slum
puna	high-altitude grassland, usually above the treeline
Punchao	a sacred idol of the sun from Cusco's Sun Temple, looted by the conquistadors
Qenko	sacred sculpted stone near Cusco
qollqa	Inca storehouse
qompi	fine fabric woven for the Inca
quebrada	deep, sheer-sided river valley
Quechua	native South American language spoken primarily in the Andes and used by the Incas, also refers to the Incas' descendants currently living in Peru
quinoa	a grain like crop grown for its edible seeds
quipus	literally 'talking knots', a recording device of knotted strings used by the Incas; could only be read by skilled interpreters, the quipucamayos
raccay	ruins
Runasimi	the Quechua word for the language, literally 'peoples' speech'
Sapa Inca	the Great Inca, the Inca emperor and ruler of Cusco and the empire, also known simply as 'the Inca'
sapo	traditional Peruvian game
selva	jungle
sol(es)	unit of Peruvian currency
soroche	altitude sickness
suyua	division of the Inca empire
Tahuantinsuyu	name of the Inca empire
tambo	an inn or rest-house
tarjeta telefónica	telephone card
taxista	taxi driver
Tiahuanaco	a pre-Inca Peruvian culture
tumi	a ceremonial Andean knife
urpu	traditional fat-bellied pot with a curved base and long spout
usno	raised ceremonial square in Inca city
vicuña	undomesticated camelid living in high alpine areas of the Andes that is related to the llama and alpaca, with very fine wool
Valle Sagrado	Sacred Valley of the Incas; lies along the Urubamba River, north of Cusco
Vilcanota	alternative name for the upper Urubamba River
Villac Umu	chief of the caste of priests in the Inca state religion
Viracocha	the creator of the Incas and a key figure in Inca mythology, also the name of one of the early Incas

APPENDIX C: RAIL INFORMATION

Traditionally, buses have been the cheapest and easiest way of getting around Peru, even if journeys take a long time and aren't always comfortable. This is especially true since the end of the twentieth century and the privatization of the rail network that saw the new owners, PeruRail, introduce restricted tourist services and much higher fares. However, there is one place the buses can't go: Aguas Calientes, the gateway to Machu Picchu. Given that there is no road access to the town and the only alternative is to walk in, the train emerges as the only real option for many visitors. Recognizing this, PeruRail have set up a series of services, all at fairly expensive rates. There's a subsidized train service for local people only; although Peruvian citizens from outside the area can occasionally use it, foreigners may not.

RAIL SERVICES

Currently three services of tourist train ply the route from the station at Poroy, eight miles (13km) outside downtown Cusco (about a 20 minute drive), through the Sacred Valley to Aguas Calientes. Sadly the trains no longer leave from the main station in Cusco meaning that you miss out on the slow, scenic zigzag as the train ascends a series of switchbacks to leave the city.

The 'budget' **Expedition** service (previously called the Backpacker) is the cheapest, with fares starting at US$48 one way or US$96 return. The **Vistadome** service has panoramic windows, complimentary drinks and snacks and takes slightly less time to complete the route but costs a little more with fares starting at US$71 one way/US$142 return. The top of the range ride is aboard the **Hiram Bingham** (US$599 round trip, US$349 from Poroy to Aguas Calientes and US$300 from Aguas Calientes to Poroy), which runs Mon-Sat. The exorbitant ticket entitles you to brunch and dinner in the opulent dining car, cocktails and live entertainment en route as well as guides, bus transfers from Cusco to Poroy and from Aguas Calientes to Machu Picchu, entrance to the ruins and afternoon tea in the plush Machu Picchu Sanctuary Lodge. That's still a lot of money for a day trip, though.

Unfortunately there aren't many ways of making this cheaper. You might consider using both bus and train to make the journey, as train fares between Ollantaytambo and Aguas Calientes and Ollantaytambo and Cusco can be substantially cheaper than Vistadome fares between Cusco and Aguas Calientes and even sometimes cheaper than the Expedition service. Public buses to and from Cusco stop in Ollantaytambo adjacent to the station. If that doesn't appeal then you are better off putting your feet up and enjoying the ride along the rails as you ease into the mountains. In real terms the train fares are representative of what you might expect to pay for such a spectacular ride elsewhere in the world; they just seem hugely inflated by Peruvian standards.

TIMETABLES AND ONLINE BOOKINGS

Bear in mind that the timetables below are subject to change at very short notice and are a guide rather than a rule. To get the most up-to-date information check locally at the train stations or try visiting PeruRail's website at 💻 **www.perurail.com**. You can also book and pay for tickets with a credit card online. Print the e-voucher and take it along with your passport to the station at least an hour ahead of departure, where you can exchange it for a ticket. The e-voucher alone is not valid for travel.

Cusco (Poroy) to Machu Picchu (Aguas Calientes)
Services are daily, except for the Hiram Bingham which does not run on Sundays.

SERVICE NAME	TRAIN No	COST ONE WAY	COST RTN	DEP CUSCO (POROY)	ARR MACHU PICCHU (AGUAS CALIENTES)
Vistadome	31	US$71	US$142	06.53	09.52
Expedition	33	US$48	US$96	07.42	10.51
Hiram Bingham	11	US$349	US$599	09.05	12.24

Machu Picchu (Aguas Calientes) to Cusco (Poroy)
Services are daily, except for the Hiram Bingham which does not run on Sundays.

SERVICE NAME	TRAIN No	COST ONE WAY	COST RTN	DEP MACHU PICCHU (AGUAS CALIENTES)	ARR CUSCO (POROY)
Vistadome	32	US$71	US$142	15.20	18.50
Expedition	34	US$56	US$96	16.43	20.13
Hiram Bingham	12	US$300	US$599	17.50	21.16

Ollantaytambo to Machu Picchu (Aguas Calientes)
For those based in the Sacred Valley, there is the option of taking the shorter, yet similarly spectacular journey from Ollantaytambo to Aguas Calientes. Prices vary according to service and also time of departure. PeruRail lays on occasional special trains between Ollantaytambo and Urubamba.

SERVICE NAME	TRAIN No	COST ONE WAY	DEP OLLANTAYTAMBO	ARR MACHU PICCHU (AGUAS CALIENTES)
Expedition	81	US$37	06:10	07:40
Vistadome	301	US$60	07:05	08:27
Vistadome	501	US$60	08.29	09:52
Servicio Especial	501	US$175	08.29	09:52
Autovagon	601	US$60	08:00	09:24
Expedition	83	US$43	08:53	10:26
Vistadome	203	US$60	10:32	12:11
Expedition	73	US$37	12:58	14:24
Vistadome	303	US$53	13:27	14:49
Vistadome	603	US$49	15:37	17:02
Expedition	75	US$33	19:00	20:43
Expedition	51	US$33	21:00	22:50

Machu Picchu (Aguas Calientes) to Ollantaytambo

SERVICE NAME	TRAIN No	COST ONE WAY	DEP MACHU PICCHU (AGUAS CALIENTES)	ARR OLLANTAYTAMBO
Expedition	50	US$33	05:35	07:44
Expedition	72	US$33	08:53	10:52
Vistadome	302	US$53	10:55	12:32
Vistadome	204	US$53	13:37	15:04
Expedition	74	US$43	14:55	16:31
Vistadome	304	US$60	15:48	17:29
Vistadome	504	US$60	16:22	18:01
Servicio Especial	504	US$175	16:22	18:01
Vistadome	604	US$60	17:27	18:56
Autovagon	606	US$60	18:10	19:45
Expedition	84	US$37	18:45	20:18
Expedition	76	US$33	21:30	23:01

Between Cusco and Puno (Lake Titicaca)

This is possibly the highest passenger railway route in the world: at its highest point, La Raya, the altitude is 4313m/14,146ft.

The luxurious **Andean Explorer** train, decorated in the style of the Pullman trains of the 1920s, leaves Cusco for Puno from Huanchac Station on Monday, Wednesday and Saturday at 8am and gets to Puno at 6pm. During the high season (Apr-Oct) there is an additional departure on Friday. Trains travelling the other way from Puno to Cusco depart on Monday, Wednesday and Saturday at 8am and arrive in Cusco at 6pm. Again, during the high season there is an additional departure on Friday.

Tickets cost US$143 one-way and include a three-course lunch.

Between Puno and Arequipa

Once a popular route, this stretch of track is currently only available for private charters. For the latest information see ⌨ www.perurail.com.

INDEX

TRAILBLAZER TREKKING GUIDES

Europe
Corsica Trekking – GR20
Dolomites Trekking – AV1 & AV2
Scottish Highlands – The Hillwalking Guide
Tour du Mont Blanc
Trekking in the Pyrenees
Walker's Haute Route: Mt Blanc to Matterhorn

South America
Inca Trail, Cusco & Machu Picchu

Africa
Kilimanjaro
Moroccan Atlas – The Trekking Guide

Australasia
New Zealand – The Great Walks

Asia
Nepal Trekking & The Great Himalaya Trail
Trekking in the Annapurna Region
Trekking in the Everest Region
Trekking in Ladakh

New Zealand – The Great Walks
Alexander Stewart, 2nd edn, £12.99
ISBN 978-1-905864-11-9, 272pp, 60 maps, 40 colour photos
New Zealand is a wilderness paradise of incredibly beautiful landscapes. There is no better way to experience it than on one of the nine designated Great Walks, the country's premier walking tracks. Also includes detailed guides to Auckland, Wellington, National Park Village, Taumarunui, Nelson, Queenstown, Te Anau and Oban.

Kilimanjaro – the trekking guide to Africa's highest mountain
Henry Stedman, 3rd edn, £12.99
ISBN 978-1-905864-24-9, 368pp, 40 maps, 30 photos
At 19,340ft the world's tallest freestanding mountain, Kilimanjaro is one of the most popular destinations for hikers visiting Africa. It's possible to walk up to the summit: no technical skills are necessary. Includes town guides to Nairobi and Dar-Es-Salaam, and a colour guide to flora and fauna. Includes Mount Meru.

Tour du Mont Blanc *Jim Manthorpe* 1st edn, £11.99
ISBN 978-1-905864-12-6, 208pp, 60 maps, 30 colour photos
At 4810m (15,781ft), Mont Blanc is the highest mountain in western Europe, and one of the most famous mountains in the world. The trail (105 miles, 168km) that circumnavigates it, passing through France, Italy and Switzerland, is the most popular long distance walk in Europe. Includes Chamonix and Courmayeur guides.

The Walker's Haute Route – Mt Blanc to the Matterhorn
Alexander Stewart, 1st edn, £12.99
ISBN 978-1-905864-08-9, 256pp, 60 maps, 30 colour photos
From Mont Blanc to the Matterhorn, Chamonix to Zermatt, the 180km (113-mile) Walker's Haute Route traverses one of the finest stretches of the Pennine Alps – the range between Valais in Switzerland and Piedmont and Aosta Valley in Italy. Includes Chamonix and Zermatt guides.

Moroccan Atlas – the Trekking Guide
Alan Palmer, 1st edn, £12.99
ISBN 978-1-873756-77-5, 268pp, 54 maps, 40 colour photos
The High Atlas in central Morocco is the most dramatic and beautiful section of the entire Atlas range. Towering peaks, deep gorges and huddled Berber villages enchant all who visit. With 44 detailed trekking maps, 10 town and village guides including Marrakech.

TRAILBLAZER GUIDES – TITLE LIST

www.trailblazer-guides.com

Peru

Trekking Routes

AND TRAIL MAP NO KEY (16 = MAP No)

M1 p211, M2 p213, M3 p215, M4 p219, M5 p224
M6 p225, M7 p234, M8 p235, M9 p237, M10 p238
M11 p239, M12 p245, M13 p247, M14 p249
M15 p254, M16 p255, M17 p266, M18 p267
M19 p269, M20 p271, M21 p273, M22 p274
M23 p275, M24 p277, M25 p281, M26 p282
M27 p289, M28 p291, M29 p293, M30 p303
M31 p306, M32 p307, M33 p308, M34 p309
M35 p315, M36 p317, M37 p319, M38 p321